Project Management for Associates with Artificial Intelligence Second Edition

Lynn Smith

ISBN: 979-8-3495-5859-7

ABOUT THE BOOK

This book offers comprehensive coverage of concepts in the 2023 Certified Associate in Project Management (CAPM) exam content outline, with expanded insights into agile methodologies, business analysis, and artificial intelligence. It includes multiple-choice questions to test your understanding of key concepts and a case study on developing a software application for a hypothetical small university, enabling readers to apply chapter concepts to a real-world scenario. Additionally, the book provides MS Project exercises to help readers manage the case study project. Through this approach, readers learn essential concepts, develop an application, and practice project management using MS Project.

CONTENTS

1 Chapter 1: Introduction to Project Management 1
2 Chapter 2: Roles and Responsibilities 31
3 Chapter 3: Stakeholder Communications 55
4 Chapter 4: Project Requirements 83
5 Chapter 5: Project Planning 119
6 Chapter 6: Predictive Plan-based Approach 154
7 Chapter 7: Agile Mindset 189
8 Chapter 8: Adaptive Approach 222
9 Chapter 9: Business Analysis 260
10 Chapter 10: Executing and Closing 290
11 Chapter 11: AI in Project Management 318
12 Chapter 12: Data Integration and Automation 354

DISCLAIMER

NOTICE OF LIABILITY

ACKNOWLEDGMENTS

We thank Dr. Youlong Zhuang for reviewing this edition and providing valuable suggestions.

Chapter 1: Introduction to Project Management

Chapter Learning Outcomes

1.1 Analyze the differences between a project, program, and portfolio.
1.2 Evaluate the distinction between a project and operations.
1.3 Compare and contrast predictive and adaptive approaches in project management.
1.4 Evaluate the significance of issues, risks, assumptions, and constraints in project management.
1.5 Review and critique the project scope.

1.1 Project and Project Management

A *project* is a temporary undertaking designed to produce a unique product, service, or result (PMI, 2021). This temporary nature distinguishes projects from ongoing operations. Projects have a clear start and end date, unlike continuous and repetitive operational work. It's important to note that 'temporary' doesn't equate to 'short.' A project's duration can range from days to years, but it will always have a defined completion.

Several key characteristics distinguish projects from ongoing operational work. A core differentiator is the concept of *unique deliverables*. Every project is undertaken to create a distinct outcome, something that hasn't been produced before in the same way.

A project's outcome can take many forms. It might produce tangible products, such as a newly constructed bridge, a software application, or a smartphone. Alternatively, results could manifest as services, such as consulting to optimize supply chains, or employee training programs. Intangible deliverables, by contrast, include outcomes like intellectual property (e.g., patents or trademarks), brand reputation enhanced through public relations, or data-driven insights from market research guiding consumer strategies. Each outcome represents a distinct value proposition, whether physical, service-based, or conceptual.

The unique nature of every project demands customized planning and execution. Project managers must tailor strategies to address each initiative's distinct requirements, whether navigating unforeseen challenges or capitalizing on emerging opportunities. This fundamental distinction between project-based work and routine operations underscores why standardized process management fails to accommodate the variable realities of temporary, goal-oriented endeavors.

Another defining characteristic is *defined objectives*. Projects are initiated with the clear intention of achieving specific, predetermined goals. These objectives serve as the compass for the project, directing all activities and providing a benchmark against which project success is measured.

A common and useful framework for defining objectives is the SMART criteria: Specific, Measurable, Achievable, Relevant, and Time-bound. "Specific" means the objective is clearly defined and unambiguous. "Measurable" implies that there are quantifiable metrics to track progress and determine if the objective has been met. "Achievable" suggests that the objective is realistic and attainable within the given constraints. "Relevant" means the objective aligns with the overall strategic goals of the organization. And "Time-bound" establishes a clear timeframe for achieving the objective. For example, instead of a vague objective like "increase sales," a SMART objective would be "increase sales of Product X by 15% in the next fiscal quarter." Understanding how project objectives drive project activities and how changes to those objectives can impact the project is a key area of focus for the project management.

The third key characteristic is *constraints*, which are limitations that restrict the project team's options and influence how the project is executed. The most commonly recognized constraints are scope, time, and cost, often referred to as the "triple constraint" or the "project management triangle."

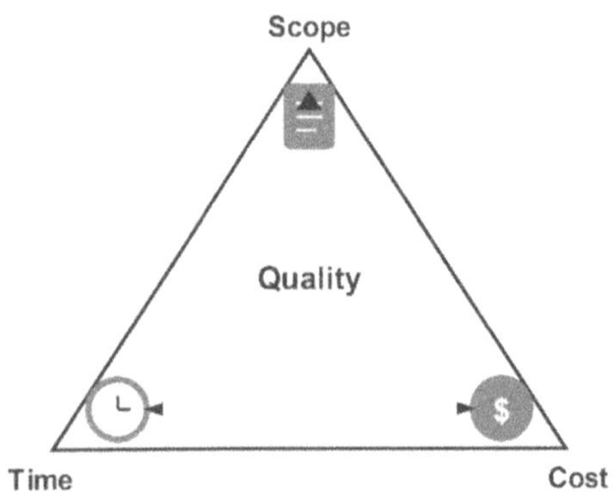

Figure 1.1 Triple constraint.

Scope defines the boundaries of the project, specifying what work will be included and, equally importantly, what will be excluded. A clear scope statement prevents "scope creep," which is the uncontrolled expansion of the project's requirements beyond the original agreement.

Time refers to the project schedule, encompassing start and end dates, key milestones, and deadlines for various tasks. Effective time management helps ensure the project is completed on schedule.

Cost represents the budget allocated to the project, covering expenses for resources (human resources, equipment, etc.), materials, and other necessary expenditures. Managing costs effectively supports staying within budget and delivering a financially viable project.

These three constraints are interconnected; a change in one constraint often necessitates adjustments to one or both of the others. For instance, if the scope of a project is increased (more work needs to be done), it will likely require more time and/or more money. Similarly, if the project needs to be completed in a shorter timeframe, it might require additional resources (increasing cost) or a reduction in scope.

While projects represent goal-driven, temporary endeavors constrained by resources and time, *project management* is the art and science of applying knowledge, skills, tools, and techniques to project activities to meet the project requirements (PMI, 2021). It's about orchestrating all elements of a project, from its initial conception to its final completion, ensuring that the project delivers its intended outcomes within the defined constraints of scope, time, and cost. At its core, project management involves using a structured approach, encompassing processes, methods, and essential skills, to effectively plan, execute, monitor, control, and ultimately close projects. This structured approach is what differentiates project management from simply doing a project.

One aspect of project management is the use of processes. Project management isn't a haphazard endeavor; it relies on a set of defined processes to manage the project lifecycle. These processes are logically grouped into five process groups (PMI, 2021): Initiating, Planning, Executing, Monitoring and Controlling, and Closing.

The *Initiating process group* defines and authorizes the project or a project phase. It includes activities like developing the project charter and identifying stakeholders. The *Planning process group* involves defining the project scope, objectives, and course of action. This includes creating the project management plan, which outlines how the project will be executed, monitored, and controlled. The *Executing process group* directs and manages the project work. This is where the project deliverables are actually created. The *Monitoring and Controlling process group* tracks, reviews, and regulates the progress and performance of the project. This involves comparing actual performance against the project plan and taking corrective actions as needed. Finally, the *Closing process group* formally completes the project or a project phase. This includes finalizing all activities, archiving project documents, and conducting post-project reviews.

Furthermore, project management employs various methods or methodologies, which provide frameworks for managing projects. These methodologies offer different approaches to project execution, each with its own strengths and weaknesses.

The *Waterfall methodology* is a traditional, sequential approach where each phase of the project is completed before the next one begins. It's often used for projects with well-defined requirements and a low tolerance for change.

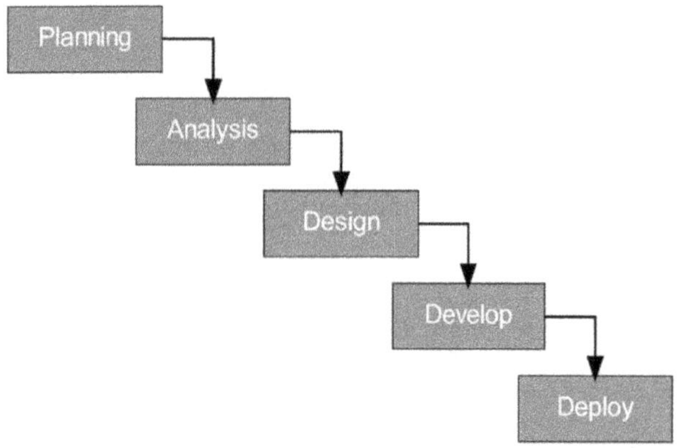

Figure 1.2 Waterfall approach.

Agile methodologies, on the other hand, are iterative and incremental, emphasizing flexibility and collaboration. Agile is well-suited for projects with evolving requirements and a need for frequent feedback. Scrum is a specific type of Agile framework that uses short iterations called sprints to deliver working increments of the product.

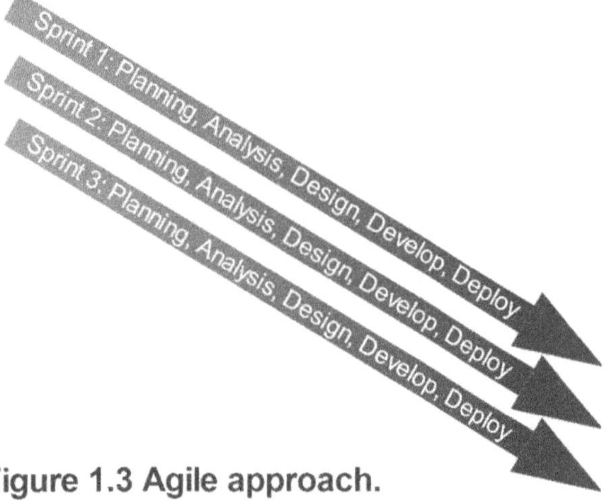

Figure 1.3 Agile approach.

Finally, effective project managers possess a range of essential skills. These skills go beyond technical knowledge and encompass interpersonal and leadership abilities. Key skills include:

Communication: Project managers must be able to communicate effectively with all stakeholders, including team members, sponsors, customers, and vendors. This involves active listening, clear and concise writing, and effective presentation skills.

Leadership: Project managers need to motivate and guide their teams to achieve project objectives. This involves setting clear expectations, providing feedback, and resolving conflicts.

Problem-Solving: Projects inevitably encounter challenges, and project managers must be able to identify problems, analyze their root causes, and develop effective solutions.

Negotiation: Project managers often need to negotiate with stakeholders to reach agreements on scope, schedule, and budget.

Test Your Understanding 1.1
What does the "SMART" criteria in project management objectives primarily ensure?

A. Strict adherence to budget.
B. Clear, measurable, and achievable goals.
C. Rapid project execution.
D. Minimal stakeholder involvement.

Test Your Understanding 1.2
Which of the following is NOT typically considered a constraint in project management?
A. Scope.
B. Time.
C. Cost.
D. Stakeholder opinions.

Test Your Understanding 1.3
Which project management methodology is characterized by sequential phases and is best suited for projects with well-defined requirements?
A. Agile.
B. Scrum.
C. Waterfall.
D. Iterative.

Test Your Understanding 1.4
What is "scope creep" in project management?
A. The uncontrolled expansion of the project's requirements.
B. A sudden reduction in the project budget without any prior indicators.
C. Delays in the project schedule.
D. Changes in the project team.

Test Your Understanding 1.5
Which of the following is an example of an intangible project deliverable?
A. A newly constructed bridge.
B. A software application.
C. Market research insights.
D. A smartphone.

Test Your Understanding 1.6
What is the significance of "temporary" in the definition of a project?
A. It implies projects are always short in duration, usually within a year.
B. It distinguishes projects from ongoing operations.
C. It means projects lack defined objectives.
D. It indicates projects are always low-budget.

1.2 Project vs. Operations

While both project and operations involve work and resources, they differ significantly in their nature and objectives. Understanding these differences helps in grasping the core concepts of project management.

Operations are the ongoing, repetitive activities that sustain a business. They are primarily concerned with the continuous delivery of products or services and the maintenance of existing business processes. A key characteristic of operations is the use of repetitive processes. These are standardized, repeatable procedures performed consistently over time. These processes are typically well-defined and documented, which contributes to efficiency and predictability. Examples of repetitive operational processes include a manufacturing assembly line, where the same steps are followed for each product; a customer service call center, where agents follow established protocols for handling customer inquiries; or daily accounting procedures, such as processing invoices and reconciling bank statements.

Another defining characteristic is continuous delivery. The main objective of operations is to provide a consistent output of products or services without a defined end date. The emphasis is on maintaining stable and predictable performance, ensuring a steady flow of value to customers or stakeholders.

Operations also place a strong focus on efficiency. This means constantly seeking ways to optimize existing processes, minimize costs, reduce waste, and improve productivity within the established operational framework. This continuous improvement maintains competitiveness and profitability.

Unlike projects, which are temporary endeavors, operations have an ongoing nature. They continue indefinitely unless a deliberate decision is made to discontinue them. In essence, operations are about performing the same tasks repeatedly, but with a constant focus on improvement and optimization, ensuring that the work is done better each time.

Though distinct from day-to-day operations, projects are closely tied to them, particularly in how their deliverables transition into operational use. Upon completion and finalization of a project's deliverables, they are typically handed over to operational teams responsible for their ongoing maintenance and utilization. This transition, or handover process, is critical for ensuring the seamless integration of the project's output into the organization's existing operations. Several key steps are commonly involved in this process.

Knowledge transfer requires the project team to share their expertise and understanding of the deliverables with the operational teams. This can be achieved through various methods, such as training sessions, comprehensive documentation, and providing ongoing support during the initial operational phase. Thorough documentation is also vital, including user manuals, maintenance procedures, system specifications, and any other relevant information necessary for the smooth operational use of the project's deliverables.

Before the formal handover, acceptance testing should be conducted by the operational teams to verify that the deliverables meet their requirements and are ready for operational deployment. This ensures that the system or product functions as expected in a real-world setting.

Ongoing support may be provided by the project team to the operational teams during a transition period. This support helps address any issues or questions that may arise during the initial stages of operational use, facilitating a smoother transition and minimizing disruptions.

Understanding this relationship supports effective project management by emphasizing that projects are not isolated events but integral components of an organization's broader strategic objectives, contributing to long-term business success.

Test Your Understanding 1.7
Which of the following BEST distinguishes a project from ongoing operations?
A. Repetitive tasks.
B. Temporary nature and unique deliverables.
C. Standardized process management.
D. Continuous workflow.

Test Your Understanding 1.8
What is a key characteristic of operational processes?
A. Flexibility and adaptability to change.
B. Repetitive and standardized procedures.
C. Unpredictable and variable outputs.
D. Short-term, goal-oriented activities.

Test Your Understanding 1.9
How do projects differ from operations in terms of their duration?
A. Projects are temporary, while operations are ongoing.
B. Projects are ongoing, while operations are temporary.
C. Both projects and operations are temporary.
D. Both projects and operations are ongoing.

Test Your Understanding 1.10
Which of the following is an example of a repetitive operational process?
A. Developing a new marketing campaign.
B. Constructing a new office building.
C. Processing invoices and reconciling bank statements.
D. Implementing a new software system for the whole business.

Test Your Understanding 1.11
Why is understanding the relationship between projects and operations important for project managers?
A. To isolate projects from organizational objectives.
B. To ensure seamless integration of project outputs into existing operations.
C. To minimize the need for acceptance testing.
D. To eliminate the need for operational team training and thus reduce the cost for business.

1.3 Project, Program, and Portfolio

The terms of projects, programs, and portfolios are often used interchangeably, but they represent distinct levels of organizational work with varying scopes and objectives. Recognizing these differences is key for effective project management and aligning project work with overall strategic goals.

A *project*, as previously discussed, is a temporary endeavor undertaken to create a unique product, service, or result. It has a defined beginning and end, specific objectives, and operates within constraints such as scope, time, and cost.

A *program*, on the other hand, is a group of related projects, subsidiary programs, and program activities managed in a coordinated way to obtain benefits not available from managing them individually. Programs are larger in scope and longer in duration than individual projects. They are designed to achieve strategic objectives by managing multiple related projects in a coordinated manner. The focus of a program is on realizing benefits, which can include cost savings, increased market share, or improved customer satisfaction.

A *portfolio* represents the highest level of organizational work. It is a collection of projects, programs, subsidiary portfolios, and operations managed as a group to achieve strategic objectives. Portfolios are not necessarily related in terms of their subject matter or technical content; rather, they are grouped together because they contribute to the organization's overall strategic goals. Portfolio management focuses on selecting and prioritizing programs and projects to optimize resource allocation and maximize the return on investment.

The key differences between projects, programs, and portfolios can be summarized by examining their scope, duration, objective, and management focus. In terms of scope, projects have the narrowest focus, concentrating on delivering a specific deliverable. Programs possess a broader scope, encompassing multiple related projects that contribute to a shared objective. Portfolios have the widest scope, encompassing all organizational investments, including projects, programs, and operations, that contribute to achieving strategic objectives.

Regarding duration, projects have a clearly defined beginning and end, making them temporary endeavors. Programs, while longer in duration than individual projects, also have a defined end date, marking the realization of the intended benefits. Portfolios, however, are ongoing and do not have a defined end date, as they represent the organization's continuous strategic investments.

The objective of each level also differs. Projects aim to produce specific deliverables, such as a product, service, or result. Programs aim to realize benefits by coordinating the related projects within them, achieving outcomes greater than the sum of individual project results. Portfolios aim to achieve strategic objectives by optimizing resource allocation across all investments, ensuring alignment with the organization's overall goals.

Finally, the management focus varies at each level. Project management concentrates on managing project constraints, such as scope, time, and cost, to deliver the defined deliverables. Program management focuses on coordinating related projects, managing interdependencies, and realizing the intended benefits of the program. Portfolio management focuses on strategic alignment, prioritizing investments, and optimizing resource allocation across all projects, programs, and operations to maximize the achievement of strategic objectives.

The relationship between these three levels is hierarchical: projects are components of programs, and programs are components of portfolios. This hierarchical structure ensures that the work performed at the project level directly contributes to the benefits realized at the program level, which in turn contributes to the achievement of the organization's overall strategic objectives at the portfolio level.

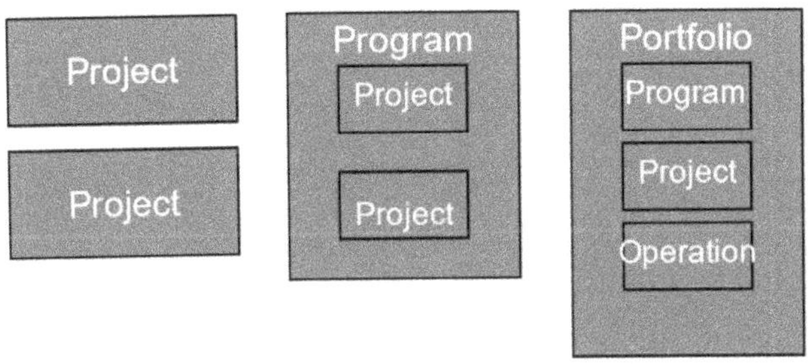

Figure 1.4 Projects, Programs, and Portfolio.

Let's illustrate these concepts with practical examples relevant to the project management:

Project: Building a new software module. This is a distinct, temporary endeavor with a defined scope, timeline, and budget. The objective is to deliver a specific piece of software functionality, such as a new reporting module for an existing application.

Program: Multiple software modules for an enterprise solution. A program could encompass the development of several related software modules that together form a complete enterprise solution, such as an integrated human resources management system. This program would consist of multiple projects, each focused on developing a specific module (e.g., payroll, benefits administration, recruitment). By managing these related projects as a program, the organization can ensure that the modules integrate seamlessly and deliver the desired overall benefits, such as streamlined HR processes and improved data management.

Portfolio: IT department initiatives to improve efficiency. A portfolio could include all of the IT department's initiatives aimed at improving organizational efficiency, such as upgrading network infrastructure, implementing new cybersecurity measures, developing mobile applications for employees, and migrating to a cloud-based platform. This portfolio is not limited to software development; it encompasses all IT-related investments that contribute to the strategic goal of improving efficiency. This could include projects related to hardware upgrades, cybersecurity training, or implementing new IT service management processes.

Test Your Understanding 1.12
Which of the following BEST describes a program?
A. A collection of coding projects, all belong to the same department.
B. A group of related projects managed in a coordinated way.
C. A single, temporary endeavor.
D. Ongoing operational activities.

Test Your Understanding 1.13
What is the primary objective of a portfolio?
A. To deliver a single, unique product.
B. To manage individual project constraints.
C. To optimize resource allocation and achieve strategic objectives.
D. To coordinate related projects within a program and meet the stakeholder requirements.

Test Your Understanding 1.14
Which organizational level has the narrowest scope?
A. Portfolio.
B. Program.
C. Project.
D. Operation.

Test Your Understanding 1.15
How does the duration of a portfolio differ from that of a project?

A. Portfolios are ongoing, while projects are temporary.
B. Projects are ongoing, while portfolios are temporary.
C. Both are temporary with defined end dates.
D. Both are ongoing without defined end dates.

Test Your Understanding 1.16
Which of the following is an example of a project?
A. Implementing an enterprise-wide HR system.
B. Building a new software module.
C. Managing all IT department initiatives.
D. Conducting daily operational tasks.

Test Your Understanding 1.17
What is the hierarchical relationship between projects, programs, and portfolios?
A. Portfolios are components of projects, and projects are components of programs.
B. Programs are components of projects, and programs are components of portfolios.
C. Projects are components of programs, and programs are components of portfolios.
D. They are independent and have no hierarchical relationship.

Test Your Understanding 1.18
What is the primary objective of project management to deliver defined deliverables?
A. To optimize resource allocation.
B. To manage project constraints.
C. To realize program benefits.
D. To achieve strategic goals.

Test Your Understanding 1.19
Which of the following is an example of a portfolio?
A. Developing a payroll software module.
B. Coordinating multiple software module projects.
C. IT department initiatives to improve efficiency.
D. Managing a single software upgrade project.

1.4 Issues, Risks, Assumptions, and Constraints

Issues are current, existing problems that are impacting or have the potential to immediately impact the project. They are unexpected challenges that require immediate attention and resolution. Unlike risks, which are potential future events, issues are happening now. They often arise from unforeseen circumstances, changes in requirements, or problems with resources. Effectively managing issues involves identifying the problem, analyzing its impact, developing a solution, implementing the solution, and monitoring its effectiveness. For example, an issue could be a key team member unexpectedly resigning, a critical piece of equipment malfunctioning, or a delay in receiving necessary materials from a supplier. These situations demand immediate action to mitigate their negative impact on the project's timeline, budget, or scope. Remember that issues are reactive; they require a response to a problem that has already occurred.

Risks are potential events or conditions that, if they occur, could have a positive or negative impact on the project objectives. Unlike issues, which are current problems, risks are future uncertainties. Risk management is a proactive process that involves identifying potential risks, analyzing their likelihood and potential impact, developing response strategies, and monitoring the effectiveness of those strategies. Risks can be categorized as either threats (negative impacts) or opportunities (positive impacts). Examples of risks include potential delays from weather conditions, changes in market demand, or the possibility of a key technology becoming obsolete. Effective risk management minimizes the negative impacts of threats and maximizes the benefits of opportunities. It's important to understand the different risk response strategies, such as avoidance, mitigation, transference, and acceptance for threats, and exploit, enhance, share, and accept for opportunities.

Assumptions are conditions or beliefs that are assumed to be true for the purpose of planning and making decisions. They are accepted as facts, even though they may not be proven. Assumptions are necessary because it's impossible to know everything about the future. However, it's important to document assumptions and regularly review their validity throughout the project lifecycle. If an assumption proves to be incorrect, it can lead to significant problems. For example, an assumption might be that a certain resource will be available at a specific time, that a particular technology will function as expected, or that certain regulatory approvals will be granted. It's important to analyze the potential impact of assumptions if they turn out to be false. This analysis can help determine the level of risk associated with each assumption and inform contingency planning. It's important to understand how to document and manage assumptions.

Constraints are limitations or restrictions that affect the project's ability to achieve its objectives. They are factors that restrict the project team's options and influence how the project is executed. As mentioned earlier, the most common constraints are scope, time, and cost, often referred to as the "triple constraint" or the "project management triangle." Other constraints can include resources (human, material, equipment), quality, and legal or regulatory requirements. For example, a constraint could be a limited budget, a tight deadline, a shortage of skilled labor, or a regulatory requirement that must be met. Changes to one constraint often impact other constraints. For instance, reducing the project timeline may require increasing the budget or reducing the scope. It's important to understand how constraints interact and how to manage them effectively.

Test Your Understanding 1.20

How do risks differ from issues in project management?
A. Risks are unexpected challenges requiring immediate resolution, while issues are future uncertainties.
B. Risks are future uncertainties, while issues are current problems impacting the project.
C. Risks and issues are both present problems that impact the project.
D. Risks require immediate action, while issues do not need to be addressed urgently.

Test Your Understanding 1.21
Which of the following is an example of an issue in project management?
A. A supplier failing to deliver materials on time, delaying project progress.
B. A project assumption that a certain resource will be available when needed.
C. A potential increase in material costs due to market fluctuations.
D. A regulatory change that may impact project deliverables in the future.

Test Your Understanding 1.22
Which of the following is an example of a project assumption?
A. The project must be completed within a fixed budget.
B. A key resource is expected to be available on the required start date.
C. The team is experiencing a delay due to software defects.
D. Regulatory approval has been granted for project execution.

Test Your Understanding 1.23
What is an example of a project constraint?
A. A key stakeholder assumes that the project will be completed on time.
B. A competitor is planning to launch a similar product.
C. A strict regulatory requirement limits the project's options.
D. A potential security breach could impact project success.

Test Your Understanding 1.24
Which of the following best describes the relationship between project constraints?
A. Constraints operate independently of each other.
B. A change in one constraint may impact other constraints.
C. Constraints only apply to project scope, time, and cost.
D. Constraints do not affect project decision-making.

Test Your Understanding 1.25
Which of the following is a valid example of a risk in project management?
A. A critical team member resigning unexpectedly.
B. A software bug that is causing system failures.
C. A mandatory legal requirement for project completion.
D. A potential delay due to extreme weather conditions.

1.5 Project Charter

The *Project Charter* is a document in project management, especially within a predictive framework, that formally authorizes the project and provides the project manager with the authority to allocate organizational resources. It essentially acts as a contract between the project sponsor, stakeholders, and the project team, ensuring alignment on the project's purpose and objectives.

This high-level document establishes the project, outlines its purpose, objectives, scope, and key stakeholders, and serves as a reference point throughout the project lifecycle. It also defines the project manager's authority and responsibility. Think of it as the project's birth certificate, officially recognizing its existence and authorizing its commencement. It is important to note that the Project Charter is not the same as a project plan; instead, it sets the stage for detailed planning and execution. Without a Project Charter, a project lacks formal standing within the organization.

The Project Charter typically includes several key components that provide a high-level overview of the project. The *Project Purpose* or Justification explains the rationale behind the project, clearly articulating the business need or opportunity it addresses. For example, a company might initiate a project to develop a new online ordering system to increase sales and improve customer convenience.

High-level *Project Objectives* define the desired outcomes of the project in measurable terms. These objectives should be SMART (Specific, Measurable, Achievable, Relevant, and Time-bound). For instance, an objective could be "Increase online sales by 15% within the next fiscal year."

High-level *Requirements* summarize the key features or functionalities that the project must deliver. These are not detailed technical specifications but rather a broad overview of what the project will produce. For a software project, a high-level requirement might be "The system must allow users to create accounts, browse products, and place orders."

The High-level *Scope* defines the boundaries of the project, clearly outlining what is included and, importantly, what is excluded. This helps to prevent scope creep later in the project. For example, a project to develop a mobile app might explicitly exclude development for desktop browsers.

High-level *Milestones* identify key dates or events in the project timeline. These are significant points in the project's progression, such as the completion of a major phase or a key deliverable. For a construction project, a milestone might be "Completion of foundation" or "Roof installation."

The Pre-assigned *Project Manager* is named in the charter, and their authority level is defined. This clarifies who is responsible for leading the project and what level of decision-making power they have.

The High-level *Budget* summarizes the estimated costs associated with the project. This is a preliminary estimate, not a detailed budget, and provides a general idea of the financial resources required.

Key Stakeholders are identified, along with their roles and responsibilities. Stakeholders are individuals or groups who have an interest in the project's outcome. Identifying them early helps to ensure their needs and expectations are considered.

Finally, the Charter includes the *Sponsor* or *Initiator*, who authorizes the project and provides overall direction and support. This individual is typically a senior manager or executive who champions the project within the organization.

The process for developing the Project Charter is an early step in the project lifecycle. It typically begins with gathering information from key stakeholders. This involves meetings, interviews, and workshops to understand their needs, expectations, and perspectives on the project.

Next, feasibility studies are often conducted to assess the viability of the project. This involves evaluating the technical, economic, and operational feasibility of the project to determine if it is worth pursuing. For example, a feasibility study might assess whether the necessary technology is available, if the project is financially viable, and if the organization has the resources to implement it.

A preliminary project scope and budget are then developed based on the information gathered. This provides a high-level overview of what the project will deliver and how much it is expected to cost. This information is then compiled into the Project Charter document, which is a concise summary of the project's key elements.

Finally, the completed Project Charter is reviewed and approved by the project sponsor or initiator. This formal approval signifies the official start of the project and authorizes the project manager to begin planning activities.

Let's create a Project Charter example for a fictional company, "FreshBrew Coffee," developing a mobile ordering app.

Project Charter: FreshBrew Coffee Mobile App
1. Project Purpose/Justification:

FreshBrew Coffee aims to increase market share and customer loyalty by providing a convenient mobile ordering platform. This app will allow customers to pre-order and pay for their coffee and food items, skipping the line and enhancing their overall experience. This initiative directly addresses the growing demand for mobile convenience and aims to capture a larger segment of the on-the-go coffee market.
2. Project Objectives:
Achieve 50,000 app downloads within the first three months of launch.
Increase average customer order value by 10% within six months of launch.
Achieve a 4.5-star average app store rating within one year of launch.
3. Requirements:
User registration and login functionality (including social media login options).
Menu browsing with customizable options (e.g., milk type, sugar level).
Secure online ordering and payment processing (integration with payment gateways like Stripe or PayPal).
Order tracking and pickup notifications.
Store locator with hours of operation and directions.
Loyalty program integration (points accrual and redemption).
4. Scope:
Included: Development of iOS and Android mobile applications.
Excluded: Development of a web-based ordering platform (desktop access) for the initial release. Integration with third-party delivery services (e.g., DoorDash, Uber Eats) will be considered in future phases.
5. Milestones:
App Design Completion: [Date - e.g., 2026-03-15]
App Development Completion: [Date - e.g., 2026-05-30]
Beta Testing Completion: [Date - e.g., 2026-06-15]
App Launch (iOS & Android): [Date - e.g., 2026-07-01]
6. Project Manager:
Project Manager Name: [- e.g., Sarah Smith]
Authority Level: Full authority to manage project budget, resources, and timelines within the defined scope. Authority to approve changes up to $5,000. Changes exceeding this amount require sponsor approval.
7. Budget:
Estimated Total Budget: $150,000
Breakdown:

* Development: $80,000
* Testing: $20,000
* Marketing & Launch: $30,000
* Contingency: $20,000

8. Key Stakeholders:
Marketing Department: Responsible for app promotion and marketing campaigns.
Development Team (Internal & External Contractors): Responsible for app development and testing.
Operations Team: Responsible for integrating the app with in-store operations.
Customer Service Team: Responsible for handling customer inquiries and support related to the app.
Executive Leadership: Responsible for overall project oversight and strategic direction.
9. Project Sponsor/Initiator:
Sponsor Name/Title: [- e.g., John Miller, Chief Operating Officer]

Test Your Understanding 1.26
What is the primary purpose of the Project Charter?
A. To create a detailed project schedule.
B. To formally authorize the project and provide the project manager with authority.
C. To manage day-to-day project activities.
D. To finalize the project budget, timeline, team members, project manager, and scope.

Test Your Understanding 1.27

What does the "High-level Scope" section of the charter define?
A. Detailed technical specifications.
B. The boundaries of the project.
C. The project team's performance reviews.
D. Day-to-day project tasks at a high level.

Test Your Understanding 1.28
What is the relationship between the Project Charter and the project plan?
A. The charter sets the stage for detailed planning.
B. The charter is the same as the project plan.
C. The project plan authorizes the project.
D. They are developed simultaneously.

Test Your Understanding 1.29
What is the importance of identifying key stakeholders in the Project Charter?
A. To finalize the project budget with the approval of all stakeholders.
B. To create the project schedule that fits all stakeholders.
C. To ensure their needs and expectations are considered.
D. To manage project risks.

Test Your Understanding 1.30
Who formally approves the completed Project Charter?
A. The project team.
B. The project manager.
C. The project stakeholders.
D. The project sponsor.

1.6 Project Scope Statement

Earlier in this chapter, we define project scope as the boundaries of the project, specifying what work will be included and what will be excluded. The Project Scope Statement defines the process for managing stakeholder expectations, preventing scope creep (i.e., uncontrolled expansion of project scope), and ensuring the project delivers its outcomes within agreed-upon constraints. A well-defined scope statement serves as a foundation for all subsequent project planning and execution activities. A well-crafted scope statement typically includes several key elements:

First, *Project Objectives* define the overall goals the project aims to achieve. They articulate the project's purpose and intended outcomes. Effective objectives should adhere to the SMART criteria. Clearly defined objectives provide a clear direction for the project team and serve as measurable benchmarks for evaluating project success. Project objectives must align with business needs and strategic goals.

Second, *Deliverables* represent the tangible or intangible outputs that the project will produce. These are the specific products, services, or results that the project is designed to deliver. Deliverables should be clearly defined and described, including their key characteristics and acceptance criteria. Acceptance criteria define the conditions that must be met for a deliverable to be formally accepted by the stakeholders. Precisely defining deliverables helps manage stakeholder expectations, ensure a shared understanding of what the project will produce, and prevent disputes later in the project lifecycle.

Third, *Boundaries (Scope Exclusions)* are equally crucial as defining what is included in the project. This section explicitly states what is not part of the project's scope. Clearly defined boundaries could prevent scope creep, which is the uncontrolled expansion of the project's scope beyond the original agreement. Scope creep can lead to project delays, cost overruns, and ultimately, project failure. For example, if a project aims to develop a mobile application exclusively for the iOS platform, the scope statement should explicitly exclude development for Android or other platforms. This clear demarcation manages stakeholder expectations and minimizes misunderstandings regarding the project's deliverables.

Finally, the scope statement includes *Assumptions and Constraints*. This section documents the assumptions made during the project planning phase and the constraints that will affect the project's execution. Documenting assumptions and constraints helps understand the project's context, identifying potential risks and issues, and developing appropriate mitigation strategies.

By clearly defining the project's objectives, deliverables, and boundaries, the scope statement helps ensure that the project is focused on delivering value that aligns with the organization's strategic objectives. It also facilitates communication and understanding among stakeholders, ensuring that everyone is on the same page regarding the project's purpose and scope. This shared understanding reduces the risk of misunderstandings, conflicts, and rework. Furthermore, by explicitly documenting assumptions and constraints, the scope statement helps to identify potential risks and challenges early in the project lifecycle, allowing for proactive mitigation and contingency planning. The scope statement is a foundational document that directly influences other project management processes, such as schedule development, cost estimation, and risk management.

Test Your Understanding 1.31
What is the primary purpose of a Project Scope Statement?
A. To establish boundaries for the project and prevent scope creep
B. To outline the approach for executing the project schedule
C. To define the roles and responsibilities of the project team

D. To define the project budget and cost management strategy

Test Your Understanding 1.32
Which of the following best describes scope creep?
A. An increase in project costs due to inflation
B. A failure to define the project budget accurately
C. A reduction in project deliverables due to cost-cutting measures
D. The uncontrolled expansion of project scope beyond the original agreement

Test Your Understanding 1.33
Which of the following is an example of an assumption in a Project Scope Statement?
A. The project must be completed within six months
B. The development will only be for iOS, excluding Android
C. Key personnel will be available throughout the project
D. The project cannot exceed a budget of $500,000

Test Your Understanding 1.34
What is the relationship between a well-defined scope statement and stakeholder communication?
A. It reduces the need for stakeholder involvement
B. It ensures all stakeholders have the same understanding of the project
C. It eliminates the possibility of scope changes
D. It primarily serves as an internal project team document

Test Your Understanding 1.35
How does the Project Scope Statement contribute to risk management?
A. It defines financial contingencies for handling risks
B. It eliminates the need for a separate risk management plan
C. It provides detailed risk response strategies
D. It helps identify assumptions and constraints that may introduce risks

1.7 Steps to Review and Critique Project Scope

A well-defined project scope requires a detailed review of the scope statement to ensure clarity, alignment with objectives, and prevention of scope creep, stakeholder misunderstandings, or project failure. The steps below outline a practical review framework (Larson and Gray, 2021, PMI 2021).

Step 1: Analyze Alignment with Project Charter. The first step is to compare the scope statement against the project charter. The project charter provides a high-level overview of the project, including its objectives, high-level requirements, and authorized project manager. Comparing the scope statement to the charter ensures that the detailed scope aligns with the initial project authorization and high-level project goals. This step confirms that the project, as defined in the scope statement, is still addressing the original business need and strategic intent outlined in the charter. This alignment emphasizes the link between project work and organizational strategy.

Step 2: Review Stakeholder Requirements. This step involves examining the documented stakeholder requirements to ensure completeness and clarity. Stakeholder requirements are the needs and expectations of individuals or groups who have an interest in the project's outcome. These requirements should be clearly articulated, measurable, and traceable back to specific business objectives. This review verifies that the scope statement adequately addresses all documented stakeholder needs and that there are no conflicting or ambiguous requirements. It also confirms alignment with business objectives, ensuring that the project delivers value to the organization.

Step 3: Evaluate Deliverables. This step focuses on assessing the feasibility and clarity of the project deliverables. Each deliverable should be clearly defined, with specific characteristics and acceptance criteria. The review should ensure that the deliverables are realistic and achievable within the project constraints. It also verifies that the deliverables meet the documented stakeholder expectations.

Step 4: Identify Gaps and Ambiguities. During this step, the review team actively looks for any gaps or ambiguities within the scope statement. This includes highlighting any unclear assumptions, missing information, or areas that require further clarification. For example, if the scope statement assumes that a specific resource will be available but doesn't specify how that availability will be secured, this would be flagged as an unclear assumption. Identifying these gaps and ambiguities early on prevents misunderstandings and potential problems during project execution.

Step 5: Validate Constraints and Assumptions. This step involves critically assessing the documented constraints and assumptions and evaluating their potential impact on the project scope. This review should determine the level of risk associated with each constraint and assumption and inform contingency planning. For example, if the project assumes a fixed price for materials, a potential price increase in the market would be a significant risk that needs to be addressed.

Step 6: Document and Communicate Findings. The final step involves documenting all findings from the scope review and communicating them to relevant stakeholders. This includes sharing recommendations for improving scope clarity, completeness, and alignment. This documentation provides a record of the review process and serves as a basis for updating the scope statement. Clear communication of the findings ensures that all stakeholders are aware of any potential issues and agree on the necessary changes. This step reinforces the importance of communication and stakeholder management.

Test Your Understanding 1.36
What is the first step in reviewing a project scope statement?
A. Documenting findings.
B. Evaluating deliverables.
C. Reviewing stakeholder requirements.
D. Analyzing alignment with the project charter.

Test Your Understanding 1.37
What is the focus of evaluating deliverables during a scope review?
A. Assessing feasibility and clarity.
B. Managing project risks.
C. Creating a communication plan.
D. Documenting project lessons learned.

Test Your Understanding 1.38
What does validating constraints and assumptions involve?
A. Creating detailed project reports.
B. Assessing potential impact on the project scope.
C. Managing project communications between the team and the stakeholders.
D. Finalizing the project budget.

Test Your Understanding 1.39
What is the purpose of documenting and communicating findings from the scope review?
A. To create a detailed task list.
B. To ensure stakeholders agree on necessary changes.
C. To manage project expenses.
D. To finalize the project schedule to ensure it is based on the documented scope.

Test Your Understanding 1.40
What does aligning the scope statement with the project charter ensure?
A. Detailed task management.
B. Management of project risks as stated in the project charter.
C. Alignment with organizational strategy.
D. Finalization of the project budget agreed in the project charter.

1.8 Project Management Code of Ethics

Ethics is a cornerstone of professional project management, influencing every aspect of a project from initiation to closure. A strong ethical foundation is not merely a desirable quality; it fosters trust, ensures accountability, and ultimately contributes to project success. The Project Management Institute (PMI) Code of Ethics and Professional Conduct provides a robust framework for ethical decision-making in project management. This code is built upon a foundation of core values that guide the professional conduct of project managers worldwide (PMI, 2021).

Responsibility signifies ownership and accountability for one's actions and decisions, as well as the consequences of those actions. In project management, this means taking ownership of project outcomes, both successes and failures. It includes fulfilling commitments, adhering to professional standards, and acting in the best interests of the project, the organization, and the profession. A responsible project manager ensures that resources are used effectively, project plans are realistic, and stakeholders are kept informed of project progress and any potential issues. For example, if a project falls behind schedule due to unforeseen circumstances, a responsible project manager will proactively communicate the delay to stakeholders, analyze the causes, and develop a revised plan to mitigate the impact.

Respect involves showing consideration and regard for the value, dignity, and perspectives of all stakeholders. This includes team members, clients, sponsors, vendors, and the public. Respectful project managers foster a collaborative and inclusive environment, valuing diverse opinions and promoting open communication. They actively listen to others, acknowledge their contributions, and treat everyone fairly and equitably. For instance, a respectful project manager will ensure that all team members have equal opportunities to contribute to the project and will address any conflicts or disagreements constructively. Respect also extends to respecting cultural differences and adhering to local laws and regulations.

Fairness refers to making impartial and objective decisions, free from bias, prejudice, or favoritism. It involves applying consistent standards and processes, ensuring equal opportunities, and disclosing any potential conflicts of interest. A fair project manager ensures that all stakeholders are treated equitably and that decisions are made based on merit, not personal relationships or other extraneous factors. For example, in a procurement process, a fair project manager will evaluate all bids objectively based on predefined criteria, without giving preferential treatment to any particular vendor. This principle is important for maintaining trust and credibility among stakeholders.

Honesty encompasses truthfulness, integrity, and transparency in all communications and actions. It involves providing accurate information, avoiding misrepresentation, and upholding ethical standards even when facing difficult situations. An honest project manager builds trust and credibility with stakeholders by being open and transparent about project progress, risks, and challenges. For instance, an honest project manager will accurately report project costs, even if they exceed the initial budget, and will promptly disclose any potential risks that could impact the project.

Ethical conduct in project management directly impacts project outcomes, stakeholder relationships, and the overall reputation of the project manager and the organization.

While the PMI Code of Ethics provides a strong ethical framework, real-world project management often presents complex situations that require careful consideration and application of these principles. Ethical dilemmas often involve conflicts between competing values or obligations, requiring project managers to make difficult choices. Here are some common ethical dilemmas encountered in project management and strategies for addressing them:

1. *Conflicts of Interest*: A conflict of interest arises when a project manager's personal interests, or the interests of a close associate, could potentially influence their professional judgment or actions. For example, a project manager might have a financial interest in a vendor bidding on a project or might be offered a personal benefit by a vendor in exchange for favorable treatment.

How to Address: Transparency and disclosure are key. Project managers should disclose any potential conflicts of interest to relevant stakeholders, such as the project sponsor or management. They should recuse themselves from any decisions where their impartiality could be questioned. Establishing clear procurement policies and procedures can also help prevent conflicts of interest.

2. *Pressure to Cut Corners*: Project managers may face pressure to cut corners to meet deadlines or budget constraints. This could involve using substandard materials, skipping essential testing procedures, or falsifying project reports.

How to Address: Project managers should resist pressure to compromise ethical standards. They should clearly communicate the potential risks and consequences of cutting corners to stakeholders. If necessary, they should escalate the issue to higher management or seek guidance from legal counsel. Emphasizing quality management processes and adhering to industry best practices can help prevent this issue.

3. *Confidentiality Breaches*: Project managers often have access to sensitive information, such as proprietary data, financial records, or personnel information. Breaching confidentiality can have serious consequences for the project and the organization.

How to Address: Project managers should respect the confidentiality of sensitive information and ensure that it is protected from unauthorized access. They should establish clear confidentiality agreements with team members and vendors and implement appropriate security measures to safeguard data.

4. *Misrepresentation of Information*: Project managers may be tempted to misrepresent project progress, risks, or challenges to stakeholders to avoid negative consequences. This could involve inflating progress reports, downplaying risks, or concealing problems.

How to Address: Honesty and transparency are crucial. Project managers should provide accurate and truthful information to stakeholders, even when it is difficult news to deliver. They should establish open communication channels and foster a culture of trust and transparency within the project team. This is directly tied to the ethical principle of honesty.

5. *Bribery and Corruption*: In some contexts, project managers may encounter situations involving bribery or corruption, such as being offered bribes to award contracts or being asked to participate in fraudulent activities.

How to Address: Project managers should refuse to participate in any form of bribery or corruption. They should report any such incidents to the appropriate authorities, both within the organization and externally if necessary. Organizations should have clear anti-corruption policies and procedures in place.

Navigating ethical challenges requires more than just knowing the rules; it demands a proactive and practical approach. Here are key strategies for applying ethical principles in your project management practice.

Consult the PMI Code: When facing an ethical dilemma, your first step should be to consult the PMI Code of Ethics and Professional Conduct. This document provides a framework built on the core values of responsibility, respect, fairness, and honesty. Use it to analyze the situation and guide your decision-making process.

Seek Guidance: You don't have to make tough decisions alone. Discuss complex ethical situations with trusted colleagues, mentors, or your organization's ethics officer. Gaining diverse perspectives can clarify the issue and help you identify the best course of action, demonstrating a commitment to professional responsibility.

Document Your Process: Thoroughly document the ethical dilemma, the options you considered, and the rationale behind your final decision. This record creates transparency and accountability, serving as a crucial reference in case of future audits or disputes.

Champion an Ethical Culture: As a project manager, you are instrumental in shaping your team's ethical culture. Foster an environment of integrity by consistently leading by example, encouraging open communication so team members feel safe voicing concerns, providing regular ethics training to build awareness, and establishing clear policies and guidelines for your team.

Test Your Understanding 1.41
What is a conflict of interest in project management?
A. Disagreements among team members, sponsors, customers, or suppliers.
B. Situations where personal interests influence professional judgment.
C. Changes in project scope.
D. Delays in project timelines.

Test Your Understanding 1.42
How should project managers address pressure to cut corners?
A. By ignoring the pressure.
B. By compromising ethical standards without increasing the project cost.
C. By escalating the issue and communicating risks.
D. By falsifying project reports.

Test Your Understanding 1.43
Which of the following is NOT a strategy for project managers when facing an ethical dilemma?
A. Consult the PMI Code of Ethics.
B. Seek advice from trusted sources.
C. Document decisions.
D. Make decisions regardless of personal gain.

Test Your Understanding 1.44
Why is documenting ethical decisions important?
A. To protect the project manager and promote transparency.
B. To avoid future disputes among team members and customers.
C. To finalize the project budget.
D. To create a detailed task list.

Test Your Understanding 1.45
What should project managers do if they encounter bribery or corruption?
A. Report the incidents to the appropriate authorities.
B. Minimizing participation in the activities whenever possible.
C. Ignore the situation.
D. Conceal the information.

1.9 Projects as Vehicles for Change

Projects are not merely isolated endeavors focused on delivering specific outputs; they are powerful drivers of organizational change and innovation (Lester and Robertson, 2017). They provide a structured mechanism for introducing new ideas, processes, and technologies, enabling organizations to adapt to evolving market conditions, improve efficiency, and achieve strategic objectives. Project managers should recognize this transformative role, as it highlights the broader context in which projects operate and their lasting impact on organizational success (Iriogbe et al., 2024).

A key strength of projects lies in their temporary nature. By establishing a focused environment with defined goals, projects allow for concentrated effort and controlled experimentation without disrupting day-to-day operations. Once a project is completed and its deliverables transition into ongoing use, the results become embedded in the organization's activities and culture, effectively becoming the "new normal" (KMI, 2021).

Projects drive change in several important ways. One significant contribution is the introduction of new technologies. Projects often involve implementing new hardware, software, or systems that can transform how an organization operates. These advancements may automate manual tasks, improve communication and collaboration, enhance data analysis, or even create entirely new products and services -- opening new markets and revenue streams. Another common focus is reengineering business processes. Organizations frequently use projects to analyze and redesign workflows, eliminating redundancies, automating repetitive tasks, and optimizing resource utilization to improve efficiency and productivity.

Projects also serve as engines for developing new products and services. From concept to market launch, they manage the full lifecycle of activities, including market research, design, development, testing, and marketing. When successful, these efforts expand market share, attract new customers, and strengthen competitive advantage. For example, a project to develop a mobile app can provide customers with easier access to services while opening entirely new business opportunities. In addition, projects can reshape organizational structures. Implementing a new project management methodology, for instance, might result in the creation of a Project Management Office (PMO) or the introduction of new roles and responsibilities within teams. These structural changes can improve governance, standardize practices, and enhance an organization's overall project management maturity.

While projects act as engines of innovation and transformation, their success depends not only on technical execution but also on how effectively the "people side" of change is managed (Kotter et al., 2025). This is the role of change management -- a structured approach to guiding individuals, teams, and organizations from a current state to a desired future state. Without it, even the most technically sound project may fail due to user resistance, lack of adoption, or integration challenges.

Effective change management involves several critical elements. Communication builds understanding and buy-in. Clearly explaining the purpose of the change, the benefits it will bring, and the impact on day-to-day work helps minimize resistance. Messages should be tailored to different groups; executives may require strategic insights, while employees may need practical guidance. Using multiple communication channels, such as meetings, emails, training, and intranet updates, ensures the message reaches all stakeholders. Training and support are equally vital. Employees must be prepared to work with new systems, processes, or tools, and training should be practical, role-specific, and ongoing, with opportunities for feedback and hands-on experience.

Stakeholder engagement further strengthens the adoption of change. Involving employees, customers, suppliers, and other interested parties early and throughout the project builds ownership and trust while also surfacing valuable insights that improve outcomes. Techniques such as surveys, workshops, and focus groups can be particularly effective in keeping stakeholders engaged. Finally, resistance management is a key part of the process. Since resistance to change is natural, project leaders must identify its sources -- whether fear of job loss, increased workload, or uncertainty -- and address them directly. Proactively responding to these concerns, rather than simply suppressing them, is far more effective in ensuring project success.

Test Your Understanding 1.46
What is a key role of projects within organizations?
A. Delivering specific outputs without affecting business operations.
B. Providing a structured mechanism for implementing change and innovation.
C. Maintaining the status quo to ensure business stability.
D. Reducing project costs by eliminating change initiatives.

Test Your Understanding 1.47
Why is the temporary nature of projects beneficial for organizations?
A. It allows for controlled experimentation without disrupting daily operations.
B. It ensures all employees are involved in every project decision.
C. It prevents long-term commitment to new ideas.
D. It minimizes the need for project planning and risk management.

Test Your Understanding 1.48
Why is change management essential for project success?
A. It ensures employees understand and support the changes introduced by the project.
B. It minimizes the need for technical implementation in projects.
C. It focuses mainly on leadership and executive-level decision-making related to the changes.
D. It removes the need for communication with stakeholders.

Test Your Understanding 1.49
What is a critical aspect of effective change management?
A. Releasing change updates only after project completion.
B. Keeping change-related information confidential.
C. Communicating the reasons for change and its benefits.
D. Assisting employees figure out the new processes on their own.

Test Your Understanding 1.50
What is an effective way to manage resistance to change in projects?
A. Avoiding communication about the upcoming changes before the project is closed.
B. Ignoring resistance and continuing project implementation as planned.
C. Removing employees who resist the new changes.
D. Identifying sources of resistance early and addressing concerns proactively.

1.10 Chapter Summary

This chapter covers the fundamental aspects of project management, including essential concepts like operations, projects, programs, and portfolios. It briefly discusses project management methodologies, such as waterfall and agile. Additionally, it addresses topics such as project issues, risks, assumptions, and constraints that play a significant role in project management. Next, the chapter explores project scope for effective project management. The project management ethical code of conduct is also discussed. Finally, the chapter explains how projects can be powerful drivers of organizational change and innovation.

1.11 Case Study

Lynn Smith University is a small university that has approximately 5000 undergraduate students and 1000 graduate students. The university has recognized the need for a web-based software application to manage the student experience from application to graduation. This application will allow students to apply for the university, register for courses, declare majors, audit degree completion timelines, and check for attendance and grades in progress and completed courses.

The university was founded in 1875 and has a strong tradition of liberal arts education. The university's mission is to provide students with a well-rounded education that prepares them for success in their chosen careers and as responsible citizens. The university has a diverse student population, with students from all 50 states and more than 50 countries. The university's campus is spread over an area of 200 acres and is known for its beautiful architecture, lush green lawns, and state-of-the-art facilities. The university has an active student life, with more than 110 student organizations, including academic clubs, honor societies, cultural groups, and recreational clubs.

To begin the project, the university must first define the project scope. The scope of this project includes the development of a web-based software application that will allow students to complete the above-mentioned tasks.

User requirements:
Secure login: The landing page has three links, one for each type of users: Administrators, faculty, and students.

Application process: The application should allow students to submit their application for the university online, including the ability to upload required documents such as transcripts and self-reported test scores. The university allows anyone to apply. However, not all applicants will be accepted. An administrator decides who to accept.

Course registration: The application should allow students (accepted applicants) to view available courses and register for them online, including checking for prerequisites and availability. Courses are offered by the semesters. There are three semesters in a year, fall, spring, and summer. The administrators are allowed to add, update, and delete courses.

Degree audit: The application should allow students to view their progress towards completing their degree, including a timeline of when they will be able to graduate. The university requires students to take any 120 credit hours for graduation as long as the grade for each course is C or above.
Grades: The application should allow students to view their grades for completed courses. The students can also view the class attendance. Faculty enters grade and attendance for courses they teach. Administrators add faculty to the system.

Reporting and analytics: The application should have reporting and analytics capabilities, so administrators can track student progress and performance. This feature may include, display all students of the university, display student enrollments by semester, display all students in a certain class, display all course status of a student, display all faculty and courses they teach.

Project Management Tasks:
1. Assemble a team of 4 to 7 individuals. Provide introductions, including information that will build trust among team members, and details about the best way to reach you and your availability for meetings.
2. Write a charter by following the sample provided in the chapter.

1.12 References

Iriogbe, H. O., Agu, E. E., Efunniyi, C. P., Osundare, O. S., & Adeniran, I. A. (2024). The role of project management in driving innovation, economic growth, and future trends. International Journal of Management & Entrepreneurship Research, 6(8)
Kotter, J. P., Akhtar, V., & Gupta, G. (2025). Change: How organizations achieve hard-to-imagine results in uncertain and volatile times. John Wiley & Sons.
Larson, E. W., & Gray, C. F. (2021). Project management: the managerial process (8th). McGraw-Hill Education, New York.
Lester, A., & Robertson, K. (2017). Project management for dummies. John Wiley & Sons.
Project Management Institute (PMI). (2021). A Guide to the Project Management Body of Knowledge (PMBOK Guide) - and the Standard for Project Management. 7th Edition.

1.13 Solutions to Test Your Understanding

1.1 B; 1.2 D; 1.3 C; 1.4 A; 1.5 C; 1.6 B; 1.7 B; 1.8 B; 1.9 A; 1.10 C; 1.11 B; 1.12 B; 1.13 C; 1.14 C; 1.15 A; 1.16 B; 1.17 C; 1.18 B; 1.19 C; 1.20 B; 1.21 A; 1.22 B; 1.23 C; 1.24 B; 1.25 D; 1.26 B; 1.27 B; 1.28 A; 1.29 C; 1.30 D; 1.31 A; 1.32 D; 1.33 C; 1.34 B; 1.35 D; 1.36 D; 1.37 A; 1.38 B; 1.39 B; 1.40 C; 1.41 B; 1.42 C; 1.43 D; 1.44 A; 1.45 A; 1.46 B; 1.47 A; 1.48 A; 1.49 C; 1.50 D;

Chapter 2: Roles and Responsibilities

Chapter Learning Outcomes

2.1 Analyze and differentiate the duties of project managers, team, and sponsors.
2.2 Examine and clarify the various functions performed by a project manager.
2.3 Analyze and distinguish between the concepts of leadership and management.
2.4 Examine emotional intelligence (EQ) and its impact on project management.

2.1 Project Manager and Project Sponsor

Every project is guided by two pivotal roles: Project Manager and Project Sponsor. While they collaborate closely, they operate at different levels and have distinct responsibilities. The Project Manager is the tactical executor, focused on the "how" of day-to-day delivery, while the Project Sponsor is the strategic champion, focused on the "why" that aligns the project with organizational goals.

The *Project Manager* serves as the primary driver of the project, responsible for its successful delivery within the defined constraints of scope, time, and cost. Their responsibilities are extensive, encompassing the operational aspects of the project from initiation to closure. This includes developing detailed project schedules, defining tasks, and allocating resources, as well as leading and coordinating the project team to foster collaboration and resolve conflicts. Furthermore, the Project Manager is tasked with managing the approved budget, controlling costs, and proactively identifying project-level risks and issues. They act as the central point of contact for stakeholder communication and are responsible for implementing quality control measures and managing all project documentation. To fulfill these duties, the Project Manager is granted operational authority, allowing them to make tactical, day-to-day decisions about task assignments and problem-solving to keep the project on track. They report directly to the Project Sponsor.

In contrast, the *Project Sponsor* is typically a senior executive who acts as the project's champion and is accountable for its success from a business perspective. Their key responsibilities are strategic in nature. They own and defend the business case that justifies the project's existence and ensure it delivers the expected value. The Sponsor also ensures the project remains aligned with evolving business priorities and adheres to organizational governance. A function is the authorization of funding and securing of necessary organizational resources, as they have the authority to approve the overall budget and resolve cross-project resource conflicts. By acting as an executive-level advocate, they promote the project's importance, secure buy-in, remove high-level obstacles, and provide support for the organizational change the project will introduce. This high-level accountability is supported by the Sponsor's strategic authority; they are not involved in daily management but make the significant decisions that shape the project's direction.

The differences between the two roles become clearest when examining their decision-making authority and collaborative processes. The distinction is sharp: the Project Manager decides on *how* to execute the work, including choosing technical approaches and making minor schedule adjustments, whereas the Project Sponsor decides on *whether* the project's direction should change. This includes approving major changes to scope or budget and, ultimately, deciding if a project should continue or be terminated.

This division of authority necessitates a formal escalation pathway for issues that exceed the Project Manager's scope. Issues are typically escalated if they involve significant budget overruns, schedule delays that impact strategic objectives, high-impact risks, or stakeholder conflicts requiring executive intervention. An example of their necessary collaboration is the creation of the project charter. The Project Manager drafts the charter with a practical foundation, and the Sponsor reviews and approves it, validating its business case and formally authorizing the project to begin.

Test Your Understanding 2.1
What is the primary responsibility of the Project Manager?
A. Securing project funding and ensuring executive buy-in.
B. Managing the execution of the project, including task assignments and resource utilization.
C. Defining the project scope and making high-level strategic decisions, assigning resources.
D. Approving significant changes to the project budget and timeline.

Test Your Understanding 2.2
Which of the following is NOT a responsibility of the Project Manager?
A. Managing the project budget within approved limits.
B. Ensuring project quality through quality control measures within the project.
C. Acting as the main point of contact for all stakeholders.
D. Providing final approval for significant changes to project scope.

Test Your Understanding 2.3
Which of the following responsibilities is primarily associated with the Project Manager rather than the Project Sponsor?
A. Controlling expenditures and ensuring the business case remains relevant throughout the project.
B. Controlling expenditures and ensuring the project stays within the approved budget.
C. Providing organizational change management support.
D. Acting as the project's advocate at the executive level.

Test Your Understanding 2.4

Why is effective stakeholder communication critical for a Project Manager?
A. It allows them to secure project funding directly from senior management.
B. It ensures that all project-related changes are approved without delays from senior management.
C. It helps in managing expectations, addressing concerns, and maintaining alignment.
D. It reduces the need for formal documentation throughout the project lifecycle.

Test Your Understanding 2.5
What best describes the Project Sponsor's authority?
A. They provide funding and strategic direction but do not manage day-to-day activities.
B. They have operational control over project execution and task prioritization.
C. They make most of all project decisions, including assigning tasks to the project team.
D. They are responsible for team performance management and motivation.

Test Your Understanding 2.6
What is a key distinction between the Project Manager and the Project Sponsor?
A. The Sponsor manages project execution, while the Manager handles stakeholder relationships.
B. The Sponsor is responsible for risk management, while the Manager handles governance.
C. The Sponsor focuses on strategic alignment, while the Manager focuses on project execution.
D. The Project Sponsor assigns daily tasks, while the Project Manager controls project funding.

Test Your Understanding 2.7
What is the primary focus of the Project Manager's decision-making scope?
A. Strategic direction and alignment of the project with business goals.
B. Portfolio-level prioritization of projects.
C. Tactical execution of project tasks and resource management.
D. Approval of major scope and budget changes.

Test Your Understanding 2.8
Which of the following decisions falls under the authority of the Project Sponsor?
A. Assigning specific team members to specific tasks of the project.
B. Implementing project risk response strategies.
C. Approving major scope changes that significantly alter deliverables.
D. Adjusting the project schedule for minor changes.

Test Your Understanding 2.9
If a project faces a budget overrun exceeding the predefined threshold, what is the appropriate escalation pathway?
A. The issue is handled at the project level by the Project Manager.
B. The issue is escalated to the Project Sponsor for resolution.
C. The issue is resolved directly by executive leadership.
D. The team members adjust their tasks to accommodate the budget overrun.

Test Your Understanding 2.10
What is one of the key responsibilities of the Project Sponsor during project initiation?
A. Drafting the project charter, including objectives and resource plans.
B. Reviewing and formally approving the project charter.
C. Defining specific project tasks and team roles.
D. Managing day-to-day project risks.

2.2 Project Team and Project Sponsor

For a project to succeed, it relies on a well-structured group of individuals, each with distinct roles and responsibilities. This group can be broadly divided into the project team, which handles the day-to-day execution, and the project sponsor, as explained in last section, who provides strategic oversight and direction. Understanding the composition of the team and its relationship with the sponsor is fundamental to effective project management.

The *project team* is responsible for the operational work of carrying out the project plan. This team is typically composed of a core team and an extended team. At the helm of the core team is the Project Manager, who holds primary responsibility and authority for the project's overall success. Supporting the Project Manager are technical team members, the subject matter experts (SMEs) who build and implement the project's deliverables, such as engineers, developers, or architects. Business Analysts play a crucial role by bridging the gap between business needs and technical solutions, gathering requirements from stakeholders to ensure the project delivers its intended value. Finally, Project Coordinators provide essential administrative support, handling tasks like scheduling meetings, managing documentation, and tracking action items, which allows other team members to focus on their core duties.

Beyond the core group, an extended team often brings specialized expertise on an as-needed basis. Quality Assurance (QA) professionals ensure deliverables meet pre-defined standards, while Risk Management specialists help identify and mitigate potential project risks. For projects that involve significant organizational change, Change Management specialists manage the "people side" of the transition, helping stakeholders adapt smoothly. Additionally, representatives from a Project Management Office (PMO) may provide templates, tools, and guidance to ensure the project aligns with broader organizational standards and best practices.

The structure in which this team operates significantly influences its dynamics. In a common matrix organization, team members report to both a functional manager (for career development) and the Project Manager (for project tasks). This requires clear communication and a well-defined project charter that outlines decision-making authority to avoid conflicts and ensure efficient governance.

While the project team operates at this tactical level, the Project Sponsor functions at a strategic one. The distinction in authority is critical: the project team makes operational decisions about task execution and problem-solving, whereas the sponsor makes strategic decisions, such as approving major scope changes, authorizing budget increases, or even terminating the project if it no longer serves its business purpose. Similarly, their stakeholder interactions differ; the team engages with those directly involved in the project, while the sponsor communicates with executive management to maintain high-level support.

Test Your Understanding 2.11
Which of the following best describes the role of Business Analysts in a project team?
A. They oversee the project's technical implementation and guide development team members
B. They bridge the gap between business needs and technical solutions by gathering and documenting requirements
C. They manage the project budget and track expenses to ensure financial compliance
D. They ensure that the project team follows best practices and adheres to organizational methodologies

Test Your Understanding 2.12
What is the primary role of the Project Management Office (PMO) in an organization?
A. Providing support by ensuring projects align with organizational standards and methodologies
B. Assigning technical resources and overseeing system development
C. Executing the project deliverables and managing the project budget
D. Conducting risk assessments and training project teams on compliance

Test Your Understanding 2.13
In a project, who is primarily responsible for managing stakeholder expectations and ensuring smooth organizational transitions?
A. Quality Assurance Specialist
B. Business Analyst
C. Project Coordinator
D. Change Management Specialist

Test Your Understanding 2.14
Which of the following best describes the authority of a Project Manager in a matrix organization?
A. The Project Manager has full authority over team members' career development
B. The Project Manager independently determines policies without consulting functional managers
C. The Project Manager has no authority over resource allocation or task assignments
D. The Project Manager and functional manager must clearly define decision-making responsibilities

Test Your Understanding 2.15
What is the primary focus of the project team within a project?
A. Executing project tasks and managing day-to-day operations
B. Setting the organization's strategic goals
C. Approving budget modifications and scope changes
D. Securing funding and organizational support

Test Your Understanding 2.16
Who is primarily responsible for securing project funding?
A. Project Manager
B. Technical Team Lead

C. Project Sponsor
D. Business Analyst

Test Your Understanding 2.17
Which of the following is NOT a role of the project sponsor?
A. Removing organizational roadblocks
B. Providing high-level oversight of the project
C. Managing the day-to-day execution of project tasks
D. Approving major scope changes

2.3 More Roles of Project Managers

Project managers not only fulfill the duties discussed previously, but also act as initiators, negotiators, listeners, coaches, team members, and facilitators (PMI, 2021).

2.3.1 As an Initiator

The initiator role of the project manager establishes the groundwork for the entire project. This role is where the project officially begins, with the project manager collaborating with the sponsor to create the project charter. Without this crucial step, the project lacks legitimacy and risks becoming disorganized or failing to secure necessary support.

A key responsibility during initiation is defining the project's scope, where the project manager works with stakeholders to clearly outline what the project will and will not deliver. The initiator role also involves defining clear and measurable project objectives, providing a target for the project team and a benchmark for assessing project success. Well-defined objectives maintain project focus and ensure the delivery of intended benefits.

Furthermore, the initiator role ensures stakeholder alignment and buy-in. During initiation, the Project Manager identifies key stakeholders who will be affected by or have an interest in the project, including internal stakeholders like team members, management, and other departments, as well as external stakeholders like customers, suppliers, and regulatory bodies. The initiator role also involves initial communication with stakeholders to understand their needs and expectations. This early engagement helps building buy-in and ensuring that the project meets stakeholder needs, while also helping to identify potential conflicts or issues early on for proactive resolution.

Resource planning and allocation are also key aspects of the initiator role. This involves outlining the project's resource requirements, including human resources, budget, equipment, and materials. This initial resource planning provides a basis for developing a more detailed project budget and schedule in later phases. The Project Manager collaborates with the sponsor to secure the initial resources needed to begin the project, which may involve obtaining funding, assigning team members, and acquiring necessary equipment or materials.

Ultimately, the initiator role is about setting the project up for success. By clearly defining the project's foundation, aligning stakeholders, and securing initial resources, the Project Manager creates a solid base upon which to build the project. A weak initiation can lead to problems throughout the project lifecycle, including scope creep, budget overruns, schedule delays, and stakeholder dissatisfaction.

2.3.2 As a Negotiator

The negotiator role goes beyond simply bargaining; it's about building consensus, managing expectations, resolving conflicts, and fostering collaboration among diverse stakeholders.

Projects often involve individuals with varying needs and priorities, and the project manager acts as a mediator, negotiating compromises and finding solutions that satisfy as many stakeholders as possible. This prevents conflicts from escalating and ensures that everyone feels heard and valued, ultimately securing buy-in and support for the project. Effective negotiation builds trust and fosters a sense of shared ownership, making stakeholders more likely to contribute to the project's success. A key aspect of this role is translating negotiated agreements into clear, documented commitments, preventing misunderstandings and ensuring everyone is aligned on scope, timelines, and deliverables.

Furthermore, the project manager often needs to negotiate for resources like budget, personnel, and equipment with various departments or external vendors. Strong negotiation skills help secure the necessary resources for successful project completion. Negotiation also optimizes resource utilization within the project, potentially requiring the project manager to negotiate with team members to adjust workloads, prioritize tasks, or resolve conflicts over resource allocation.

Conflicts are inevitable in projects, especially those with multiple stakeholders or complex technical challenges. The project manager uses negotiation skills to resolve these conflicts constructively, finding solutions that address the concerns of all parties involved. Negotiation also encourages creative problem-solving by exploring different options and finding mutually beneficial solutions, allowing the project manager to find innovative ways to overcome obstacles and keep the project on track (Hishamuddin and Aminuddin, 2025).

When changes to the project scope, schedule, or budget are required, the project manager must negotiate these changes with stakeholders, explaining the reasons, discussing the potential impact, and reaching an agreement on how to proceed. Effective negotiation can minimize disruption caused by these changes, ensuring the project remains on track and stakeholders remain satisfied.

Ultimately, successful negotiation builds trust and rapport with stakeholders, creating stronger working relationships essential for effective collaboration and communication throughout the project lifecycle. Even when disagreements occur, skillful negotiation can help maintain positive relationships, which helps long-term project success and future collaborations. Therefore, the negotiator role isn't just about haggling; it's about building consensus, managing expectations, resolving conflicts, and fostering collaboration, making it a key competency for project managers.

2.3.3 As a Listener

Active listening promotes effective communication and stakeholder management, particularly during requirements gathering. By carefully listening to stakeholders, the project manager accurately captures their needs, expectations, and concerns, preventing misunderstandings and ensuring the project delivers intended value, a critical aspect of the clear scope definition.

Furthermore, active listening enhances the management of stakeholder expectations by identifying discrepancies among their often diverse and sometimes conflicting needs, allowing the project manager to proactively address these differences and prevent future dissatisfaction and conflicts. Demonstrating respect and empathy through active listening fosters trust and rapport with stakeholders, strengthening relationships and creating a more collaborative project environment, crucial for navigating the various stakeholder influences.

Within the project team, active listening helps the project manager understand individual members' concerns, challenges, and ideas, leading to better team management, improved morale, and increased productivity. By creating a safe space for open and honest communication, the project manager facilitates better communication flow, improving problem-solving and decision-making. When conflicts arise within the team, active listening helps uncover root causes and facilitate resolutions that address all parties' concerns, maintaining team cohesion and project momentum.

Active listening also supports risk and issue management. Stakeholders often provide valuable insights into potential risks and issues, and by actively listening to their concerns, the project manager can identify risks and issues that might otherwise be overlooked, aligning with the proactive risk management. Furthermore, active listening helps the project manager understand the potential impact of risks and issues on the project, enabling more effective risk response planning and issue resolution.

Finally, active listening aids continuous improvement and the capturing lessons learned. By gathering feedback from stakeholders throughout the project lifecycle, the project manager can improve project processes and ensure the project meets stakeholder needs. At project closure, active listening helps capture valuable lessons learned that can be applied to future projects. The listener role is not just a soft skill but a fundamental competency contributing to effective communication, stakeholder management, team dynamics, risk management, and continuous improvement. It demonstrates an understanding of the human element in project management. By actively listening, the project manager fosters a more collaborative, efficient, and ultimately successful project environment.

2.3.4 As a Coach

The project manager's role as a coach is increasingly recognized as a vital aspect of effective project leadership, a perspective reflected in the emphasis on interpersonal skills. The coach role centers on developing and empowering the project team to achieve peak performance. A project manager acting as a coach helps team members develop their skills and competencies through training, mentoring, and constructive feedback. This investment in team development enhances overall team capabilities and improves project outcomes (Cox and Ireland, 2017).

This coaching approach also motivates and engages team members by recognizing their contributions, providing encouragement, and fostering a positive work environment, leading to a more productive and committed team, which contributes to positive team dynamics. Furthermore, it empowers team members to take ownership of their work and make decisions within their responsibilities, fostering accountability and increasing their commitment to the project.

A project manager adopting a coaching style facilitates open and honest communication within the team, creating a safe space for sharing ideas, concerns, and feedback, which improves communication flow and strengthens team cohesion. Coaching also helps build strong relationships within the team based on trust and mutual respect, fostering a more collaborative and supportive work environment. When conflicts arise, a coaching approach helps team members develop their problem-solving skills by guiding them through the process, helping them identify root causes and develop effective solutions. The project manager can also facilitate constructive dialogue during conflicts, helping team members understand each other's perspectives and find mutually acceptable solutions.

Finally, a coaching approach promotes a culture of learning and growth within the project team, encouraging team members to reflect on their experiences, identify areas for improvement, and develop new skills. It also facilitates the capture of lessons learned during the project, guiding team members in reflecting on what went well, what could have been done differently, and how to apply these lessons to future projects. The coach role highlights the importance of developing and empowering project teams. This focus on the human element in project management demonstrates that successful project management involves not just technical skills but also strong interpersonal and leadership skills.

2.3.5 As a Working Member

While the project management emphasizes the project manager's leadership, planning, and organizational skills, it also recognizes situations where the project manager may need to function as a "working member" of the team, contributing directly to project tasks alongside other team members without relinquishing their management responsibilities.

This dual role is particularly relevant in smaller projects or those with limited resources. In smaller projects or organizations with limited resources, the project manager may possess specific technical skills necessary for project execution, and by acting as a working member, they can fill skill gaps and prevent project delays due to a lack of expertise. In resource-constrained environments, having the project manager contribute directly can be more cost-effective than hiring additional resources.

By working directly on project tasks, the project manager gains a deeper understanding of the technical challenges and complexities involved, enhancing their ability to make informed decisions, manage risks, and communicate effectively with the technical team. This hands-on experience also provides valuable insights into task durations, dependencies, and potential bottlenecks, improving their ability to estimate project timelines and develop realistic project plans.

When the project manager works alongside the team, it can foster a stronger sense of camaraderie and teamwork, improving team morale and communication (Meng and Boyd, 2017). By contributing directly, the project manager demonstrates their commitment to the project's success and gains the respect of the team, improving motivation and engagement.

In situations where urgent issues arise requiring immediate attention, the project manager can step in as a working member to help resolve the problem quickly, preventing project delays and maintaining momentum. When facing tight deadlines, the project manager's direct contribution can help the team meet critical milestones and avoid schedule slippage. However, it's important to emphasize that the working member role should not replace the project manager's core responsibilities of planning, organizing, leading, and controlling the project.

The Project Manager must balance their direct contributions with their management duties to ensure the project stays on track. When acting as a working member, the project manager must communicate clearly with the team about their dual role and ensure that tasks are properly delegated to other team members to prevent confusion and maintain clear lines of responsibility.

The working member role is often temporary or limited to specific tasks or project phases, and the project manager should transition back to their primary management responsibilities as soon as possible. The "working member" role is not about replacing dedicated technical staff but about strategically contributing when necessary to address resource constraints, gain deeper project understanding, enhance team dynamics, or maintain project momentum during critical periods, demonstrating adaptability and a willingness to contribute at all levels while still prioritizing core management functions.

2.3.6 As a Facilitator

A facilitator guides processes and discussions, ensuring effective communication, collaboration, and decision-making among team members and stakeholders, focusing less on direct instruction and more on enabling effective teamwork (Raelin, 2013). Facilitation enhances effective communication and collaboration, particularly in meetings and workshops where the project manager ensures these sessions are productive, focused, and inclusive, allowing all participants to contribute effectively. By facilitating open communication and knowledge sharing, the project manager helps create a more informed and collaborative project environment, ensuring everyone has access to necessary information.

Furthermore, facilitation plays a key role in stakeholder management, particularly in managing conflicting interests. The project manager, as a facilitator, helps mediate differences and facilitates discussions to find mutually acceptable solutions, crucial for managing stakeholder expectations and building consensus. Facilitation also helps build consensus among stakeholders by ensuring everyone has a voice and all perspectives are considered, increasing stakeholder buy-in and support.

Within team dynamics and performance, facilitation techniques can be used to improve team dynamics and build stronger working relationships. By facilitating team-building activities and discussions, the project manager helps create a more cohesive and collaborative team. When conflicts arise within the team, the project manager can act as a facilitator to help team members resolve their differences constructively, creating a safe space for open communication, helping team members understand each other's perspectives, and guiding them towards mutually acceptable solutions.

Facilitation also enhances problem-solving and decision-making. The project manager can facilitate structured problem-solving sessions using techniques like brainstorming, root cause analysis, and decision matrices, ensuring problems are addressed systematically and effective solutions are identified. Facilitation also helps improve the quality of group decision-making by ensuring all relevant information is considered and all team members have the opportunity to contribute. Finally, facilitation enhances process improvement. At the end of a project or phase, the project manager can facilitate lessons learned sessions to identify areas for improvement in future projects, contributing to organizational learning and continuous improvement.

Test Your Understanding 2.18
Which of the following best describes the project manager's role as an initiator?
A. Outlining project risks and assigning mitigation strategies.
B. Securing funding and assigning team members to specific tasks and events.
C. Establishing project scope, objectives, and stakeholder alignment.
D. Directly performing tasks within the project.

Test Your Understanding 2.19
What is a key outcome of defining clear and measurable project objectives?
A. Reducing the project scope to minimize work.
B. Providing a benchmark for assessing project success.
C. Guaranteeing that no scope changes will occur.
D. Eliminating the need for a change management plan.

Test Your Understanding 2.20
How does a project manager use negotiation when securing project resources?
A. By bargaining with vendors for the lowest cost services.
B. By engaging stakeholders to optimize resource allocation.
C. By ensuring team members agree with all project decisions.
D. By reallocating all resources to optimize resources distribution.

Test Your Understanding 2.21
Which of the following is a key skill for project managers when negotiating stakeholder agreements?
A. Avoiding conflict at all costs.
B. Documenting commitments clearly to prevent misunderstandings.
C. Delegating all stakeholder discussions to the sponsor.
D. Making all decisions for the benefits of the project and all team members.

Test Your Understanding 2.22
Why is negotiation important when changes to project scope, schedule, or budget are required?
A. It prevents unnecessary disruptions and keeps the project on track.
B. It allows the project manager to avoid all stakeholder disagreements.
C. It eliminates the need for stakeholder approvals.
D. It ensures the project is always delivered under budget.

Test Your Understanding 2.23
Which statement best describes the importance of active listening in stakeholder management?
A. It helps in capturing stakeholder needs and expectations accurately.
B. It eliminates potential project conflicts.
C. It ensures all stakeholders are equally satisfied with project decisions.
D. It removes the need for formal documentation of requirements.

Test Your Understanding 2.24
How does active listening contribute to project risk management?
A. It allows the project manager to ignore low-priority risks.
B. It replaces the need for a formal risk register.
C. It prevents all risks from materializing.
D. It helps identify risks that might otherwise be overlooked.

Test Your Understanding 2.25
Which of the following is a key function of the project manager in the coaching role?
A. Performing all project tasks independently.
B. Assigning tasks without explanation for time-based competition.
C. Providing training and mentoring to develop the team.
D. Avoiding feedback to prevent conflict among team members.

Test Your Understanding 2.26
How does a coaching approach support conflict resolution within a project team?
A. By avoiding discussions about disagreements.
B. By helping team members develop problem-solving skills.
C. By instructing team members to resolve conflicts independently.
D. By reducing the number of team meetings.

Test Your Understanding 2.27

In which type of project is the project manager most likely to take on a working member role?
A. A large-scale project with abundant resources.
B. A project with outsourced technical execution.
C. A government-funded infrastructure project.
D. A small project with limited resources.

Test Your Understanding 2.28
How does taking on a working member role benefit the project manager?
A. It provides direct insight into technical challenges.
B. It eliminates the need for team collaboration.
C. It allows the project manager to micromanage team members.
D. It ensures all work is completed without delegation.

Test Your Understanding 2.29
Which of the following best describes the role of a facilitator in project management?
A. A facilitator provides direct instruction to team members to ensure task completion.
B. A facilitator focuses on executing tasks rather than enabling team collaboration.
C. A facilitator makes all project decisions to prevent stakeholder disagreements.
D. A facilitator aids productive and inclusive meetings where all participants contribute effectively.

2.4 Ledership and Management

Leadership in project management is about inspiring and motivating the project team and stakeholders towards a shared vision. It involves influencing, guiding, and empowering individuals to achieve project objectives, even amidst challenges and uncertainties. This emphasizes interpersonal skills, effective communication, and the ability to build and maintain strong relationships (Kotter, 1996; Robbins, et al., 2015).

Effective project leaders inspire trust, foster collaboration, and cultivate a positive and supportive team environment. They articulate the project vision clearly and passionately, ensuring that every member understands the project's goals and their individual role in achieving them. They empower team members to take ownership of their work by providing them with the necessary autonomy, resources, and support to succeed. This empowerment encourages initiative, creativity, and a sense of responsibility within the team.

Furthermore, project leaders excel at navigating the complexities of stakeholder relationships, building consensus among diverse groups, and effectively managing conflicting interests. They recognize the importance of communication and employ various techniques to keep stakeholders informed, engaged, and supportive throughout the project lifecycle. This includes active listening, clear and concise communication, and tailoring communication styles to different audiences.

Project managers can adopt various leadership styles (Northouse, 2013). An *autocratic* leader makes decisions independently, without team input. A *transformational* leader inspires and motivates the team towards project goals. A *laissez-faire* leader provides minimal direction, allowing the team autonomy. Conversely, a *servant* leader prioritizes the team's needs, supporting them in achieving their objectives. These styles offer diverse approaches to managing project teams, allowing leaders to adapt to different situations.

Project leaders adapt their leadership style to different situations and team members, understanding that a single approach is rarely universally effective. They demonstrate flexibility and adaptability in their leadership approach, recognizing that different situations require different responses. They also understand the importance of emotional intelligence, the ability to understand and manage their own emotions and the emotions of others. This is vital for building strong relationships, resolving conflicts constructively, and motivating teams effectively.

Leadership in project management is about creating a positive and productive project environment where team members are intrinsically motivated to achieve project objectives and stakeholders are actively engaged and supportive.

While leadership inspires and motivates, management focuses on the practical application of processes, tools, and techniques to achieve project objectives. It's about planning, organizing, directing, and controlling resources to ensure the project is delivered within the defined scope, schedule, and budget constraints. Management emphasizes efficiency, predictability, and adherence to established procedures (Kerzner, 2017).

In project management, management encompasses a wide range of activities. This includes developing the project management plan, which serves as a roadmap for project execution. This plan details how the project will be executed, monitored, and controlled, and it includes subsidiary plans for scope management, schedule management, cost management, risk management, and other key areas.

Management also involves defining project scope, breaking down the project into manageable tasks, and creating a work breakdown structure (WBS). This ensures that all project work is identified and accounted for. Resource management is another critical aspect of management, involving acquiring, allocating, and managing resources such as human resources, equipment, and materials. This includes developing resource calendars, assigning tasks to team members, and tracking resource utilization.

Furthermore, management includes developing and managing the project schedule, defining task dependencies, estimating task durations, and creating a project timeline. This ensures that the project is completed within the agreed-upon timeframe. Cost management is also a management function, involving estimating project costs, developing a budget, and controlling expenditures throughout the project lifecycle. This ensures that the project is completed within the approved budget. Risk management, from a management perspective, involves identifying, assessing, and responding to project risks. This includes developing risk response plans and implementing mitigation strategies.

Finally, management includes monitoring and controlling project progress, tracking key performance indicators (KPIs), and taking corrective actions as needed to keep the project on track. This involves using project management tools and techniques to monitor schedule, cost, and scope performance.

Distinguishing between leadership and management in project management enables a clearer understanding of their distinct yet intertwined approaches to achieving project success. Management focuses on the practical application of processes, tools, and techniques to ensure projects are delivered within defined constraints. It's about planning, organizing, directing, and controlling resources, emphasizing efficiency, predictability, and adherence to established procedures. Leadership, on the other hand, centers on inspiring and motivating individuals towards a shared vision. It's about influencing, guiding, and empowering teams and stakeholders, emphasizing interpersonal skills, communication, and relationship building.

A key difference lies in their focus. Management focuses on the "how"-- how to execute the project efficiently and effectively. This involves creating detailed plans, managing budgets, tracking schedules, and controlling risks. It's about maintaining stability and order within the project. Leadership, conversely, focuses on the "why" -- why the project is important and what it aims to achieve. It's about communicating the project's vision, inspiring commitment, and motivating individuals to overcome challenges. Leaders create a sense of purpose and shared ownership, fostering a positive and collaborative environment.

Another key difference is in their approach to people. Management emphasizes control and direction, focusing on assigning tasks, monitoring performance, and enforcing rules. Leaders, however, emphasize influence and empowerment, focusing on building relationships, fostering trust, and motivating individuals to perform at their best. They empower team members to take ownership of their work and provide them with the support and autonomy they need to succeed.

Decision-making also differs between the two. Management often involves making decisions based on data and analysis, following established procedures and protocols and risk mitigation. Leaders, while also considering data, often make decisions based on intuition, vision, and a deep understanding of the people involved (empathy). They are willing to take calculated risks to navigate ambiguity and embrace change when necessary. Both roles may overlap in practice, but their decision-making emphasis reflects distinct priorities.

Project managers ideally possess both strong management and leadership skills. They use management skills to plan and organize the project and leadership skills to motivate and inspire the team. They use management to maintain control and leadership to adapt to change. Recognizing these distinct yet complementary roles is essential for anyone seeking to become an effective project manager.

Test Your Understanding 2.30
What is the primary focus of leadership in project management?
A. Enforcing strict adherence to project schedules.
B. Motivating teams toward a shared vision.
C. Developing detailed risk management plans.
D. Allocating financial resources efficiently.

Test Your Understanding 2.31
Which activity is MOST closely associated with project management's "management" function?
A. Empowering team members to take ownership of tasks.
B. Creating a work breakdown structure (WBS).
C. Building consensus among stakeholders.
D. Adapting leadership styles to team dynamics.

Test Your Understanding 2.32
How does leadership decision-making differ from management decision-making?
A. Leaders prioritize data analysis over intuition.
B. Leaders rely on established protocols for all decisions.
C. Leaders emphasize intuition, vision, and empathy.
D. Leaders avoid risks to maintain project stability.

Test Your Understanding 2.33
Which skill is MOST critical for a project leader to resolve conflicts constructively?
A. Proficiency in scheduling software.
B. Risk mitigation strategies.
C. Budget forecasting expertise.
D. Emotional intelligence.

Test Your Understanding 2.34
Which of the following is a key emphasis of management in projects?
A. Adherence to established procedures.
B. Inspiring creativity through autonomy.

C. Building long-term stakeholder relationships.
D. Encouraging risk-taking to drive innovation.

Test Your Understanding 2.35
Why are both leadership and management skills essential for project success?
A. Leadership ensures strict compliance with schedules, while management inspires teams.
B. Management prioritizes intuition over data analysis.
C. Leadership eliminates the need for risk management.
D. Management provides structure, while leadership motivates teams.

Test Your Understanding 2.36
Which leadership style involves making decisions independently without seeking input from the team?
A. Transformational
B. Servant
C. Laissez-faire
D. Autocratic

Test Your Understanding 2.37
A project manager who inspires and motivates the team toward achieving project goals is exhibiting which type of leadership style?
A. Transformational
B. Autocratic
C. Servant
D. Laissez-faire

Test Your Understanding 2.38
A leader who prioritizes the team's needs and supports them in achieving their objectives is practicing which style?
A. Autocratic
B. Transformational
C. Laissez-faire
D. Servant

Test Your Understanding 2.39
According to the author, when managing a highly skilled and self-motivated team, which leadership style would be most effective?
A. Autocratic
B. Transformational
C. Servant
D. Laissez-faire

2.5 Emotional Intelligence

Emotional Intelligence (EQ) refers to the ability to understand and manage one's own emotions and the emotions of others. It encompasses a range of skills that contribute to effective communication, collaboration, and leadership within project teams (Salovey and Mayer, 1990; Goleman, 1998).

Self-awareness is the foundation of EQ. It involves understanding one's own emotions, recognizing what triggers those emotions, and understanding how these emotions impact decision-making. Self-awareness also includes assessing one's strengths and limitations, which is crucial for personal and professional development. For a Project Manager, self-awareness might involve recognizing when they are feeling stressed due to a project deadline and understanding how that stress might affect their communication with the team.

Self-regulation builds upon self-awareness and involves managing emotional responses effectively. This includes developing stress management techniques to cope with project pressures, adapting to changing circumstances, and maintaining professional composure even in challenging situations. For example, a Project Manager with strong self-regulation skills can remain calm and focused when a critical risk materializes, effectively leading the team through the crisis.

Motivation, in the context of EQ, refers to the internal drive that propels individuals towards achieving their goals. It involves maintaining a goal-oriented mindset, demonstrating resilience and persistence in the face of obstacles, and maintaining a positive attitude even during difficult times. A motivated project manager inspires the team and fosters a sense of shared purpose, driving project success.

Empathy is the ability to understand and share the feelings of others. It involves understanding others' perspectives, reading emotional cues, demonstrating cultural sensitivity, and showing compassion. A project manager with high empathy can build strong relationships with team members and stakeholders, fostering trust and collaboration. For instance, if a team member is struggling with a personal issue that is affecting their work, an empathetic project manager can offer support and understanding.

Finally, *social skills* encompass a range of interpersonal skills that facilitate effective communication and collaboration. This includes relationship building, network development, conflict resolution, and team collaboration. A project manager with strong social skills can build and maintain strong relationships with stakeholders, resolve conflicts constructively, and foster a positive and productive team environment. For example, a project manager with strong conflict resolution skills can effectively mediate disagreements between team members, finding solutions that address the concerns of all parties involved. The principles of EQ underpin many aspects of effective project management, such as stakeholder management, team management, communication, and leadership.

EQ is a key enabler for building trust with stakeholders. Trust development strategies include consistent communication, ensuring stakeholders are kept informed of project progress, challenges, and decisions. Demonstrating reliability by consistently meeting commitments and deadlines builds credibility. Transparency practices, such as openly sharing project information and being honest about project challenges, further enhance trust. Fulfilling commitments, even small ones, reinforces reliability and strengthens stakeholder confidence.

EQ is equally vital for maintaining professional boundaries in stakeholder relationships. Boundary-setting strategies involve recognizing appropriate interaction limits, actively listening to stakeholders' needs, and responding empathetically to their concerns. Clear communication practices, such as delivering messages concisely and interpreting non-verbal cues, foster mutual respect. Upholding these boundaries consistently strengthens trust and supports healthy, productive stakeholder relationships.

Furthermore, EQ is crucial in managing team dynamics and conflict resolution. Understanding group behavior and the dynamics of team interaction allows the project manager to anticipate potential issues and proactively manage team dynamics. Effective team morale management involves creating a positive and supportive work environment, recognizing team members' contributions, and providing opportunities for team building. EQ also informs the use of effective motivation techniques, understanding what drives individual team members and tailoring motivational strategies accordingly. This contributes to performance optimization, maximizing team effectiveness and achieving project objectives.

When conflicts inevitably arise, EQ aids in early detection, allowing the project manager to address issues before they escalate. De-escalation techniques, such as active listening and empathetic communication, help manage conflict constructively. Mediation processes, facilitated by the project manager, can help conflicting parties reach mutually acceptable solutions. Effective resolution strategies focus on addressing the root cause of the conflict and finding solutions that prevent future occurrences.

Team development benefits significantly from EQ, by building psychological safety, creating an environment where team members feel comfortable expressing their ideas and concerns without fear of judgment. Fostering collaboration through open communication and shared goals creates a more productive team environment. Encouraging innovation by valuing diverse perspectives and creating opportunities for creative problem-solving leads to better project outcomes. Supporting growth through mentorship, training, and feedback helps team members develop their skills and contribute more effectively to the project.

Developing EQ is a continuous process, and it's particularly valuable for project managers. Understanding how to develop EQ enhances practical project management skills. Several practical strategies can be employed to improve EQ.

Active listening techniques involve giving full attention to the speaker, minimizing distractions, and focusing on understanding their message. Asking clarifying questions ensures accurate comprehension and demonstrates engagement. Reflection methods, such as paraphrasing and summarizing, confirm understanding and allow the speaker to clarify their points. Providing feedback, both positive and constructive, reinforces communication and helps the speaker understand how their message is being received. For instance, instead of simply saying "I understand," a project manager might say, "So, if I understand correctly, you're concerned about the timeline because of the potential vendor delay?"

Mindfulness practices cultivate present moment awareness, allowing individuals to observe their thoughts and emotions without judgment. This enhances emotional regulation by creating a space between a trigger and a reaction. Mindfulness techniques, such as meditation and deep breathing, can also contribute to stress reduction and focus enhancement, which are beneficial for project managers dealing with project pressures. For example, a short mindfulness exercise before a stressful meeting can help a project manager maintain composure and focus.

Feedback mechanisms promotes personal and professional growth. This involves not only delivering constructive feedback effectively but also being receptive to receiving feedback from others. 360-degree assessments, which gather feedback from multiple sources such as supervisors, peers, and subordinates, provide a holistic view of an individual's strengths and weaknesses. This continuous improvement loop is vital for developing EQ. For instance, a project manager might solicit feedback from their team on their communication style and then use that feedback to improve their communication effectiveness.

A *structured development framework* can further enhance EQ development. This starts with assessment tools, such as validated EI measurement instruments, self-assessment questionnaires, peer evaluations, and professional assessments. These tools provide a baseline understanding of an individual's current EQ levels and identify areas for improvement. Based on the assessment results, growth planning involves setting specific development goals, creating action plans with concrete steps, tracking progress towards those goals, and adjusting strategies as needed. For example, after a self-assessment reveals a weakness in empathy, a project manager might set a goal to actively practice perspective-taking in team meetings.

Finally, *professional development* opportunities play a significant role in EQ development. Training programs focusing on communication, conflict resolution, and leadership can provide valuable skills and knowledge. Mentoring relationships provide guidance and support from experienced professionals. Coaching opportunities offer personalized feedback and support for developing specific EQ skills. Experiential learning, such as taking on challenging projects or participating in simulations, provides opportunities to practice EQ skills in real-world settings.

Test Your Understanding 2.40
What is the foundation of Emotional Intelligence (EQ) according to the text?
A. Social skills
B. Self-regulation
C. Self-awareness
D. Motivation

Test Your Understanding 2.41
Which EQ component enables a project manager to remain calm during a project crisis?
A. Empathy
B. Self-regulation
C. Motivation
D. Social skills

Test Your Understanding 2.42
What does empathy in EQ primarily involve?
A. Understanding others' perspectives and feelings
C. Prioritizing data-driven decisions
B. Setting strict project deadlines
D. Delegating tasks efficiently

Test Your Understanding 2.43
Which activity is MOST directly part of developing social skills in emotional intelligence (EQ)?
A. Facilitating team brainstorming sessions
B. Providing constructive feedback during performance reviews
C. Analyzing stakeholder communication preferences
D. Resolving conflicts constructively

Test Your Understanding 2.44
What is a key purpose of 360-degree assessments in emotional intelligence (EQ) development?
A. To enhance active listening skills through role-playing exercises
B. To identify personal values aligning with leadership goals
C. To measure team performance metrics for project success
D. To gather feedback from multiple sources

Test Your Understanding 2.45
What is a critical element of psychological safety in project teams?
A. Establishing clear role definitions for team members

B. Promoting individual accountability for task completion
C. Encouraging open expression of ideas
D. Implementing structured decision-making processes

Test Your Understanding 2.46
Which activity is an example of active listening?
A. Paraphrasing the speaker's message
B. Taking detailed notes during a conversation
C. Offering empathetic responses to build rapport
D. Asking probing questions to guide the discussion

Test Your Understanding 2.47
What is a key outcome of strong motivation in a project manager?
A. Strict adherence to protocols
B. Resilience in overcoming obstacles
C. Elimination of stakeholder meetings
D. Automation of task assignments

2.6 Chapter Summary

This chapter discusses the roles and responsibilities of project managers, teams, and sponsors, and examines their relationships with one another. We delve deeper into the specific roles of project managers, including initiators, negotiators, listeners, coaches, team members, and facilitators. It then compares and contrasts management and leadership. The chapter concludes with a review of emotional intelligence and its importance in project management.

2.7 Case Study

Revisit the case study in Chapter 1. Perform the following tasks:

1. Prepare a 2-page document for the roles and responsibilities of the project manager, team members, and sponsor, specifically relating to the project described in the case study.
2. Compose a 3-page project scope statement, using the key elements provided in Chapter 1.
3. Follow the steps outlined in Chapter 1 to review and critique the scope statement created above.

2.8 References

Cox, J. & Ireland, L. (2017). An Introduction to Project Management. Sixth Edition. New Jersey, USA: John Wiley & Sons.
Goleman, D. (1998). Working with emotional intelligence. Bantam.
Hishamuddin, H. A., & Aminuddin, F. A. (2025). The Potential of Project Managers Taking Roles in

Conflict Settlement and Dispute Resolution. International Journal of Research and Innovation in Social Science, 9(4), 270-283.
Kerzner, H. (2017). Project management: A systems approach to planning, scheduling, and controlling. John Wiley & Sons.
Kotter, J. P. (1996). Leading change. Harvard Business Review, 74(2), 59-67.
Meng, X., & Boyd, P. (2017). The role of the project manager in relationship management. International Journal of Project Management, 35(5), 717-728.
Northouse, P. G. (2013). Leadership: theory and practice. Sage publications.
Project Management Institute. (2021). A Guide to the Project Management Body of Knowledge (PMBOK Guide), 7th edition. Newtown Square, PA: Project Management Institute.
Raelin, J. A. (2013). The manager as facilitator of dialogue. Organization, 20(6), 818-839.
Robbins, S. P., Judge, T. A., & DeCenzo, D. A. (2015). Fundamentals of management. Pearson.
Salovey, P., & Mayer, J. D. (1990). Emotional intelligence. Imagination, cognition and personality, 9(3), 185-211.
Wateridge, J. (2017). The role of the project sponsor in ensuring project success. International Journal of Project Management, 35(2), 191-201. doi: 10.1016/j.ijproman.2016.06.007

2.9 Solutions to Test Your Understanding

2.1 B; 2.2 D; 2.3 B; 2.4 C; 2.5 A; 2.6 C; 2.7 C; 2.8 C; 2.9 B; 2.10 B; 2.11 B; 2.12 A; 2.13 D; 2.14 D; 2.15 A; 2.16 C; 2.17 C; 2.18 C; 2.19 B; 2.20 B; 2.21 B; 2.22 A; 2.23 A; 2.24 D; 2.25 C; 2.26 B; 2.27 D; 2.28 A; 2.29 D; 2.30 B; 2.31 B; 2.32 C; 2.33 D; 2.34 A; 2.35 D; 2.36 D; 2.37 A; 2.38 D; 2.39 D; 2.40 C; 2.41 B; 2.42 A; 2.43 D; 2.44 D; 2.45 C; 2.46 A; 2.47 B;

Chapter 3: Stakeholder Communications

Chapter Learning Outcomes

3.1 Classify the various categories of stakeholders.
3.2 Construct a stakeholder analysis plan.
3.3 Organize and administer the management of stakeholders.
3.4 Justify the requirement for precise and well-defined roles and obligations of stakeholders.
3.5 Evaluate and choose the suitable modes of communication for stakeholder engagement.

3.1 Role of Business Analysis

Business analysis is the practice of enabling change in an organizational context, by defining needs and recommending solutions that deliver value to stakeholders. This involves a set of tasks, knowledge, and techniques required to identify business needs and determine solutions to business problems. These solutions often, but not always, involve a systems development component.

A key aspect of business analysis is understanding the "why" behind a project. It's not simply about implementing a solution, but about understanding the underlying business problem or opportunity that needs to be addressed. This involves eliciting, analyzing, documenting, and managing requirements. Requirements are the documented needs of stakeholders that must be met to achieve the project objectives. Effective business analysis ensures that projects are aligned with business goals and deliver the intended benefits. It's important to recognize that business analysis is a distinct discipline from project management, although they often work closely together. While project managers focus on managing the project's scope, time, and budget, business analysts focus on understanding the business needs and ensuring that the project delivers value (Harris and Clark, 2023).

Let's illustrate this with an example. Imagine a company experiencing a decline in customer satisfaction due to a slow and inefficient order processing system. A business analyst would be brought in to investigate this issue. They would conduct interviews with customers, sales representatives, and operations staff to understand the pain points in the current system. They would analyze data on order processing times, error rates, and customer complaints. Based on this analysis, they would document the requirements for a new order processing system, specifying features such as online order tracking, automated email notifications, and integration with the company's inventory management system. This detailed analysis and documentation ensures that the project team builds a solution that truly addresses the business problem and improves customer satisfaction.

Furthermore, business analysis plays a critical role in risk management. By thoroughly understanding the business needs and requirements, business analysts can identify potential risks and issues early in the project lifecycle. For instance, if a requirement is unclear or ambiguous, it could lead to misinterpretations and costly rework later on. A business analyst can mitigate this risk by ensuring that all requirements are clearly defined, documented, and agreed upon by stakeholders. They also help in evaluating the feasibility of proposed solutions, considering factors such as cost, technical feasibility, and business impact.

Test Your Understanding 3.1
What is the primary role of business analysis in an organization?
A. Managing project budgets and schedules to enure the success of the project
B. Defining needs and recommending solutions that deliver stakeholder value
C. Designing technical architectures for new systems
D. Overseeing the hiring of project team members

Test Your Understanding 3.2
Which of the following best distinguishes business analysis from project management?
A. Business analysis focuses on documenting risks, while project management avoids risks.
B. Business analysis defines solutions, while project management selects vendors.
C. Business analysis ensures business value, while project management manages scope, time, and budget.
D. Business analysis tracks expenses, while project management sets project objectives.

Test Your Understanding 3.3
In the example of improving customer satisfaction (Section 3.1), which of the following would NOT be a task performed by the business analyst?
A. Interviewing customers and staff to understand issues
B. Documenting requirements for a new system
C. Implementing the technical features of the system
D. Analyzing data on processing times and error rates

Test Your Understanding 3.4
Why is understanding the "why" behind a project essential in business analysis?
A. It clarifies the underlying business problem or opportunity
B. It ensures the project stays within budget
C. It allows for faster project completion
D. It reduces the number of stakeholders involved

Test Your Understanding 3.5
How can unclear requirements pose a risk in projects?
A. They may lead to resource overallocation due to competing priorities
B. They could delay progress due to insufficient team expertise
C. They might result in scope creep from uncontrolled changes

D. They could cause misinterpretations and costly rework

Test Your Understanding 3.6
When evaluating the feasibility of proposed solutions, which factors might a business analyst consider?
A. Cost, technical feasibility, and business impact
B. Team size, color schemes, and competitor branding
C. CEO preferences, project deadline, and location of stakeholders
D. Industry trends, stock prices, and marketing slogans

3.2 Types of Stakeholder

In project management, *stakeholders* are individuals, groups, or organizations that have an interest in or are affected by the project's outcomes, either positively or negatively (Miles, 2017). They can influence the project, be impacted by it, or both. Stakeholders may include people within the organization (internal stakeholders) as well as external parties. The previous chapter discussed several stakeholder types, including project managers, sponsors, and team members. This section introduces additional stakeholders who play distinct roles in driving project success. Distinguishing between these roles enables clear communication, effective collaboration, and ultimately, project success.

A *Process Owner* is responsible for the overall effectiveness and efficiency of a specific business process. They are concerned with how work gets done and are accountable for its performance. For example, the process owner for order fulfillment would be responsible for ensuring that orders are processed accurately and efficiently. They focus on continuous improvement and often initiate projects to optimize their processes. This contrasts with the *Product Owner*, a key role in agile projects, who is responsible for maximizing the value of the product resulting from the work of the development team. They define and prioritize the product backlog, representing the voice of the customer and ensuring that the product meets market needs.

The *Operations Manager* is responsible for the day-to-day running of a specific department or function. They focus on maintaining operational stability and efficiency. They are often impacted by projects that introduce new systems or processes and are therefore important stakeholders. A *Technical Architect* is responsible for the overall technical design and implementation of a system. They ensure that the technical solution meets the business requirements and is scalable, secure, and maintainable. They work closely with the development team to provide technical guidance and resolve technical issues.

Product manager defines the strategy, roadmap, and features of a product or product line, conducting market research and defining the product vision, often collaborating with agile product owners for strategic direction. This contrasts with *process managers*, who focus on improving business processes rather than products, optimizing efficiency and effectiveness using methodologies like Lean or Six Sigma. *Process owners*, unlike process managers, are accountable for a process's overall performance and strategic direction, defining the "what" and "why," while process managers focus on the "how" of daily execution and operational improvement.

A *Subject Matter Expert (SME)* possesses specialized knowledge and expertise in a particular area. They provide valuable input to the project team, helping to define requirements, validate solutions, and resolve technical issues. They are often consulted on complex or specialized topics. A *compliance/legal representative* ensures that the project complies with all relevant laws, regulations, and industry standards. They identify potential legal and compliance risks and provide guidance on how to mitigate them. This is especially important in regulated industries such as healthcare or finance.

End Users/Customers are the ultimate beneficiaries of the project. They use the product or service that the project delivers. Their feedback ensures that the project meets their needs and expectations. Engaging with end users throughout the project lifecycle, through methods like user testing and feedback sessions, is essential for delivering a successful product. Recognizing the differences between a Product Owner and a Product Manager, or a Process Owner and a Process Manager, for example, demonstrates a strong grasp of project dynamics.

Beyond the internal team and direct users, several external entities hold significant influence over a project. *Suppliers and vendors* are instrumental stakeholders who provide the essential goods, services, and resources required for project execution. Their performance and reliability directly impact the project's timeline, budget, and quality, making vendor relationship management a critical function. In a different capacity, *government and regulatory bodies* establish the legal and compliance framework the project must operate within. While an internal compliance representative interprets their rules, these external bodies have the authority to impose penalties or halt work, making their requirements non-negotiable. Lastly, *investors and shareholders* are primary financial stakeholders whose main interest lies in the project's financial viability and its expected return on investment. They provide the capital that makes the project possible and are ultimately concerned with how its success will contribute to the organization's bottom line and market value.

Test Your Understanding 3.7
Which of the following best describes a Process Owner in project management?

A. A stakeholder who defines the strategy, roadmap, and features of a product
B. A stakeholder responsible for providing technical design and architecture
C. A stakeholder who manages the day-to-day operations of a department
D. A stakeholder responsible for the overall effectiveness and efficiency of a business process

Test Your Understanding 3.8
How does a Product Owner differ from a Product Manager?
A. Product Owners define strategy, while Product Managers manage the backlog
B. Product Owners focus on processes, while Product Managers focus on products
C. Product Owners maximize product value through backlog prioritization, while Product Managers set product strategy and vision
D. Product Owners ensure compliance, while Product Managers oversee legal risks

Test Your Understanding 3.9
What is the primary responsibility of an Operations Manager as a stakeholder?
A. Providing specialized technical expertise to validate solutions
B. Ensuring daily operational stability and efficiency of a department or function
C. Managing suppliers and vendors to maintain reliable service delivery
D. Monitoring financial performance and return on investment

Test Your Understanding 3.10
Why are Suppliers and Vendors considered important stakeholders?
A. Their goods, services, and performance directly affect project cost, quality, and timelines
B. They set legal standards and compliance regulations
C. They define customer requirements and provide user feedback
D. They provide specialized technical expertise to development teams

3.3 Stakeholder Analysis

Stakeholder analysis is a process in project management that involves identifying all individuals or groups impacted by or who can impact a project, and then analyzing their interests, influence, and potential impact on the project's success (Aaltonen, 2011). This analysis allows project managers to effectively manage stakeholder expectations, build support, and mitigate potential risks. It's not simply about creating a list of names; it's about understanding the complex web of relationships and influences that can affect a project's trajectory.

The first step in stakeholder analysis is *stakeholder identification.* This involves brainstorming and documenting all individuals, groups, or organizations that could be affected by the project or who could affect the project. This can include internal stakeholders like project team members, managers, and executives, as well as external stakeholders such as customers, suppliers, government agencies, and community groups. Techniques like brainstorming, stakeholder registers, and organizational charts can be used for this purpose. A stakeholder register is a document that lists all identified stakeholders and includes information about their contact details, roles, interests, influence, and potential impact.

Once stakeholders are identified, the next step is *stakeholder analysis and prioritization*. This involves analyzing each stakeholder's interest in the project, their level of influence or power, and their potential impact (positive or negative) on the project. Several tools and techniques can be used for this analysis, including:

Power/Interest Grid: This grid classifies stakeholders based on their level of power (ability to influence the project) and their level of interest (concern about the project's outcomes). This helps prioritize stakeholder engagement efforts. For example, stakeholders with high power and high interest require close management, while those with low power and low interest require minimal effort.

Influence/Impact Grid: Similar to the power/interest grid, this grid assesses stakeholders based on their influence on the project and the potential impact the project could have on them.

Salience Model: This model categorizes stakeholders based on their power, urgency (need for immediate attention), and legitimacy (their involvement is appropriate). This model helps prioritize stakeholders who demand immediate attention.

Understanding stakeholder influence is crucial. Some stakeholders may have formal authority, while others may exert influence through informal networks or expertise. For example, a senior executive has formal power, while a subject matter expert might have significant influence due to their specialized knowledge. Project managers need to identify stakeholder influence and determine the appropriate engagement strategy.

Finally, stakeholder analysis informs the development of a *stakeholder engagement plan*. This plan outlines how the project team will communicate and interact with each stakeholder or stakeholder group throughout the project lifecycle. It defines the communication methods, frequency, and content that will be used to keep stakeholders informed and engaged. This plan should be tailored to each stakeholder's specific needs and interests, as identified during the analysis phase. For instance, a high-power, high-interest stakeholder might require regular face-to-face meetings and detailed progress reports, while a low-power, low-interest stakeholder might only need occasional email updates. By effectively conducting stakeholder analysis and developing a robust engagement plan, project managers can significantly increase the likelihood of project success and effectively navigate the complex stakeholder landscape.

The process of stakeholder analysis helps determine who needs to be involved in the project and what they need to do. For example, identifying a senior executive as a high-power, high-interest stakeholder necessitates assigning them the role of project sponsor, with responsibilities like providing high-level direction, securing funding, and removing roadblocks. Conversely, identifying a group of end-users as high-interest but low-power stakeholders might lead to establishing user acceptance testing (UAT) groups with responsibilities for providing feedback on the deliverables and ensuring they meet their needs. This demonstrates how the analysis directly drives the need for specific roles and responsibilities.

Test Your Understanding 3.11
Which of the following BEST describes the purpose of stakeholder analysis in project management?
A. To document all stakeholders' names in a register
B. To evaluate risks and opportunities within project deliverables
C. To identify, analyze, and prioritize stakeholders based on interests and influence
D. To assign project tasks and responsibilities to team members

Test Your Understanding 3.12
A project manager is preparing a stakeholder register. Which of the following would MOST likely be included in this document?
A. Stakeholder contact information, interests, influence, and potential impact
B. Project scope statement, deliverables, and acceptance criteria
C. Work breakdown structure and resource assignments
D. Communication methods and meeting schedules

Test Your Understanding 3.13
A subject matter expert (SME) does not hold formal authority but strongly influences technical decisions due to specialized knowledge. This is an example of:
A. Legitimate power based on position
B. Informal influence through expertise
C. Urgency within the salience model
D. Stakeholder disinterest due to low power

Test Your Understanding 3.14
The Salience Model classifies stakeholders based on which three attributes?
A. Power, interest, and communication frequency
B. Power, urgency, and legitimacy
C. Influence, impact, and authority
D. Role, responsibility, and decision-making capacity

Test Your Understanding 3.15
During stakeholder analysis, end-users were identified as high-interest but low-power stakeholders. Which engagement approach is MOST appropriate?
A. Assign them as project sponsors to secure funding
B. Exclude them from decision-making processes
C. Provide only occasional status updates via email
D. Include them in user acceptance testing (UAT) groups for feedback

3.4 Stakeholder Management

Following stakeholder analysis, which identifies and analyzes stakeholders and their potential impact on a project, stakeholder management becomes the next step. *Stakeholder management* encompasses the processes required to effectively engage stakeholders throughout the project lifecycle. It's not simply about communicating with stakeholders; it's about proactively managing their expectations, addressing their concerns, and ensuring their continued support for the project. Effective stakeholder management maximizes positive influences and mitigates negative ones, significantly increasing the likelihood of project success.

Stakeholder management comprises several key processes that ensure effective engagement throughout the project lifecycle (Pandi-Perumal et al., 2015). These processes are iterative and interconnected, forming a continuous cycle of engagement and improvement.

The first process, *Identifying Stakeholders*, as previously detailed in the section on stakeholder analysis, involves recognizing all individuals, groups, or organizations that could be affected by the project (positively or negatively) or that could affect the project's outcome. Techniques like brainstorming, stakeholder registers, and organizational charts are commonly used for this identification. It's important to be thorough in this step, as overlooking a key stakeholder can lead to unforeseen challenges later in the project.

The second process, *Planning Stakeholder Engagement*, centers around developing the stakeholder engagement plan. This plan, directly informed by the stakeholder analysis, details the strategies for engaging stakeholders based on their identified needs, interests, influence, and potential impact. The plan specifies communication methods, frequency, content, escalation paths, key messages, responsible parties, and metrics for monitoring engagement effectiveness. For example, the plan might specify that the project sponsor receives monthly face-to-face updates, while the project team receives daily stand-up meetings and updates via project management software.

Managing Stakeholder Engagement, the third process, involves putting the stakeholder engagement plan into action. This includes carrying out the planned communication and engagement activities, such as conducting meetings, sending updates, addressing concerns, managing expectations, and resolving conflicts. This process requires strong interpersonal skills, communication skills, and negotiation skills from the project manager and the project team. It's about building and maintaining positive relationships with stakeholders, proactively addressing their concerns, and ensuring their continued support for the project.

The final process, *Monitoring Stakeholder Engagement*, focuses on tracking stakeholder satisfaction, identifying any emerging issues, and making necessary adjustments to the engagement plan. This continuous monitoring ensures that the engagement strategies remain effective and aligned with the project's evolving needs. Techniques like stakeholder surveys, feedback sessions, and communication logs can be used to monitor engagement effectiveness. This iterative approach to stakeholder management ensures that stakeholders remain engaged and supportive throughout the project lifecycle.

As mentioned earlier, a core element of stakeholder management is developing and implementing a robust *stakeholder engagement plan*. This plan serves as a roadmap for effectively engaging stakeholders throughout the project lifecycle. It's not a static document but rather a living artifact that should be reviewed and updated as needed. The plan outlines the strategies, actions, communication methods, frequency, content, and escalation paths tailored to each stakeholder or stakeholder group. This targeted approach ensures that communication is relevant, timely, and effective, maximizing positive stakeholder influence and minimizing negative impacts.

A comprehensive stakeholder engagement plan should include the following key elements:

Stakeholder Identification and Classification: This section summarizes the stakeholder analysis, listing each stakeholder or stakeholder group and classifying them based on their power, interest, influence, or other relevant criteria (e.g., impact, urgency, legitimacy). This provides a quick reference for understanding each stakeholder's position and engagement needs.

Engagement Objectives: For each stakeholder or stakeholder group, define specific engagement objectives. What do you want to achieve by engaging with them? Examples include gaining support for the project, gathering feedback on deliverables, managing expectations, or resolving conflicts. These objectives should be SMART (Specific, Measurable, Achievable, Relevant, and Time-bound).

Engagement Strategies/Communication Strategies: This section outlines the overall approach for engaging with each stakeholder group. It describes how you will work with them to achieve the engagement objectives. This includes defining the level of engagement (e.g., actively involved, kept informed, monitored), the types of activities you will undertake (e.g., meetings, workshops, reviews), and the overall tone and approach of your interactions. This is the core of the plan and details how you will communicate with each stakeholder.

Escalation Paths: Clearly define the process for escalating issues or conflicts that may arise. This should include identifying who to escalate to, under what circumstances, and the expected response time. This ensures that issues are addressed promptly and effectively.

Key Messages: Define the key messages that you want to communicate to each stakeholder. These messages should be consistent and aligned with the project's overall objectives.

Responsible Parties: Assign specific individuals or roles responsible for carrying out the engagement activities. This ensures accountability and prevents confusion.

Metrics and Monitoring: Define how you will measure the effectiveness of your stakeholder engagement efforts. This could include tracking stakeholder satisfaction, monitoring engagement activity frequency, and analyzing feedback received. This data allows for continuous improvement of the engagement plan.

For example, a high-power, high-interest stakeholder like a project sponsor might require monthly face-to-face meetings with detailed progress reports and direct access to the project manager. A medium-power, medium-interest stakeholder like a department manager might receive weekly email updates and participate in monthly project status meetings. A low-power, low-interest stakeholder like a community group might only receive quarterly newsletters or public announcements.

By developing and diligently implementing a well-defined stakeholder engagement plan, project managers can foster strong stakeholder relationships, build support for the project, and effectively manage expectations, significantly contributing to project success. This is a skill that emphasizes the importance of proactive and strategic stakeholder management.

Effective stakeholder management requires strong communication skills, interpersonal skills, and negotiation skills. Project managers must be able to communicate effectively with diverse stakeholder groups, build trust and rapport, and resolve conflicts diplomatically. They must also be able to adapt their communication style to the specific needs of each stakeholder. For instance, communicating with a technical stakeholder might require using technical jargon, while communicating with a business stakeholder might require focusing on business benefits.

Furthermore, stakeholder management is not a one-time activity; it's an ongoing process throughout the project lifecycle. As the project progresses, stakeholder needs and interests may change, and new stakeholders may emerge. Therefore, it's essential to regularly review and update the stakeholder engagement plan to ensure that it remains relevant and effective.

Test Your Understanding 3.16
Which of the following BEST describes the primary purpose of stakeholder management?
A. To ensure all project deliverables meet stakeholder requirements and quality standards
B. To proactively engage stakeholders, manage expectations, and gain continued support
C. To document all communication methods in the stakeholder register
D. To monitor risks and assign contingency responses

Test Your Understanding 3.17
You are managing a software development project. A new government regulation emerges mid-project, and a regulatory agency becomes a key stakeholder. What should you do FIRST?
A. Add the regulatory agency to the stakeholder register and update the engagement plan
B. Escalate the issue to the project sponsor immediately
C. Send a status report to the agency explaining current progress
D. Delay project activities until the agency's requirements are clarified and sponsor approves

Test Your Understanding 3.18
Which process involves tracking stakeholder satisfaction, identifying emerging issues, and making necessary adjustments to the engagement plan?
A. Planning Stakeholder Engagement
B. Managing Stakeholder Engagement
C. Monitoring Stakeholder Engagement
D. Identifying Stakeholders

Test Your Understanding 3.19
A project sponsor expects monthly face-to-face meetings with detailed reports, while a department manager prefers weekly emails. How should the project manager address these differing needs?
A. Provide both stakeholders the same type of communication to maintain consistency
B. Escalate the conflict to the steering committee for resolution
C. Tailor the stakeholder engagement plan to match each stakeholder's preferences
D. Reduce communication frequency to avoid overburdening the project team

Test Your Understanding 3.20
Which of the following elements is LEAST likely to be included in a stakeholder engagement plan?
A. Escalation paths for issue resolution
B. SMART objectives for each stakeholder group
C. Metrics for monitoring engagement effectiveness
D. Detailed Work Breakdown Structure (WBS) for project deliverables

Test Your Understanding 3.21
During project execution, several stakeholders report dissatisfaction with how their concerns are being addressed. As project manager, what is the BEST course of action?
A. Revisit the stakeholder engagement plan, gather feedback, and adjust strategies accordingly
B. Hold an urgent meeting with the project sponsor to reassign responsibilities

C. Increase the frequency of all stakeholder communications
D. Remove dissatisfied stakeholders from the project register to reduce conflict

3.5 Stakeholder Communication

A crucial aspect of the effective stakeholder communication is selecting the most appropriate communication channel or tool for each stakeholder or stakeholder group, considering their individual needs, preferences, and the nature of the information being conveyed (Alsulaimi and Abdullah, 2020). Simply sending every update via email, for example, is unlikely to be effective. A well-defined communication plan, informed by stakeholder analysis, should outline the specific communication methods to be used with each stakeholder group.

Choosing the right communication channel depends on several factors, including the urgency of the message, the complexity of the information, the audience's familiarity with the topic, and the desired level of interaction. For instance, if a critical risk has been identified that requires immediate action, a face-to-face meeting or a phone call would be more appropriate than an email or a written report. This allows for immediate discussion, clarification, and decision-making. Conversely, for routine project updates or progress reports, email, newsletters, or project management software updates might suffice. These methods are efficient for disseminating information to a large audience without requiring immediate interaction.

Selecting the right communication channel is a key skill for project managers. Different communication channels have varying strengths and weaknesses, making them suitable for different purposes and audiences. Choosing the appropriate channel ensures that the message is received and understood as intended. Here are examples of common communication channels and their appropriate uses within a project context:

Face-to-face meetings: These are highly effective for complex discussions, conveying sensitive information, resolving conflicts, and building rapport. As a high-context communication method, face-to-face interactions allow for the interpretation of nonverbal cues like body language and facial expressions, facilitating deeper understanding and trust. Examples in a project setting include project kickoff meetings to establish team dynamics and project goals, stakeholder review meetings to gather feedback on deliverables, one-on-one discussions with key stakeholders to address specific concerns, and negotiation sessions to resolve disputes. However, remember that while highly effective, face-to-face meetings can be time-consuming and resource-intensive.

Presentations: Presentations are ideal for conveying key project information to a larger audience in a structured and engaging manner. They are effective for project status updates to keep stakeholders informed of progress, stakeholder briefings to provide high-level overviews, and project closure meetings to formally present the project's outcomes. Incorporating visual aids like charts, graphs, and images can significantly enhance understanding and engagement, especially when presenting complex data. Consider presentations as a good way to disseminate information broadly but less effective for in-depth discussions.

Email: Email is suitable for routine updates, distributing documents, confirming decisions, and sending reminders. It provides a written record of communication, which can be useful for future reference. However, email is less effective for complex or sensitive information, as it lacks the nuances of face-to-face communication and can easily lead to misinterpretations if not carefully worded. Remember that while efficient, email can contribute to information overload and may not be the best choice for urgent or sensitive matters.

Reports: Reports are valuable for providing detailed information, documenting progress against baselines, tracking key metrics, and providing a formal record of project activities. Reports can be formal or informal, depending on the audience and the purpose. Examples include weekly status reports to track progress against the project schedule, monthly progress reports to provide a higher-level overview to management, and final project reports to document project outcomes and lessons learned. Reports are important for formal communication and documentation but may not be the most engaging way to communicate with all stakeholders.

Project Management Software: Tools like Jira, Asana, Microsoft Project, and Trello facilitate collaboration, task management, and communication within the project team. They provide a central repository for project information, including tasks, schedules, documents, and updates. These tools enhance transparency and streamline communication within the project team, making them essential for managing complex projects. Understand that these tools primarily facilitate internal team communication and collaboration.

Video conferencing: Video conferencing platforms like Zoom, Microsoft Teams, and Google Meet offer a good alternative to face-to-face meetings when physical proximity is not possible. They allow for visual and auditory interaction, making them more engaging and effective than phone calls. Video conferencing is suitable for remote team meetings, virtual stakeholder reviews, and online training sessions. Recognize video conferencing as a good compromise between face-to-face meetings and less interactive methods.

Instant messaging: Instant messaging platforms like Slack or Microsoft Teams are useful for quick questions, informal communication, and coordinating tasks within the project team. They facilitate rapid communication and can be useful for addressing urgent issues. However, instant messaging is generally not suitable for formal communication, sensitive information, or complex discussions. Understand that instant messaging is primarily for informal, quick communication within the project team.

For project managers, it's important to understand the strengths and weaknesses of different communication channels and be able to recommend the most appropriate channel for specific scenarios. For instance, if a stakeholder requires detailed technical information, a written report or a technical presentation would be more appropriate than a brief email update. Similarly, if a stakeholder is resistant to change, a face-to-face meeting to address their concerns and build trust would be more effective than simply sending an email announcing the change.

Test Your Understanding 3.22
Which of the following factors should a project manager consider when selecting the most appropriate communication channel for a stakeholder?
A. The cost of the communication method
B. The urgency, complexity, and audience familiarity with the information
C. The number of communication channels used in the project and the cost of the method
D. The project manager's personal preference

Test Your Understanding 3.23
A critical risk has been identified, and immediate action is required. Which communication method is MOST appropriate for addressing this situation?
A. Send an email to all stakeholders
B. Issue a formal report documenting the risk
C. Schedule a face-to-face meeting or phone call with key decision-makers
D. Post an update on project management software and allow all relevant parties to see it.

Test Your Understanding 3.24
Which of the following is a PRIMARY advantage of using project management software for communication?
A. It is best for resolving conflicts between stakeholders
B. It provides a central repository for tasks, schedules, and updates
C. It eliminates the need for face-to-face meetings
D. It is the most appropriate channel for communicating sensitive issues

Test Your Understanding 3.25
During execution, a stakeholder expresses resistance to an upcoming process change. What communication method should the project manager use FIRST to address this concern?
A. Send an email outlining the business benefits of the change
B. Conduct a face-to-face meeting to discuss concerns and build trust

C. Include the stakeholder in weekly project updates via reports
D. Add a note in project management software for transparency

Test Your Understanding 3.26
Which communication channel is MOST effective for quick, informal team coordination but is NOT suitable for formal communication or sensitive topics?
A. Instant messaging
B. Reports
C. Presentations
D. Video conferencing

3.6 Effective Communication

Effective communication is essential for project success, particularly in the collaborative partnership between a project manager and a business analyst. The business analyst (BA) is responsible for clarifying the "what" and "why" of a project, acting as a bridge between business needs and the development team. The project manager, in turn, must communicate the "who," "when," and "how," orchestrating the resources and timeline. This dual-stream of information ensures everyone is aligned (Rajhans, 2018).

One key area where communication is crucial is in the elicitation and documentation of requirements. The business analyst works with business stakeholders, such as process owners, subject matter experts, and end-users, to understand their needs and translate them into specific, measurable, achievable, relevant, and time-bound (SMART) requirements. This process requires active listening, probing questions, and clear documentation.

Effective communication ensures that all stakeholders have a shared understanding of the requirements and that no critical needs are overlooked. For example, a business analyst might use techniques like interviews, workshops, and surveys to gather information from stakeholders and then document these requirements in a format that is easily understood by the development team, such as user stories, use cases, or process flow diagrams. This clear communication prevents ambiguity and reduces the risk of rework later in the project.

Communication is equally important between the business analyst and the development team. The business analyst must communicate the requirements clearly and concisely to the development team, ensuring that they understand what needs to be built and why. This involves explaining the business context, clarifying any ambiguities, and answering questions from the development team.

Regular communication throughout the development process helps address issues as they arise and ensures the final product meets the requirements. For instance, the business analyst might participate in daily stand-up meetings with the development team to answer questions and provide clarification on requirements. They might also conduct regular reviews of the developed software to ensure that it aligns with the documented requirements.

Furthermore, effective communication facilitates change management. Projects often involve changes to business processes or systems, and these changes can be disruptive to stakeholders. The business analyst plays a key role in communicating these changes to stakeholders and managing their expectations. This involves explaining the reasons for the changes, the benefits they will bring, and how they will be implemented. Effective communication can help minimize resistance to change and ensure a smooth transition. For example, the business analyst might conduct training sessions for end-users on how to use a new system or create communication materials that explain the changes in a clear and concise manner.

Test Your Understanding 3.27
Which of the following best describes the distinct communication responsibilities of the business analyst (BA) and the project manager (PM)?
A. The BA focuses on schedules and budgets, while the PM clarifies the purpose of the project.
B. The BA clarifies the "what" and "why," while the PM communicates the "who," "when," and "how."
C. The BA manages timelines, while the PM documents business needs.
D. The BA ensures tasks are assigned, while the PM validates requirements with stakeholders.

Test Your Understanding 3.28
A business analyst is running a workshop with end-users to clarify requirements. After the session, the BA creates detailed user stories and process flow diagrams for the development team. Which key principle is this scenario illustrating?
A. Stakeholder conflict resolution
B. Risk monitoring and control
C. Requirements elicitation and documentation
D. Quality assurance and testing

Test Your Understanding 3.29
During daily stand-up meetings, the development team raises questions about ambiguous requirements. The BA answers these questions immediately and later reviews the developed features to confirm alignment with the requirements. What is the primary purpose of this approach?
A. To reduce rework by ensuring clarity and continuous alignment
B. To accelerate testing and reduce quality assurance effort
C. To shorten the project schedule regardless of stakeholder needs
D. To prevent scope creep by avoiding stakeholder input

Test Your Understanding 3.30
A project introduces a new system that changes existing business processes. Some employees resist using the

system. How should the business analyst address this issue according to the text?
A. Enforce mandatory usage without explanation.
B. Focus only on technical training for the development team.
C. Communicate reasons, benefits, and provide stakeholder training.
D. Ask the project manager to handle all communications.

3.7 The Need for Roles and Responsibilities

Establishing distinct roles and responsibilities within a project team and among stakeholders provides a framework for accountability, communication, efficiency, task delegation, decision-making, problem-solving, and collaboration (Kerzner, 2025).

Clearly defined roles and responsibilities significantly improve accountability (Shamim, 2022). It eliminates ambiguity, ensuring that individuals are held accountable for their specific contributions. When team members understand their duties and obligations, tracking progress becomes easier, bottlenecks are more readily identified, and performance issues can be addressed effectively. This heightened accountability fosters a sense of ownership among team members, encouraging proactive participation and ultimately leading to higher quality work and improved project outcomes.

Clearly defined roles and responsibilities also enhance communication within a project by streamlining communication channels. When everyone knows who to contact for specific information or decisions, confusion is reduced and communication flows more efficiently. Establishing clear points of contact eliminates the need for individuals to guess who is responsible for what, creating a more structured and predictable communication environment. This structured communication minimizes miscommunication, reduces the risk of information silos forming within the project, and ensures that all team members and stakeholders are on the same page. For instance, if a team member has a question regarding a specific requirement, they know to contact the business analyst, whose clearly defined role designates them as the liaison between the business stakeholders and the development team.

Additionally, clearly defined roles and responsibilities increase project efficiency by ensuring that tasks are assigned to the most appropriate individuals based on their skills and expertise. This targeted assignment of work prevents duplicated effort, reduces wasted time spent on tasks outside of an individual's core competencies, and maximizes the utilization of project resources. By allowing team members to focus on their strengths, productivity and overall project efficiency are enhanced. For example, assigning complex technical tasks to developers with the relevant expertise ensures that these tasks are completed efficiently and effectively, rather than assigning them to someone with less experience who might require additional time, training, or rework.

Clear roles and responsibilities enable effective task delegation within a project. When roles are clearly defined, managers can confidently delegate tasks, knowing that individuals understand their responsibilities and possess the necessary authority to complete them successfully. This clarity empowers team members, fostering a greater sense of ownership over their work and increasing their engagement. Furthermore, effective delegation frees up managers to focus on higher-level strategic activities, such as planning, risk management, and stakeholder communication. Clearly defined roles also mitigate the risk of micromanagement, as individuals understand their scope of authority and are empowered to make decisions within their defined area of responsibility, promoting autonomy and efficiency.

Clearly defined roles and responsibilities significantly improve decision-making and problem-solving within a project. When roles are clear, so too is the associated decision-making authority, preventing confusion and minimizing delays in the decision-making process. This clarity ensures that decisions are made by the individuals with the most relevant expertise and the appropriate level of authority. Similarly, when problems arise, clearly defined roles and responsibilities quickly identify who is responsible for addressing the issue and implementing a solution. This prevents confusion and ensures that problems are resolved promptly and effectively, minimizing potential negative impacts on the project.

Finally, defining roles and responsibilities fosters a stronger collaborative environment within a project by clarifying how individuals should interact and work together. Establishing clear interfaces between different roles promotes a mutual understanding of each team member's contributions and responsibilities. This, in turn, fosters teamwork, improves communication flow, and cultivates a shared sense of purpose among the project team. When every individual understands their specific role within the larger project context and how their work contributes to the overall objective, they are significantly more likely to collaborate effectively and efficiently to achieve project success.

Test Your Understanding 3.31
During a software project, a developer receives conflicting instructions from two stakeholders about how to implement a feature. The confusion delays work. Which project management principle could have prevented this issue?
A. Defining clear escalation procedures
B. Establishing clearly defined roles and responsibilities
C. Increasing the project budget

D. Applying stricter quality assurance testing for every step of the project lifecycle

Test Your Understanding 3.32
A project manager delegates testing responsibilities to a quality assurance (QA) lead who is skilled in that area. The QA lead feels ownership of the task and is empowered to make decisions about testing methods. What project benefit is being demonstrated here?
A. Effective task delegation supported by clear roles
B. Improved accountability through monitoring
C. Reduced project scope through role specialization
D. Improved budget control through resource constraints

Test Your Understanding 3.33
A project team is struggling with collaboration because team members are unsure how their work connects to the project's overall goals. What action should the project manager take to address this?
A. Reassign the team members to different tasks.
B. Redefine the project scope to reduce confusion.
C. Clarify each member's role and how it contributes to the project objectives.
D. Increase the project's communication frequency without clarifying responsibilities.

3.8 Factors Influencing Channel Choice

Selecting the appropriate communication channel is a critical skill for project managers. Choosing the right channel significantly impacts the effectiveness of communication and, consequently, the success of the project. Several key factors influence the choice of communication channel in project management, and understanding them supports effective stakeholder engagement and project execution (Shakeri and Khalilzadeh, 2020).

One primary factor is the *urgency* of the message. For time-sensitive information requiring immediate action, direct and immediate channels like face-to-face meetings, phone calls, or instant messaging are most appropriate. For instance, if a critical risk has been identified that requires immediate mitigation, a phone call or a meeting with key stakeholders is necessary to discuss the issue and determine a course of action. Conversely, for routine updates or less time-sensitive information, channels like email, reports, or project management software updates are sufficient. Remember that urgency dictates the need for synchronous (real-time) versus asynchronous (delayed) communication.

The *complexity* of the message is another important consideration. Complex or technical information is best conveyed through high-context communication methods that allow for detailed explanations, questions, and immediate feedback. Face-to-face meetings, presentations, and video conferences are well-suited for this purpose. These methods allow for visual aids, demonstrations, and clarification of any misunderstandings.

Simpler messages, on the other hand, can be effectively communicated through lower-context channels like email or written reports. For example, detailed technical specifications are better communicated through a formal report than a brief email.

The audience's *familiarity* with the topic also plays a role. If the audience is unfamiliar with the subject matter, a more detailed and explanatory approach is necessary. This might involve using presentations, training sessions, or one-on-one discussions. If the audience is already knowledgeable about the topic, a more concise and direct approach, such as email or a brief report, may be sufficient. For better communication, consider the audience's technical background and their level of understanding of project management concepts.

The *size of the audience* determines the most suitable communication channel. For large audiences, broadcast channels such as email or intranet are more suitable. These channels allow for a one-way communication to reach many people at once. For small audiences, such as a small team or a limited number of stakeholders, more interactive channels, such as video conferencing or instant messaging, are more appropriate. These channels allow for real-time interaction and discussion.

The *level of interaction* can affect the choice of tools. If real-time interaction and non-verbal cues are important, then video conferencing may be the best choice. For communication that requires real-time interaction and verbal cues, channels such as telephone are more appropriate. These channels allow for direct and interactive communication. For one-way communications, such as updates or reports, email or intranet would be more suitable. These channels allow for asynchronous communication, where the recipient can respond at their convenience.

Project *constraints* such as time, budget, and resource availability also influence communication channel choice. Face-to-face meetings, while highly effective, can be time-consuming and expensive, especially if stakeholders are geographically dispersed. In such cases, video conferencing or phone calls might be a more practical alternative. Similarly, the availability of technology and infrastructure can also limit communication options. For example, if some stakeholders have limited internet access, email or online collaboration tools might not be suitable.

Stakeholder *preferences* should also be taken into account. Some stakeholders may prefer receiving information through email, while others may prefer phone calls or meetings. Understanding these preferences and tailoring communication accordingly can improve stakeholder engagement and satisfaction.

This information can be gathered during stakeholder analysis. Rremember that stakeholder satisfaction is a key project objective.

Finally, *confidentiality and sensitivity* of the information must be considered. Sensitive or confidential information should be communicated through secure and private channels, such as face-to-face meetings or encrypted email. Public forums or open communication channels are not appropriate for such information. Be aware of ethical considerations related to communication, especially when dealing with confidential information.

By considering these factors -- urgency, complexity, audience familiarity, audience size, level of interaction, project constraints, stakeholder preferences, and confidentiality -- project managers can select the most appropriate communication channels for each situation, leading to more effective communication, improved stakeholder engagement, and ultimately, greater project success.

Test Your Understanding 3.34
Which factor most directly determines whether synchronous (real-time) or asynchronous (delayed) communication is required?
A. Audience familiarity
B. Urgency of the message
C. Project budget
D. Confidentiality of the information

Test Your Understanding 3.35
A project manager needs to inform stakeholders about a critical system failure that requires immediate mitigation. Which communication channel is most appropriate?
A. Posting an update in the project management software
B. Sending a weekly report
C. Emailing all stakeholders
D. Calling key stakeholders for a meeting

Test Your Understanding 3.36
What is the best channel to use when communicating complex or highly technical information that requires clarification and feedback?
A. Video conferencing or presentations
B. Short text messages
C. A brief email
D. An intranet announcement

Test Your Understanding 3.37
A project manager is preparing a short progress update for 120 employees in a large organization. Which channel would be most effective?
A. Email broadcast

B. One-on-one phone calls
C. Video conference with all employees
D. Instant messaging group chat

Test Your Understanding 3.38
Which of the following factors would most influence whether to use face-to-face meetings versus video conferencing for stakeholder discussions?
A. Level of technical expertise of stakeholders
B. Size of the development team
C. Stakeholder preferences and project constraints
D. Type of project management methodology used

3.9 Stakeholder Register

The stakeholder register is a document that formally documents all identified project stakeholders. It serves as a central repository of information about each stakeholder, providing a structured way to track their contact details, roles, interests, influence, and potential impact on the project. This document is a key output of the "Identify Stakeholders" process and forms the foundation for effective stakeholder engagement and management throughout the project lifecycle. It's not simply a list of names; it's a dynamic tool that helps project managers understand the complex web of relationships and influences surrounding the project.

A typical Stakeholder Register includes several key components:

Stakeholder Identification Information: This includes basic details such as the stakeholder's name, organization, position/role, contact information (phone number, email address, physical address if relevant), and location. This information ensures that the project team can easily contact stakeholders when needed.
Assessment Information: This is the core of the Stakeholder Register and includes an analysis of each stakeholder's:

Interest: What are the stakeholder's concerns, expectations, and motivations related to the project? This could include financial interests, business objectives, personal interests, or concerns about potential negative impacts.

Influence/Power: What is the stakeholder's ability to influence the project, either positively or negatively? This could be based on their formal authority, their position within the organization, their expertise, or their access to resources.

Impact: What is the potential impact of the project on the stakeholder? This could be positive (e.g., increased profits, improved efficiency) or negative (e.g., job losses, disruption to operations).

Stakeholder Classification: Based on the assessment of interest and influence (or other criteria like power/urgency/legitimacy using the Salience Model), stakeholders are classified into categories to help prioritize engagement efforts. Common classifications include:

Classifications	Examples	Engagement Efforts
High Power/High Interest	Project Sponsor/Executive Key Customer/Client Steering Committee	These stakeholders require close management and regular communication.
High Power/Low Interest	Senior Management (indirectly involved) Regulatory Bodies Government Agencies	These stakeholders need to be kept satisfied and informed, but less frequently than high power/high interest stakeholders.
Low Power/High Interest	Project Team Members (non-managers) Local Community Groups (e.g., construction project) End Users	These stakeholders need to be kept informed and engaged, as they can influence other stakeholders.
Low Power/Low Interest	General Public External Consultants (limited scope) Some Administrative Staff	These stakeholders require minimal monitoring and communication.

Table 3.1 Stakeholder classifications

Stakeholder Engagement Strategy: This section outlines the planned approach for engaging with each stakeholder, including communication methods, frequency, and key messages. This is directly linked to the Stakeholder Engagement Plan.

The Stakeholder Register is a living document that should be updated throughout the project lifecycle as new stakeholders are identified, stakeholder interests change, or the project progresses. Regular reviews and updates ensure that the information remains accurate and relevant. This is particularly important, as it emphasizes the dynamic nature of projects and the need for continuous monitoring and adaptation.

Project managers may be presented with scenarios where they need to identify stakeholders, analyze their influence, and recommend appropriate engagement strategies based on the information contained in a Stakeholder Register. The Stakeholder Register is not just a document; it's a tool that empowers project managers to proactively manage stakeholder relationships and contribute significantly to project success.

Here's a simplified example of a stakeholder register for a software development project creating a mobile app for ordering food from local restaurants:

Project Name: Mobile Food Ordering App

Name/ Group	Organization	Role/ Position	Contact Info	Interest	Influence/Power	Impact on Project	Stakeholder Classif.	Engagement Strategy	Key Messages
John Smith	Local Restaurant Association	President	[email address removed], (555) 123-4567	High (Increased restaurant orders, visibility)	High (Represents many restaurants, can influence adoption)	Positive (Potential for increased revenue for restaurants)	High Power/ High Interest	Regular meetings (monthly), presentations at association meetings, dedicated support channel.	Emphasize increased revenue, ease of use for restaurants, marketing support.
Maria Garcia	Individual Restaurant Owner (Maria's Tacos)	Owner/Manager	[email address removed], (555) 987-6543	High (Direct impact on her business)	Medium (Individual restaurant has less influence than the association)	Positive (Potential for increased orders, new customers)	Low Power/High Interest	Regular email updates, training sessions, direct support contact.	Focus on ease of use, cost-effectiveness, and customer acquisition.
David Lee	Venture Capital Firm (TechInvest)	Investor	[email address removed], (555) 555-1212	High (Return on investment)	High (Provides funding for the project)	Positive (Potential for high ROI if the app is successful)	High Power/High Interest	Monthly progress reports, quarterly meetings with project leadership.	Emphasize project milestones, market penetration, and financial projections.
Susan Chen	Mobile App Development Team	Lead Developer	[email address removed]	High (Success of the project, career progression)	Medium (Expertise in app development, influences technical decisions)	Positive (Opportunity to showcase skills, build a successful product)	Low Power/High Interest	Daily stand-up meetings, regular code reviews, clear requirements documentation.	Focus on technical challenges, clear communication of requirements, and opportunities for professional development.
Robert Brown	Local Community Group (Foodies United)	Community Representative	[email address removed]	Medium (Access to local restaurants, convenience)	Low (Limited direct influence on the project)	Positive (Increased convenience for ordering food)	Low Power/Low Interest	Occasional email updates, public announcements about app launch.	Emphasize convenience, support for local businesses, and community benefits.
City Council (represented by Jane Doe)	City Government	Regulatory Body	[email address removed], (555) 111-2222	Medium (Compliance with local regulations, permits)	High (Can grant or deny permits for certain aspects of the business)	Neutral (Ensures compliance with regulations; no direct impact on profits)	High Power/Low Interest	Formal reports on compliance, meetings as needed for permits/approvals.	Focus on compliance with local regulations, adherence to permit requirements.
App Users (Target demographic)	General Public	End Users	N/A	High (Ease of use, variety of restaurants, reliable service)	Low (Individual users have little direct influence)	Positive (Convenient way to order food)	Low Power/High Interest	App store reviews, social media feedback, in-app feedback mechanisms.	Focus on user experience, app features, and customer support.

Table 3.2 A simplified sample stakeholder register.

Please note that a real-world register would typically contain more detailed information than a simplified example here, including specific communication preferences (e.g., preferred communication channels, frequency of updates), risk tolerance (e.g., their comfort level with project risks), and more detailed engagement plans outlining specific strategies for interacting with each stakeholder. Regular updates ensure the register remains accurate and relevant throughout the project lifecycle, reflecting any changes in stakeholder influence, interest, or project circumstances. Maintaining confidentiality is also critical, as some information contained within the register may be sensitive and should be handled with appropriate discretion. Finally, while spreadsheets can be used, project management software often provides built-in features specifically designed for managing stakeholder registers, offering greater efficiency and functionality for tracking and analyzing stakeholder data.

Test Your Understanding 3.39
Which process in project management produces the stakeholder register as a key output?
A. Manage Stakeholder Engagement
B. Identify Stakeholders
C. Plan Communications Management
D. Monitor Stakeholder Engagement

Test Your Understanding 3.40
A project manager is reviewing the stakeholder register and notices that one stakeholder has high power but low interest. How should the project manager engage this stakeholder?
A. Provide daily project updates to maintain close engagement
B. Keep the stakeholder satisfied through occasional updates
C. Monitor the stakeholder with minimal communication
D. Involve the stakeholder in all technical decision-making

Test Your Understanding 3.41
Which of the following best describes the stakeholder register?
A. A list of names and phone numbers of people involved in the project
B. A communication plan for reporting progress to stakeholders
C. A formal project charter authorizing stakeholder involvement
D. A dynamic tool for analyzing stakeholder roles, interests, influence, and engagement strategies

Test Your Understanding 3.42
A stakeholder with low power but high interest is classified in which category?
A. Keep informed
B. Keep satisfied
C. Monitor only
D. Manage closely

Test Your Understanding 3.43
In the sample stakeholder register of the book, the City Council is classified as high power/low interest. What engagement strategy is most appropriate?

A. Daily progress reports and frequent meetings
B. Occasional updates only when convenient
C. Formal reports on compliance and meetings as required
D. No direct communication unless requested

Test Your Understanding 3.44
During project execution, a new stakeholder emerges who has significant interest in the project outcomes but minimal influence. What should the project manager do?
A. Update the stakeholder register to include the new stakeholder
B. Exclude the stakeholder since their influence is low
C. Immediately escalate the situation to senior management
D. Reclassify all stakeholders to rebalance the engagement plan

Test Your Understanding 3.45
A project manager wants to prioritize stakeholders based on power, urgency, and legitimacy. Which model is being applied?
A. Salience Model
B. RACI Matrix
C. Power/Interest Grid
D. Responsibility Assignment Model

3.10 Chapter Summary

This chapter introduces business analysis frameworks with a focus on the topic of stakeholders, starting with the classification of various types of stakeholders. It then goes on to explore stakeholder analysis and management techniques. The significance of establishing well-defined stakeholder roles and responsibilities is emphasized throughout the chapter. Followed by a discussion on the different communication channels available for stakeholders and the appropriate use of each in different scenarios. The chapter concludes with a discussion of stakeholder register which is a tool for stakeholder management.

3.11 Case Study

Revisit the case study in Chapter 1. Perform the following task:
Create a stakeholder register based on a college or university you've studied at (use the real names, positions, and contacts for next chapter's case study.). Use the details from Table 3.2 to guide your entries.

3.12 MS Project Exercise 1

Getting Started with Microsoft Project

Part 1: Setting Up a New Project
1. Open Microsoft Project.

2. Click on Blank Project to start.
Part 2: Enter the Project Information
3. With your new project open, navigate to the Project tab in the Ribbon. In the Properties group, click on Project Information. A dialog box will appear with fields for Start date, Finish date, Status date, and more.
4. In the Start date field, click the dropdown icon and select the desired project start date, preferably the first working day of the current month for practice purposes.
5. The Project Calendar field allows you to choose working times, days, and holidays. By default, it's set to Standard (Project Calendar). To change it, click the dropdown menu and select a different calendar if needed.
6. Add the Project Title by going to File > Info > Project Information > Advanced Properties. In the Title field of the Summary tab, type "Exercise 1" for your project's name. Click OK to save the changes.

Part 3: Understanding the Interface
7. Ribbon: The top area of the Microsoft Project interface with tabs like File, Task, Resource, and Project, each containing specific commands.
8. Entry Table: The left-hand side of the main workspace below the Ribbon. It's a spreadsheet-like area labeled Gantt Chart where task details like names, durations, start dates, and finish dates can be entered. Enter Task1 for one day and Task2 for three days, setting Task1 as a predecessor of Task2.
9. Gantt Chart: The right-hand side of the main workspace, providing a visual representation of your project schedule.
10. Timeline: An optional feature located above the Entry Table and Gantt Chart, offering a high-level overview of your project's schedule. To add tasks to the Timeline, select them in the Entry Table, go to the Task tab in the Ribbon, and click Add to Timeline. Add both tasks you added above to the timeline.

Part 4: Adding a Resource to the Project
15. Click on View > Resource Sheet. Enter "Student1" as Resource Name, select "Work" as Type, and set the standard rate to $40 per hour.
16. Return to the Gantt Chart, click on Task1, and go to Task > Properties > Information. On the resource tab, select "Student1" as the resource name for Task1. Repeat the process for Task2.
17. To view the current cost for this project, click Project > Project Information > Statistics.

Part 5: Creating Custom Calendar
You can set a custom calendar in MS Project to reflect specific working hours and days. Here are the steps to create a custom calendar:
18. Click the Project tab and then click the Change Working Time button.
19. In the upper right corner of the Change Working Time dialog, click the Create New Calendar button.
20. Give the new calendar a Name, “My Calendar”, select Create new base calendar, and then click OK.
21. Click the Work Weeks tab, and then click Details.
22. Select the days that you want to change the working times for, and then choose whether you want them to be working or nonworking time.
23. For practice, chose Set day(s) to these specific working times, use the From and To columns to set the working times for the selected days.
24. Click OK to return to the Change Working Time dialog box, and then click OK again.
25. Go back to the calendar (Part 2 Step 5) to apply “My calendar” to the project.

3.13 References

Aaltonen, K. (2011). Project stakeholder analysis as an environmental interpretation process. *International journal of project management*, *29*(2), 165-183.
Alsulaimi, A., & Abdullah, T. (2020, March). Management of stakeholder communications in IT projects. In *2020 3rd International Conference on Computer Applications & Information Security (ICCAIS)* (pp. 1-6). IEEE.
Harris, A., & Clark, C. (2023). Understanding the Diffusion of Business Analysis Responsibilities. Journal of Computer Information Systems, 1-11.
Kerzner, H. (2025). *Project management: a systems approach to planning, scheduling, and controlling*. John Wiley & Sons.
Miles, S. (2017). Stakeholder theory classification: A theoretical and empirical evaluation of definitions. *Journal of business ethics*, *142*(3), 437-459.
Pandi-Perumal, S. R., Akhter, S., Zizi, F., Jean-Louis, G., Ramasubramanian, C., Edward Freeman, R., & Narasimhan, M. (2015). Project stakeholder management in the clinical research environment: How to do it right. *Frontiers in psychiatry*, *6*, 130129.
Rajhans, K. (2018). Effective communication management: A key to stakeholder relationship management in project-based organizations. *IUP Journal of Soft Skills*, *12*(4), 47-66.
Shakeri, H., & Khalilzadeh, M. (2020). Analysis of factors affecting project communications with a hybrid DEMATEL-ISM approach (A case study in Iran). *Heliyon*, *6*(8).
Shamim, M. I. (2022). Exploring the Success Factors of Project Management. American Journal of Economics and Business Management, 5(7), 64-72.

3.14 Solutions to Test Your Understanding

3.1 B; 3.2 C; 3.3 C; 3.4 A; 3.5 D; 3.6 A; 3.7 D; 3.8 C; 3.9 B; 3.10 A; 3.11 C; 3.12 A; 3.13 B; 3.14 B; 3.15 D; 3.16 B; 3.17 A; 3.18 C; 3.19 C; 3.20 D; 3.21 A; 3.22 B; 3.23 C; 3.24 B; 3.25 B; 3.26 A; 3.27 B; 3.28 C; 3.29 A; 3.30 C; 3.31 B; 3.32 A; 3.33 C; 3.34 B; 3.35 D; 3.36 A; 3.37 A; 3.38 C; 3.39 B; 3.40 B; 3.41 D; 3.42 A; 3.43 C; 3.44 A; 3.45 A;.

Chapter 4: Project Requirements

Chapter Learning Outcomes

4.1 Recognize the different tools utilized in collecting stakeholder requirements.
4.2 Evaluate the appropriate tool to use for gathering requirements based on a given scenario.
4.3 Construct product roadmaps.

4.1 User Stories

User stories provide a simple yet powerful way to capture user needs and drive development. They serve as a bridge between business requirements and technical implementation, ensuring that the development team focuses on delivering value to the end-user. The concept of user stories originated within Agile methodologies, particularly Extreme Programming (XP), as a way to shift the focus from lengthy, formal requirements documents to concise, user-centric descriptions of desired functionality (Cockburn, 2001). This shift emphasizes collaboration and continuous feedback, allowing for greater flexibility and adaptability throughout the project lifecycle.

A *user story* is a short, simple statement describing a desired piece of functionality from the perspective of the end-user. It typically follows a standard template: "As a [user type], I want [some goal] so that [some reason]." For example, "As a website visitor, I want to be able to search for products by keyword so that I can quickly find what I'm looking for." This structure ensures that the story is user-centric, outcome-oriented, and provides context for the development team. This format ensures that the team understands *who* is using the system, *what* they want to achieve, and *why* it's important to them. This "why" is crucial for prioritization and helps the team understand the value proposition of each feature.

Each user story should include acceptance criteria, which define its boundaries and ensure it meets the intended requirements. They act as a checklist for the development team and the product owner, confirming when a story is considered "done." Understanding acceptance criteria enables project managers to manage scope, control quality, and communicate effectively with stakeholders. Clearly defined acceptance criteria can prevent scope creep, ensure that delivered features meet user expectations, and provide a basis for testing and validation.

The primary purpose of acceptance criteria is to ensure clarity and completeness. They provide a precise definition of what constitutes a successful implementation of the user story. Acceptance criteria help to avoid ambiguity by explicitly stating the conditions that must be met for the story to be considered complete. This clarity is invaluable during testing, as testers use the acceptance criteria to design test cases and verify that the implemented functionality behaves as expected. For instance, if a user story is "As a user, I want to be able to reset my password so that I can regain access to my account if I forget it," without specific acceptance criteria, it's unclear what "resetting the password" actually entails. Does it involve email verification? Does it have password complexity requirements? Acceptance criteria address these questions.

A commonly used and effective format for writing acceptance criteria is the Given-When-Then format, also known as Behavior-Driven Development (BDD) or Gherkin syntax (James, 2024). This format provides a structured way to describe the expected behavior of the system under specific conditions. "Given" sets the initial context or preconditions. "When" describes the action taken by the user or the system. "Then" specifies the expected outcome or result. This structure makes the acceptance criteria easy to understand and implement. For example, consider the user story mentioned earlier about resetting a password. Using the Given-When-Then format, we can define the following acceptance criteria:

Given I am on the password reset page, When I enter a valid email address and click the "Reset Password" button, Then I should receive an email with a password reset link.
Given I am on the password reset page, When I enter an invalid email address and click the "Reset Password" button, Then I should see an error message indicating that the email address is not found.
Given I click the password reset link in the email, When I enter a new password that meets the complexity requirements (e.g., at least 8 characters, including one uppercase letter, one number, and one special character) and confirm it, Then my password should be updated, and I should be redirected to the login page.
Given I click the password reset link in the email, When I enter a new password that does not meet the complexity requirements, Then I should see an error message indicating the password requirements.

Using user stories provides several benefits. First, they enhance the understanding of user needs by focusing on the user's perspective. This prevents the development team from building features that are technically complex but ultimately don't address real user needs. Second, they improve communication within the team and between the team and stakeholders. The simple language and clear structure of user stories facilitate effective communication and reduce misunderstandings. This shared understanding reduces rework and ensures that everyone is on the same page.

Third, user stories facilitate the prioritization of work based on value. By focusing on the "why" behind each story, the product owner can prioritize features that deliver the most value to the business and the users, maximizing the return on investment. This is particularly relevant for project managers, as understanding value delivery is a key aspect of project management. For example, in a financial application, a user story like "As an investor, I want to see real-time stock quotes so that I can make informed trading decisions" would likely be prioritized higher than a story about aesthetic changes to the application's interface. Project managers should understand how user stories contribute to scope management, requirements gathering, and stakeholder communication.

Test Your Understanding 4.1
Which of the following best describes the primary purpose of user stories in Agile methodologies?
A. To document all technical details of system architecture
B. To capture user needs and guide development through concise, user-focused statements
C. To replace project charters and stakeholder registers of the waterfall approach in Agile projects
D. To serve as a legal contract between developers and stakeholders

Test Your Understanding 4.2
A product manager is drafting a user story for a mobile banking app. Which of the following best follows the standard user story format?
A. "As a customer, I want to transfer money between my accounts so that I can manage my finances conveniently."
B. "The system must allow users to transfer money between accounts quickly."
C. "Developers should implement a transfer feature with confirmation messages."
D. "Users need money transfers because it is an essential part of mobile banking."

Test Your Understanding 4.3
Why are acceptance criteria important in user stories?
A. They define the technical architecture of the system.
B. They are only used for testing after the product is released.
C. They eliminate the need for stakeholder feedback.
D. They act as a checklist to confirm when a story is complete.

Test Your Understanding 4.4
A development team delivers a "reset password" feature, but users complain it does not check for password complexity. The team argues that complexity rules were never specified. What most likely caused this issue?
A. The product owner did not prioritize the story correctly.
B. The developers skipped unit testing.
C. The acceptance criteria for the story were incomplete.
D. The team did not conduct a sprint retrospective.

Test Your Understanding 4.5
In the Given-When-Then format for acceptance criteria, what does the "Then" component specify?
A. The precondition that sets the initial state
B. The action performed by the user or system
C. The expected outcome of the action
D. The rationale for why the feature is needed

Test Your Understanding 4.6
You are a project manager working on a financial application. Two user stories are under discussion:
Story A: "As an investor, I want to see real-time stock quotes so that I can make informed trading decisions."
Story B: "As a user, I want the application to display a new color scheme for improved aesthetics."
Which should be prioritized higher, and why?
A. Story A, because it delivers higher business value.
B. Story B, because aesthetics improve customer satisfaction.
C. Story A, because it requires less development effort.
D. Story B, because it can be implemented faster.

4.2 Product Backlogs

The product backlog is an artifact in Agile project management, serving as a dynamic, prioritized list of all the work that needs to be done on a project. It acts as the single source of truth for requirements and provides a roadmap for the development team. The product backlog directly relates to scope management, planning, and stakeholder communication. A well-maintained product backlog ensures that the project stays focused on delivering value and that everyone involved has a shared understanding of the project's goals and priorities.

The *product backlog* is a centralized repository for all work items in an Agile project. It's not a static document but rather a living, evolving artifact that is continuously refined and updated throughout the project lifecycle. This dynamic nature allows the project to adapt to changing requirements and priorities. The product owner is responsible for managing and prioritizing the product backlog, ensuring that it reflects the needs of the business and the users. This ownership helps maintain focus and ensure alignment with the project's objectives.

Several components typically make up the product backlog. The most common are user stories, which, as discussed previously, are short, user-centric descriptions of desired functionality. These stories form the basis of much of the development work. In addition to user stories, the product backlog also includes technical tasks. These are tasks that are necessary for the implementation of the user stories but are not directly visible to the end-user. Examples include setting up development environments, writing unit tests, or refactoring code. These tasks help ensure the quality and maintainability of the software.

Bugs and improvements also find their place in the product backlog. Bugs represent defects or errors in the existing functionality that need to be fixed. Improvements represent enhancements or changes to existing features that are not necessarily fixing a bug but are aimed at improving the user experience or performance of the system. These can range from minor UI tweaks to significant performance optimizations. Sometimes, especially in projects with a strong technical focus, the backlog may also contain "Enablers," which are tasks that don't directly add business value but are necessary to enable future development. Examples include researching a new technology or upgrading a development tool.

The product backlog's importance stems from several key functions it performs. First and foremost, it acts as a single source of truth for all project requirements. This eliminates confusion and ensures that everyone is working from the same understanding of what needs to be built. This single source of truth is a critical aspect of scope management.

Second, the product backlog facilitates prioritization and planning. By prioritizing items in the backlog, the product owner ensures that the team focuses on delivering the most valuable features first. This prioritization informs sprint planning, where the team selects a subset of items from the top of the backlog to work on during the upcoming sprint. This iterative approach to planning and execution is a hallmark of Agile methodologies.

Managing the product backlog ensures that the development team is working on the right things at the right time and that the project remains aligned with business objectives. Product backlog management directly relates to scope management, stakeholder management, and project planning. Effective backlog management contributes significantly to delivering value and achieving project goals.

The product owners manage the product backlog. They are ultimately responsible for its content, prioritization, and maintenance. This ownership means the product owner makes decisions about what features are included in the product, what order they should be developed in, and when they should be released. Prioritization is a key responsibility, as the product owner must constantly balance competing demands and ensure that the team is working on the most valuable items first. This often involves making tough choices and saying "no" to some requests.

The product owner also acts as the primary liaison between the development team and stakeholders, including customers, business users, and management. This collaboration supports feedback gathering, requirement clarification, and alignment with stakeholder needs. The product owner translates business needs into user stories and acceptance criteria, ensuring that the development team has a clear understanding of what needs to be built. This continuous communication and collaboration are key for maintaining alignment and preventing misunderstandings.

Backlog grooming, also known as backlog refinement, is an ongoing activity that keeps the product backlog healthy and manageable. It involves regularly reviewing the items in the backlog, ensuring they are still relevant, appropriately sized, and clearly defined. This is not a one-time event but rather a continuous process that occurs throughout the project lifecycle.

One of the key aspects of backlog grooming is breaking down large user stories, often referred to as epics, into smaller, more manageable stories. This makes it easier for the development team to estimate the effort required and to complete the work within a single sprint. For instance, an epic like "Implement online payment functionality" could be broken down into smaller stories such as "Allow users to pay with credit cards," "Allow users to pay with PayPal," and "Implement secure transaction processing."

During grooming, the product owner also adds details to the user stories, including acceptance criteria, descriptions, and any relevant attachments. Estimates are also added, typically using story points or other relative sizing techniques. This estimation helps the team plan sprints and track progress. Finally, priorities are reviewed and adjusted as needed, based on changing business needs or feedback from stakeholders. The frequency of backlog grooming sessions varies depending on the project, but typically occurs once or twice per sprint.

Several tools are available to help manage product backlogs, ranging from simple spreadsheets to sophisticated project management software. Jira is a popular choice for many Agile teams, offering features like issue tracking, workflow management, and reporting. Trello is another widely used tool, known for its visual Kanban board interface, which provides a clear overview of the work in progress. Microsoft Project, while traditionally used for waterfall projects, can also be adapted for Agile projects and offers robust planning and scheduling features.

The choice of tool depends on the specific needs of the project and the team. For smaller projects, a simple spreadsheet or Trello board may suffice, while larger, more complex projects may benefit from the more advanced features of Jira or similar tools.

Test Your Understanding 4.7
Which of the following best describes the purpose of the product backlog in Agile project management?

A. A static requirements document maintained by the project manager
B. A dynamic, prioritized list of all the work required for the project
C. A detailed contract between stakeholders and the development team
D. A record of completed tasks for auditing purposes

Test Your Understanding 4.8
A project's business stakeholders request a new feature midway through development. The development team is unsure how to prioritize it. Where should this request be captured?
A. In the sprint backlog
B. In the project charter
C. In the product backlog
D. In the release notes

Test Your Understanding 4.9
Which of the following is NOT typically found in a product backlog?
A. User stories
B. Technical tasks
C. Completed sprint deliverables
D. Bugs and improvements

Test Your Understanding 4.10
During sprint planning, the team identifies the need to refactor existing code to support a new feature. Where should this refactoring task be placed?
A. In the risk register
B. In the business case as a technical task
C. In the sprint retrospective notes
D. In the product backlog as a technical task

Test Your Understanding 4.11
Which of the following is a primary responsibility of the product owner?
A. Estimating the effort required for each backlog item
B. Writing all test cases for acceptance criteria
C. Assigning tasks to individual developers
D. Prioritizing backlog items based on business value

Test Your Understanding 4.12
A stakeholder approaches the development team directly with a new request. What should the development team do first?
A. Add the request directly into the sprint backlog
B. Direct the stakeholder to the product owner
C. Immediately start implementing the request
D. Escalate the request to project governance

Test Your Understanding 4.13
Which of the following best describes backlog grooming (refinement)?
A. A continuous process of reviewing, clarifying, and prioritizing backlog items
B. Reviewing backlog items once at project initiation
C. The process of archiving completed backlog items
D. A retrospective activity for identifying process improvements

Test Your Understanding 4.14
The product backlog contains the epic "Implement online payment functionality." Which of the following represents an effective refinement activity?
A. Splitting it into smaller stories like “Pay with credit card” and “Pay with PayPal”
B. Moving the epic to the risk register until resources are available
C. Adding it directly to the sprint backlog without changes
D. Rewriting the epic as a project objective in the charter

4.3 Use Cases

Use cases offer a structured approach to capturing system requirements from a user's perspective, focusing on how users interact with a system to achieve specific goals. They provide a detailed narrative of the interactions between actors (users or external systems) and the system itself. This approach originated in object-oriented software engineering and has become a valuable tool in various project management methodologies, including both traditional and Agile approaches.

Use cases describe the sequence of actions a user performs and the system's responses, offering a more detailed view than high-level requirements or user stories (Cockburn, 2002). This granular level of detail helps uncover hidden requirements and is particularly useful in complex projects where understanding intricate user interactions is crucial. A well-defined use case provides a clear blueprint for development, testing, and ultimately, project success.

Several key components make up a use case, providing a structured way to describe how users interact with a system to achieve specific goals. *Actors* are external entities that interact with the system. They can be human users/external system initiating the interaction (primary actors) or other systems (secondary actors). A primary actor initiates the interaction to achieve a specific goal, while a secondary actor supports the system in fulfilling the primary actor's goal.

The *system* is the subject of the interaction -- the software or application being described. The *goals* represent what the actor wants to achieve by interacting with the system. These goals should be clearly defined and measurable, such as "Withdraw Cash," "Make a Payment," or "View Transaction History." The *steps* or *scenarios* describe the sequence of actions that occur between the actor and the system to achieve the goal. These steps are typically described in a numbered list, outlining the flow of events. This flow can be further visualized using a *use case diagram*.

A use case diagram provides a graphical representation of the interactions between actors and the system. This visual representation helps stakeholders quickly grasp the scope of the system and how different actors interact with it. Here is an example of use case diagram for online shopping. A customer wants to purchase a product online, and the use case describes the steps they will take, such as browsing the website, adding items to their cart, checking out, placing order, and creating account.

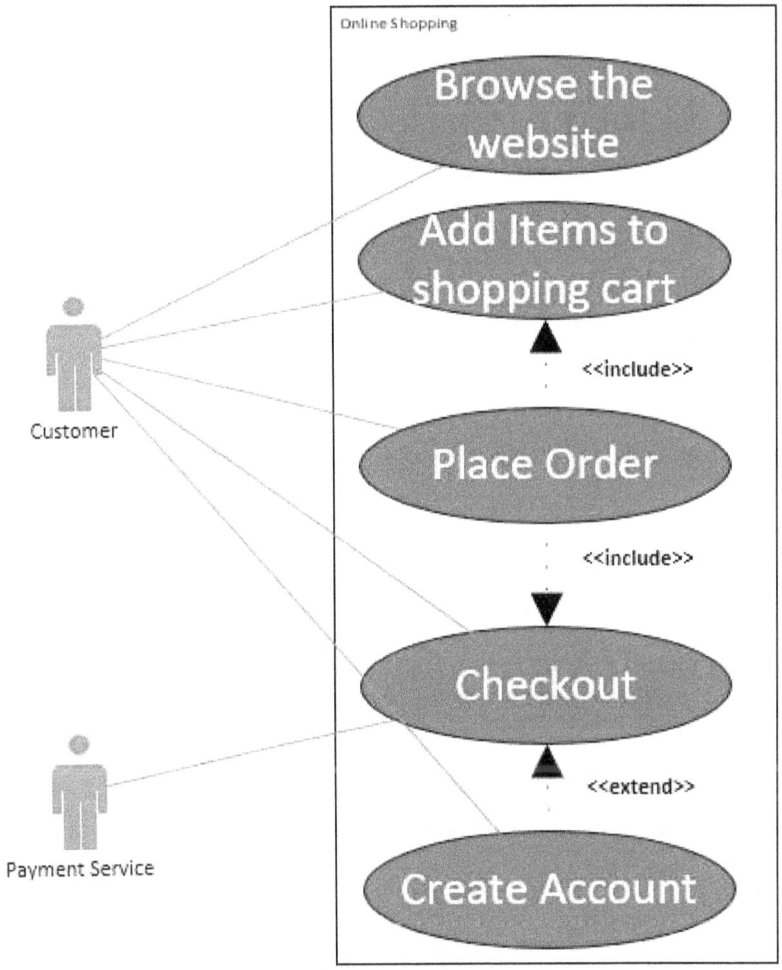

Figure 4.1 A use case diagram of online shopping.

In a use case diagram, a use case is typically represented with an oval shape, which indicates a specific feature or function of the application that can be performed by a user or system. An actor is represented with a stick figure or other appropriate graphic that indicates a person or system that interacts with the use case.

The "include" and "extend" relationships are two types of associations that can be used to connect use cases in a use case diagram. However, they have different meanings and are used in different ways.

The "include" relationship is used to show that one use case (the "included" use case) is part of another use case (the "including" use case). The included use case is a necessary step in achieving the functionality of the including use case. For example, a use case for "place order" may include a use case for "add items to shopping cart".

The "extend" relationship is used to show that one use case (the "extended" use case) can be optionally extended by another use case (the "extending" use case). The extending use case is optional and provides additional functionality beyond the basic functionality of the extended use case. For example, a use case for "create a new user account" may be extended by a use case for "checkout".

The importance of use cases in project management stems from their ability to enhance communication between stakeholders and provide a clear understanding of system functionality. By describing user interactions in a clear and concise manner, use cases facilitate communication between technical and non-technical stakeholders. They provide a common language that everyone can understand, reducing the risk of misunderstandings and misinterpretations.

This improved communication is particularly valuable during requirements elicitation and validation, ensuring that all stakeholders have a shared understanding of the system's intended behavior. Furthermore, use cases provide a clear understanding of system functionality by outlining the steps involved in each user interaction. This detailed description helps developers understand what needs to be built and testers understand what needs to be tested. This clarity is essential for ensuring that the system is developed correctly and meets the needs of its users.

Test Your Understanding 4.15
What is the primary purpose of a use case in project management?
A. To document technical requirements of the system in agile projects
B. To provide a structured narrative of user interactions with the system
C. To replace user stories entirely in Agile projects
D. To outline project risks and mitigation strategies

Test Your Understanding 4.16
A project team is building a mobile banking application. During requirements gathering, they realize users want to receive SMS confirmations after transactions, which was not initially stated. Which tool is most useful for uncovering such hidden requirements?
A. Use cases
B. Gantt charts
C. Risk registers

D. Work breakdown structures

Test Your Understanding 4.17
In a use case, who or what is considered the **primary actor**?
A. The stakeholder who funds the project
B. The primary project team members who develop the software application
C. The project manager who defines the scope of the project
D. The human or external system initiating the interaction to achieve a goal

Test Your Understanding 4.18
A team is designing an online shopping system. The use case "Place Order" must always include "Add Items to Cart." However, the use case "Create Account" may optionally allow users to extend it by performing "Checkout." Which statement is correct?
A. "Place Order" uses an extend relationship with "Add Items to Cart."
B. "Create Account" uses an include relationship with "Checkout."
C. "Place Order" uses an include relationship with "Add Items to Cart."
D. Both use cases should use the include relationship.

Test Your Understanding 4.19
In a use case diagram, how are actors and use cases typically represented?
A. Actors as ovals and use cases as rectangles
B. Actors as stick figures and use cases as ovals
C. Actors as diamonds and use cases as circles
D. Actors as rectangles and use cases as stick figures

Test Your Understanding 4.20
During a system design meeting, non-technical stakeholders struggle to understand technical requirements written in system specification documents. Which approach would best improve shared understanding?
A. Using use cases to describe user interactions in plain language and diagrams
B. Providing stakeholders with detailed code documentation
C. Having the project manager summarize the system architecture verbally
D. Replacing all user stories with technical specifications

4.4 Stakeholder Interviews

Stakeholder interviews are a technique for gathering information through structured or semi-structured conversations with individuals or groups affected by a project. These interviews help understand perspectives, build relationships, and elicit information about project objectives, requirements, and potential impacts, contributing to a shared understanding of goals, risks, and opportunities.

The primary purpose of stakeholder interviews is to gather detailed information about stakeholders' needs, expectations, and concerns related to the project. They provide an opportunity for stakeholders to express their views in their own words, offering rich qualitative data that may not be captured through other methods like surveys or questionnaires. These interviews are particularly valuable during the early stages of a project, such as initiation and planning, as they help to define project scope, identify key requirements, and establish a baseline understanding of stakeholder priorities. By engaging stakeholders early on, potential conflicts and misunderstandings can be identified and addressed proactively. This process ensures that the project aligns with the needs and expectations of those who have a vested interest in its outcome.

Planning for stakeholder interviews begins with stakeholder identification, using tools like stakeholder registers and power/interest grids to document and analyze stakeholders based on their influence and interest in the project. After identification, clear interview objectives must be defined and aligned with project goals, focusing on gathering relevant information about scope, requirements, and potential impacts.

The preparation process continues with creating an interview plan that addresses scheduling, participant selection, and format choice (in-person, virtual, or hybrid). The final step involves drafting effective interview questions, using a mix of open-ended, closed-ended, and probing questions while avoiding leading or ambiguous ones. Questions typically cover areas such as goals and expectations, pain points and challenges, and success criteria, all designed to elicit comprehensive and honest responses from stakeholders.

Conducting effective stakeholder interviews begins with creating a positive environment by setting the right tone, clearly outlining the agenda, and establishing trust through respectful engagement and appropriate body language. Active listening is crucial, involving careful attention to both verbal and non-verbal communication, along with paraphrasing and summarizing to ensure mutual understanding.

The interview process relies on asking effective questions, starting with broad, open-ended inquiries before narrowing to specific topics, and using follow-up questions to gain deeper insights. When managing difficult stakeholders who may show resistance or hold conflicting viewpoints, interviewers should remain professional, listen carefully to concerns, provide clear information, and use techniques like negotiation and mediation to find mutually acceptable solutions.

Documenting stakeholder input requires effective recording methods during interviews, including detailed note-taking, audio/video recording (with explicit consent), and real-time collaboration tools for virtual meetings. The information gathered must then be organized by categorizing inputs into themes or priorities, creating clear summaries, and developing visual representations like mind maps or affinity diagrams to make the data more accessible and meaningful.

The documentation process concludes with stakeholder verification, where interview notes or summaries are shared with stakeholders for review and feedback. This step ensures accuracy, prevents misunderstandings, and demonstrates respect for stakeholder input while allowing them to clarify points or provide additional information.

Analyzing stakeholder interview results begins with synthesizing information by identifying common themes, patterns, and crucial requirements or constraints from the collected data. This synthesis process often employs tools like affinity diagrams to visually group related ideas and establish clear patterns across stakeholder feedback. The next step involves prioritizing stakeholder needs using techniques such as the MoSCoW method (Must have, Should have, Could have, Won't have) (Kravchenko et al., 2022) and RACI analysis (Responsible, Accountable, Consulted, Informed) to determine which requirements are most critical and who should be involved in addressing them. "Must have" features are essential for the product to be considered viable. "Should have" features are important but not critical. "Could have" features are desirable but can be deferred. "Won't have" features are those that are not planned for the current release.

The analysis concludes with *integrating results into project requirements* by translating stakeholder insights into actionable items within project documentation. This involves updating requirements documents or product backlogs with clear, concise, and testable requirements that directly reflect stakeholder needs. For example, general feedback about user-friendly interfaces would be translated into specific, measurable requirements like "The system shall provide intuitive navigation" or "The system shall use consistent terminology," ensuring stakeholder input directly shapes the project's deliverables.

Stakeholder interviews offer several significant benefits to a project. First, they help in *clarifying project objectives.* By engaging in direct conversations with stakeholders, the project team can gain a deeper understanding of what the project aims to achieve and how it aligns with broader organizational goals. This clarity helps define the project's scope and ensure that everyone is working towards the same objectives.

Second, interviews are invaluable in *identifying constraints and expectations.* Stakeholders can provide insights into potential limitations, such as budget constraints, time constraints, resource constraints, or technical limitations. They can also articulate their expectations regarding project deliverables, timelines, and communication. Identifying these constraints and expectations early on allows the project team to develop realistic plans and manage stakeholder expectations effectively.

Finally, stakeholder interviews play a crucial role in *building relationships with stakeholders.* By engaging in face-to-face or virtual conversations, the project team can establish rapport, build trust, and foster a sense of collaboration. These strong relationships support effective communication and conflict resolution throughout the project lifecycle. When stakeholders feel heard and understood, they are more likely to support the project and contribute to its success.

Test Your Understanding 4.21
What is the primary purpose of stakeholder interviews in a project?
A. To finalize the project schedule and cost estimates
B. To gather detailed information about stakeholder needs and expectations
C. To confirm compliance with regulatory requirements relevant to the project
D. To document project lessons learned

Test Your Understanding 4.22
During the initiation phase of a project, a project manager wants to avoid potential misunderstandings and conflicts later on. Which technique would be most valuable at this stage?
A. Conducting stakeholder interviews
B. Finalizing the project charter
C. Performing earned value analysis
D. Completing procurement negotiations

Test Your Understanding 4.23
When planning stakeholder interviews, what is the first step the project manager should take?
A. Drafting interview questions
B. Identifying stakeholders using tools like registers or grids
C. Scheduling meetings with high-power stakeholders only
D. Choosing between in-person or virtual formats

Test Your Understanding 4.24
Which of the following best demonstrates active listening during a stakeholder interview?
A. Taking notes silently without interrupting
B. Repeating every word the stakeholder says
C. Paraphrasing key points to confirm understanding
D. Focusing only on verbal communication and ignoring body language

Test Your Understanding 4.25
Which tool is most commonly used to visually group related ideas from stakeholder interviews into patterns and themes?
A. Work breakdown structure (WBS)
B. Fishbone diagram
C. Responsibility assignment matrix (RAM)
D. Affinity diagram

4.5 Stakeholder Surveys

Stakeholder surveys are a structured method for efficiently gathering input from a large and diverse group of stakeholders. Unlike interviews, which provide in-depth qualitative insights from a select few, surveys are ideal for collecting quantitative data, such as stakeholder preferences, satisfaction levels, or opinions on project features. This data can be analyzed statistically to identify trends, patterns, and areas of consensus or disagreement. Surveys are particularly useful for validating requirements identified through other methods, such as interviews or workshops, or for gathering initial input from a broader audience.

Choosing between surveys and interviews depends on project needs. Interviews are better suited for exploring complex issues and gaining detailed qualitative insights, while surveys are more effective for reaching a geographically dispersed audience and collecting measurable feedback. They are also time-and cost-efficient, making them ideal for assessing stakeholder satisfaction, gathering feedback on proposed changes, or identifying training needs. For example, in a large-scale IT implementation, a survey could help gauge employee satisfaction with existing systems and expectations for new ones.

A well-designed survey begins with identifying the target audience, segmenting stakeholders based on influence and interest, and defining clear objectives aligned with project goals. Choosing the right survey format--online or paper-based, anonymous or attributed--ensures accessibility and honest feedback.

Effective survey design includes a mix of open-ended and closed-ended questions, avoiding bias and ensuring clarity. Distribution through appropriate channels, setting response deadlines, and encouraging participation through reminders or incentives (where appropriate and ethical) enhance response rates. Once collected, survey data is analyzed using quantitative and qualitative methods, with visualizations aiding interpretation. Integrating survey findings into project requirements ensures stakeholder feedback is effectively used to guide decisions, complementing insights from interviews and workshops for a well-rounded understanding of needs and priorities.

Stakeholder surveys offer several key benefits. First, they allow for efficiently collecting feedback from multiple stakeholders. This scalability is a major advantage over interviews, which are more time-consuming and resource-intensive. Second, surveys provide quantifiable and structured data for decision-making. The structured nature of survey questions allows for easy analysis and comparison of responses. This quantitative data can be used to support project decisions and track changes over time. For example, survey data can be used to measure the effectiveness of a training program by comparing pre-training and post-training scores. Finally, surveys can offer anonymity, which can lead to more honest responses. When stakeholders feel that their responses will be kept confidential, they are more likely to provide candid feedback, even if it is critical of the project or its stakeholders. This honest feedback can be invaluable for identifying potential problems and improving project outcomes.

Several best practices can further enhance the effectiveness of stakeholder surveys. Keeping surveys concise and relevant helps maximize response rates and minimize respondent fatigue. Only ask questions that are directly relevant to the project and avoid unnecessary or redundant questions. Using clear and accessible language ensures that all stakeholders can understand the questions. Avoid technical jargon, complex sentence structures, and ambiguous wording.

Testing the survey before full distribution is a critical step in identifying and correcting any problems with the questions or the survey design. This pilot testing allows for feedback from a small group of stakeholders, which can be used to improve the survey before it is distributed to the wider audience. Following up with key stakeholders for clarifications can be helpful for gathering more detailed information or resolving any ambiguities in their responses. This follow-up can be done through email, phone calls, or brief interviews.

Test Your Understanding 4.26
Which of the following is the primary advantage of stakeholder surveys compared to interviews?
A. They provide more detailed qualitative insights.
B. They allow for efficiently collecting feedback from a large group.
C. They reduce the need for defining clear project objectives.
D. They eliminate the need for follow-up with stakeholders.

Test Your Understanding 4.27
You are managing a global IT implementation project with stakeholders located across multiple countries. You need to gather measurable feedback on employee satisfaction with the current system. Which method is most appropriate?
A. One-on-one interviews with all employees.
B. A paper-based survey distributed to only local offices.
C. An online survey designed for a geographically dispersed audience.
D. Workshops held in each regional office.

Test Your Understanding 4.28
Which of the following best describes the role of anonymity in stakeholder surveys?
A. It prevents bias by hiding the survey's objectives.
B. It ensures stakeholders only provide positive feedback.
C. It increases the likelihood of honest, candid responses.
D. It eliminates the need to analyze qualitative data.

Test Your Understanding 4.29
Which of the following is a best practice for ensuring survey effectiveness?

A. Using pilot testing, as it may delay the survey launch.
B. Using only open-ended questions to gain rich insights.
C. Using only close-ended questions to gain rich insights.
D. Limiting responses to senior stakeholders only.

Test Your Understanding 4.30
During a project, survey results revealed mixed feedback about a proposed system change. Some stakeholders strongly supported it, while others were opposed. What should the project manager do NEXT?
A. Disregard the survey since responses were inconsistent.
B. Assume the majority opinion reflects the correct decision.
C. Conduct another survey with the same questions.
D. Follow up with stakeholders for clarification and deeper insights.

4.6 Stakeholder Workshops

Stakeholder workshops serve the purpose of bringing key stakeholders together in a structured setting to collaboratively define and refine project requirements. They differ from interviews and surveys in their approach and objectives. Interviews are typically one-on-one conversations focused on gathering individual perspectives, while surveys are used to collect structured data from a large number of stakeholders. Workshops, on the other hand, emphasize group interaction and collaborative problem-solving. They provide a forum for stakeholders to share their ideas, discuss different viewpoints, and reach a shared understanding of project goals and requirements. This collaborative environment fosters a sense of ownership and commitment among stakeholders.

Effective stakeholder workshops require careful planning and facilitation to generate valuable insights and build consensus. Planning begins with *defining clear objectives* that align with project requirements, such as identifying key features of a new product or assessing business process impacts. *Selecting the right participants* ensures diverse perspectives by involving stakeholders with varying expertise and influence. The *workshop format* -- in-person or virtual, structured or unstructured -- should be chosen based on project needs. A well-prepared *agenda and materials*, including discussion points and interactive exercises, help keep the session focused and productive.

Skilled facilitation supports stakeholder engagement and ensures balanced participation. Techniques such as brainstorming, mind-mapping, and prioritization frameworks (e.g., MoSCoW, Kano model) help guide discussions. Facilitators must also manage conflicts by fostering open communication and finding common ground. Documenting key insights through note-taking, shared documents, or visual aids ensures that critical discussions are captured. Post-workshop, findings should be structured and validated with participants to confirm accuracy and agreement.

To maximize impact, workshop outcomes must be integrated into project requirements. This includes aligning insights with stakeholder expectations, converting discussions into actionable requirements, and cross-referencing data from interviews and surveys. A structured approach ensures that stakeholder input is well-documented and effectively informs project decisions.

Stakeholder workshops provide several benefits. First, they facilitate collaborative decision-making. By bringing stakeholders together in a collaborative environment, workshops encourage open communication, idea sharing, and joint problem-solving. This leads to better-informed decisions that are more likely to be supported by all stakeholders. Second, workshops are highly effective in aligning stakeholders on project requirements. The interactive nature of workshops allows for real-time clarification and discussion, ensuring that everyone has a shared understanding of what needs to be delivered. Finally, workshops help in reducing misunderstandings and conflicts. By providing a forum for stakeholders to express their viewpoints and discuss their concerns, workshops can help identify and resolve potential conflicts early on.

While stakeholder workshops offer significant advantages for requirements gathering, they also present certain challenges and limitations that project managers must address to ensure their effectiveness. One common challenge is managing large groups and diverse opinions. When a large number of stakeholders are involved, it can be difficult to ensure that everyone has an opportunity to contribute and that discussions remain focused. Diverse opinions and conflicting viewpoints can also create challenges in reaching consensus. Another challenge is time constraints and scheduling issues. Coordinating the schedules of multiple stakeholders can be difficult, and workshops often have limited time allocated for achieving their objectives. This can put pressure on the facilitator to keep the discussions moving and ensure that all important topics are covered. Overcoming dominant or passive participants is another potential challenge. Some stakeholders may dominate the discussion, preventing others from contributing, while others may be passive and reluctant to share their ideas. This can lead to biased input and a less comprehensive understanding of stakeholder needs.

Several strategies can be implemented to mitigate these challenges. To manage large groups and diverse opinions, the facilitator can use techniques such as breaking the group into smaller subgroups for focused discussions, using structured brainstorming techniques, and employing voting or prioritization methods to reach consensus. To address time constraints and scheduling issues, it's important to plan the workshop carefully, set a realistic agenda, and stick to the allocated time for each activity. Pre-workshop communication can also help to set expectations and ensure that stakeholders come prepared. To overcome dominant or passive participants, the facilitator can use techniques such as round-robin discussions, encouraging quieter participants to share their ideas in writing, and gently redirecting dominant participants. The facilitator should also create a safe and inclusive environment where all stakeholders feel comfortable contributing.

Test Your Understanding 4.31
Which of the following best differentiates a stakeholder workshop from interviews and surveys?
A. Workshops focus on structured data collection, unlike interviews.
B. Workshops emphasize group interaction and collaborative problem-solving.
C. Workshops provide only individual perspectives, unlike surveys.
D. Workshops eliminate the need for other requirement-gathering techniques.

Test Your Understanding 4.32
A project manager is preparing to run a stakeholder workshop for a new product launch. Which of the following actions would best ensure the workshop is productive?
A. Allow discussions to develop organically without an agenda.
B. Invite only senior management to maintain efficiency.
C. Prepare a clear agenda, discussion points, and interactive exercises.
D. Avoid pre-workshop communication to prevent bias.

Test Your Understanding 4.33
Which facilitation technique would be most appropriate if a few stakeholders dominate discussions during a workshop?
A. Canceling the session and rescheduling with fewer participants.
B. Using round-robin discussions to give everyone a chance to speak.
C. Limiting participation only to those with decision-making authority.
D. Avoiding intervention to maintain the natural flow of conversation.

Test Your Understanding 4.34
During a stakeholder workshop, participants are struggling to prioritize requirements. Which tool would be most effective for reaching consensus?
A. SWOT analysis
B. Earned Value Management
C. PESTLE analysis
D. MoSCoW prioritization

Test Your Understanding 4.35
You are facilitating a workshop where stakeholders express conflicting opinions about business process changes. Tension is rising, and progress has stalled. What should you do as the facilitator?
A. Encourage open communication and help stakeholders find common ground.
B. End the workshop early and resolve the conflict later one-on-one.
C. Proceed with majority voting to avoid wasting time.
D. Avoid addressing the conflict to maintain neutrality.

Test Your Understanding 4.36

Which of the following is NOT listed as a challenge commonly faced in stakeholder workshops?
A. Large groups with diverse opinions.
B. Time constraints and scheduling issues.
C. Difficulty in documenting workshop insights.
D. Dominant or passive participants.

4.7 Lessons Learned

Lessons learned are defined as the knowledge gained during a project that can be used to improve future performance. They encompass both positive and negative experiences, capturing what worked well, what didn't work well, and what could be done differently in the future. The significance of lessons learned in project management lies in their contribution to continuous improvement. By systematically capturing and applying lessons learned, organizations can avoid repeating past mistakes, replicate successful strategies, and enhance their project management processes.

Effective stakeholder lessons learned sessions capture valuable insights to drive continuous improvement. Planning begins with defining objectives -- such as identifying best practices, evaluating risk mitigation, or assessing project estimates -- to ensure focused discussions. Engaging key stakeholders across roles provides diverse perspectives, while choosing the right format (in-person vs. virtual, structured vs. informal) enhances participation. Preparing guiding questions and documentation tools -- like templates and collaboration platforms -- streamlines data collection.

Strong facilitation supports open and productive discussions. Facilitators should encourage participation, use SWOT analysis to structure insights, and apply prioritization techniques like dot voting (Dalton, 2018). Managing conflicts professionally ensures constructive dialogue. Documenting takeaways using structured formats, mind maps, or digital notes helps organize key insights. Synthesizing feedback into actionable recommendations and validating findings with stakeholders enhances accuracy.

To maximize impact, lessons learned must be implemented and shared. Updating processes, integrating insights into risk management, and maintaining a knowledge repository ensures long-term organizational learning. Communicating findings via reports, training, and workshops fosters continuous improvement.

Involving stakeholders in lessons learned sessions captures diverse perspectives and uncovers overlooked issues, leading to comprehensive insights. Their participation also increases buy-in for future improvements, fostering a culture of continuous learning and enhancing the effectiveness of implemented changes.

Timing is key -- sessions can be held post-project for a full review or phase-based for timely adjustments. Compared to other engagement methods, lessons learned sessions provide a structured approach to translating insights into action. For example, identifying communication gaps in a post-project session can lead to improved protocols for future projects.

Stakeholder lessons learned sessions are valuable but come with challenges that project managers must address to ensure effectiveness. *Resistance to honest feedback* can hinder meaningful discussions, as stakeholders may fear blame or repercussions. *Biased or limited participation* may result in dominant voices overshadowing others, leading to an incomplete view of project experiences. Additionally, *failure to implement lessons learned* reduces their impact -- without clear action plans and follow-ups, valuable insights risk being ignored.

To mitigate these challenges, creating a *safe, blame-free environment* encourages open communication. Facilitators should use techniques like round-robin discussions, anonymous feedback, and targeted outreach to ensure diverse participation. To ensure *actionable follow-ups*, assign responsibilities, set deadlines, and integrate lessons learned into project methodologies and training programs.

Best practices further enhance effectiveness. *Fostering a culture of continuous improvement* helps organizations value learning from both successes and failures. Sessions should be *structured yet flexible* to cover key topics while allowing room for unexpected insights. Leveraging *technology for documentation and knowledge retention*, such as shared repositories and project management tools, ensures lessons are accessible and actionable.

Test Your Understanding 4.37
What is the primary purpose of conducting lessons learned sessions in project management?
A. To evaluate stakeholder satisfaction after project closure
B. To document only the failures of a project for future avoidance
C. To capture knowledge that improves future project performance
D. To ensure compliance with organizational audit requirements

Test Your Understanding 4.38
During a lessons learned meeting, one stakeholder dominates the conversation, while others remain passive. What is the best approach for the facilitator?
A. Allow the dominant stakeholder to continue speaking to save time.
B. Use round-robin discussions or invite quieter participants to share in writing.
C. End the session early and request written feedback later.
D. Remove the dominant stakeholder from the meeting to restore balance.

Test Your Understanding 4.39

A post-project lessons learned session identifies recurring communication gaps that delayed deliverables. What is the best way to maximize the impact of these findings?

A. Develop improved communication protocols and integrate them into future projects.
B. Share the findings only with the core project team.
C. Highlight them in the project closure report and archive it.
D. Revisit the issue only if it arises in another project.

4.8 Project Requirements Traceability Matrix

The Requirements Traceability Matrix (RTM) is a key tool in requirements management. It provides a structured way to track requirements throughout the project lifecycle, linking them to their origin, their development, and their verification. An RTM is a table or spreadsheet that maps each requirement to other project artifacts, such as design documents, test cases, and deliverables. This traceability ensures that all requirements are implemented, tested, and delivered. The RTM also supports project quality assurance by providing a clear audit trail of requirements and their associated work products.

An RTM typically includes several key components: a *unique requirement ID* to identify each requirement uniquely; a clear and concise *requirement description* that explains what the requirement entails; the *source* of the requirement (e.g., a specific stakeholder, a regulatory body, or a business need); the *priority* of the requirement (e.g., high, medium, low) and its *classification* (e.g., functional, non-functional); the *relationship to project deliverables* (e.g., which deliverable implements this requirement); and the *verification and validation criteria* that will be used to determine if the requirement has been met.

For example, a requirement might be "The system shall allow users to log in with a username and password." The RTM would link this requirement to its source (e.g., a stakeholder interview), its priority (e.g., high), its classification (e.g., functional), the relevant design document, the corresponding test cases, and the criteria for verifying that the login functionality works correctly.

Creating an RTM involves several key steps. The process begins with identifying and documenting requirements. This involves gathering requirements from various sources, such as stakeholders, user stories, use cases, and business needs. Each requirement should be uniquely identified and clearly described. The next step is mapping requirements to project objectives. This ensures that each requirement contributes to achieving the overall project goals. This mapping helps to prioritize requirements and ensure that the project delivers the intended business value. Finally, establishing tracking mechanisms helps maintain the RTM throughout the project lifecycle. This involves defining how changes to requirements will be tracked, approved, and implemented. This may involve using version control, change request forms, or other tracking tools.

Using an RTM offers several benefits. It helps in ensuring completeness and accuracy of requirements by providing a clear overview of all requirements and their relationships. This helps to prevent requirements from being missed or misinterpreted. An RTM also assists in tracking changes and maintaining control by providing a clear audit trail of all changes made to requirements. This helps to prevent scope creep and ensure that changes are implemented in a controlled manner. Finally, an RTM simplifies compliance and audits by providing a readily available record of all requirements and their traceability. This is particularly important for projects that are subject to regulatory requirements or internal audits.

Understanding how the RTM is used in different methodologies, particularly Waterfall and Agile, supports effective requirements management. In Waterfall projects, which follow a sequential, linear approach, the RTM is typically used to track requirements from the initial requirements gathering phase through design, development, testing, and deployment. It's often highly detailed and formally documented, serving as a key document for change control and configuration management. Because Waterfall emphasizes up-front planning and detailed documentation, the RTM is usually established early in the project and maintained throughout the project lifecycle, with minimal changes expected once the requirements are baselined.

In Agile projects, which embrace iterative development and flexibility, the use of the RTM is adapted to suit the iterative nature of the methodology. While the core principle of traceability remains important, the way it's implemented differs. Agile projects prioritize working software over comprehensive documentation, so the RTM might not be as formal or detailed as in Waterfall projects (Rempel and Mäder, 2015).

Differences in requirement tracking in iterative models mean that requirements are often captured as user stories in a product backlog and then broken down into smaller tasks for each iteration (sprint). The RTM in Agile is often used to track the relationship between user stories, tasks, and test cases within each iteration. The product backlog itself serves as a high-level representation of requirements, but the RTM can provide a more detailed level of traceability, particularly for regulatory requirements or complex features. In some Agile implementations, a simplified RTM might be used to track the acceptance of user stories and their alignment with sprint goals.

Deciding when to use an RTM versus a Product Backlog depends on the project type and needs. An RTM is more suitable for projects with strict regulatory requirements, complex dependencies, or a need for detailed documentation. It's also often used in projects where changes to requirements are expected to be minimal. A Product Backlog is more suitable for projects that require flexibility, iterative development, and frequent feedback from stakeholders. In some cases, a hybrid approach might be used, where a high-level RTM is used to track key requirements and their alignment with business objectives, while a Product Backlog is used to manage the details of user stories and tasks within each iteration.

Test Your Understanding 4.40
What is the primary purpose of a Requirements Traceability Matrix (RTM)?
A. To document lessons learned from requirements gathering sessions
B. To link requirements to project artifacts and ensure they are implemented and verified
C. To replace the product backlog in Agile projects
D. To provide a communication tool between only the development and testing teams

Test Your Understanding 4.41
A project team is preparing for an external compliance audit. The auditors request proof that all stakeholder requirements were tested and met. Which tool would best provide the necessary audit trail?
A. Stakeholder register
B. Work Breakdown Structure (WBS)
C. Requirements Traceability Matrix (RTM)
D. Project schedule

Test Your Understanding 4.42
During a workshop, a stakeholder specifies: "The system must allow users to reset their password via email." In the RTM, this requirement would most likely be linked to:
A. The business case and cost baseline
B. Design documents, test cases, and verification criteria
C. The project charter and milestone list
D. Procurement documents and vendor contracts

Test Your Understanding 4.43
How is the RTM typically applied in Waterfall projects?
A. As an informal log maintained only during testing
B. As a backlog prioritization tool updated at daily stand-ups
C. As a high-level list of user stories used during sprints
D. As a detailed, formally documented tool maintained from requirements through deployment

Test Your Understanding 4.44
Which statement best describes the use of an RTM in Agile projects?
A. It is identical to the RTM used in Waterfall, with no adaptation needed.
B. It is typically unnecessary because the product backlog serves as full traceability.
C. It may be simplified, focusing on linking user stories, tasks, and test cases in iterations.
D. It replaces sprint goals and becomes the main Agile planning tool.

Test Your Understanding 4.45
A project involves a medical device subject to strict regulatory oversight. The sponsor insists on detailed documentation of requirements and their verification. Which approach is most appropriate?

A. Use an RTM to track requirements and a backlog for sprint planning
B. Rely on the product backlog alone for traceability
C. Eliminate traceability to focus on iterative development speed
D. Create only informal notes of requirements to reduce overhead

Test Your Understanding 4.46
Which benefit of the RTM directly supports preventing scope creep?
A. Linking requirements to test cases
B. Providing a structured method for lessons learned
C. Maintaining an audit trail of requirement changes
D. Classifying requirements as functional or non-functional

4.9 Match Tools to Scenarios

Selecting the right tools for managing project requirements ensues efficiency, accuracy, and stakeholder satisfaction. The right tools streamline requirements gathering, documentation, and tracking, reducing risks and increasing project success. Aligning tools with project needs enhances traceability and minimizes rework, allowing teams to focus on delivering value rather than managing logistical challenges.

Several factors should be considered when selecting tools for managing project requirements. Project size and complexity are primary considerations. Larger and more complex projects typically require more sophisticated tools with advanced features for tracking, reporting, and change management. Smaller projects may be adequately managed with simpler tools or even spreadsheets.

The methodology used (Waterfall vs. Agile) also influences tool selection. Waterfall projects, with their emphasis on detailed up-front planning and documentation, often benefit from tools that support comprehensive requirements documentation and traceability, such as dedicated requirements management software or detailed templates within project management software. Agile projects, with their focus on iterative development and flexibility, often rely on tools that support user story management, product backlogs, and sprint planning, such as Jira or Trello.

Stakeholder involvement and collaboration needs also play a role. If the project involves a large number of stakeholders or requires frequent collaboration, tools that support online collaboration, shared documents, and easy communication are essential. For instance, if stakeholders are geographically dispersed, online survey tools and video conferencing for workshops become more suitable. In contrast, if stakeholders are co-located, in-person workshops with physical whiteboards might be more effective.

The previously discussed project requirements tools can be categorized into two types. Stakeholder engagement tools, such as interviews, surveys, workshops, and lessons learned methodologies, are used to gather information and feedback from stakeholders. Requirements documentation and tracking tools, including use cases, user stories, product backlogs, and requirements traceability matrices, are employed to document, organize, and track project requirements.

One common scenario is initiating a new project with unclear requirements. This situation often presents several challenges. A lack of clarity about what the project should deliver is a primary concern. Stakeholders may have different ideas about the project's goals, scope, and functionality, leading to confusion and uncertainty. Multiple stakeholders with diverse perspectives and needs can further complicate the process. Gathering and reconciling these different viewpoints can be challenging. Finally, evolving needs are common in new projects, as stakeholders' understanding of the project and its potential evolves over time. This requires a flexible approach to requirements management that can accommodate changes and refinements.

In this scenario of unclear initial requirements, a combination of tools is often most effective. Stakeholder interviews are invaluable for gaining initial insights and understanding individual stakeholder perspectives. These one-on-one conversations allow for in-depth exploration of needs, concerns, and expectations. They are particularly useful for gathering qualitative data and building rapport with key stakeholders. Surveys can be used to gather broad input from a larger group of stakeholders, providing a wider perspective on potential requirements. Surveys are particularly useful for collecting quantitative data and identifying trends or patterns in stakeholder feedback. Workshops are highly effective for facilitating collaborative requirement discussions. Bringing stakeholders together in a structured workshop setting allows for open communication, brainstorming, and consensus-building. Workshops are particularly useful for resolving conflicting viewpoints and developing a shared understanding of project goals.

If the project is following an Agile approach, user stories are a powerful tool for early requirement formulation. User stories provide a concise and user-centric way to capture requirements, focusing on the value that the project will deliver to the end-user. They are also flexible and adaptable, allowing for changes and refinements as the project progresses.

For example, imagine a university deciding to create a new online portal for students. Initially, the requirements are vague. By conducting interviews with students, faculty, and administrators, the project team can gather initial insights into their needs and expectations for the portal. A survey can then be distributed to a larger student population to gather broader feedback on desired features and functionalities. A workshop can be held with representatives from different departments to discuss and prioritize the collected requirements. Finally, user stories can be created to capture the agreed-upon requirements in a user-centric format, such as "As a student, I want to be able to access my grades online so that I can track my academic progress." This combination of tools allows the project team to effectively gather requirements, build consensus among stakeholders, and establish a solid foundation for the project.

Adapting requirements management techniques to specific project methodologies facilitates project success. Agile methodologies, with their iterative and incremental approach, require a different set of tools and techniques compared to traditional Waterfall projects. Managing requirements in Agile projects requires flexibility, adaptability, and collaboration. Since requirements evolve through iterative development, teams need tools that support ongoing refinement without disrupting progress. User stories help structure requirements by capturing specific functionalities. The product backlog serves as a dynamic, prioritized repository, ensuring alignment with evolving stakeholder needs. Workshops facilitate ongoing discussions, clarify acceptance criteria, and refine user stories, while sprint retrospectives help teams continuously improve by identifying lessons learned.

Effective requirements management is critical across various project types, each demanding tailored tools and approaches to address their unique challenges. Compliance-driven projects in regulated industries such as healthcare, finance, and government face stringent requirements that demand meticulous traceability and extensive documentation. Regulatory constraints dictate specific procedures for project scope, design, development, and testing, requiring strict adherence to standards. Ensuring traceability is crucial, as projects must demonstrate that all regulatory requirements have been implemented, tested, and validated. Additionally, these projects are documentation-heavy, with records serving as evidence of compliance during audits and inspections.

To manage these challenges, several tools are particularly effective. A Requirements Traceability Matrix (RTM) links regulatory requirements to project deliverables, ensuring compliance and facilitating audits. Use cases provide detailed functional documentation, outlining how users interact with the system to meet regulatory standards. Stakeholder surveys help identify compliance gaps by gathering insights from those familiar with the regulatory landscape. Finally, the lessons learned methodology enables continuous improvement, allowing organizations to refine compliance strategies after each phase or audit.

Large-scale infrastructure and engineering projects, such as bridge construction, pipeline development, or enterprise IT system deployment, face significant challenges in requirements management. These projects involve multiple stakeholders with diverse interests, extended timelines that introduce evolving requirements, and intricate interdependencies between components.

To address these challenges, several tools are particularly effective. Use cases capture different stakeholder perspectives by outlining how various groups will interact with the infrastructure or system, ensuring their needs are met. Stakeholder interviews provide in-depth insights into specific requirements, helping to align priorities and expectations. A RTM ensures that all project needs are tracked, managed, and validated over time, crucial for long-duration projects with evolving requirements. Workshops facilitate collaboration among cross-functional teams, resolving conflicts and fostering a shared understanding of project goals.

For instance, in developing a high-speed rail system, stakeholders include government agencies, construction firms, engineers, and local communities. Use cases define how passengers, operators, and maintenance crews will interact with the system, while stakeholder interviews gather detailed input from each group. An RTM tracks regulatory, technical, and stakeholder requirements throughout the project, ensuring alignment. Workshops help coordinate design, construction, and testing efforts, keeping the project on track despite its complexity and extended duration.

Improving an existing product or service requires careful requirements management, as it involves enhancing functionalities, addressing user feedback, and adapting to evolving market needs. Unlike new projects, these initiatives must balance existing constraints while implementing meaningful improvements. Key challenges include understanding user feedback from sources like customer support logs and surveys, balancing business goals with user needs to ensure enhancements align with strategic objectives, and managing incremental updates that require a flexible approach to accommodate frequent changes and releases.

To address these challenges, several tools are particularly effective. Surveys collect quantitative and qualitative user insights, helping identify areas for improvement. Workshops bring stakeholders together to brainstorm and prioritize feature enhancements collaboratively. The lessons learned methodology ensures that past improvement efforts are analyzed to refine future processes. User stories and the product backlog help prioritize and manage incremental updates, ensuring controlled and efficient implementation of enhancements.

For instance, an e-commerce company aiming to improve its website could use surveys to gather customer feedback on navigation and checkout processes. Workshops with product managers, developers, and UX designers could explore potential enhancements. A lessons learned session could review past updates to identify successes and areas for refinement. Finally, user stories -- such as adding a price filter to improve search functionality -- would be prioritized in the product backlog and implemented in future updates.

Test Your Understanding 4.47
A project manager is leading a small internal project with limited requirements. Which tool would likely be sufficient for managing requirements?
A. Advanced requirements management software
B. A complex RTM with version control
C. A simple spreadsheet
D. A product backlog with sprint boards

Test Your Understanding 4.48
Which methodology typically requires tools that emphasize detailed documentation and traceability?
A. Agile
B. Waterfall
C. Scrum
D. Kanban

Test Your Understanding 4.49
In Agile projects, which tool is MOST commonly used to capture evolving requirements?
A. Use cases
B. Product backlog
C. Requirements traceability matrix
D. Work breakdown structure

Test Your Understanding 4.50
Stakeholder interviews, surveys, workshops, and lessons learned are best categorized as:
A. Documentation and tracking tools
B. Change control tools
C. Scheduling and cost control tools
D. Stakeholder engagement tools

Test Your Understanding 4.51
A university is creating a new online portal with unclear requirements. Which combination of tools would BEST help clarify requirements early?
A. Stakeholder interviews, surveys, and workshops
B. Lessons learned sessions and earned value analysis
C. Work breakdown structure and cost baseline
D. RTM and project charter

Test Your Understanding 4.52
A healthcare project requires compliance with strict government regulations. Which tool would be most critical for demonstrating requirements traceability during an audit?
A. Product backlog
B. Whiteboard brainstorming
C. Stakeholder interviews

D. Requirements Traceability Matrix (RTM)

Test Your Understanding 4.53
In large-scale infrastructure projects, what is the role of use cases?
A. They help capture how different stakeholders will interact with the system
B. They measure earned value to track project performance
C. They serve as a high-level repository of evolving requirements
D. They provide the cost breakdown of project deliverables

Test Your Understanding 4.54
An e-commerce company wants to enhance its website by improving navigation and checkout. Which tools would BEST support this improvement initiative?
A. Surveys, workshops, lessons learned, and user stories
B. Cost-benefit analysis and earned value reports
C. Regulatory compliance checklists and RTM
D. Business case and milestone charts

Test Your Understanding 4.55
What is the key requirement management challenge in long-duration infrastructure projects?
A. Lack of access to stakeholder interviews
B. The difficulty of handling evolving requirements and interdependencies
C. Limited need for documentation
D. The inability to track project costs effectively

4.10 Product Roadmap

A product roadmap is a high-level visual summary that outlines the vision, direction, priorities, and progress of a product over time, serving as a strategic communication tool to align stakeholders on its evolution. Unlike a project plan, which is tactical and details the "how," "when," and "who" of specific deliverables over a shorter timeframe, a product roadmap is strategic, focusing on the "what" and "why" of product development over months or years. It helps teams prioritize tasks, allocate resources, and manage expectations, ensuring efficient project and product management. For example, a roadmap might set the goal of launching a mobile app with offline functionality within a year, while the project plan would break down the necessary sprints and resources.

Several key components comprise a robust product roadmap (Layton et al., 2025). The foundation is the *product vision and strategic objectives.* This defines the long-term goal of the product and how it aligns with the overall business strategy. For example, a vision might be "to become the leading provider of cloud-based project management software," with a strategic objective to increase market share by 20% in the next two years.

The roadmap then outlines the *key features and capabilities* necessary to achieve this vision. These are the specific functionalities that will be developed and delivered to users. For instance, features might include Gantt charts, Kanban boards, and team collaboration tools. A release timeline and milestones provide a high-level schedule for when these features will be available. These milestones are not as granular as project plan milestones, but rather represent significant releases or phases of development.

Dependencies and constraints, such as resource availability, budget limitations, or technical dependencies, must also be considered and documented. Stakeholder alignment and communication are vital. The roadmap should be shared and discussed with all relevant stakeholders, including customers, management, development teams, and marketing, to ensure everyone is on the same page. Finally, it's essential to define *metrics for measuring success*. These could include user adoption rates, customer satisfaction scores, or revenue growth. These metrics help track progress and demonstrate the value of the product roadmap.

Product roadmaps can be categorized into several types, each serving a specific purpose. A strategic roadmap provides a high-level overview of the product's direction, aligning with overall business goals. This roadmap is typically used for executive communication and long-term planning. A feature-based roadmap focuses on the delivery of key features and is useful for communicating planned functionalities to internal teams and external stakeholders. A technology roadmap outlines the technical infrastructure, upgrades, and enhancements required to support the product's development. A release roadmap maps out incremental software or product releases, providing a timeline for when specific versions or updates will be available. Lastly, a portfolio roadmap aligns multiple projects or products within a company, ensuring they work together to achieve overall business objectives.

A product roadmap is a dynamic tool that aligns stakeholders, guides development, communicates priorities, manages dependencies, and adapts to market changes. It ensures a shared vision across teams -- development, marketing, sales, executives, and customers -- reducing conflicts and fostering collaboration.

As a development guide, a roadmap prioritizes features based on business value, customer demand, and feasibility, helping teams focus, estimate timelines, and allocate resources effectively. It prevents scope creep by defining release content and provides long-term direction, especially in Agile environments, where sprints contribute to a larger product vision.

A roadmap also sets clear expectations for product teams and stakeholders, fostering trust and accountability. Internally, it keeps teams aligned on goals, while externally, it helps manage customer expectations by confirming delivery timelines and generating anticipation for releases. Additionally, it visualizes dependencies, allowing teams to coordinate efforts and prevent bottlenecks.

Finally, a flexible roadmap is essential in a rapidly evolving market. While providing structure, it must allow adjustments based on customer feedback, competitive moves, and business priorities. For example, if a competitor releases a key feature, the roadmap can be updated to incorporate a similar or differentiating feature to maintain an edge. This adaptability ensures long-term product success and a proactive approach to product management.

Test Your Understanding 4.56
Which of the following best distinguishes a product roadmap from a project plan?
A. A roadmap details tasks, schedules, and assigned resources, while a project plan focuses on long-term product strategy.
B. A roadmap provides a strategic vision for product development, while a project plan is tactical, focusing on execution details.
C. A roadmap measures progress through earned value metrics, while a project plan measures through customer satisfaction.
D. A roadmap is used only in Agile projects, while a project plan applies only to Waterfall projects.

Test Your Understanding 4.57
Which of the following is NOT typically included in a robust product roadmap?
A. Technical specifications for each feature and detailed task assignments
B. Metrics for success such as adoption rates or revenue growth
C. Dependencies and constraints such as budget or resource availability
D. Milestones representing significant releases or development phases

Test Your Understanding 4.58
A competitor has just launched a major feature that directly threatens your market position. According to best practices for product roadmaps, what should your team do?
A. Ignore the competitor's move and stay rigid to the original roadmap.
B. Immediately add the competitor's feature to the next sprint backlog.
C. Update the roadmap to consider incorporating a similar or differentiating feature while staying aligned with strategic goals.
D. Delay roadmap updates until the next quarterly planning cycle.

Test Your Understanding 4.59
Which of the following types of roadmaps would best help align multiple ongoing projects within the same company to achieve a unified business objective?
A. Portfolio roadmap
B. Feature-based roadmap
C. Release roadmap
D. Technology roadmap

4.11 Determining Release Components with Roadmaps

One aspect of product roadmap management is determining which features and functionalities to include in each release (Brewer et al., 2025). This involves a structured approach to prioritization, considering various factors such as business value, customer needs, technical feasibility, and market dynamics. Several frameworks and techniques can aid in this process. One popular method is the MoSCoW method, which categorizes features into four categories: Must have, Should have, Could have, and Won't have.

Another useful framework is the Kano model, which classifies features based on their impact on customer satisfaction. It distinguishes between three types of features: Basic needs (must-be qualities), Performance features (one-dimensional qualities), and Exciters (attractive qualities). Basic needs are fundamental features that customers expect; their absence leads to dissatisfaction, but their presence doesn't necessarily increase satisfaction. Performance features are those where customer satisfaction is directly proportional to the level of functionality; more of these features leads to higher satisfaction. Exciters are unexpected features that delight customers and create a sense of wow; their absence doesn't cause dissatisfaction, but their presence significantly boosts satisfaction. Understanding these different types of features helps prioritize development efforts and focus on features that will have the greatest positive impact on customer perception.

Weighted scoring models provide a more quantitative approach to prioritization. This method involves assigning weights to different criteria, such as business value, customer impact, development effort, and risk. Each feature is then scored against these criteria, and a weighted score is calculated. Features with higher scores are prioritized for inclusion in the release. This approach offers a more objective and data-driven way to compare features and make informed decisions.

Alongside prioritization, feature mapping and dependency analysis clarify feature relationships and uncover dependencies. For instance, Feature A might depend on the completion of Feature B. Identifying these dependencies helps plan releases and ensure that features are developed in the correct order. This also helps in managing cross-functional dependencies, where different teams might be responsible for different parts of the product. Developing features in the wrong order due to dependency mismanagement can cause rework, delays, and inefficiency.

Identifying high-impact and time-sensitive features is another important consideration. Some features might have a significant impact on the business or customer satisfaction but are not time-sensitive. Others might be crucial for meeting a specific deadline or capitalizing on a market opportunity. Balancing these factors is essential for creating a successful release plan.

Finally, deciding between incremental and big-bang releases is a key strategic decision. Incremental releases involve delivering smaller sets of features in frequent releases, allowing for faster feedback and adaptation. This approach offers several advantages, including reduced risk, faster time to market for some features, and the ability to incorporate customer feedback early in the development process. However, it can also lead to increased development overhead and require more frequent communication with stakeholders. Big-bang releases, on the other hand, involve delivering a large set of features in a single release. This approach can be more efficient for certain types of products or projects but carries a higher risk of delays and requires more extensive testing and integration.

Choosing between a major release versus continuous delivery depends on various factors, including the nature of the product, the development process, and the market environment. Continuous delivery, a practice often associated with Agile and DevOps, involves releasing small updates frequently, often multiple times a day. This approach allows for rapid iteration and continuous improvement but requires a high degree of automation and a mature development process. A major release might be more appropriate for products with complex dependencies or when significant new features are being introduced.

Test Your Understanding 4.60
A product manager is using the MoSCoW method to categorize features. Which category should include features that are essential for the product to function and cannot be compromised?
A. Should have
B. Must have
C. Could have
D. Won't have

Test Your Understanding 4.61
During a customer feedback session, users emphasized that while a feature's absence would frustrate them, its presence wouldn't significantly increase satisfaction. According to the Kano model, how should this feature be classified?
A. Exciter
B. Performance feature
C. Basic need
D. Optional add-on

Test Your Understanding 4.62
A company is deciding between incremental and big-bang releases. The product has several interdependent features, and the business wants to minimize integration risk while incorporating customer feedback frequently. Which release strategy is most suitable?
A. Incremental release

B. Big-bang release
C. One-time delivery
D. Continuous freeze release

Test Your Understanding 4.63
Feature A depends on Feature B's completion. If the team mistakenly schedules Feature A before Feature B, what is the most likely risk?
A. Customer dissatisfaction due to missing performance features
B. Reduced business value of all features
C. Over-prioritization of exciters
D. Increased project costs due to rework and delays

4.12 Chapter Summary

This chapter covers several ways of gathering requirements, including user stories, use cases, stakeholder interviews, surveys, workshops, lessons learned, and a project requirements traceability matrix. We then explain how to match the appropriate tool to each scenario in order to ensure accurate requirement capture and project alignment. The chapter concludes with an introduction to product roadmaps, which are high-level visual representations of a product's strategy and vision over time.

4.13 Case Study

Revisit the case study in Chapter 1. Perform the following tasks:
1. Gather requirements from the stakeholders you identified in Chapter 3 using at least two of the methods discussed in this chapter.
2. Develop product backlog with user stories including acceptance criteria prioritized and estimated.
3. You are expected to complete the project in X (your instructor may decide) week-long sprints. Find the total story points from Item 1 above and divided it by X. That will serve as your team velocity.

4.14 References

Brewer, J. L., Dittman, K. C., & Thomas, P. J. (2025). *Methods of IT project management*. Purdue University Press.
Cockburn, A. (2001). Agile software development. Boston, MA: Addison-Wesley.
Cockburn, A. (2002). Writing Effective Use Cases. Addison-Wesley Professional.
Dalton, J. (2018). Dot voting. In *Great Big Agile: An OS for Agile Leaders* (pp. 165-166). Berkeley, CA: Apress.
James, C. (2024). Introduction to Test-Driven Development (TDD) and Behavior-Driven Development (BDD): Definitions, Differences, and Core Principles.
Kravchenko, T., Bogdanova, T., & Shevgunov, T. (2022, April). Ranking requirements using
Layton, M. C., Ostermiller, S. J., & Kynaston, D. J. (2025). *Agile project management for dummies*. John Wiley & Sons.

MoSCoW methodology in practice. In *Computer Science On-line Conference* (pp. 188-199). Cham: Springer International Publishing.
Rempel, P., & Mäder, P. (2015, March). Estimating the implementation risk of requirements in agile software development projects with traceability metrics. In *International Working Conference on Requirements Engineering: Foundation for Software Quality* (pp. 81-97). Cham: Springer International Publishing.

4.15 Solutions to Test Your Understanding

4.1 B; 4.2 A; 4.3 D; 4.4 C; 4.5 C; 4.6 A; 4.7 B; 4.8 C; 4.9 C; 4.10 D; 4.11 D; 4.12 B; 4.13 A; 4.14 A; 4.15 B; 4.16 A; 4.17 D; 4.18 C; 4.19 B; 4.20 A; 4.21 B; 4.22 A; 4.23 B; 4.24 C; 4.25 D; 4.26 B; 4.27 C; 4.28 C; 4.29 A; 4.30 D; 4.31 B; 4.32 C; 4.33 B; 4.34 D; 4.35 A; 4.36 C; 4.37 C; 4.38 B; 4.39 A; 4.40 B; 4.41 C; 4.42 B; 4.43 D; 4.44 C; 4.45 A; 4.46 C; 4.47 C; 4.48 B; 4.49 B; 4.50 D; 4.51 A; 4.52 D; 4.53 A; 4.54 A; 4.55 B; 4.56 B; 4.57 A; 4.58 C; 4.59 A; 4.60 B; 4.61 C; 4.62 A; 4.63 D;

Chapter 5: Project Planning

Chapter Learning Outcomes

5.1 Recall basic definitions and key terms related to cost, quality, schedule, and risk.
5.2 Explain the significance of cost, quality, schedule and risk to the success of a project.
5.3 Compare project and product by identifying and contrasting their key characteristics.
5.4 Identify the differences and similarities between tasks and milestones.
5.5 Recall the basic categories of resources typically required for a project.
5.6 Create a project plan that incorporates effective cost, quality, schedule, and risk management practices.

5.1 Cost Management

The core objective of project cost management is to ensure project completion within the approved budget. This involves a series of interconnected processes, beginning with cost planning. Effective cost planning serves several purposes that contribute to project success (Zhang, 2024).

One of the most significant benefits of cost planning is the ability to minimize project overruns. By developing accurate cost forecasts, project managers can anticipate potential cost risks. These risks could stem from various sources, such as inaccurate initial estimates, changes in market prices for materials or labor, scope creep, or unforeseen technical challenges. Proactive identification of these risks allows project managers to develop and implement mitigation strategies.

These strategies might include contingency reserves (budget buffers for unexpected expenses), alternative sourcing options for materials, or revised project schedules. This proactive approach helps prevent unexpected expenses that could jeopardize the project's financial viability and lead to significant cost overruns. For example, if a project relies on a specific material whose price is volatile, the project manager might secure a fixed-price contract with a supplier or explore alternative materials.

Furthermore, sound cost management practices enable the optimization of resource allocation. By understanding the true cost of each project activity, including labor, materials, equipment, and other resources, project managers can allocate resources strategically. This involves assigning the right resources to the right tasks at the right time, maximizing their utilization and minimizing waste. For instance, if two tasks require similar skills, scheduling them consecutively can reduce idle time and improve resource efficiency. Cost management provides the data needed to make these informed decisions. This efficient resource utilization maximizes the return on investment (ROI) by ensuring that resources are used effectively and efficiently, avoiding unnecessary expenditures.

Accurate cost data is also essential for facilitating informed decision-making throughout the project lifecycle. This data provides valuable insights that allow project managers to evaluate trade-offs between different project approaches, select the most cost-effective solutions, and make necessary adjustments to the project scope or schedule. For example, if a project is facing budget constraints, the project manager might use cost data to evaluate the impact of reducing the scope of certain deliverables or extending the project timeline.

Effective cost management establishes a framework for project control. By tracking actual project expenditures against the approved budget, project managers can identify cost variances early on. These variances, which represent deviations from the planned budget, can be either positive (under budget) or negative (over budget). Early identification of negative variances allows for prompt corrective actions to be taken to bring the project back on track. These actions might involve renegotiating contracts, implementing cost-cutting measures, or adjusting the project schedule. Consistent monitoring and control of costs ensures that the project remains within its financial boundaries and maximizes the chances of successful completion within the allocated budget.

Diligent cost management offers numerous benefits that contribute directly to project success. One key advantage is enhanced project profitability. By effectively controlling costs and delivering projects within budget, organizations maximize their returns on investment. This means more efficient use of resources and greater financial gains from the project. This is particularly important in competitive markets where profit margins are often tight.

Furthermore, well-managed costs contribute significantly to increased stakeholder satisfaction. Meeting budget expectations helps maintain positive relationships with all stakeholders. Clients are satisfied when they receive the agreed-upon deliverables at the agreed-upon price. Sponsors are pleased when their investment yields the expected returns. Team members are more motivated when they are part of a well-managed and financially stable project. This positive sentiment fosters collaboration, trust, and long-term partnerships.

Effective cost management enhances project predictability. Accurate cost forecasting, a key component, improves the ability to anticipate project outcomes. With a clear understanding of required financial resources, project managers can create realistic schedules, allocate resources efficiently, and identify potential challenges early. This reduces uncertainty, strengthens decision-making, and provides better control over the project's trajectory. Improved predictability also extends to related aspects, such as scheduling and resource availability, which are closely tied to costs.

Finally, successful cost management enhances the organization's reputation. Consistently delivering projects on time and within budget demonstrates strong project management capabilities. This builds a positive reputation among clients, partners, and the wider industry. A reputation for financial responsibility and project delivery excellence can lead to new business opportunities, attract top talent, and strengthen the organization's competitive advantage. This reputation becomes a valuable asset in the long term, contributing to sustained growth and success.

Test Your Understanding 5.1
A project manager is concerned about volatile steel prices that could increase costs unexpectedly. Which proactive cost management strategy would be most effective?
A. Extending the project schedule according to the prices
B. Securing a fixed-price contract with a supplier
C. Reducing the project scope immediately
D. Eliminating contingency reserves

Test Your Understanding 5.2
One key benefit of accurate cost data in project management is that it allows the project manager to:
A. Avoid creating contingency reserves
B. Ensure that all tasks are completed ahead of schedule
C. Eliminate stakeholder disagreements
D. Evaluate trade-offs between different project approaches

Test Your Understanding 5.3
Why does effective cost management directly contribute to increased stakeholder satisfaction?
A. It ensures that the project is always completed early.
B. It guarantees all risks are eliminated.
C. It delivers agreed-upon outcomes at the agreed-upon cost.
D. It prevents the need for scope changes.

Test Your Understanding 5.4
A consulting firm consistently delivers projects on time and within budget. As a result, it gains more clients and attracts skilled employees. Which benefit of cost management does this illustrate?
A. Enhanced reputation and competitive advantage
B. Increased contingency reserves
C. Reduced scope creep
D. Improved team utilization as the team experiences more success.

5.2 Purpose and Importance of Quality

Quality in project management is defined as the degree to which a set of inherent characteristics fulfills requirements. This definition, derived from ISO 9000, emphasizes that quality is not simply about "goodness" or "luxury," but rather about meeting the agreed-upon needs and expectations of the stakeholders. In a project, requirements may include functionality, performance, reliability, usability, durability, and standards compliance. Furthermore, quality is different from grade; a low-grade product can still be of high quality if it meets its intended purpose and specifications. For example, a basic economy car might not have the features of a luxury car (low grade), but it can still be of high quality if it is reliable, safe, and performs as expected within its design parameters.

The primary purpose of quality management in a project is to ensure that the project deliverables meet the defined quality requirements and satisfy stakeholder expectations (Holovko, 2025). This involves a systematic approach that includes quality planning, quality assurance, and quality control. Quality planning involves defining the quality standards relevant to the project and determining how they will be met. Quality assurance focuses on the processes used to manage quality, ensuring that the project is following the defined standards and procedures. This is often done through audits and process analysis.

Quality control involves monitoring specific project results to determine if they comply with relevant quality standards and identifying ways to eliminate causes of unsatisfactory performance. This is achieved through inspections, testing, and other evaluation methods. By focusing on these three areas, quality management strives to:

Prevent defects: Proactive quality planning and assurance processes aim to prevent defects from occurring in the first place, which is significantly more cost-effective than correcting them later.
Meet customer requirements: Ensuring that the project delivers what the customer or sponsor expects is paramount to project success and satisfaction.
Improve project efficiency: By minimizing rework and defects, quality management reduces wasted time and resources, leading to improved project efficiency and potentially lower costs.
Increase stakeholder satisfaction: Delivering high-quality deliverables that meet or exceed expectations builds trust and strengthens relationships with stakeholders.

The importance of quality in project management cannot be overstated. High quality contributes directly to project success in several ways. Firstly, it enhances customer satisfaction. When project deliverables meet or exceed expectations, it leads to positive feedback, repeat business, and a strong reputation. Secondly, quality reduces costs. Preventing defects is far less expensive than fixing them after they occur. Rework, scrap, and warranty claims can significantly impact project budgets.

Thirdly, quality improves project performance. When processes are well-defined and followed, it leads to smoother execution, fewer delays, and better overall project outcomes. Fourthly, quality enhances organizational reputation. Consistently delivering high-quality projects builds trust and credibility, which is a valuable asset for any organization.

Finally, in some industries, quality is not just a desirable outcome but a mandatory requirement due to regulatory standards or safety concerns. For example, in the pharmaceutical or aerospace industries, stringent quality control ensures product safety and compliance. By prioritizing quality throughout the project lifecycle, project managers can significantly increase the likelihood of project success and create lasting value for their organizations.

Test Your Understanding 5.5
Which of the following best illustrates the difference between quality and grade in project management?
A. A luxury sports car with many advanced features is considered high grade and high quality.
B. A basic economy car with limited features that consistently performs as expected and is safe.
C. A project deliverable that has exceeded its budget but includes premium materials.
D. A high-grade product that is automatically of high quality because of its expensive components.

Test Your Understanding 5.6
A project team is conducting an audit to ensure that established processes are being followed during development. Which aspect of quality management does this activity represent?
A. Quality planning
B. Quality assurance
C. Quality control
D. Quality improvement

Test Your Understanding 5.7
Which of the following is the primary purpose of quality control?
A. To evaluate whether deliverables comply with quality standards
B. To establish relevant quality standards for the project
C. To ensure processes are consistently followed throughout the project
D. To develop long-term organizational reputation

Test Your Understanding 5.8
A software project has started experiencing significant rework due to defects being found late in testing. What would have been the most effective proactive strategy to prevent this problem?
A. Adding more testing staff at the end of the project

B. Increasing stakeholder meetings to review final deliverables
C. Strengthening quality planning and assurance earlier in the project
D. Extending the project schedule to allow for more bug fixing

Test Your Understanding 5.9
A pharmaceutical project team emphasizes rigorous inspections and compliance with regulatory standards to ensure patient safety. Which statement best explains why quality is critical in this context?
A. Quality is desirable but not mandatory in regulated industries.
B. Meeting grade expectations ensures compliance with safety laws.
C. High quality guarantees stakeholder satisfaction without additional oversight.
D. Quality is mandatory due to regulatory and safety requirements.

5.3 Risk Management

As noted in Chapter 1, project management defines risk as an uncertain event or condition that, if it occurs, impacts project objectives like scope, time, cost, or quality positively or negatively. Risk is not simply a negative event; it encompasses both threats (negative impacts) and opportunities (positive impacts). A threat could be a delay in receiving critical materials, while an opportunity might be the emergence of a new technology that could improve project efficiency. This definition emphasizes the uncertainty associated with risk; if an event is certain to happen, it's considered an issue, not a risk. It also highlights the potential impact on project objectives, meaning that a risk is only relevant if it could affect the project's success criteria.

The primary purpose of risk management is to increase the probability and impact of positive events (opportunities) and decrease the probability and impact of negative events (threats) on the project. This is achieved through a systematic process that includes risk planning, risk identification, qualitative risk analysis, quantitative risk analysis, risk response planning, risk implementation, and risk monitoring (Khalilzadeh et al., 2024).

Risk planning involves defining how risk management will be conducted throughout the project. Risk identification focuses on determining which risks might affect the project. Qualitative risk analysis prioritizes risks for further analysis or action by assessing their probability of occurrence and their potential impact. Quantitative risk analysis numerically analyzes the overall effect of identified risks on project objectives. Risk response planning develops options and actions to enhance opportunities and reduce threats to project objectives. Risk implementation is the process of executing risk response plans. Risk monitoring tracks identified risks, monitors residual risks, identifies new risks, and evaluates risk process effectiveness.

By following these steps, risk management aims to:

Increase the likelihood of project success: By proactively addressing potential issues and capitalizing on opportunities, risk management increases the chances of achieving project objectives within the defined constraints.

Minimize negative impacts: By identifying and mitigating threats, risk management reduces the potential for costly delays, budget overruns, and quality issues.

Maximize positive impacts: By identifying and exploiting opportunities, risk management can enhance project outcomes and create additional value.

Improve decision-making: Risk management provides valuable information that supports informed decision-making throughout the project lifecycle.

Improve stakeholder communication: By openly discussing risks and mitigation strategies, risk management fosters transparency and builds trust among stakeholders.

Effective risk management practices significantly enhance project outcomes and substantially reduce the probability of project failure. By proactively identifying, analyzing, and responding to potential risks, project managers can navigate uncertainty more effectively and steer the project toward successful completion. Conversely, ignoring or neglecting risk management can have severe and far-reaching consequences, jeopardizing the project's objectives and potentially leading to its downfall.

One significant consequence of inadequate risk management is cost overruns. Unforeseen events, such as changes in market prices for materials, unexpected regulatory changes, or unforeseen technical challenges, can lead to unexpected expenses that push the project beyond its allocated budget. These overruns can erode profitability, strain stakeholder relationships, and even lead to financial losses.

Another common consequence of neglecting risk management is schedule delays. Risks can disrupt the planned sequence of project activities, leading to delays in task completion and pushing back the overall project completion date. For instance, if a critical piece of equipment is delayed in delivery, it can impact all subsequent activities that depend on it, causing a ripple effect throughout the project schedule. Such delays can have cascading effects, impacting other projects and potentially incurring penalties for late delivery.

Unmanaged risks can also contribute to scope creep, which refers to uncontrolled changes or expansion of the project scope beyond its originally defined boundaries. When risks related to requirements gathering or change management are not adequately addressed, it can lead to stakeholders requesting additional features or functionalities that were not initially planned. This expansion of scope can strain resources, extend the project timeline, and increase costs, making it difficult to deliver the project within the original constraints.

Furthermore, risks can negatively impact the quality of project deliverables. For example, if a risk related to inadequate testing is not addressed, it can lead to defects or errors in the final product. These quality issues can necessitate costly rework, delay project completion, and result in customer dissatisfaction, potentially damaging the organization's reputation.

In the most severe cases, unmanaged risks can lead to outright project failure. A combination of cost overruns, schedule delays, scope creep, and quality issues can overwhelm the project, making it impossible to achieve its intended objectives. This can result in significant financial losses, damage to stakeholder relationships, and reputational harm for the organization.

By proactively identifying, analyzing, and developing appropriate responses to risks, project managers can significantly increase the probability of project success. This includes developing risk response strategies like avoidance, mitigation, transference, and acceptance.

Developing risk response strategies involves choosing the most appropriate action for each identified threat. Avoidance is the most direct strategy, where one completely eliminates the risk by choosing not to engage in the activity that causes it. A less drastic approach is mitigation, which focuses on reducing the likelihood of a risk occurring or minimizing its impact if it does. Alternatively, a risk can be handled through transference, where the financial consequences are shifted to a third party, most commonly through an insurance policy or outsourcing. Finally, acceptance is the conscious decision to take no action, a suitable strategy when the potential impact is low or the cost of addressing the risk outweighs the potential benefit.

Test Your Understanding 5.10
The main purpose of risk management is to:
A. Eliminate all threats before they occur
B. Increase opportunities while reducing threats
C. Avoid stakeholder disagreements during the project
D. Ensure projects are always completed ahead of schedule

Test Your Understanding 5.11
A software project team decides to buy insurance to cover potential financial losses from cyberattacks instead of developing their own mitigation measures. Which risk response strategy is being used?
A. Acceptance
B. Avoidance
C. Mitigation

D. Transference

Test Your Understanding 5.12
What is the primary focus of qualitative risk analysis?
A. Assigning numerical values to risks to calculate overall project impact
B. Developing risk response strategies and contingency plans
C. Prioritizing risks by assessing probability and impact
D. Executing risk response actions during the project

Test Your Understanding 5.13
A project experiences uncontrolled additions of new features because risks in requirements gathering were not properly managed. Which negative outcome of poor risk management does this illustrate?
A. Schedule delays
B. Cost overruns
C. Scope creep
D. Quality defects

Test Your Understanding 5.14
A project manager notices that unexpected technical challenges are causing frequent defects, requiring costly rework. Which proactive risk management practice would have been most effective in preventing this?
A. Stronger risk identification and early mitigation planning
B. Extending the project deadline to allow more defect fixing
C. Adding more stakeholders late in the project lifecycle
D. Reducing scope after defects have already occurred

5.4 Purpose and Importance of Schedule

A schedule represents the planned timing of project activities and milestones. It outlines when each activity will start and finish, their dependencies on one another, and the overall project duration. A project schedule is typically visualized using tools like Gantt charts, network diagrams (PERT or CPM), and milestone charts. These tools provide a clear visual representation of the project timeline, allowing stakeholders to understand the sequence of work, identify critical path activities (the sequence of activities that determines the shortest possible project duration), and track progress against the plan. A well-defined schedule considers factors such as resource availability, task dependencies, and potential constraints (Nguyen and Nguyen, 2024).

The primary purpose of schedule management is to ensure that the project is completed within the agreed-upon timeframe. This involves a series of processes, including plan schedule management (establishing policies, procedures, and documentation for planning, developing, managing, executing, and controlling the project schedule), define activities (identifying the specific actions needed to produce the project deliverables), sequence activities (determining and documenting the dependencies among the project activities), estimate activity durations (estimating the number of work periods needed to complete individual activities), develop schedule (analyzing activity sequences, durations, resource requirements, and schedule constraints to create the project schedule), and control schedule (monitoring the status of the project to update the project schedule and manage changes to the schedule baseline).

Effective schedule management serves several purposes that contribute to smooth project execution and positive outcomes. One aim is to provide a clear roadmap for project execution. The project schedule acts as a guide for the entire project team, clearly outlining the sequence of work, establishing dependencies between tasks, and providing specific deadlines for each activity. This roadmap ensures that everyone understands their responsibilities and the overall project timeline, promoting a shared understanding of the project's progression.

Furthermore, effective schedule management facilitates communication and coordination among project team members, stakeholders, and other involved parties. By providing a common reference point for project timelines and milestones, the schedule ensures that everyone is on the same page regarding project progress and upcoming activities. This shared understanding minimizes misunderstandings, reduces conflicts, and promotes effective collaboration. Regular schedule updates and communication ensure that all stakeholders are kept informed of any changes or adjustments to the project timeline.

Another purpose of schedule management is to track project progress. By comparing actual progress against the planned schedule, project managers can identify any deviations or variances early on. This allows for timely intervention and corrective actions to be taken to bring the project back on track.

Effective schedule management also helps manage resources effectively. The schedule helps in planning and allocating resources, such as personnel, equipment, and materials, efficiently. By knowing when each activity is scheduled to take place, project managers can ensure that the necessary resources are available when needed and avoid resource conflicts or shortages. This optimized resource allocation maximizes resource utilization and minimizes idle time, leading to cost savings and improved project efficiency.

Because delays can often lead to cost overruns, effective schedule management is also a key tool for controlling project costs. By adhering to the schedule and minimizing delays, project managers can avoid incurring additional expenses related to extended project durations, such as increased labor costs, equipment rental fees, and potential penalties for late delivery. This proactive approach to schedule control helps in keeping the project within its budget constraints.

Finally, the project schedule provides valuable information that supports informed decision-making throughout the project lifecycle. It allows project managers to evaluate the impact of potential changes, assess the feasibility of different options, and make informed decisions about resource allocation, task prioritization, and potential schedule adjustments. For example, if a critical task is delayed, the project manager can use the schedule to assess the impact on subsequent tasks and determine the best course of action to mitigate the delay. This data-driven approach to decision-making enhances project control and increases the likelihood of project success.

Test Your Understanding 5.15
Which of the following best describes the critical path in a project schedule?
A. The sequence of activities that determines the shortest possible project duration.
B. The path that contains the most resource-intensive activities.
C. The path that contains the activities with the most slack or float.
D. The sequence of activities that must be completed in parallel to shorten project duration.

Test Your Understanding 5.16
A construction project is halfway through, and the project manager compares actual progress with the baseline schedule. Several deviations are found, but corrective measures are still possible. Which process is the manager performing?
A. Define activities
B. Control schedule
C. Develop schedule
D. Plan schedule management

Test Your Understanding 5.17
One of the main benefits of effective schedule management is:
A. Ensuring the project scope is met without changes.
B. Avoiding the need for communication with stakeholders.
C. Guaranteeing that all risks are eliminated before the project begins.
D. Providing a clear roadmap that outlines the sequence of work and deadlines.

Test Your Understanding 5.18
A software development team is working on multiple modules. The project manager uses a Gantt chart to coordinate resource allocation and ensure developers are not assigned overlapping tasks. What purpose of schedule management is being demonstrated here?
A. Tracking project progress
B. Facilitating communication and coordination
C. Managing resources effectively
D. Controlling project costs

Test Your Understanding 5.19
A project manager is considering a stakeholder's request to delay a non-critical task by one week. To assess the impact on the overall timeline, the manager consults the project schedule. Which purpose of schedule management does this illustrate?
A. Facilitating communication

B. Tracking project progress
C. Supporting informed decision-making
D. Controlling costs

5.5 Interdependence of Cost, Quality, Risk, Schedule, and Scope

Project cost, quality, risk, schedule, and scope are all interdependent factors in any project. Changes in one area can have an impact on the others, and it's essential to manage each area carefully to ensure the overall success of the project. Project managers need to manage the interdependency to ensure the project's overall success. By understanding how these factors affect each other, project managers can make informed decisions that balance the competing demands of these factors to achieve the project's objectives (Slaeat, 2024). The following paragraphs explain how each of these factors can affect each other.

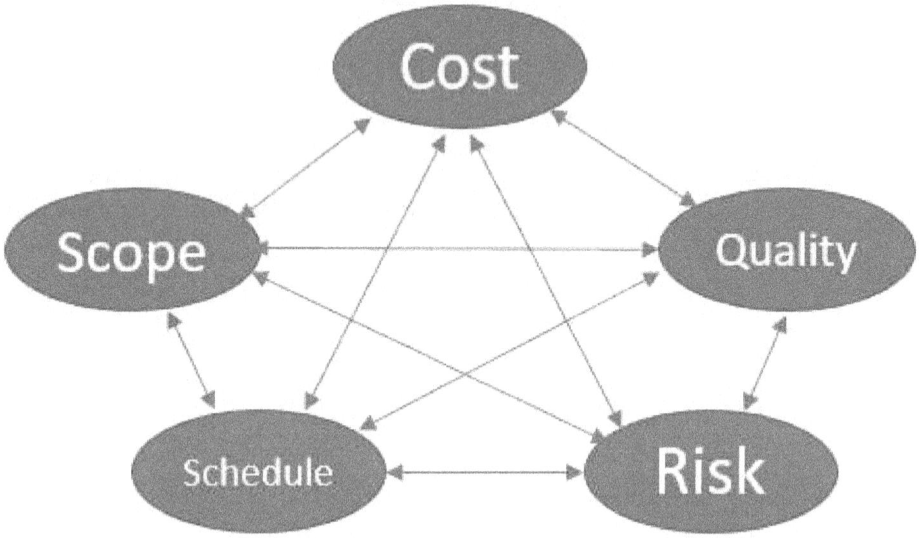

Figure 5.1 Interdependence of cost, quality, risk, schedule, and scope.

Cost: The cost of a project is affected by several factors, including the scope of the project, the quality of the work, and the schedule. For example, if the project's scope is increased, the cost may also increase to accommodate the additional work. Similarly, if the project timeline is shortened, it may increase the cost because the team may have to work overtime or hire additional resources.

Quality: The quality of a project is determined by several factors, including the project's scope, the schedule, and the level of risk. For example, if the project scope is reduced, it may be possible to deliver a higher quality product within the same timeline and budget. On the other hand, if the project's schedule is tight, it may impact the quality of work, as the team may have to rush to complete the project.

Risk: The level of risk in a project can impact the project's cost, quality, schedule, and scope. For example, if the project's risk is high, the team may need to spend more time and resources on risk management, which can increase the project's cost and timeline. Additionally, high-risk projects may require a more robust scope to ensure that all potential risks are considered.

Schedule: The project schedule is closely tied to the project's cost, quality, and scope. For example, if the project schedule is shortened, the team may need to increase the budget to accommodate the additional resources required to complete the project on time. Similarly, if the project's scope is increased, the schedule may also need to be adjusted to accommodate the additional work.

Scope: The project scope can have a significant impact on the project's cost, quality, schedule, and risk. For example, if the project's scope is increased, the project may take longer to complete, require more resources, and increase the level of risk associated with the project. Conversely, if the scope is reduced, the project may be completed faster, at a lower cost, and with a lower level of risk.

Project Cost and Quality: The cost of a project and its quality are often closely linked. In general, higher quality usually means higher costs. For example, using higher-quality materials or employing more skilled workers can increase project costs. However, delivering a high-quality project can also result in cost savings in the long run. For instance, a project with high-quality deliverables is less likely to experience issues that require costly rework or maintenance.

Project Cost and Schedule: Project cost and schedule are directly related. If a project takes longer to complete, the costs associated with it will likely increase. This could be due to a variety of factors such as labor costs, materials costs, or equipment rental fees. Similarly, if the project budget is limited, it may be necessary to reduce the schedule or cut back on the scope of work to stay within budget.

Project Quality and Risks: The level of project quality can affect the risks associated with the project. For example, if a project has poor quality deliverables, there is a higher chance that the project will fail or experience issues that could lead to additional costs or delays. Additionally, risks associated with a project may affect its quality. For instance, if a project is rushed to meet a tight deadline, there may be a higher likelihood of errors or defects in the deliverables.

Project Schedule and Risks: The project schedule can have a significant impact on the risks associated with a project. A tight schedule can lead to rushed work, which increases the likelihood of errors or defects. Additionally, a schedule that is too aggressive may lead to unrealistic expectations and the potential for missed deadlines.

Test Your Understanding 5.20
A project manager is informed that the project must be delivered two months earlier than originally planned. To meet the new deadline, the team will need overtime and possibly outside contractors. Which factor is most directly impacted alongside schedule?
A. Scope
B. Risk
C. Cost
D. Quality

Test Your Understanding 5.21
Which statement about the relationship between quality and risk is most accurate?
A. Higher quality always eliminates project risks.
B. Poor quality deliverables can increase the likelihood of project failure.
C. Reducing risk guarantees higher quality.
D. Risks only affect cost and schedule, not quality.

Test Your Understanding 5.22
A construction project decides to use premium materials and highly skilled labor to reduce future maintenance issues. While this increases immediate project costs, it reduces the risk of long-term failures. Which trade-off does this scenario demonstrate?
A. Cost vs. Quality
B. Schedule vs. Scope
C. Risk vs. Scope
D. Quality vs. Schedule

Test Your Understanding 5.23
A project team is pressured to meet a very aggressive schedule. As a result, tasks are rushed, and errors begin appearing in deliverables. Which factor is being most negatively impacted by the tight schedule?
A. Scope
B. Risk
C. Cost
D. Quality

5.6 Project and Product Management Planning

Project management planning is the process of defining how a project will be executed, monitored, controlled, and closed. It involves creating a detailed roadmap that outlines the project's objectives, scope, deliverables, timelines, budget, resources, and risk management strategies. This planning phase establishes a foundation for the project. It transforms high-level goals into actionable steps, providing a framework for the project team to follow throughout the project lifecycle.

Effective planning provides several benefits. It clarifies project objectives, ensuring that everyone involved has a shared understanding of what needs to be achieved. It also defines the project scope, preventing uncontrolled expansion and keeping the project focused. Planning establishes a realistic timeline and budget, providing a baseline for tracking progress and controlling costs. It also identifies potential risks and develops mitigation strategies, minimizing the likelihood and impact of negative events. Furthermore, planning facilitates communication and coordination among project team members and stakeholders, ensuring that everyone is informed and aligned.

It's important to differentiate between project management and product management, as these two disciplines, while related, have distinct focuses. Project management is concerned with the temporary endeavor undertaken to create a unique product, service, or result. It focuses on the efficient execution of a defined scope within a specific timeframe and budget. Product management, on the other hand, is concerned with the entire lifecycle of a product, from conception to retirement. It focuses on understanding market needs, defining product strategy, and managing the product roadmap. While a project might be undertaken to develop a new product or enhance an existing one, the project itself is a temporary undertaking within the broader context of product management (Attah et al., 2024).

This distinction leads to the creation of two distinct plans: the Project Management Plan and the Product Management Plan. The Project Management Plan is a formal, approved document that defines how the project will be executed, monitored, controlled, and closed. It includes subsidiary plans such as scope management plan, schedule management plan, cost management plan, quality management plan, resource management plan, communications management plan, risk management plan, and stakeholder engagement plan. The Product Management Plan, conversely, outlines the long-term vision and strategy for a product. It encompasses market analysis, product roadmap, competitive analysis, and product lifecycle management.

The key differences between these plans lie in their focus and timeframe. The Project Management Plan focuses on the execution of a specific project with a defined start and end date, while the Product Management Plan focuses on the long-term management of a product throughout its lifecycle. The Project Management Plan is concerned with delivering a specific set of deliverables within constraints, while the Product Management Plan is concerned with maximizing the value and success of the product in the market.

Despite these differences, the two plans complement each other. The Project Management Plan provides the tactical execution needed to bring the product vision outlined in the Product Management Plan to life. Projects are often the vehicles through which product strategies are implemented. For example, a Product Management Plan might identify a need for a new feature in an existing software product. A project would then be initiated with a Project Management Plan to develop and release that specific feature. This symbiotic relationship ensures that product strategy is effectively translated into tangible results, contributing to both project and product success.

Project management and product management, while distinct, often work in tandem. This distinction is reflected in the key deliverables produced by each discipline's planning processes. The Project Management Plan, focused on the execution of a specific project, generates several deliverables. The project charter formally authorizes the project and documents high-level information, including the project's purpose, objectives, key stakeholders, and high-level requirements. It essentially provides the project manager with the authority to proceed.

The work breakdown structure (WBS) decomposes the project scope into smaller, manageable work packages, providing a hierarchical structure for organizing and managing project work. This is crucial for scope management and tracking progress. Gantt charts and schedules visually represent the project timeline, outlining the sequence of activities, their durations, and dependencies. These tools are essential for schedule management and tracking project progress against deadlines. Budget reports track project expenditures against the approved budget, providing insights into cost performance and enabling cost control.

Finally, risk assessment reports document identified risks, their potential impact, and planned response strategies. These reports allow proactive risk management and mitigating potential threats to project success. Other deliverables often included in a Project Management Plan include a scope statement, a communications plan, a resource management plan, and a stakeholder engagement plan.

In contrast, the Product Management Plan, focused on the long-term vision and strategy for a product, produces a different set of deliverables. The product requirements document (PRD) details the features, functionalities, and performance requirements of the product. It serves as a blueprint for the development team and ensures that everyone is aligned on the product vision.

Market research reports provide insights into market trends, customer needs, and competitive landscape. These reports inform product strategy and ensure that the product meets market demands. Prototypes and wireframes are visual representations of the product's user interface and user experience (UI/UX). They are used to test and refine the product's design before development begins. Product launch plans outline the activities and timelines for launching the product to market. These plans include marketing strategies, sales plans, and distribution channels.

Finally, customer feedback and iteration reports document customer feedback on the product and track iterations or updates made based on that feedback. This feedback loop is important for continuous product improvement and ensuring customer satisfaction. Other common product management deliverables include a product roadmap, a competitive analysis document, and a product marketing plan.

While a project might be initiated to develop a new product (and thus utilize a Project Management Plan), the ongoing management and evolution of that product after its launch falls under the purview of product management and its associated deliverables. The Project Management Plan is temporary, ending when the project is completed. The Product Management Plan is ongoing, guiding the product throughout its lifecycle. This distinction is key for understanding the interplay between project and product management.

Test Your Understanding 5.24
A project manager notices that team members are unclear about project objectives and some stakeholders are suggesting new features that were never agreed upon. Which part of the planning process would have helped prevent this issue?
A. Developing a project charter.
B. Creating a stakeholder engagement plan.
C. Defining the project scope.
D. Drafting a product requirements document.

Test Your Understanding 5.25
Which statement best describes the difference between project management and product management?
A. Project management ensures long-term product evolution, while product management handles temporary initiatives.
B. Project management focuses on temporary, unique endeavors, while product management focuses on a product's lifecycle.
C. Project management always involves developing new products, while product management focuses on budgets.
D. Project management emphasizes market analysis, while product management emphasizes scheduling.

Test Your Understanding 5.26
Your company is developing a new mobile app. The Product Management Plan outlines the long-term roadmap, including future versions. However, the first release must be completed within six months with a fixed budget. Which document should guide this initial release?
A. The market research report.
B. The Work Breakdown Structure (WBS).

C. The Product Management Plan.
D. The Project Management Plan.

Test Your Understanding 5.27
Which of the following is typically included in a Project Management Plan but NOT in a Product Management Plan?
A. Work Breakdown Structure (WBS).
B. Product roadmap.
C. Market research reports.
D. Prototypes and wireframes.

Test Your Understanding 5.28
A project manager is tracking progress using Gantt charts and budget reports. Meanwhile, the product manager is preparing a competitive analysis and customer feedback report. What does this scenario illustrate?
A. Duplication of roles between project and product management.
B. Misalignment between execution and strategy.
C. Complementary responsibilities of project and product management.
D. Ineffective communication between the two disciplines.

Test Your Understanding 5.29
A software company's Product Management Plan identifies the need for a new reporting feature to stay competitive. A project is launched to build the feature. What role does the Project Management Plan play here?
A. It replaces the Product Management Plan for strategic direction.
B. It ensures the product's lifecycle continues after launch.
C. It provides the tactical roadmap to execute the feature's development.
D. It determines the product's market success.

5.7 Milestones vs. Task Duration

A task represents a distinct unit of work that contributes to the overall project completion. Tasks are characterized by several key features: they require a certain amount of time to complete, they are assigned to specific team members or resources, and they often have dependencies on other tasks (meaning they cannot start until another task is finished) and produce specific deliverables. Practical examples of tasks include writing a piece of code, conducting a market research survey, assembling a physical product, or preparing a project report. Each of these activities requires effort, has a defined output, and is assigned to an individual or team.

Task duration, as the name suggests, refers to the amount of time required to complete a specific task. It is typically measured in units of time such as hours, days, or weeks, depending on the scale and complexity of the project. Several factors can influence task duration. Task complexity plays a significant role; a more complex task will naturally require more time than a simpler one. Resource availability is another critical factor; if resources (personnel, equipment, or materials) are limited, it can extend the time needed to complete the task. Dependencies on other tasks also affect duration; a task cannot begin until its predecessor tasks are completed, which can create delays if those preceding tasks are behind schedule. A practical example of task duration would be "Develop login module – 5 days," which clearly defines the estimated time required for that specific task. This estimate is crucial for creating the project schedule.

A milestone, in contrast to a task, represents a significant point or event in a project. It marks the completion of a phase, a major deliverable, or a key decision point. A crucial characteristic of a milestone is that it has zero duration; it is instantaneous, representing a moment in time rather than a period of work. Milestones serve as important checkpoints for tracking project progress and communicating achievements to stakeholders. They provide a clear indication of how the project is progressing against the planned timeline. Examples of milestones include "Project kickoff completed," "Design approval received," "Prototype finalized," or "Phase 1 testing complete." These events signify significant progress in the project lifecycle but do not themselves consume any time. They are used to mark the completion of a set of tasks.

The dependency aspect further differentiates tasks and milestones. A task can be dependent on other tasks, meaning it cannot start until its predecessor tasks are finished. This creates a chain of dependencies that influences the overall project schedule. Milestones, however, often mark the completion of a group of related tasks. They serve as a summary of progress, indicating that a significant portion of work has been completed. The purpose of defining task duration is to represent the actual work being performed, while the purpose of a milestone is to represent a checkpoint in the project, signaling the completion of a phase or a key deliverable. Task duration represents the "doing" of the project, while milestones represent the "done," providing key progress markers along the project timeline.

Test Your Understanding 5.30
Which of the following best distinguishes a milestone from a task in project management?
A. A milestone consumes less time than a task.
B. A milestone has zero duration and marks a significant event, while a task requires time and effort.
C. A milestone requires fewer resources, while a task requires more resources.
D. A milestone is optional, while a task is always required.

Test Your Understanding 5.31
A project manager is scheduling tasks for developing a mobile app. The login module is estimated to take 5 days, but it cannot start until the user interface (UI) design is complete. What concept does this scenario best illustrate?

A. Task deliverables
B. Task complexity
C. Task dependencies
D. Milestone tracking

Test Your Understanding 5.32
A project team has completed “Phase 1 testing.” This achievement is recorded in the project plan but did not require additional work time to mark it. How should this event be categorized?
A. A task with short duration
B. A dependency between testing activities
C. A deliverable requiring final approval
D. A milestone marking a project checkpoint

Test Your Understanding 5.33
A project manager estimates that writing a market research survey will take longer than expected because only one qualified analyst is available. Which factor is primarily influencing the task duration?
A. Resource availability
B. Task deliverables
C. Milestone placement
D. Dependency relationships

5.8 Type of Resources

Resources refer to the tools, equipment, people, and time required to complete a project. Project managers must carefully assess the types of resources needed for a project and develop a plan to allocate these resources effectively (Kerzner, 2025). In this section, we will discuss the three types of resources commonly used in project management: work resources, materials resources, and cost resources.

5.8.1 Work Resources

The term "work resources" encompasses both the equipment and personnel essential for completing a project. A defining characteristic of work resources is that they are measured and managed based on time. For human resources, tracking time allows project managers to understand how much effort is being dedicated to specific tasks, identify potential schedule slippages, and accurately calculate labor costs. Similarly, for equipment resources, tracking usage time helps determine availability, schedule maintenance, calculate depreciation, and allocate costs associated with their operation. This time-based tracking is fundamental for resource leveling and smoothing, which are techniques used to optimize resource utilization and avoid overallocation.

Human resources, a subset of work resources, refer to the individuals who contribute their skills and expertise to the project. This group includes a variety of roles, each with specific responsibilities. The project manager is responsible for the overall oversight of the project. Team members are responsible for executing specific tasks and working towards achieving the project goals. Stakeholders may have varying levels of involvement and influence on the project. Contractors can bring expertise in areas such as engineering, construction, IT, or legal services. Effective management of human resources involves clear communication, defined roles and responsibilities, and appropriate motivation to ensure optimal performance.

Equipment resources, another essential category of work resources, consist of the physical tools, machinery, and other types of equipment needed to complete project tasks. These can range from heavy construction machinery like excavators and cranes to smaller items like computers, specialized tools, laboratory equipment, vehicles, and standard office equipment. The management of equipment resources involves scheduling their usage, ensuring their availability when needed, performing regular maintenance to prevent breakdowns, and managing associated costs like rental fees, fuel, and repairs.

5.8.2 Material Resources

Material resources constitute a distinct category of resources measured by quantity rather than time. These resources are typically tangible items consumed or incorporated into the project's deliverables. This distinguishes them from work resources, which are managed based on the time they are utilized. Unlike work resources, where effort and duration are key metrics, material resources are assigned and tracked based on their physical quantity -- units, weight, volume, or other relevant measures. This focus on quantity supports accurate procurement, inventory management, and cost control.

Consider various project scenarios to illustrate this concept. In a construction project, the project manager needs specific quantities of raw materials like steel beams, bags of cement, cubic yards of concrete, and board feet of lumber. The project's success hinges on having the right amount of these materials available at the right time. Similarly, in a painting project, the project manager must procure a specific quantity of paint (gallons or liters), brushes (number and type), rollers, and drop cloths. In an interior design project, the project manager manages quantities of carpet (square yards or meters), furniture items (number and type), fabric (yards or meters), and decorative accessories. These examples highlight how diverse material resources can be, depending on the project's nature.

Measuring material resources by quantity allows project managers to accurately estimate material needs, ensuring sufficient stock for project completion without excessive surplus. This precise estimation also contributes to effective cost management by preventing overspending on materials. Furthermore, it helps ensure that materials are available when needed, preventing project delays due to material shortages. Beyond quantity, project managers must also verify that the acquired materials meet the required quality standards and specifications outlined in the project documentation. This might involve inspections, testing, or certifications to ensure materials conform to industry standards or project-specific requirements.

Examples of material resources can be categorized into several types. Raw materials are unprocessed or minimally processed substances used as inputs for manufacturing or construction, such as wood, cement, steel, sand, and gravel. Consumables are items used up or depleted during the project execution, such as adhesives, sealants, lubricants, cleaning supplies, and safety equipment like gloves, masks, and goggles. These items support project activities but are not incorporated into the final product. Finally, office supplies, while often overlooked in larger projects, are also material resources. These include items like paper, pens, printer ink, stationery, and other administrative supplies needed for project documentation and communication.

5.8.3 Cost Resources

Cost resources represent a distinct category of resources defined solely by their associated costs, independent of time or quantity variables. This differentiates them from work resources (managed by time) and material resources (managed by quantity). Cost resources are not tracked based on usage duration or the number of units consumed, but rather by the actual monetary expenditure incurred. Several types of expenses fall under this category.

Travel expenses are a common example of cost resources, especially in projects that involve geographically dispersed teams or require travel to project sites. These expenses encompass various costs, including airfare, hotel accommodations, ground transportation (such as taxis, rental cars, or public transport), meals, and incidentals. These costs are typically incurred when team members travel for meetings, training sessions, site visits, or other project-related activities. Accurate estimation and tracking of travel expenses are vital for maintaining budget control and ensuring that travel arrangements are cost-effective.

Costs associated with permits and licenses also fall under the category of cost resources. These are expenses incurred to obtain the necessary legal authorizations and regulatory approvals required for the project. Examples include building permits for construction projects, environmental permits for projects with potential environmental impact, zoning permits for land use, and other industry-specific licenses. These costs are often fixed and are incurred regardless of the project's duration or the quantity of materials used.

Training and development costs are another type of cost resource. These expenses are incurred when project team members participate in training sessions, workshops, conferences, or other professional development activities to enhance their skills and knowledge relevant to the project. These costs can include course fees, travel expenses related to training events, and the cost of training materials. Investing in training and development can improve team performance and project outcomes, but these costs must be carefully budgeted and tracked.

Finally, costs associated with end-of-project celebrations, while seemingly less critical than other expenses, are also considered cost resources. These are expenses incurred to acknowledge and celebrate the successful completion of a project. Examples include team dinners, parties, or other celebratory events. While these expenses are typically smaller compared to other project costs, they contribute to team morale and can be an important part of project closure. Understanding how these costs are budgeted, tracked, and controlled helps effective project cost management.

Test Your Understanding 5.34
Which of the following best describes work resources in project management?
A. Items measured by physical units like weight or volume.
B. Expenses such as training, permits, and celebrations.
C. People and equipment managed primarily by time.
D. Supplies that are consumed during project execution.

Test Your Understanding 5.35
A project manager notices that equipment like cranes and computers are being overbooked for multiple tasks. Which technique should the manager use to balance this issue?
A. Resource leveling or smoothing
B. Earned value analysis
C. Quality inspections
D. Material procurement

Test Your Understanding 5.36
Which of the following is an example of a material resource?
A. Project manager’s time overseeing tasks
B. Gallons of paint purchased for a renovation
C. Travel costs for stakeholder meetings
D. Software license fees

Test Your Understanding 5.37

In a construction project, the team requires 200 bags of cement. This requirement should be tracked as:
A. A work resource
B. A material resource
C. A cost resource
D. A project milestone

Test Your Understanding 5.38
Which factor primarily differentiates cost resources from work and material resources?
A. Cost resources are measured by time.
B. Cost resources are measured by quantity.
C. Cost resources are defined only by monetary expenditure.
D. Cost resources always include consumables.

Test Your Understanding 5.39
A software development project requires renting a specialized server for 3 weeks. How should this be classified?
A. Work resource (equipment)
B. Material resource
C. Cost resource
D. Stakeholder requirement

Test Your Understanding 5.40
A project manager sets aside $5,000 for team training sessions during project execution. This allocation represents what type of resource?
A. Work resource
B. Material resource
C. Cost resource
D. Deliverable resource

Test Your Understanding 5.41
During project closure, the team organizes a celebratory dinner to recognize their success. Which type of resource is this classified under?
A. Work resource
B. Material resource
C. Cost resource
D. Quality resource

Test Your Understanding 5.42
A project manager must ensure equipment like bulldozers and cranes are available when needed and undergo regular maintenance. What type of resource management is this?
A. Human resource management
B. Material resource management
C. Cost resource management
D. Equipment (work) resource management

Test Your Understanding 5.43
Which of the following is an example of a consumable material resource?
A. Excavator
B. Adhesive
C. Office printer

D. Permit fee

Test Your Understanding 5.44
A project team needs to purchase software licenses before coding can begin. These costs are one-time fees and not tied to usage duration. How should they be classified?
A. Cost resources
B. Material resources
C. Work resources
D. Stakeholder requirements

Test Your Understanding 5.45
A project manager is preparing for a design phase. The team will need 10 computers, 500 sheets of paper, and $2,000 for travel. How should these resources be categorized?
A. Computers = work, paper = material, travel = cost
B. Computers = material, paper = work, travel = cost
C. Computers = cost, paper = material, travel = work
D. Computers = work, paper = cost, travel = material

5.9 Risk Register

A risk register is a document that serves as a centralized repository for all identified project risks, their analysis, and planned responses. The primary purpose of a risk register is threefold. First, it provides a structured and systematic approach to risk tracking throughout the project lifecycle. This structured approach ensures that no identified risk is overlooked and that all relevant information about each risk is documented and readily accessible.

Second, the risk register enhances communication and decision-making by providing a clear and concise overview of potential project threats and opportunities. This information allows project managers and stakeholders to make informed decisions about resource allocation, project scope, and overall project strategy. Third, and perhaps most importantly, the risk register ensures proactive risk mitigation. By documenting planned responses to identified risks, the risk register enables project teams to take timely action to prevent or minimize negative impacts on project objectives.

A well-constructed risk register contains several key components, each serving a specific purpose.
In addition to the general description of a risk register above, the rest of this section explores specific components of a risk register with examples. A typical risk register is a table that may include the following columns:

Risk ID/number: This is just a unique number to identify each risk.

Formatted risk statement: A risk statement is a concise description of a potential risk in a project. Risk statements are typically required to be in a certain format because this helps to ensure consistency and clarity in the communication of risks. We recommend this format:

```
Because of <one or more causes>, <risk event> might occur, which would lead
to <one or more effects>.
```

Here are two examples of a risk statement:

Example 1:

Because of potential software conflicts, the risk event of project delays or system downtime might occur, which would lead to increased project costs and potential damage to the organization's reputation.

Example 2:

Because of inadequate data backup procedures, the risk event of data loss or corruption might occur, which would lead to significant data loss, potential legal or compliance issues, and damage to the organization's reputation.

Probability: This refers to a numerical value between 0 and 1 that indicates the likelihood of a risk occurring.

The rationale for probability: This is an explanation of why a particular numerical value between 0 and 1 reflects the likelihood of a risk occurring.

Example 1:

The probability of potential software conflicts resulting in project delays or system downtime is 0.7. This value was determined based on a review of historical data on similar software conflicts, and an assessment of the project team's ability to identify and mitigate conflicts before they cause significant delays or downtime (number in the examples may not reflect similar case in your work).

Example 2:

The probability of data loss or corruption due to inadequate data backup procedures is 0.9. This value was determined based on a review of the organization's current backup procedures, which were found to be insufficient, as well as an assessment of the potential consequences of data loss or corruption (number in the examples may not reflect similar case in your work).

The impact value of a risk: This is a numerical value between 1 and 10 that indicates the degree to which the risk may affect the project.

The rationale for impact: This is an explanation of why a particular numerical value between 1 and 10 reflects the degree to which the risk may affect the project.

Example 1:

The impact value of potential software conflicts resulting in project delays or system downtime is 8. This value was determined based on an assessment of the potential impact on the project timeline, budget, and stakeholder satisfaction, as well as an analysis of the organization's ability to recover from delays or downtime.

Example 2:

The impact value of data loss or corruption due to inadequate backup procedures is 9. This value was determined based on an assessment of the potential impact on the organization's operations, reputation, and legal or regulatory compliance.

The risk score: This is the product of probability and impact. For the two examples above, the risk score for the first example is 5.6 (explanation: 0.7 of probability times impact score of 8) and the risk score for the second example is 8.1.

The *Risk Owner* is the individual or team responsible for monitoring the risk and implementing the planned responses. This ensures accountability and ownership of risk management activities.

The *Risk Response Strategy* outlines the planned action to address the risk. Common strategies include: Avoid (eliminating the risk by changing the project plan), Mitigate (reducing the probability or impact of the risk), Transfer (shifting the risk to a third party, such as through insurance), and Accept (acknowledging the risk and taking no action unless it occurs).

Based on the two examples provided earlier, here are some risk strategies that a project manager may consider:

Example 1:

Risk Strategy: The project team should implement a robust software testing process to identify potential conflicts and reduce the likelihood of delays or downtime. The team should also develop a contingency plan to address any conflicts that do occur, such as allocating additional resources or adjusting the project schedule.

Example 2:

Risk Strategy: The organization should implement a comprehensive data backup and recovery plan to minimize the impact of data loss or corruption. This may include regular data backups, redundant data storage, and data recovery procedures. Additionally, the organization should review and update its data backup procedures regularly to ensure they remain effective.

The *Mitigation Plan* details the specific steps to be taken to reduce the probability or impact of a threat. It includes specific actions, timelines, and responsible parties. The *Contingency Plan* describes alternative actions that will be taken if the risk materializes despite mitigation efforts. This provides a backup plan to minimize the negative consequences. Finally, the *Status* field tracks the current progress in managing the risk, indicating whether the risk is open, in progress, or closed. This provides a real-time view of the risk landscape and allows project managers to prioritize their efforts. Maintaining an up-to-date risk register is a continuous process throughout the project lifecycle.

A risk register is not a static document; it is a dynamic tool that is actively used throughout the project lifecycle. Its effective use involves a continuous cycle of identification, analysis, response planning, monitoring, and updating. The first step in utilizing a risk register is identifying potential risks. Several techniques can be employed for this purpose. Brainstorming sessions with the project team and stakeholders can generate a wide range of potential risks. Expert judgment, drawing on the experience of subject matter experts, can identify risks that might not be obvious to others. Historical data analysis, reviewing past project records, can reveal recurring risks or patterns that can inform current risk identification efforts.

Once risks have been identified, the next step is to analyze them. This involves assessing both the probability of each risk occurring and the potential impact it could have on project objectives. This analysis can be performed using either qualitative or quantitative methods. Qualitative risk analysis uses descriptive scales, such as low, medium, and high, to assess probability and impact. Quantitative risk analysis uses numerical values, such as percentages or monetary values, to assess probability and impact. This allows for more precise calculations of risk exposure and can be used to perform techniques like Monte Carlo simulations. Combining probability and impact results in a risk score, which helps prioritize risks for response planning.

After analyzing the risks, the next step is to develop appropriate risk responses. This involves selecting mitigation strategies to reduce the probability or impact of negative risks (threats) or enhance the probability or impact of positive risks (opportunities). For the example risk of supplier delays, a mitigation strategy could be securing backup suppliers or establishing buffer stock. The chosen strategy should be documented in the risk register, along with specific actions, timelines, and responsible parties. Contingency plans should also be developed for high-priority risks, outlining alternative actions to be taken if the risk materializes despite mitigation efforts.

Finally, the risk register must be continuously monitored and updated throughout the project lifecycle. This involves regularly reviewing the risk register in project status meetings, tracking the status of identified risks, identifying new risks that may emerge, and adjusting risk responses as necessary. This dynamic approach ensures that the risk register remains a relevant and effective tool for managing project uncertainty.

Test Your Understanding 5.46
Which of the following is NOT one of the three primary purposes of a risk register?
A. Structured risk tracking throughout the project lifecycle
B. Enhancing communication and decision-making
C. Ensuring proactive risk mitigation
D. Eliminating all risks from the project

Test Your Understanding 5.47
A project team identifies a potential supplier delay and decides to secure backup suppliers and establish buffer stock. Which risk response strategy are they applying?
A. Avoid
B. Mitigate
C. Transfer
D. Accept

Test Your Understanding 5.48
If a risk has a probability of 0.6 and an impact score of 7, what is the risk score?
A. 3.5
B. 4.2
C. 7.6
D. 8.1

Test Your Understanding 5.49
A project sponsor is worried about potential data loss from inadequate backup procedures. To address this, the project team purchases cyber insurance so the financial burden of data recovery would fall on the insurer. Which response strategy is being applied?
A. Transfer
B. Avoid
C. Mitigate
D. Accept

Test Your Understanding 5.50
During a project status meeting, the project manager updates the risk register by marking one risk as "closed," adding a new risk from a recent brainstorming session, and adjusting the mitigation plan for another. What does this illustrate?
A. The static nature of the risk register
B. The importance of contingency planning only
C. The dynamic and continuous use of the risk register
D. The avoidance of risks by eliminating them at the start

5.10 Quality Management Plan

Quality management ensures that a project meets agreed-upon requirements and stakeholder expectations.

A quality management plan is a comprehensive document that defines quality standards, expectations, and the processes to achieve them. It is a critical component of any successful project, particularly in a predictive environment, as it provides a structured approach to maintaining quality. The plan should be developed early in the project planning phase and regularly reviewed and updated throughout the project lifecycle.

One of the foundational elements of a quality management plan is defining clear quality objectives. These objectives translate high-level quality goals into measurable standards. They should be specific, measurable, achievable, relevant, and time-bound (SMART). For example, instead of a vague objective like "improve software quality," a SMART objective would be "reduce the number of critical software defects found during user acceptance testing by 20% within the next three months." These measurable objectives provide a clear target for the project team and allow for objective assessment of quality performance.

The quality management plan also identifies relevant quality standards and compliance requirements. These can include internationally recognized standards like ISO 9001, which sets requirements for quality management systems, or methodologies like Six Sigma, which focuses on reducing process variation and defects. Other standards include the Capability Maturity Model Integration (CMMI), often used in software development, and various industry-specific regulations, such as those imposed by the FDA in the pharmaceutical industry or the FAA in the aviation industry. Identifying these standards and compliance requirements early in the project ensures that the project deliverables meet all necessary criteria.

Defining and tracking quality metrics is another essential aspect of the quality management plan. These metrics provide measurable criteria for assessing quality performance. Examples of common quality metrics include defect rate (the number of defects found per unit of work), cycle time (the time it takes to complete a process), compliance percentage (the percentage of deliverables that meet the specified requirements), and customer satisfaction scores. Tracking these metrics throughout the project lifecycle provides valuable insights into quality trends and allows for proactive identification and resolution of quality issues.

Additionally, the quality management plan defines the roles and responsibilities in quality management, clearly distinguishing between Quality Assurance (QA) and Quality Control (QC). Quality assurance focuses on preventing defects by implementing processes and procedures that ensure quality throughout the project lifecycle. It is process-oriented. Quality control, on the other hand, focuses on detecting defects in deliverables through inspections, testing, and other quality control techniques. It is product-oriented. The quality management plan should clearly define the roles and responsibilities of project managers, quality managers (if applicable), and other stakeholders in both QA and QC activities. This ensures that everyone understands their contribution to achieving project quality objectives. For example, a quality manager might be responsible for developing quality standards and conducting audits, while the project manager is responsible for ensuring that the project team follows the defined quality processes.

Finally, quality improvement processes encompass the strategies and methods used to continuously enhance project quality. These may include process optimization and continuous improvement initiatives to refine the quality management plan and achieve better outcomes. By implementing these processes, the project team can consistently improve quality performance and meet or exceed the established quality standards.

A quality management plan offers several benefits. The first benefit is that it helps to ensure that the project meets the agreed-upon requirements and expectations of stakeholders. By setting clear quality objectives and standards, the project team can work towards meeting the expectations of stakeholders and delivering a product or service that satisfies their needs.

The second benefit of a quality management plan is that it provides a clear understanding of the quality standards that will be used to measure the quality of the project. This helps to establish a common understanding of what constitutes acceptable quality for the project, ensuring that all team members and stakeholders are on the same page.

The third benefit of a quality management plan is that it facilitates communication and collaboration between team members and stakeholders. By establishing a common understanding of the quality expectations for the project, team members can work together more effectively and communicate more clearly with stakeholders.

The fourth benefit of a quality management plan is that it improves the overall efficiency and effectiveness of the project. By identifying and addressing quality issues early in the process, the project team can avoid delays and rework, reducing the overall project timeline and costs.

Finally, a quality management plan increases customer satisfaction by delivering a high-quality product or service. By ensuring that the final product meets or exceeds the quality standards set out in the plan, the project team can deliver a product that meets the expectations of the customer, resulting in increased customer satisfaction and loyalty.

Test Your Understanding 5.51

Which of the following best describes the purpose of a quality management plan in a project?
A. To ensure all project team members follow the same coding standards.
B. To define quality standards, objectives, and processes for achieving them.
C. To create a detailed schedule for testing project deliverables.
D. To provide a list of risks and mitigation strategies.

Test Your Understanding 5.52
A project manager is leading a pharmaceutical project. During planning, the team identifies compliance with FDA regulations as a key requirement. Where should this compliance requirement be documented?
A. In the project risk register.
B. In the stakeholder engagement plan.
C. In the quality management plan.
D. In the change control log.

Test Your Understanding 5.53
Which of the following is an example of a SMART quality objective?
A. Improve software quality.
B. Ensure project deliverables meet stakeholder expectations.
C. Reduce critical software defects during user acceptance testing by 20% within three months.
D. Deliver a reliable product that includes artificial intelligence to handle different quality issues.

Test Your Understanding 5.54
During a software project, the quality manager notices that defects are repeatedly being introduced due to inconsistent coding practices. Which quality management activity should be emphasized to prevent such defects?
A. Quality control through final product inspections.
B. Quality assurance through process improvements.
C. Quality metrics tracking customer satisfaction.
D. Quality audits after delivery to clients.

Test Your Understanding 5.55
Which of the following best distinguishes Quality Assurance (QA) from Quality Control (QC)?
A. QA is performed at the end of the project; QC is ongoing.
B. QA is product-oriented; QC is process-oriented.
C. QA and QC are identical in purpose but use different tools.
D. QA prevents defects through process focus; QC detects defects through inspections.

Test Your Understanding 5.56
A project team is tracking defect rates, cycle time, and customer satisfaction scores during execution. What is the main purpose of tracking these quality metrics?
A. To identify and resolve quality issues proactively.
B. To satisfy contractual obligations with suppliers.
C. To complete the quality audit checklist.
D. To update the work breakdown structure (WBS).

5.11 Chapter Summary

This chapter covers key aspects of project planning, including costs, quality, risks, and scheduling. Costs represent the financial resources needed to achieve project objectives. Quality measures how well a deliverable meets required standards. Risks are uncertain events that may impact project outcomes. A schedule outlines project activities, durations, and dependencies. The chapter also examines project vs. product differences, essential resources, and the use of a risk register. Finally, it explains the components and benefits of a Quality Management Plan.

5.12 Case Study

Revisit the case study in Chapter 1. Perform the following tasks:

1. Write a project plan that includes the following sections:
   - Project Overview
     - Provide a brief introduction to the project, including its purpose, goals, and objectives.
     - Define the scope of the project and the deliverables that will be produced.
     - Describe the stakeholders involved in the project and their roles and responsibilities.
   - Project Schedule
     - Develop a detailed timeline for the project, including major milestones and deadlines.
     - Identify the tasks to be completed, and assign specific start and end dates and dependencies.
   - Resource Allocation
     - Identify the resources (e.g. work, materials, and cost) required for the project.
     - Allocate the resources to specific tasks and activities.
   - Risk Management
     - Identify potential risks and challenges that could impact the project.
     - Develop a risk register for mitigating these risks and responding to any issues that arise.
   - Communication Plan
     - Define a communication strategy for the project, including the frequency and channels.
     - Develop a stakeholder register.
   - Quality Management
     - Define the quality standards and expectations for the project deliverables.
     - Develop a plan for monitoring and managing quality throughout the project.
   - Project Budget
     - Develop a detailed budget for the project, including all expenses and resources required.
     - Identify any contingencies or unexpected expenses and develop a plan for managing them.
   - Project Evaluation
     - Define the criteria for evaluating the success of the project.
     - Develop a plan for conducting regular evaluations and reviews throughout the project.
2. Develop Sprint 1 backlog with sprint goals and user stories.
3. Work on Sprint 1, update the backlog, and turn in the increment in pre-defined time-box.

Note: Sprint work will be excluded from future case studies to allow for greater flexibility.

5.13 MS Project Exercise 2

Adding and Linking Tasks

Start by creating a new project named "Exercise 2".

Part 1: Creating Sprints as Summary Tasks
1. Navigate to the "Task" tab in the Ribbon at the top.
2. Click on "Summary" in the "Insert" group.
3. In the "Task Name" field, type "Sprint 1".
4. Repeat the above step for "Sprint 2", "Sprint 3", and "Sprint 4". Ensure these sprints are at the same level as "Sprint 1".

Part 2: Adding Stories to Each Sprint
5. Add stories to each sprint directly beneath it. For instance, to insert a story under "Sprint 1", select the row under "Sprint 1". Clicking on "Task" in the "Insert" group will create a new task. Enter the story's name in the "Task Name" field. Repeat this for all stories in "Sprint 1". Repeat this for all other sprints.
6. Group summary tasks and story tasks together. You can indent story tasks beneath it to designate them as subtasks. To do this, select the task you want to convert into a subtask, then click on "Task" in the Ribbon and select "Indent Task" in the "Schedule" group.
7. The summary task will automatically calculate the duration based on the start and finish dates of the subtasks. Remember, a summary task is a collection of subtasks and displays their combined information.
8. Enter the duration, predecessors, or start date for each task. The remainder of this exercise provides more details on predecessors. The aim of setting predecessors is to accurately depict the sequence of activities in your project, which aids in effective project scheduling and tracking.
9. Next, create dependencies using the "Predecessors" column in the Gantt chart view.
10. Understand task dependencies. Depending on the tasks in your sprint, you may have one of the four types of dependencies (The examples below are based on a simple project of organizing a conference):
10a. Finish-to-Start (FS): This is the most common type of dependency. The successor task can't start until the predecessor task has finished. For example, you can't start "Send invitations" (successor) until you finish "Book venue" (predecessor). In the "Predecessors" column, you would just enter the ID of the predecessor task.
10b. Start-to-Start (SS): The successor task can't start until the predecessor task has started. For example, let's say you want to start "Confirm attendees" at the same time you start "Send invitations". In the "Predecessors" column, you would enter the ID of the predecessor task, followed by SS. For example, if "Send invitations" is task 2, you would enter "2SS".
10c. Finish-to-Finish (FF): The successor task can't finish until the predecessor task has finished. For example, let's say you can't finish "Arrange catering" until "Confirm attendees" has finished. In the "Predecessors" column, you would enter the ID of the predecessor task, followed by FF. For example, if "Confirm attendees" is task 3, you would enter "3FF".
10d. Start-to-Finish (SF): The successor task can't finish until the predecessor task has started. This is a rare type of dependency, but to illustrate, let's say you can't finish "Book venue" until "Send invitations" has started. In the "Predecessors" column, you would enter the ID of the predecessor task, followed by SF. For example, if "Send invitations" is task 2, you would enter "2SF".

5.14 References

Attah, R. U., Garba, B. M. P., Gil-Ozoudeh, I., & Iwuanyanwu, O. (2024). Best Practices in Project Management for Technology-Driven Initiatives: A Systematic Review of Market Expansion and Product Development Technique. *Int J Eng Res Dev*, *20*(11), 1350-61.
Holovko, V. (2025). Development of an integrated approach to the implementation of IT project quality management.

Kerzner, H. (2025). *Project management: a systems approach to planning, scheduling, and controlling*. John Wiley & Sons.
Khalilzadeh, M., Banihashemi, S. A., & Božanić, D. (2024). A step-by-step hybrid approach based on multi-criteria decision-making methods and a bi-objective optimization model to project risk management. *Decision Making: Applications in Management and Engineering*, *7*(1), 442-472.
Nguyen, T. A., & Nguyen, T. A. (2024). Building information modeling (BIM) for construction project schedule management: a review. *Engineering, Technology & Applied Science Research*, *14*(2), 13133-13142.
Slaeat, F. (2024). The impact of poor planning on the duration and cost of the projects: The implications of poor planning on the projects. *Mesopotamian Journal of Civil Engineering*, *2024*, 60-81.
Zhang, X. (2024). Research on optimization strategies for enterprise cost management in the context of the digital economy. *Journal of Applied Economics and Policy Studies*, *7*, 1-5.

5.15 Solutions to Test Your Understanding

5.1 B; 5.2 D; 5.3 C; 5.4 A; 5.5 B; 5.6 B; 5.7 A; 5.8 C; 5.9 D; 5.10 B; 5.11 D; 5.12 C; 5.13 C; 5.14 A; 5.15 A; 5.16 B; 5.17 D; 5.18 C; 5.19 C; 5.20 C; 5.21 B; 5.22 A; 5.23 D; 5.24 C; 5.25 B; 5.26 D; 5.27 A; 5.28 C; 5.29 C; 5.30 B; 5.31 C; 5.32 D; 5.33 A; 5.34 C; 5.35 A; 5.36 B; 5.37 B; 5.38 C; 5.39 A; 5.40 C; 5.41 C; 5.42 D; 5.43 B; 5.44 A; 5.45 A; 5.46 D; 5.47 B; 5.48 B; 5.49 A; 5.50 C; 5.51 B; 5.52 C; 5.53 C; 5.54 B; 5.55 D; 5.56 A;

Chapter 6: Predictive, Plan-based Approach

Chapter Learning Outcomes

6.1 Assessing the fit of the predictive approach for various organizational structures.
6.2 Construct a Work Breakdown Structure (WBS)
6.3 Use Critical Path Method (CPM) techniques
6.4 Identify the work packages for a project
6 5 Evaluate and interpret the cost variance and schedule variance

6.1 Introduction to Predictive Approach

Predictive, plan-based project management, often referred to as the Waterfall methodology, emphasizes comprehensive upfront planning to define the project's scope, schedule, and cost before execution begins. This approach relies on sequential project phases, where each phase must be completed and approved before the next one starts. This structured, linear progression contrasts sharply with adaptive (Agile) and hybrid methodologies, which embrace iterative development and flexibility to accommodate changing requirements (Thesing et al., 2021).

Predictive project management aims to minimize uncertainty by meticulously planning every aspect of the project beforehand. This detailed planning includes creating a Work Breakdown Structure (WBS) to decompose the project into manageable tasks, developing a detailed project schedule using techniques like Gantt charts and the Critical Path Method (CPM), and establishing a comprehensive budget using techniques like bottom-up estimating, which estimating the cost and duration of each task, and then aggregating these estimates to determine the overall project budget and timeline.

.

The predictive approach is most suitable for projects with clearly defined requirements, minimal uncertainty, and stable environments. These projects often involve well-understood technologies, established processes, and minimal external influences. It is frequently the preferred approach for projects governed by strict regulatory or compliance requirements, such as in the pharmaceutical, aerospace, and nuclear power industries. These sectors often require extensive documentation and rigorous change control, which are strengths of the predictive approach.

Large-scale infrastructure, construction, and manufacturing projects also frequently benefit from this methodology due to their inherent complexity, long durations, and the need for meticulous planning and coordination. These projects often involve significant investments and require strict adherence to budgets and timelines, making the predictability offered by this approach particularly valuable.

The benefits of a predictive approach stem from its structured nature. It provides a clear framework with well-defined deliverables at each stage, enhancing predictability in scheduling and budgeting. This predictability enables stakeholders to make accurate forecasts for resource allocation and financial planning. The emphasis on thorough documentation and risk management ensures that potential issues are identified and addressed proactively, minimizing disruptions during execution. This robust documentation also supports auditing, compliance, and knowledge transfer.

However, the predictive approach also presents challenges. Its inherent rigidity makes it difficult to accommodate changes once the project is underway. This can lead to delays, cost overruns, and even project failure in dynamic environments where requirements evolve rapidly. The heavy reliance on initial assumptions can also be a significant weakness, as inaccurate or outdated assumptions can undermine the entire project plan. Therefore, before choosing a predictive approach, project managers must carefully assess the project's characteristics and the stability of its environment. Project managers should be able to identify scenarios where its strengths are most valuable and where its weaknesses could pose significant risks.

Test Your Understanding 6.1
Which of the following characteristics makes a project most suitable for the predictive approach?
A. Requirements are evolving rapidly and stakeholder input is ongoing.
B. The project involves well-understood technologies and stable environments.
C. The project team expects frequent scope changes during execution.
D. The customer prefers working software delivered in short iterations.

Test Your Understanding 6.2
A project manager is overseeing the construction of a nuclear power facility. Given the strict regulatory requirements, detailed planning, and need for extensive documentation, which project management approach is most appropriate?
A. Predictive (Waterfall)
B. Adaptive (Agile)
C. Hybrid
D. Incremental

Test Your Understanding 6.3
Which of the following is a key benefit of predictive project management?
A. Flexibility in adapting to changes during execution.

B. Reduced reliance on upfront assumptions.
C. Enhanced predictability in cost and schedule forecasting.
D. Ability to quickly deliver partial results to stakeholders.

Test Your Understanding 6.4
A project team is building a factory using a predictive approach. Halfway through, new environmental regulations require significant design changes. What is the most likely challenge the team will face?
A. Difficulty incorporating the changes due to rigidity of the methodology.
B. Over-allocation of resources to parallel activities.
C. Lack of documentation to justify compliance.
D. Failure to create a detailed project schedule.

6.2 Suitability on Organizational Structure

The suitability of a predictive, plan-based approach varies depending on the organizational structure within which the project is executed. Hierarchical, or functional, organizations, characterized by clear lines of authority and specialized departments, are generally well-suited for predictive project management. The structured, sequential nature of the predictive approach aligns seamlessly with the top-down management style and established reporting hierarchies typical of these organizations. This structure facilitates clear communication, well-defined roles and responsibilities, and strong alignment with traditional project governance processes (Nizma et al., 2024).

Matrix organizations, where team members report to both functional managers and project managers, present a more complex scenario. The effectiveness of a predictive approach in a matrix structure depends heavily on the balance of power between functional and project managers. In a weak matrix, where functional managers hold more authority, implementing a predictive approach can be challenging due to potential conflicts over resource allocation and prioritization.

A balanced matrix offers a more even distribution of authority, requiring careful coordination and communication between functional and project teams. A strong matrix, where project managers have significant authority, is more conducive to the predictive approach, as project managers can effectively enforce adherence to the project plan and manage resources accordingly.

Projectized organizations, where team members report directly to project managers and are dedicated to specific projects, are well-suited for predictive project management. This structure supports the predictive approach's sequential and hierarchical processes, enabling efficient execution of large, long-term projects. Project managers in these organizations have clear authority over resources and can enforce adherence to the project plan without interference from functional managers. This setup is commonly found in industries like consulting firms and construction companies, where projects are the primary focus.

The project environment also significantly influences outcomes. Virtual teams and remote work settings can pose challenges for predictive projects due to their reliance on rigid communication structures and the potential for miscommunication without face-to-face interaction. Successful implementation in these environments requires strong documentation, robust communication tools (like project management software with integrated communication features), and well-defined communication protocols.

On the other hand, colocated teams, where team members work in the same physical location, enhance collaboration in predictive projects. The ease of face-to-face communication and interaction makes it easier to maintain structured workflows, facilitate quick decision-making, and address issues promptly.

Test Your Understanding 6.5
In which type of organizational structure is the predictive approach most naturally aligned due to its sequential and hierarchical nature?
A. Weak matrix organization
B. Projectized organization
C. Functional organization
D. Virtual team environment

Test Your Understanding 6.6
Which organizational structure provides project managers full authority over resources and is therefore highly conducive to predictive project management?
A. Strong matrix organization
B. Functional organization
C. Projectized organization
D. Balanced matrix organization

Test Your Understanding 6.7
A predictive project team is distributed across multiple countries with limited face-to-face interaction. What is the best way to mitigate communication challenges in this environment?
A. Rely primarily on informal instant messaging among team members
B. Increase reliance on Agile practices to replace documentation
C. Reduce documentation to speed up communication and decision-making
D. Use robust project management software with integrated communication tools and clear protocols

6.3 Project Lifecycle

The Project Management Institute (PMI) defines five process groups that represent the lifecycle of a project:

Initiating, Planning, Executing, Monitoring and Controlling, and Closing. In a predictive, plan-based approach, these process groups are executed in a largely linear, sequential manner, closely aligned with the Waterfall methodology. This sequential flow is a key characteristic distinguishing predictive project management from iterative or adaptive approaches (Angeleski et al., 2025).

The Initiating Process Group sets the foundation for the project. Key activities include developing the project charter, which formally authorizes the project and defines its high-level objectives, scope, and constraints. Identifying key stakeholders and their influence on the project is also a critical part of initiation. This process group results in the approved project charter and the Stakeholder Register.

The Planning Process Group is the heart of a predictive project. Here, the project team develops a detailed project management plan, which serves as a comprehensive roadmap for executing, monitoring, controlling, and closing the project. This plan encompasses defining the project scope in detail using a Work Breakdown Structure (WBS), establishing schedule and cost baselines using techniques like Gantt charts, network diagrams, and cost estimating methods, identifying potential project risks and developing mitigation strategies, and creating subsidiary plans for quality management, communications management, resource management, and procurement management. Key deliverables of this process group include the WBS, which decomposes the project into manageable work packages, the Project Schedule and Budget, and the Risk Management Plan.

The Executing Process Group is where the project work is actually carried out. This involves directing and managing the project work as defined in the Project Management Plan, implementing quality assurance processes to ensure that deliverables meet the required standards, managing stakeholder engagement to maintain effective communication and address concerns, and acquiring and managing the resources necessary for project execution. Deliverables of this process group include the completed project deliverables themselves, as well as work performance data.

The Monitoring and Controlling Process Group tracks project performance against the established baselines. This involves monitoring scope, schedule, and cost performance, managing changes to the project plan, conducting quality control activities to verify that deliverables meet quality standards, and assessing the effectiveness of risk responses. This process group also involves generating status reports and performance updates to keep stakeholders informed of project progress. Key deliverables include performance reports that summarize project status and performance, as well as change requests and updates to the project plan to reflect approved changes. Earned Value Management (EVM) is a key technique used in monitoring and controlling, providing objective measures of project performance in terms of cost and schedule.

The Closing Process Group formally completes the project. This includes validating project deliverables with the customer or sponsor to obtain formal acceptance, documenting lessons learned and best practices for future projects, and closing contracts and administrative processes. Key deliverables of this process group include the final project report and lessons learned documentation.

Test Your Understanding 6.8
Which of the following best describes the primary output of the Initiating Process Group?
A. The Work Breakdown Structure (WBS) and Project Management Plan
B. The Project Charter and Stakeholder Register
C. The Risk Management Plan
D. The Final Project Report

Test Your Understanding 6.9
A project manager is leading a predictive project for a government infrastructure program. The stakeholders want a highly detailed plan with cost, schedule, and risk baselines before execution begins. Which process group should the manager focus on at this stage?
A. Planning
B. Executing
C. Monitoring and Controlling
D. Closing

Test Your Understanding 6.10
Midway through a project, the earned value analysis shows the project is behind schedule and over budget. The sponsor requests a performance update and corrective actions. Which process group is responsible for producing these outputs?
A. Executing
B. Closing
C. Planning
D. Monitoring and Controlling

Test Your Understanding 6.11
A predictive project follows a largely linear, step-by-step process flow. Which methodology is this most closely aligned with?
A. Agile methodology
B. Iterative prototyping
C. Waterfall methodology
D. Hybrid methodology

6.4 Predictive vs. Agile: A Component Comparison

Understanding project component differences in predictive versus Agile approaches enables effective decision-making for project managers. In a predictive approach, these components are defined and planned upfront, providing a stable baseline for execution. This contrasts sharply with Agile approaches, which embrace flexibility and iterative development.

Project Scope in a predictive approach is meticulously defined at the beginning of the project using a scope statement and a work breakdown structure (WBS). The scope statement clearly outlines the project's boundaries, defining what is included and excluded. The WBS decomposes the project into smaller, manageable work packages. Any changes to the scope require a formal change control process, ensuring that changes are evaluated for their impact on schedule, cost, and other project constraints. This control supports maintaining project stability. In contrast, agile methodologies allow the scope to evolve continuously based on feedback from the customer and the development team.

Project Schedule in a predictive approach is detailed and comprehensive, typically created using Gantt charts, the Critical Path Method (CPM), or Program Evaluation and Review Technique (PERT). Task dependencies and milestones are clearly defined upfront, providing a roadmap for project execution. Deviations from the schedule require formal adjustments and may necessitate a change request. Agile methodologies, on the other hand, employ more flexible scheduling techniques, focusing on iterative releases and short sprints. This allows for adjustments to the schedule based on changing priorities and feedback.

Project Cost and Budgeting in a predictive approach involves estimating costs before execution and establishing a Cost Baseline, which serves as the approved budget for the project. Strict budget control mechanisms are put in place to monitor spending and ensure that the project stays within budget. Earned Value Management (EVM) is often used to track cost performance against the baseline. Agile approaches use rolling-wave budgeting, where budgets are planned for shorter iterations or releases, allowing for adjustments as the project evolves and more information becomes available.

Risk Management in a predictive approach is proactive, with risks identified during the planning phase and documented in a Risk Register. Risk mitigation strategies are developed and incorporated into the Risk Management Plan. Risks are monitored and controlled throughout project execution. Agile teams take a more iterative approach to risk management, assessing risks at the beginning of each iteration and adapting to emerging challenges.

Quality Management in a predictive approach involves defining quality requirements upfront in a Quality

Management Plan. Quality assurance and control activities are performed throughout the project to ensure compliance with these standards. Agile methodologies emphasize continuous testing and feedback loops to refine quality throughout the development process.

Stakeholder Engagement in a predictive approach involves setting stakeholder expectations early in the project and following a structured Communication Plan to keep stakeholders informed. Agile prioritizes frequent stakeholder collaboration and feedback throughout the project lifecycle.

Project Communication in a predictive approach is typically formal and structured, following a pre-defined Communication Plan. This plan outlines who needs to receive what information, when, and how. Communication methods might include regular status reports, formal meetings, and documented updates. The emphasis is on clear, documented communication to maintain control and ensure everyone is informed. In Agile, communication is more informal and frequent, emphasizing face-to-face interactions, daily stand-up meetings, and continuous feedback loops. The focus is on rapid communication and collaboration within the team and with the customer.

Finally, Procurement and Vendor Management in a predictive approach involves defining contractual agreements upfront and following a structured acquisition process. Agile approaches allow for more flexible vendor selection and collaboration, often working closely with vendors in a more collaborative manner.

Test Your Understanding 6.12
In a predictive project, which tool is primarily used to break down the scope into smaller, manageable work packages?
A. Gantt Chart
B. Risk Register
C. Work Breakdown Structure (WBS)
D. Earned Value Management (EVM)

Test Your Understanding 6.13
A project manager on a government IT project is using a predictive approach. The schedule is defined upfront with task dependencies and milestones. Midway, a key task slips by two weeks. How should the project manager address this?
A. Adjust the schedule informally with the team to save time.
B. Create a new sprint plan to reprioritize work.
C. Submit a formal change request to update the schedule baseline.
D. Immediately work with the team to crash the critical path to recover the two weeks without changing the baseline.

Test Your Understanding 6.14

Which budgeting approach is most closely associated with Agile methodologies?
A. Fixed Cost Baseline established at project start
B. Rolling-wave budgeting for short iterations
C. Earned Value Management (EVM)
D. Program Evaluation and Review Technique (PERT)

Test Your Understanding 6.15
During planning, a project manager creates a document listing identified risks along with mitigation strategies. Later, the team monitors these risks throughout execution. Which approach is being applied here?
A. Agile approach with risk assessed each iteration
B. Informal risk handling through daily stand-up discussions
C. Hybrid approach balancing predictive and adaptive techniques
D. Predictive approach with proactive risk management

Test Your Understanding 6.16
How does communication differ between predictive and Agile methodologies?
A. Predictive uses structured communication plans; Agile uses frequent, informal interactions.
B. Predictive emphasizes face-to-face communication; Agile emphasizes structured reports.
C. Predictive requires daily stand-ups; Agile requires monthly status reports.
D. Predictive communication is primarily for stakeholder updates; Agile communication is primarily for team coordination.

6.5 Critical Path Method (CPM)

The Critical Path Method (CPM) is a tool used in project management to figure out the fastest way to finish a project. It does this by identifying the *critical path*, which is the longest sequence of dependent activities that must be completed on time for the project to finish on schedule. Think of it like a chain: if one link in the chain (an activity) is delayed, the whole chain (the project) is delayed. The critical path is the longest of these chains.

The CPM offers numerous advantages in project management, primarily by providing a clear visual representation of project activities and their interdependencies. This visualization allows for effective monitoring and control of the project's progress. A key benefit of CPM is its ability to identify the critical path. By pinpointing this critical path, project managers can readily identify potential delays and risk areas that could impact the overall project timeline. This understanding enables proactive risk management and mitigation. Furthermore, CPM facilitates more effective resource allocation by highlighting which activities are most critical to the project's timely completion, allowing resources to be prioritized accordingly.

Specifically, CPM empowers project managers in several key areas: Planning, by visually mapping the sequence of activities and their dependencies; Scheduling, by determining the shortest possible project duration and establishing crucial milestones; Monitoring, by tracking progress against the schedule and identifying potential delays on the critical path; and Controlling, by enabling corrective actions to address any deviations from the schedule, especially those affecting the critical path. By concentrating efforts and resources on the activities along the critical path, project managers ensure that the most crucial tasks are completed on time, ultimately contributing to the project's timely completion.

Example:

A software development company is planning to develop a new web-based application. The project manager needs to apply CPM to determine the minimum time required to complete the project.

Step 1: Define the Project Scope

The first step in applying CPM is to define the project scope. This involves identifying the project objectives, deliverables, and constraints. The project scope includes developing a new web-based application with specific features, within a budget of $500,000, and with a completion date of 8 months.

Step 2: Identify Project Activities

The next step is to identify all the activities required to complete the project. These are the individual tasks that need to be done to complete the project. These activities should be specific, measurable, and time-bound. The project manager identifies the following activities:

Activity 1: Conduct market research
Activity 2: Prepare requirements specification
Activity 3: Design the database
Activity 4: Develop the user interface
Activity 5: Develop the backend
Activity 6: Test the application
Activity 7: Deploy the application
Activity 8: Provide user training

Step 3: Determine Activity Sequences

The project activities should be arranged in a logical sequence based on their interdependencies. This involves determining the predecessor and successor activities for each activity. The project manager determines the following activity sequences:

Activity 1 must be completed before Activity 2
Activity 2 must be completed before Activities 3 and 4
Activity 3 must be completed before Activity 5
Activities 4 and 5 must be completed before Activity 6

Activity 6 must be completed before Activity 7
Activity 7 must be completed before Activity 8

Step 4: Establish Activity Durations

Once the activity sequences have been determined, the next step is to establish the duration of each activity. This involves estimating the time required to complete each activity. The project manager estimates the following activity durations (in weeks):

Activity 1: 3 weeks; Activity 2: 5 weeks; Activity 3: 3 weeks; Activity 4: 6 weeks; Activity 5: 8 weeks; Activity 6: 4 weeks; Activity 7: 3 weeks; Activity 8: 4 weeks

Step 5: Develop the Project Schedule

The project schedule is developed by constructing a network diagram that shows the relationships between the activities. The critical path is determined by identifying the longest path through the network. The project manager constructs a network diagram and determines the critical path as follows:

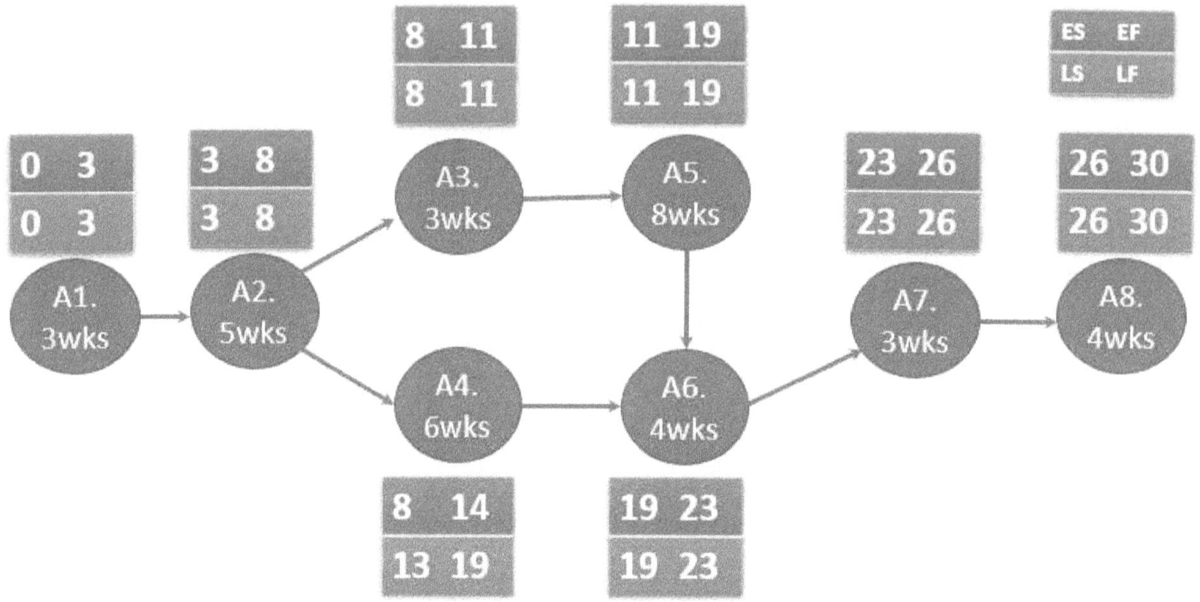

Figure 6.1 Network diagram in Critical Path Method (CPM).

The four numbers in the box are early start (ES), early finish (EF), late start (LS), and late finish (LF).

ES	EF
LS	LF

Early Start (ES) is the earliest possible time an activity can begin, assuming all its preceding activities are completed as early as possible. Imagine you have to bake a cake. You can't start baking (the activity) until you've gathered all the ingredients (preceding activity). The moment you have all the ingredients is your

Early Start for baking.

Early Finish (EF) is the earliest possible time an activity can be completed. It's calculated by adding the activity's duration to its Early Start. Using the cake example, if gathering ingredients takes 30 minutes (ES) and baking takes 45 minutes (duration), the Early Finish for baking is 1 hour and 15 minutes (ES + Duration = EF).

These two (ES and EF) are calculated by moving forward through the project schedule. In the network diagram example, Activity 1 starts at week 0, the duration is 3 wks, so its early finish is Week 3.

0	3

Activity 2 starts at Week 3, the duration is 5wks, so its early finish is Week 8.

3	8

Activity 3 starts at Week 8, the duration is 3wks, so its early finish is Week 11.

8	11

Activity 4 also starts at Week 8, the duration is 6wks, so its early finish is Week 14.

8	14

Late Finish (LF) is the latest possible time an activity can be completed without delaying the entire project. It's determined by working backward from the project's end date. If the cake needs to be ready by 3 PM (the project end date), that's the Late Finish for the last activity (perhaps "frosting the cake").

Late Start (LS) is the latest possible time an activity can begin without delaying the entire project. It's calculated by subtracting the activity's duration from its Late Finish. If frosting takes 15 minutes (duration) and needs to be done by 3 PM (LF), the Late Start for frosting is 2:45 PM (LF - Duration = LS).

These two (LS and LF) are calculated by moving backward through the project schedule. In the network example, the calculation starts with Activity 8.

26	30

For Activity 8, the late finish is Week 30, the duration is 4wks, so the late start is Week 26.

26	30
26	30

For Activity 7, the late finish is Week 26, the duration is 3wks, so the late start is Week 23.

23	26
23	26

For Activity 6, the late finish is Week 23, the duration is 4wks, so the late start is Week 19.

19	23
19	23

For Activity 4, the late finish is Week 19, the duration is 6wks, so the late start is Week 13.

8	14
13	19

The difference between the Early Start and Late Start (or Early Finish and Late Finish) is called "float" or "slack." This represents how much an activity can be delayed without impacting the project's overall completion date. Activities on the critical path have zero float, meaning any delay in these activities will directly delay the project.

The critical path is the sequence of activities with zero float. These are the activities that must be kept on schedule to avoid project delays. Activity 1 to 2 to 3 to 5 to 6 to 7 to 8 (activities with the same early start and early finish; duration = 30 weeks). This is the critical path, and it determines the minimum time required to complete the project. Activity 4 is not on the critical pay and may be delayed by 5 weeks (13 – 8 = 5) without delay the project.

Step 6: Monitor and Control Project Progress

Once the project schedule has been developed, the next step is to monitor and control project progress. This involves comparing actual project performance with the planned schedule, identifying any deviations, and taking corrective action to get the project back on track.

Test Your Understanding 6.17

Which of the following best defines the critical path in the Critical Path Method (CPM)?

A. The sequence of activities with the shortest duration in the project
B. The longest sequence of dependent activities that determines the project duration
C. The sequence of activities with the highest resource demand
D. The list of activities that have maximum slack

Test Your Understanding 6.18
A project manager is reviewing a network diagram and sees that Activity 4 has an Early Start (ES) of Week 8 and a Late Start (LS) of Week 13. What does this indicate?
A. Activity 4 is on the critical path and cannot be delayed
B. Activity 4 should be prioritized above Activity 5
C. Activity 4 must start in Week 8 or the project will be delayed
D. Activity 4 has a float of 5 weeks and can be delayed without affecting the project end date

Test Your Understanding 6.19
What is the main purpose of calculating Early Start (ES) and Early Finish (EF) times in CPM?
A. To determine which tasks have the highest cost
B. To identify the latest time an activity can begin
C. To estimate the earliest possible timeline for project completion
D. To allocate additional resources to non-critical activities

Test Your Understanding 6.20
In a web application development project, the project manager finds that Activities 1, 2, 3, 5, 6, 7, and 8 form the critical path. If Activity 5 (duration 8 weeks) is delayed by 2 weeks, what is the likely impact?
A. No impact since other activities may absorb the delay
B. The project will be delayed by 2 weeks
C. Activity 4 will have to start earlier to make up for lost time
D. Activity 4 will need to be shortened to stay on track

Test Your Understanding 6.21
A project manager notices that the Late Finish (LF) of Activity 7 is Week 26, while its Early Finish (EF) is Week 26. What does this mean?
A. Activity 7 has 0 float and lies on the critical path
B. Activity 7 can be delayed by several weeks without impact
C. Activity 7 is the shortest activity in the project
D. Activity 7 must be rescheduled to avoid resource conflicts

6.6 Earned Value Management (EVM)

Earned Value Management (EVM) is a technique for measuring project performance and progress. It integrates scope, schedule, and cost data to provide a comprehensive view of the project's health. Unlike traditional methods that only compare actual costs to budgeted costs, EVM considers the value of the work actually completed. This allows for more accurate forecasting and better decision-making, especially in predictive, plan-based projects.

EVM revolves around three key values. Planned Value (PV), also known as the Budgeted Cost of Work Scheduled (BCWS), represents the authorized budget assigned to the scheduled work, reflecting the value of the work planned for completion up to a specific point in time. Earned Value (EV), also known as the Budgeted Cost of Work Performed (BCWP), measures the value of the work actually completed up to a specific point in time and is calculated by multiplying the percentage of work completed on each task by its budgeted cost. Finally, Actual Cost (AC), also known as the Actual Cost of Work Performed (ACWP), represents the actual costs incurred for the work completed up to a specific point in time.

Using these three values, several key metrics can be calculated to assess project performance: Schedule Variance (SV), Cost Variance (CV), Schedule Performance Index (SPI), and Cost Performance Index (CPI).

Schedule Variance (SV) is calculated as SV = EV - PV. A positive SV indicates that the project is ahead of schedule, meaning more work has been completed than was planned for that point in time. A negative SV indicates that the project is behind schedule, meaning less work has been completed than planned.

Example 1:

Suppose a project's PV is $100,000 and the EV is $120,000, the SV is $20,000, indicating the project is ahead of schedule.

Example 2:

A project has a budget of $200,000 and a planned duration of 10 weeks. After 8 weeks, the project has completed $150,000 worth of work.
PV = $200,000 * (8/10) = $160,000
EV = $150,000
SV = EV - PV = $150,000 - $160,000 = -$10,000
The negative value of SV indicates that the project is behind schedule. Project managers need to investigate the causes of the variance and take corrective actions to get the project back on track.

Cost Variance (CV) is calculated as CV = EV - AC. A positive CV indicates that the project is under budget, meaning the value of the work completed is greater than the actual cost incurred. A negative CV indicates that the project is over budget, meaning the actual cost incurred is greater than the value of the work completed.

Example1:

Suppose a project's EV is $100,000 and the AC is $90,000, the CV is $10,000, indicating the project is under budget.

Example 2:

Suppose a construction project was planned to take 300 days with a budget of $2.1 million. After 100 days (one third completed), it was determined that the actual cost incurred was $0.6 million. What is the cost variance? CV = EV - AC = $0.7 million - $0.6 million = $100,000
In the example, the earned value is one third of the budget, which is $0.7 million. The cost variance is $100,000 which indicates that the project is currently $100,000 under budget.

The Schedule Performance Index (SPI) is calculated as SPI = EV / PV. An SPI greater than 1 indicates that the project is ahead of schedule, meaning the project is completing work faster than planned. An SPI less than 1 indicates that the project is behind schedule, meaning the project is completing work slower than planned. For instance, if the EV is $120,000 and the PV is $100,000, the SPI is 1.2, indicating the project is ahead of schedule. If the EV is $80,000 and the PV is $100,000, the SPI is 0.8, indicating the project is behind schedule.

The Cost Performance Index (CPI) is calculated as CPI = EV / AC. A CPI greater than 1 indicates that the project is under budget, meaning the project is getting more value for each dollar spent. A CPI less than 1 indicates that the project is over budget, meaning the project is spending more than planned for the value of work completed. For example, if the EV is $100,000 and the AC is $80,000, the CPI is 1.25, indicating the project is under budget. If the EV is $100,000 and the AC is $125,000, the CPI is 0.8, indicating the project is over budget. These EVM metrics provide valuable insights into project performance and allow project managers to take corrective actions as needed to keep the project on track in terms of both schedule and budget.

Earned Value Management (EVM) is not only useful for tracking current project performance but also for forecasting the final project cost and completion date. Several key metrics are used for forecasting, including Estimate at Completion (EAC), Estimate to Complete (ETC), and Variance at Completion (VAC).

The Estimate at Completion (EAC) represents the forecasted total cost of the project upon its completion. There are several formulas to calculate EAC, and the appropriate formula depends on the project's performance trends and assumptions about future performance. One of the most common and straightforward formulas is EAC = BAC / CPI, where BAC is the Budget at Completion (the original total planned budget for the project) and CPI is the Cost Performance Index. This formula assumes that future cost performance will be similar to the current cost performance. For example, if the BAC is $500,000 and the CPI is 0.8, the EAC would be $500,000 / 0.8 = $625,000. This indicates that the project is currently projected to be $125,000 over budget.

The Estimate to Complete (ETC) represents the estimated cost required to complete all the remaining project work. A common formula for ETC is ETC = EAC - AC. Using the previous example where EAC is $625,000 and Assume the current AC is $300,000 for this example. The ETC would be $625,000 - $300,000 = $325,000, indicating an additional $325,000 is estimated to complete the project. Another formula for

ETC is ETC = (BAC - EV)/(CPI). This formula assumes that future cost performance will be similar to the current cost performance.

The Variance at Completion (VAC) represents the difference between the original budget (BAC) and the forecasted total cost (EAC). It is calculated as VAC = BAC - EAC. Using the same example where BAC is $500,000 and EAC is $625,000, the VAC would be $500,000 - $625,000 = -$125,000. A negative VAC indicates a projected cost overrun, while a positive VAC indicates a projected cost underrun.

Example:

A project has a BAC of $200,000. At the halfway point, the EV is $80,000, and the AC is $100,000. Calculate the EAC using the BAC/CPI formula. First, calculate the CPI: CPI = EV / AC = $80,000 / $100,000 = 0.8. Then, calculate the EAC: EAC = BAC / CPI = $200,000 / 0.8 = $250,000. This tells us the project is now forecasted to cost $250,000, a $50,000 overrun.

One of the advantages of EVM is objective performance measurement. EVM provides quantifiable metrics, such as Schedule Variance (SV), Cost Variance (CV), Schedule Performance Index (SPI), and Cost Performance Index (CPI), which offer a clear and unbiased view of project progress. This reduces reliance on subjective assessments, which can be prone to bias and inaccuracies. Instead of relying on gut feelings or vague progress reports, EVM offers concrete data that can be used to assess project health.

Another benefit is early problem detection. By consistently tracking EVM metrics, project managers can identify potential schedule and cost overruns at an early stage. For instance, a consistently declining CPI would signal a potential cost overrun, while an SPI consistently below 1 would indicate schedule slippage. This early warning system allows for timely corrective actions to be taken, minimizing the impact of these issues on the project's overall success. This proactive approach is much more effective than reacting to problems only after they have become significant.

EVM also facilitates improved forecasting. By using metrics like Estimate at Completion (EAC), Estimate to Complete (ETC), and Variance at Completion (VAC), project managers can develop more accurate forecasts of project costs and completion dates. These forecasts enable better decision-making regarding resource allocation, scope adjustments, and other project management strategies. Accurate forecasting also helps in managing stakeholder expectations and securing continued support for the project.

Finally, EVM enhances communication by providing a common language for communicating project performance to stakeholders. EVM metrics offer a standardized way to report on project progress, making it easier for stakeholders to understand the project's status and make informed decisions. This consistent and objective communication improves transparency and fosters better collaboration among project stakeholders. For example, presenting stakeholders with a CPI of 0.9 clearly communicates that the project is currently getting 90 cents of value for every dollar spent, which is a clear indicator of a potential cost overrun.

While EVM is a powerful tool, it's essential to acknowledge its limitations. One significant limitation is that EVM requires accurate data. The reliability of EVM metrics depends heavily on the accuracy and timeliness of the data used to calculate them. If the data on project progress, actual costs, or planned value is inaccurate or outdated, the resulting EVM metrics will be misleading and could lead to incorrect conclusions. Therefore, implementing robust data collection and validation processes helps effective EVM implementation.

Another limitation is implementation complexity. Implementing EVM effectively can be complex, requiring careful planning, training for project team members, and the use of appropriate project management tools or software. Organizations need to invest time and resources in setting up EVM processes and ensuring that project teams understand how to use them correctly. Without proper training and support, EVM can become a cumbersome and ineffective process.

Finally, EVM has a focus on measurable work. It is most effective for projects with well-defined scopes and measurable deliverables. In projects with highly uncertain or evolving scopes, such as some Agile projects, applying EVM can be challenging. EVM works best when work packages and deliverables can be easily quantified and measured, allowing for accurate calculation of earned value. Recognizing these limitations helps determine whether EVM is the right tool for a specific project and for implementing it effectively.

Test Your Understanding 6.22
Which of the following best describes the primary purpose of Earned Value Management (EVM)?
A. Comparing actual costs to the original project budget only
B. Tracking project scope without considering schedule or cost
C. Integrating scope, schedule, and cost data to assess project performance
D. Forecasting final project duration without analyzing costs

Test Your Understanding 6.23
A construction project has a BAC of $2,100,000 and duration of 300 days. After 100 days, AC = $600,000. What is the Cost Variance (CV)?
A. -$100,000 (over budget)

B. $100,000 (under budget)
C. $200,000 (under budget)
D. $1,500,000 (remaining budget)

Test Your Understanding 6.24
You are a project manager, and your SPI is consistently below 1.0. What does this suggest, and what should you do first?
A. The project is ahead of schedule; continue current execution.
B. The project is behind schedule; investigate reasons for delays.
C. The project is over budget; reduce scope immediately.
D. The project is under budget; accelerate spending.

Test Your Understanding 6.25
If EV = $80,000 and AC = $100,000, what is the Cost Performance Index (CPI)?
A. 0.8 (over budget)
B. 1.25 (under budget)
C. 1.0 (on budget)
D. 1.8 (far under budget)

Test Your Understanding 6.26
A project has BAC = $500,000, EV = $200,000, AC = $220,000. The CPI is less than 1. Which is the most accurate conclusion?
A. The project is under budget.
B. The project is over budget.
C. The project is ahead of schedule.
D. The project is delivering higher value per dollar spent.

Test Your Understanding 6.27
What formula is commonly used to forecast the Estimate at Completion (EAC) when assuming future cost performance is consistent with current trends?
A. EAC = EV / PV
B. EAC = (BAC - AC) / CPI
C. EAC = AC - EV
D. EAC = BAC / CPI

Test Your Understanding 6.28
A project has BAC = $200,000, EV = $80,000, and AC = $100,000. Calculate the EAC using the BAC/CPI formula.
A. $160,000
B. $200,000
C. $250,000
D. $300,000

Test Your Understanding 6.29
A project team reports strong progress, but the SPI is 0.75. What is the best interpretation?
A. The project is spending too much money.
B. The project is at risk due to poor cost tracking.
C. The project is ahead of schedule but under budget.
D. The project is completing work slower than planned.

Test Your Understanding 6.30
Which of the following is NOT a limitation of Earned Value Management (EVM)?
A. It primarily focuses on qualitative assessments of project team morale.
B. It requires significant training and tool support to implement effectively.
C. It relies heavily on the accuracy and timeliness of project data.
D. It is less effective on projects with evolving or uncertain scopes.

6.7 Work Package

Work packages are fundamental building blocks in project management, especially within the predictive approach. They represent the smallest, most manageable units of work within a project, serving as the foundation for planning, scheduling, budgeting, and controlling project activities. A work package can be defined as a discrete portion of the project work that is assigned to a specific team or individual, has a defined scope, and produces a measurable deliverable. Essentially, it's the "work" that gets done to create the project's "product."

Work packages provide a clear breakdown of the project scope into manageable units, allowing for more accurate estimation of effort, resources, and duration. By assigning work packages to specific individuals or teams, accountability is established, fostering ownership and responsibility for completing the assigned tasks. This assignment also clarifies roles and responsibilities within the project team, promoting efficient collaboration and communication. Furthermore, work packages serve as control points for tracking progress. Because they have defined deliverables and estimated durations, project managers can easily monitor the completion status of each work package and identify any potential delays or issues.

Work packages fit directly into the Work Breakdown Structure (WBS). The WBS is a hierarchical decomposition of the total scope of work, where the highest level represents the entire project, and each subsequent level breaks the project down into smaller components. Work packages reside at the lowest level of the WBS, representing the individual tasks or activities required to produce a specific deliverable. The WBS provides the overall framework for organizing the project scope, while work packages define the specific tasks within that framework. For example, if a project involves building a house, the WBS might include branches like "Foundation," "Framing," and "Roofing." Within the "Foundation" branch, work packages might include "Excavate site," "Pour footings," and "Install rebar."

Each work package has a direct relationship with one or more project deliverables. The completion of a work package results in a specific deliverable, which contributes to the overall project objective. This relationship ensures that all project work is aligned with the desired outcomes. For instance, the "Pour footings" work package in the house construction example would result in the "Completed footings" deliverable. This clear link between work packages and deliverables provides a traceable path from individual tasks to the final project product.

Several characteristics define a work package. First, it is the smallest unit of work in the WBS, representing a task that cannot be further broken down. Second, it has a defined scope and deliverables, clearly specifying what needs to be done and what output is expected. Third, it has specific time and cost estimates, allowing for accurate budgeting and scheduling. Fourth, it is assigned to a responsible team or individual, establishing clear accountability. Finally, it is measurable and trackable within the project schedule, enabling progress monitoring and control.

Here are the steps you can follow to create work packages:

Identify the work required to complete the project.
Break down the work into smaller, manageable portions.
Assign each portion of the work to an individual or team.
Define the deliverables for each work package.
Develop a schedule for each work package, including a start and end date, and assign resources as needed.

To see an example, let's consider a project to develop a new mobile application for a company. A work package in this project could be the development of the user registration and login feature. This work package would include tasks such as:

Designing the user interface for the registration and login screens, including wireframes and mockups.
Writing front-end and back-end code to enable user registration and login, integrated with a secure database.
Implementing security measures, such as password hashing and HTTPS encryption, to protect user data.
Conducting unit, integration, and user acceptance testing to ensure the feature functions as expected.

The deliverables for this work package might include:

A fully functional and tested user registration and login feature.
User-facing help text or documentation for the registration and login process.
A testing report documenting any bugs or issues found during testing and their resolutions.
Technical documentation for the codebase to support future maintenance.

Test Your Understanding 6.31
Which of the following best defines a work package in project management?
A. The largest unit of work in the Work Breakdown Structure (WBS)
B. A discrete, smallest manageable portion of work assigned to a team or individual
C. A grouping of related projects managed in a coordinated way
D. A checklist of tasks used for quality assurance

Test Your Understanding 6.32
A company is developing a new mobile application. One work package involves implementing the user registration and login feature. Which of the following would NOT be considered a deliverable for this work package?
A. A functional and tested registration/login feature integrated with the database
B. A test report documenting bugs and their resolutions
C. Technical documentation for the codebase
D. A marketing campaign plan to promote the new app

Test Your Understanding 6.33
In the hierarchy of the Work Breakdown Structure (WBS), where do work packages fit?
A. At the top level, representing the entire project
B. At the middle level, representing broad project phases
C. At the lowest level, representing individual tasks or deliverables
D. Outside the WBS, used only in scheduling tools

Test Your Understanding 6.34
A project manager notices that progress tracking is inconsistent because certain tasks lack defined deliverables and cost estimates. What step should the project manager take to correct this?
A. Revisit and properly define the work packages with clear scope, deliverables, and estimates.
B. Combine smaller work elements into larger phases for simplicity.
C. Assign the tasks directly to external vendors without further breakdown.
D. Move the undefined tasks out of the WBS and track them separately.

6.8 Work Breakdown Structure (WBS)

The Work Breakdown Structure (WBS) is a tool in project management, particularly within predictive methodologies, serving as a hierarchical decomposition of the total scope of work to be carried out by the project team to accomplish the project objectives and create the required deliverables. The WBS organizes and defines the project scope into manageable work packages, providing a structured framework for planning, scheduling, budgeting, and controlling the project. Each work package is broken down into specific tasks or activities to complete the deliverables.

The primary purpose of the WBS is to break down complex projects into smaller, more manageable components. This decomposition makes it easier to define and assign responsibilities, estimate costs and durations, and track progress. A well-constructed WBS ensures that no aspect of the project is overlooked and provides a clear picture of all the work required. It's not just a list of tasks; it's a structured, hierarchical representation of all the work. For example, if the project is "Build a House," the WBS might have branches like "Foundation," "Framing," "Electrical," "Plumbing," and "Finishing," each of which would be further broken down into smaller tasks.

The WBS is directly linked to the project schedule. By breaking the project into smaller, manageable work packages, it becomes possible to accurately estimate the effort and resources required for each task. These estimates are then used to develop the project schedule, defining task dependencies, durations, and milestones. The WBS provides the framework for organizing and sequencing project activities, ensuring that the project schedule is realistic and achievable. It essentially provides the "what" that needs to be done, which then informs the "when" and "how" in the schedule.

The WBS supports project planning by providing a clear definition of the project scope and deliverables. It serves as the basis for developing the project schedule, budget, and resource allocation plan. During project execution, the WBS acts as a roadmap, guiding the project team in completing the defined work packages. For monitoring and control, the WBS provides a framework for tracking progress against the plan. By monitoring the completion of work packages, project managers can identify potential delays or issues early on and take corrective action. The WBS also facilitates communication among project stakeholders by providing a common understanding of the project scope and deliverables. It's a cornerstone of effective project management, enabling a structured and controlled approach to even the most complex projects.

Let's consider an example of an IT project to redesign a website.

The top-level objectives of the project could be defined as:

1.0 Redesign the company's website

Next, the objectives could be broken down into deliverables, such as:

1.1. Create a new website design
1.2. Develop a functional prototype of the new website
1.3. Develop the final version of the website
1.4. Perform website testing and quality assurance
1.5. Perform a successful launch of the new website

The deliverables could then be further broken down into activities, such as:

1.1.1. Conduct a design review with stakeholders
1.1.2. Create wireframes for the new website
1.1.3. Develop a high-fidelity website design
1.2.1. Develop a functional prototype of the new website
1.3.1. Develop the front-end user interface of the website
1.3.2. Develop the back-end database and server-side logic

1.4.1. Perform functional testing on the website
1.4.2. Perform accessibility testing on the website
1.5.1. Coordinate with marketing to launch the new website
1.5.2. Address website bugs and issues reported by users

Finally, the activities can be broken down into individual tasks, such as:

1.1.1.1. Schedule a design review meeting with stakeholders
1.1.2.1. Create wireframes for the homepage of the website
1.1.2.2. Create wireframes for the product page of the website
1.1.3.1. Develop the new website design using Adobe Photoshop
1.2.1.1. Develop a working prototype of the new website using HTML, CSS, and JavaScript
1.3.1.1. Develop the homepage of the website using HTML, CSS, and JavaScript
1.3.1.2. Develop the product page of the website using HTML, CSS, and JavaScript
1.3.2.1. Design the database schema for the website
1.3.2.2. Write the server-side logic for the website
1.4.1.1. Test the website to ensure that all links and buttons work as expected
1.4.2.1. Test the website using a screen reader to ensure accessibility
1.5.1.1. Coordinate with marketing to create a launch plan for the new website
1.5.1.2. Debug and fix website bugs reported by users

Test Your Understanding 6.35
Which of the following best describes the primary purpose of a Work Breakdown Structure (WBS) in project management?
A. To provide a list of all tasks in the project without hierarchy
B. To identify project risks and create a mitigation plan
C. To decompose project scope into manageable components
D. To develop a detailed communication management plan

Test Your Understanding 6.36
A project manager is leading a construction project to "Build a House." She creates a WBS with top-level elements like "Foundation," "Framing," "Plumbing," and "Finishing." What is the main advantage of this approach?
A. It ensures that project costs are minimized.
B. It guarantees that the project schedule will not slip.
C. It provides a structured way to organize deliverables.
D. It eliminates the need for stakeholder communication.

Test Your Understanding 6.37
A project manager notices that while developing the WBS, some team members keep creating a "to-do list" of activities without grouping them into higher-level components. What risk does this approach create?
A. It may make the schedule overly flexible.
B. It could lead to missing parts of the project scope.
C. It ensures better cost estimates but delays risk management.
D. It creates too much emphasis on milestones.

Test Your Understanding 6.38
How is the WBS directly connected to the project schedule?

A. It provides task dependencies and critical path details.
B. It eliminates the need for estimating task durations.
C. It ensures the schedule includes all project risks.
D. It defines the "what" that informs the "when" and "how."

6.9 Gantt Charts

A Gantt chart is a type of bar chart that illustrates the start and finish dates of the terminal elements (work packages) and summary elements of the Work Breakdown Structure (WBS). It offers a clear graphical overview of the project schedule, showcasing the sequence of activities, their durations, and their dependencies.

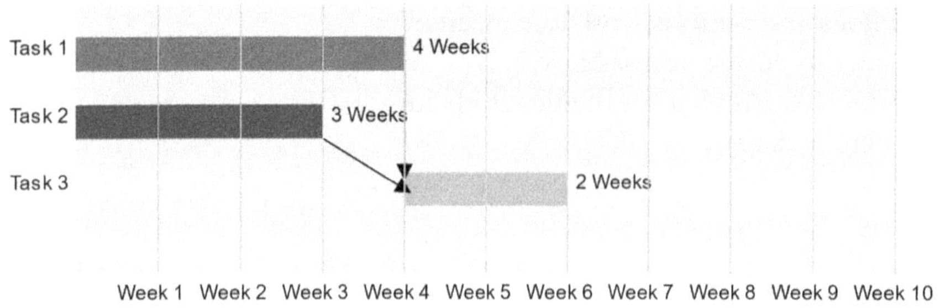

Figure 6.2 Sample Gantt chart.

Several key components work together to make these charts effective communication and management tools. Tasks or activities, derived directly from the work packages in the Work Breakdown Structure (WBS), form the vertical axis of the chart. Each row typically represents a specific task, and summary tasks, which represent higher levels of the WBS, can also be included to provide a hierarchical view. This direct link to the WBS ensures that all planned work is represented in the schedule.

The horizontal axis of the Gantt chart displays the timeline, representing the project's duration. This timeline can be scaled to show days, weeks, months, or even years, depending on the project's overall length and the level of detail required. Choosing the appropriate scale enhances readability and effective project management. For short projects, a daily or weekly scale might be appropriate, while longer projects might benefit from a monthly or quarterly scale.

Perhaps one of the most important aspects of a Gantt chart is its ability to depict task dependencies or relationships. Lines or arrows connecting tasks illustrate these dependencies, showing which tasks must be completed before others can begin. Several types of dependencies exist: Finish-to-Start (the most common, where one task must finish before the next can start), Start-to-Start (where two tasks can start simultaneously), Finish-to-Finish (where two tasks must finish together), and Start-to-Finish (where one task cannot finish until another has started). Understanding and correctly representing these dependencies helps accurately determining the project's critical path and managing the project schedule effectively.

Milestones are often represented by diamonds or other distinct symbols on the Gantt chart. These milestones typically mark the completion of key deliverables, phases, or critical decision points in the project. They provide checkpoints for tracking progress and communicating with stakeholders.

Progress tracking is another key feature. The bars representing each task can be filled in or shaded to indicate the percentage of completion. This visual cue allows for a quick assessment of project progress at any given point in time. Project management software often automates this process, updating the progress bars based on reported task completion.

Finally, while not always included, some Gantt charts incorporate resource allocation information. This shows which team members or resources are assigned to each task, providing a clear view of resource utilization and responsibilities. This information can be invaluable for resource leveling and ensuring that the right people are working on the right tasks at the right time. By combining all these elements, Gantt charts become powerful tools for planning, scheduling, tracking, and communicating project information, contributing significantly to project success.

Gantt charts are invaluable tools for project managers due to the numerous benefits they offer in planning, executing, and controlling projects. One of the most significant advantages is the visual overview of the schedule. Gantt charts provide a clear and easy-to-understand representation of the entire project schedule, allowing project managers and stakeholders to quickly grasp the project timeline, task durations, and dependencies at a glance. This visual representation simplifies complex project schedules, making it easier to communicate and understand the project's overall plan.

Gantt charts excel at dependency management. They explicitly show task dependencies, highlighting which tasks rely on the completion of others. This visualization of task relationships is crucial for understanding the project's flow and identifying potential bottlenecks. By clearly illustrating which tasks are dependent on others, project managers can anticipate potential delays and proactively manage dependencies to keep the project on track. For example, if "Install Plumbing" is dependent on "Pour Foundation," the Gantt chart will visually show this relationship, alerting the project manager to ensure the foundation is completed on time to avoid delaying the plumbing work.

Progress Tracking is another key benefit. By updating the Gantt chart with actual start and finish dates, project managers can easily track project progress and identify any deviations from the planned schedule. Progress can be indicated by visually filling in a percentage of completion on the task bars or by marking completed tasks. This allows for quick identification of tasks that are behind schedule, enabling timely intervention and corrective actions. Many project management software tools automate this process, updating the Gantt chart based on team member input and progress updates.

Gantt charts are an effective tool for communication and collaboration. Their visual nature clearly displays the project schedule, helping team members, stakeholders, and clients understand the timeline and their responsibilities. This shared understanding fosters teamwork, as everyone works from the same visual representation of the project plan.

Critical path analysis is another powerful capability. Gantt charts, especially when used with project management software, can help identify the critical path. Focusing on the critical path helps keep the project on schedule because any delay on a critical path task will directly delay the entire project. Gantt charts visually highlight the critical path, allowing project managers to prioritize their efforts and resources on the most crucial activities.

Finally, Gantt charts are useful for "What-If" analysis. They can be used to simulate the impact of potential delays or changes on the project schedule. This allows project managers to proactively assess risks and develop contingency plans. By manipulating task durations or dependencies on the Gantt chart, project managers can quickly see how changes might affect the overall project timeline and make informed decisions about how to respond to potential issues.

Creating a Gantt chart typically involves the following steps:

1. Define Activities: List all the activities or tasks required for the project (derived from the WBS).
2. Sequence Activities: Determine the dependencies between activities. Which tasks must be completed before others can start?
3. Estimate Activity Durations: Estimate the time required to complete each activity.
4. Develop the Gantt Chart: Use project management software or a spreadsheet to create the chart, plotting the activities, their durations, and their dependencies on the timeline.
5. Track and Update: Regularly update the Gantt chart to reflect actual progress, making necessary

adjustments as the project progresses.

Test Your Understanding 6.39
A project manager notices that "Install Electrical Wiring" cannot begin until "Pour Foundation" is finished. Which dependency type does this relationship represent?
A. Finish-to-Finish
B. Start-to-Start
C. Finish-to-Start
D. Start-to-Finish

Test Your Understanding 6.40
On a Gantt chart, milestones are most often represented by which symbol?
A. Circle
B. Diamond
C. Square
D. Triangle

Test Your Understanding 6.41
During a project review meeting, a stakeholder asks how much progress has been made on a task. The project manager refers to the Gantt chart and points to a bar that is half-shaded. What does this represent?
A. The task is on hold
B. The task is 50% complete
C. The task is delayed
D. The task has two dependencies

Test Your Understanding 6.42
Which of the following is NOT a direct benefit of using a Gantt chart in project management?
A. Visual overview of the project schedule
B. Identification of task dependencies
C. Tracking of progress
D. Automatic allocation of financial budgets

Test Your Understanding 6.43
A project manager notices that a delay in one critical path task will cause the entire project to finish late. What feature of the Gantt chart is being used here?
A. Critical path analysis
B. Milestone tracking
C. Resource allocation
D. Dependency scaling

Test Your Understanding 6.44
Your team wants to test the impact of extending the "Testing Phase" by two weeks. You use the Gantt chart to model the change and see how it shifts the project's end date. What capability are you using?
A. What-if analysis
B. Dependency analysis
C. Progress tracking
D. Milestone adjustment

Test Your Understanding 6.45
In a software development project, system testing can begin as soon as coding starts, and both can proceed in parallel. What type of dependency does this describe?
A. Finish-to-Finish
B. Start-to-Start
C. Start-to-Finish
D. Finish-to-Start

Test Your Understanding 6.46
In a construction project, the task "Install Windows" must be completed at the same time as "Seal Window Frames" to ensure proper installation. Which dependency type applies?
A. Finish-to-Finish
B. Finish-to-Start
C. Start-to-Start
D. Start-to-Finish

Test Your Understanding 6.47
A new customer support system is being launched. The old system cannot be shut down until the new system has started. Which type of dependency does this represent?
A. Finish-to-Start
B. Finish-to-Finish
C. Start-to-Start
D. Start-to-Finish

6.10 Integration Management Plan

Project Integration Management is the overarching function that coordinates all other project management areas. It's the glue that holds the project together, ensuring that all elements work harmoniously towards the project's objectives. It provides the framework for unifying all project components, from scope and schedule to cost, resources, risk, quality, and stakeholder engagement.

The Integration Management Plan encompasses several key elements. The Project Charter serves as the foundational document, formally authorizing the project and outlining high-level objectives, scope, and stakeholders. The Project Management Plan itself is the overarching guide for managing project integration. A robust Change Management Process handles project modifications effectively.

Effective integration management also requires a clear Issue Resolution and Decision-Making Framework. This framework outlines how project issues will be identified, analyzed, and resolved, ensuring smooth project execution and preventing issues from escalating and impacting project success. It also defines the decision-making process, clarifying who has the authority to make decisions and how those decisions will be communicated.

Knowledge Management and Documentation capture lessons learned and best practices throughout the project lifecycle. Documenting these insights allows the organization to learn from past experiences and improve future project performance. This includes maintaining project records, documenting decisions, and capturing any valuable knowledge gained during the project.

Integration Management enhances project scheduling by aligning the project schedule with scope, cost, and quality requirements. It ensures that the schedule is realistic and achievable, considering all project constraints and dependencies. It also facilitates the coordination of dependencies across different workstreams, ensuring that tasks are sequenced logically and that resources are available when needed. For example, if one workstream is dependent on the completion of another, integration management ensures that this dependency is clearly defined and managed within the schedule.

Furthermore, integration management helps in managing schedule constraints and trade-offs. Integration management provides the framework for making these decisions in a way that minimizes the overall impact on the project. Finally, integration management helps coordinate milestones. By clearly defining milestones and their dependencies, it ensures that the project stays on track and that key deliverables are completed as planned.

The integration management plan is typically created at the beginning of a project and is continually updated throughout the project life cycle. The plan serves as a guide for the project team to ensure that all project management processes work together to achieve the project objectives.

Test Your Understanding 6.48
Which of the following best describes the primary purpose of Project Integration Management?
A. To ensure that the project follows a strict schedule and budget.
B. To coordinate all project elements so they work harmoniously toward objectives.
C. To resolve conflicts among team members and stakeholders.
D. To manage project risks and uncertainties effectively.

Test Your Understanding 6.49
Which of the following activities is MOST associated with the Knowledge Management and Documentation aspect of Integration Management?
A. Assigning work packages to team members.
B. Reviewing and approving budget adjustments.
C. Defining milestones and dependencies in the project schedule.
D. Maintaining project records and capturing lessons learned.

6.11 Project Controls

Project controls are the processes, tools, and techniques used to measure progress, identify variances, forecast outcomes, and take corrective actions to ensure project success. In predictive environments, where detailed planning occurs upfront, robust project controls help maintain the project's course and minimize deviations from the established baseline. They provide the structure for monitoring performance, governing changes, and ultimately delivering the intended outcomes.

The importance of project controls in predictive methodologies stems from the sequential nature of these projects. Because each phase builds upon the previous one, any deviation early in the project can have a cascading effect, impacting subsequent phases and potentially jeopardizing the entire project. Project controls act as an early warning system, enabling project managers to identify potential issues before they escalate and implement corrective actions to keep the project on track. They also provide a mechanism for managing changes, which are inevitable in any project, ensuring that changes are assessed for their impact and incorporated in a controlled manner. Effective project controls demonstrate accountability to stakeholders and ensure that resources are used efficiently.

Several key project control processes guide predictive projects. *Scope Control* focuses on managing scope creep, which is the uncontrolled expansion of the project scope beyond its original boundaries. It involves defining the project scope clearly, establishing a change control process, and carefully monitoring any proposed changes to ensure they are justified and do not negatively impact the project's objectives.

Schedule Control involves tracking the project's progress against the established schedule baseline. It includes activities like monitoring task completion, identifying schedule variances, and taking corrective actions to address any delays. Techniques like critical path method (CPM) and Gantt charts are often used in schedule control. *Cost Control* focuses on managing the project budget. It includes activities like cost estimating, budgeting, forecasting, and variance analysis. Earned Value Management (EVM) is a powerful tool used in cost control to measure project performance against the budget baseline.

Quality Control ensures that project deliverables meet the defined quality standards. It involves activities like quality inspections, testing, and audits to verify that the project's outputs are of acceptable quality. *Risk Control* involves identifying, assessing, and mitigating project risks. It includes developing a risk management plan, monitoring risks throughout the project lifecycle, and implementing risk response strategies.

Change Control provides a structured process for handling changes to the project. It ensures that all changes are formally requested, evaluated for their impact, and approved before being implemented. A well-defined change control process prevents uncontrolled changes that can disrupt the project. Finally, *Communication Control* ensures consistent reporting and stakeholder updates. It involves establishing a communication plan, distributing project information to stakeholders regularly, and managing stakeholder expectations. These control processes, working in concert, provide the necessary framework for managing predictive projects effectively and achieving successful outcomes.

Test Your Understanding 6.50
What is the primary role of project controls in predictive environments?
A. To ensure team members complete tasks in the correct order.
B. To guarantee that no changes will occur during the project lifecycle.
C. To eliminate all project risks before execution begins.
D. To provide tools and techniques to measure progress and implement corrective actions.

Test Your Understanding 6.51
You are managing a construction project in a predictive environment. During the foundation phase, a deviation from the baseline schedule is identified. Why is early detection of this issue critical?
A. Because it prevents stakeholder communication from being disrupted.
B. Because deviations in early phases can cascade and impact later phases.
C. Because it allows the project to completely avoid scope creep.
D. Because once the baseline is set, it cannot be changed.

6.12 Artifacts

In predictive, plan-based projects, meticulous documentation helps maintain control and ensure successful project delivery. Documentation takes the form of "artifacts," which in project management terms are any tangible or digital outputs created throughout the project lifecycle. These artifacts serve as evidence of project work, provide a historical record, and facilitate communication among stakeholders.

Several essential artifacts are commonly used in predictive projects. The *project charter*, as previously discussed, formally authorizes the project and outlines its objectives, high-level scope, and key stakeholders. The *project management plan* is a comprehensive document that covers all aspects of project execution, monitoring, controlling, and closure. It integrates all subsidiary plans, providing a detailed roadmap for managing the project.

The *work breakdown structure* (WBS) is a hierarchical decomposition of the project's scope, breaking down deliverables into manageable work packages. The *Gantt Chart* provides a visual representation of the project schedule, showing task dependencies, durations, and milestones.

Baseline documents measure project performance. The scope baseline comprises the WBS, WBS Dictionary (which provides detailed information about each work package), and the scope statement. These documents define the approved scope of work against which actual performance is measured. The schedule baseline is the approved project schedule, used as the benchmark for tracking schedule performance. The cost baseline represents the approved budget for the project, used for tracking cost performance. These baselines, once established, are only changed through a formal change control process.

The *risk register* documents all identified project risks, their potential impact, and planned response strategies. The *change log* records all approved and rejected changes to the project, providing a history of modifications and their impact. The *issue log* tracks ongoing project issues and their resolutions, helping to manage and resolve problems effectively.

Performance reports provide regular updates on project status. Status reports summarize the project's current progress compared to the plan, highlighting any areas of concern. Variance reports detail schedule and cost deviations from the baseline, explaining the reasons for the variances and any corrective actions taken. *Forecasting reports*, often based on earned value analysis, project future performance based on current trends.

Quality control checklists are used to ensure that deliverables meet predefined quality standards. They provide a structured way to verify that all required quality checks have been performed. Finally, the *lessons learned register* captures knowledge gained during the project, both positive and negative, for future projects. It's a valuable resource for continuous improvement in project management practices. These documented artifacts are not merely administrative overhead; they are tools that empower project managers to maintain control, make informed decisions, and deliver successful projects.

Test Your Understanding 6.52
A project manager is preparing a document that authorizes the project, outlines its objectives, defines the high-level scope, and identifies the key stakeholders. Which artifact is the manager creating?
A. Work Breakdown Structure (WBS)
B. Project Charter
C. Project Management Plan
D. Scope Baseline

Test Your Understanding 6.53
A stakeholder requests to increase the project budget by 10% to add new functionality. Which artifact would formally record the approval or rejection of this modification?
A. Change Log
B. Cost Baseline
C. Variance Report
D. Lessons Learned Register

6.13 Chapter Summary

This chapter provided an overview of the predictive, plan-based approach to project management, also known as the waterfall approach. While this traditional approach is still popular in certain scenarios, its effectiveness can be influenced by the organizational structure. Additionally, we explored the five process groups of project management and the activities involved in each process. You also learned about work package, work breakdown structure, critical path method, Gantt chart, cost variance, schedule variance, and project components. We concluded the chapter with a discussion on the integration management plan and project controls.

6.14 Case Study

Revisit the case study in Chapter 1. Perform the following tasks:
Assuming that your team has decided to use the predictive approach for this project, create a Work Breakdown Structure (WBS) and identify the critical path. Determine the estimated time required to complete the project, and ensure that you use the work package and network diagram.

6.15 MS Project Exercise 3

Resource Setup and Assignment

Before you begin, ensure that you have "Exercise 2" open.

Part 1: Creating a Resource List
1. Navigate to the "View" tab at the top of the screen.
2. Select "Resource Sheet". This action will open a new view for resource input.
3. In the "Resource Name" field, input the name of your resource. This could be an individual, a team, or equipment—essentially, anything that will be utilized to complete project tasks.
4. If necessary, provide additional details such as the resource's "Max. Units" (the resource's maximum capacity) and "Std. Rate" (the standard pay rate for the resource).

Part 2: Assigning Resources to Tasks
5. Return to the "Gantt Chart" view by selecting "Gantt Chart" from the "View" tab.
6. Open the "Task Information" dialog box by double-clicking on a task.
7. Navigate to the "Resources" tab within the dialog box.
8. From the "Resource Name" dropdown, select the resource you wish to assign to the task. Note that it's possible to assign multiple resources to a single task.
9. Close the dialog box by clicking "OK". The resource is now assigned to the task. You should see the resource name next to the task in the "Gantt Chart" view, indicating that the resource has been assigned.
10. Repeat this process for all tasks.

Part 3: Viewing Resource Assignments
11. To view a summary of resource assignments, navigate to the "View" tab and select either "Resource Usage" or "Task Usage". These views display how each resource is allocated across all tasks.
12. Identify any overallocated resources. In Microsoft Project, resources that are overallocated are highlighted in red in the "Resource Sheet" view. Overallocation occurs when a resource is assigned to more tasks than they can concurrently handle based on their availability. For instance, if a resource named "Developer" is assigned to two overlapping tasks—"Design Phase" (10 days duration) and "Development Phase" (20 days duration)—and both tasks are scheduled to occur simultaneously, the "Developer" is overallocated because they're expected to work on two tasks at once.
13. Level Resources: Resource leveling is the process of resolving resource overallocation. By clicking on "Resource > Level All", Microsoft Project will automatically adjust the schedule to eliminate overallocations.
14. After leveling, review the results. Microsoft Project makes decisions based on algorithms and may not consider real-world implications. Ensure that the new schedule is still practical for your project.

6.16 References

Angeleski, M., Kostoska, O., & Zdraveski, D. (2025). Project Management Life Cycle Approaches for Software Development. *BNEJSS*, 11(2), 64-70.
Nizma, C., Bangun, R., Benhur, B., Cahyoginarti, C., & Zuardi, M. (2024). The role of organizational structure in project management. *Jurnal Syntax Transformation*, *5*(3), 512-519.
Thesing, T., Feldmann, C., & Burchardt, M. (2021). Agile versus waterfall project management: decision model for selecting the appropriate approach to a project. *Procedia Computer Science*, *181*, 746-756.

6.17 Solutions to Test Your Understanding

6.1 B; 6.2 A; 6.3 C; 6.4 A; 6.5 C; 6.6 C; 6.7 D; 6.8 B; 6.9 A; 6.10 D; 6.11 C; 6.12 C; 6.13 C; 6.14 B; 6.15 D; 6.16 A; 6.17 B; 6.18 D; 6.19 C; 6.20 B; 6.21 A; 6.22 C; 6.23 B; 6.24 B; 6.25 A; 6.26 B; 6.27 D; 6.28 C; 6.29 D; 6.30 A; 6.31 B; 6.32 D; 6.33 C; 6.34 A; 6.35 C; 6.36 C; 6.37 B; 6.38 D; 6.39 C; 6.40 B; 6.41 B; 6.42 D; 6.43 A; 6.44 A; 6.45 B; 6.46 A; 6.47 D; 6.48 B; 6.49 D; 6.50 D, 6.51 B, 6.52 B, 6.53 A,.

Chapter 7: Agile Mindset

Chapter Learning Outcomes

7.1 Describe the evolution of methodology from waterfall to agile.
7.2 Identify various agile frameworks and methodologies.
7.3 Compare agile planning with predictive project planning.
7.4 List agile team roles and responsibilities.
7.5 Explain the concept of self-organizing teams.

7.1 Traditional Approach

Project management methodologies have evolved significantly over time, adapting to the changing needs of projects and industries. The Waterfall methodology, discussed in the last chapter, is characterized by its linear, phase-by-phase structure. Each phase of the project is completed sequentially before moving on to the next, much like water flowing down a waterfall. This rigid structure emphasizes detailed upfront planning and documentation, with a strong focus on adhering to the initial plan. A key characteristic of Waterfall is that testing typically occurs relatively late in the project lifecycle, which can make it more difficult and costly to fix defects discovered at that stage.

The *planning* phase involves defining the project's scope, objectives, deliverables, timelines, budget, resources, and risk management strategy. A comprehensive project plan is developed, outlining how the project will be executed, monitored, and controlled. This plan serves as the roadmap for the project team and is the benchmark against which project performance is measured. In an office building example, this phase would involve the client and project team defining the project goals (e.g., build a modern, energy-efficient office building within a specific budget and timeframe), conducting feasibility studies, developing a detailed project plan with schedules, budgets, resource allocation, and risk assessments.

The *requirements gathering/ systems analysis* phase focuses on collecting and documenting all the project requirements. This involves interviewing stakeholders, conducting surveys, analyzing existing systems, and using various elicitation techniques to understand what the project needs to achieve. The outcome of this phase is a comprehensive requirements document (or a set of documents) that serves as the foundation for all subsequent phases. For the office building, this would involve detailed discussions with the client about their needs, including the number of offices, types of spaces (conference rooms, break rooms, etc.), desired amenities, accessibility requirements, sustainability goals, budget limitations, and regulatory compliance needs.

In the *design* phase, the project team creates a detailed design based on the approved requirements. This translates the "what" of the requirements into the "how" of the solution. This includes architectural designs, system specifications, user interface mockups, database schemas, and other design documents, depending on the nature of the project. For the office building, this would involve architects creating detailed blueprints, structural engineers designing the building's framework and systems (HVAC, electrical, plumbing), interior designers planning the layout and aesthetics, and landscape architects designing the surrounding grounds.

The *development* phase involves building the actual product or system based on the approved design. Developers write code, construct physical structures, or create the deliverables as specified in the design documents. In the office building example, this would be the actual construction of the building, including site preparation, laying the foundation, erecting the walls, installing building systems, finishing the interior, and landscaping the grounds.

Once the development phase is complete, the product or system is thoroughly *tested* to ensure it meets the specified requirements and is free of defects. This phase can involve various types of testing, such as unit testing, integration testing, system testing, and user acceptance testing. For the building, this would involve inspections of all systems (electrical, plumbing, HVAC), structural integrity tests, safety inspections, and final walk-throughs with the client to ensure everything meets their expectations and complies with building codes.

After successful testing, the product or system is *deployed* or released to the end-users or client. This may involve installing software, launching a new website, or handing over the keys to a newly constructed building. This phase marks the transition from project development to operational use. For the office building, this would be the official handover of the building to the client, obtaining necessary occupancy permits, and its opening for use by the tenants.

Even after deployment, projects often require ongoing *maintenance* to fix bugs, address user issues, and implement any necessary updates or enhancements. This phase ensures the continued operation and effectiveness of the delivered product or system. For the office building, this would include ongoing repairs, preventative maintenance of building systems, landscaping, and potential renovations or additions in the future.

The sequential nature of these phases in Waterfall means that each phase must be fully completed and approved before the next phase can begin. This rigidity, while providing structure and control, can also make it difficult to accommodate changes in requirements or address issues discovered late in the project. A core problem is that Waterfall requires the client to know and articulate all their needs upfront, often before they have a clear understanding of what is truly possible or desirable. This can lead to a mismatch between the final product and the client's evolving needs. The relatively late testing phase, in particular, can be problematic, as defects discovered at this stage can be expensive and time-consuming to fix, often requiring rework of earlier phases.

This is compounded by the fact that Waterfall's structure makes it difficult, if not impossible, to go back and revise earlier phases once they are "complete." Any changes, even small ones, necessitate a formal change request process, which can be slow and bureaucratic. In Waterfall, each phase is treated as a distinct step, and the output of one phase becomes the input for the next. Once a phase is signed off, it's considered "frozen." This rigidity stems from the emphasis on upfront planning and documentation. However, in reality, requirements often evolve, or new information comes to light during development.

Furthermore, the clear delineation between roles in Waterfall projects can sometimes lead to a lack of communication and collaboration between different groups, such as programmers and testers. This can create silos where individuals focus primarily on their specific phase without a strong sense of shared ownership for the overall project success. For example, programmers might not be as invested in the testing process, and testers might not have sufficient insight into the code being developed, hindering early detection of potential issues. This lack of cross-functional collaboration can exacerbate the problems caused by late testing, as issues are often identified later and require more extensive rework because the original developers may have moved on to other tasks.

Test Your Understanding 7.1

A software development team using Waterfall is frustrated because testers feel disconnected from the development process, and programmers are not involved in quality checks. Which limitation of Waterfall does this scenario illustrate?

A. Excessive flexibility in requirements gathering.
B. A lack of formal documentation to support handoffs.
C. Too much emphasis on iterative feedback loops.
D. Silos between roles leading to weak cross-functional collaboration.

Test Your Understanding 7.2
In the office building example, which activity best represents the design phase of the Waterfall methodology?
A. Conducting feasibility studies to confirm project viability.
B. Erecting the walls, installing plumbing, and finishing interiors.
C. Creating blueprints and structural engineering plans.
D. Performing inspections and client walk-throughs.

Test Your Understanding 7.3
A project manager emphasizes that once the planning phase is signed off, the scope and budget will be considered "frozen." What is the main benefit of this rigidity in Waterfall?
A. It provides clear structure and control for monitoring performance.
B. It ensures that requirements can evolve easily during development.
C. It reduces the need for stakeholder input during execution.
D. It guarantees that no change requests will be necessary.

7.2 Agile Approaches

Agile project management represents a significant shift from traditional, plan-driven approaches like Waterfall. It's an iterative and incremental methodology that emphasizes flexibility, collaboration, and rapid delivery of value. Instead of long, sequential phases, Agile projects are broken down into short cycles, called sprints or iterations, typically lasting one to four weeks. Each sprint involves a complete cycle of planning, execution, testing, and review, resulting in a potentially shippable product increment. This iterative approach allows for continuous feedback and adaptation, making Agile well-suited for projects with evolving requirements, complex environments, and a need for frequent adjustments.

Agile is not a single methodology but rather a collection of frameworks and practices that embody these principles. Popular Agile frameworks include Scrum, Kanban, and Extreme Programming (XP). While each framework has its specific practices, they all share a common focus on iterative development, frequent feedback, and close collaboration with stakeholders.

The "why" behind Agile is compelling, as it offers numerous benefits and addresses the shortcomings of traditional methodologies in certain situations. One of the advantages is increased flexibility. Agile's iterative nature allows projects to adapt to changing requirements and market conditions quickly. Instead of being locked into a rigid plan, Agile teams can incorporate feedback and adjust the project direction as needed.

Another benefit is faster time to market. By delivering working increments frequently, Agile projects can get valuable products or features into the hands of users sooner. This allows for early validation of ideas and faster realization of business value.

Agile also promotes improved quality. The emphasis on frequent testing and continuous integration helps to identify and address defects early in the development process, reducing the cost and impact of fixing them later. The close collaboration with stakeholders throughout the project also ensures that the delivered product meets their needs and expectations.

Furthermore, Agile fosters increased team morale and productivity. The collaborative and self-organizing nature of Agile teams empowers team members, leading to greater job satisfaction and increased productivity. Agile teams are often more motivated and engaged because they have a greater sense of ownership and responsibility.

Finally, Agile offers better risk management. By breaking the project into smaller iterations, risks are identified and addressed more frequently. This reduces the likelihood of large-scale problems occurring late in the project, minimizing the overall project risk.

Agile is well-suited for projects with evolving requirements, meaning the needs of the customer or the market are likely to change during the project's lifecycle. This is common in rapidly changing industries or when developing innovative products where initial understanding of the final product may be incomplete. For example, a startup developing a new mobile app might initially have a core set of features in mind, but as they gather user feedback and see how the market responds, they'll likely need to add, modify, or remove features. Agile's iterative nature and adaptability make it ideal for these dynamic scenarios.

Agile also thrives in complex environments like software development and medical equipment design, where intricate components and dependencies require collaboration, frequent communication, and continuous integration. Its iterative approach, using short cycles and working prototypes, enables teams to adapt to issues, integrate changes, and validate early, reducing late-stage risks.

A need for rapid delivery is another key driver for choosing Agile. In today's fast-paced business world, getting a product or feature to market quickly provides competitive advantage. Agile's iterative approach and focus on delivering working increments frequently allows for faster time to market compared to traditional methodologies. Instead of waiting for the entire product to be completed, Agile teams can release smaller, functional pieces, getting value to customers sooner and gaining valuable feedback early on.

Finally, Agile is most effective in organizations that foster a collaborative culture, where the project team and stakeholders are willing to work closely together. Agile emphasizes frequent communication, shared ownership, and close collaboration between developers, product owners, and customers. This collaborative environment helps to build trust, ensure that everyone is aligned on the project goals, and facilitates quick decision-making.

Examples of projects where Agile is often a good fit include software development, web design, marketing campaigns, research and development projects, and even hardware development in some circumstances. However, Agile is not a one-size-fits-all solution. The choice of project management methodology should depend on the specific characteristics of the project, including its size, complexity, and, most importantly, the stability of its requirements. For projects with very stable and well-defined requirements, where changes are unlikely, a more traditional approach like Waterfall might still be appropriate. The key is to carefully assess the project context and choose the methodology that best aligns with its needs.

Test Your Understanding 7.4
During a sprint review, a client requests a change that alters the product's direction. How should the Agile team respond?
A. Reject the change since the sprint scope is already defined.
B. Pause the sprint and restart planning to accommodate the change.
C. Escalate the issue to senior management to decide.
D. Note the change and consider it for the next sprint planning session.

Test Your Understanding 7.5
A medical device project involves multiple complex dependencies and requires frequent communication between engineers and regulators. Why would Agile be an effective fit here?
A. Because Agile avoids the need for regulatory compliance.
B. Because Agile prevents any requirement changes.
C. Because Agile fosters collaboration and iterative validation.
D. Because Agile eliminates the need for testing prototypes.

Test Your Understanding 7.6
A project team using Agile reports higher job satisfaction and stronger motivation. Which Agile principle explains this?
A. Empowerment of self-organizing teams.
B. Eliminating the need for customer collaboration.
C. Shifting accountability away from the team to management.
D. Prioritizing contracts over trust-based collaboration.

Test Your Understanding 7.7
Which type of project is least suitable for Agile?

A. A marketing campaign requiring iterative testing and feedback.
B. A web design project where requirements are evolving.
C. A software product launch with unclear customer needs.
D. A construction project with fixed regulations and stable requirements.

7.3 Agile Principles and Mindset

Agile project management isn't just about adopting a set of practices; it's about embracing a set of principles and a specific mindset. These principles and the Agile mindset guide decision-making and shape the way Agile teams work. At the heart of Agile lies the Agile Manifesto, a concise document that articulates the core values and principles that underpin Agile methodologies (Alzahrani, 2024).

The Agile Manifesto consists of four core values and twelve supporting principles. The four values emphasize:

Individuals and interactions over processes and tools: Agile values direct communication and collaboration among team members over strict adherence to rigid processes and tools. While processes and tools are important, they should support, not hinder, human interaction.
Working software over comprehensive documentation: The primary measure of progress in Agile is working software. While documentation is important, it should be concise and focused on supporting the development of working software, not replacing it.
Customer collaboration over contract negotiation: Agile prioritizes continuous collaboration with the customer throughout the project lifecycle. This ensures that the delivered product meets the customer's evolving needs and expectations. Contract negotiations are important, but they shouldn't overshadow the ongoing dialogue with the customer.
Responding to change over following a plan: Agile recognizes that change is inevitable in complex projects. It emphasizes adaptability and encourages teams to embrace change, even late in development, rather than rigidly adhering to an outdated plan.

These four values are further elaborated in twelve supporting principles, which provide more specific guidance on how to put the values into practice. These principles cover areas like iterative development, frequent feedback, continuous delivery, self-organizing teams, and technical excellence. They emphasize delivering working software frequently, welcoming changes in requirements, fostering collaboration, and building projects around motivated individuals.

Agile thinking is characterized by iterative and incremental development. Instead of delivering the entire product at once, Agile projects deliver small, working increments at regular intervals. Each iteration, or sprint, is a mini-project in itself, involving all the necessary activities to produce a potentially shippable product increment. This iterative approach allows for frequent feedback and validation, ensuring that the project is on track and meeting the customer's needs. The incremental nature of Agile means that the product is built up gradually, with each iteration adding new features or improvements.

Agile culture is built on collaboration, adaptability, and a strong customer focus. Agile teams are typically self-organizing and cross-functional, with members working closely together to achieve common goals. Collaboration extends beyond the development team to include the customer and other stakeholders. Agile teams embrace change and are constantly looking for ways to improve their processes and deliver value more effectively. A strong customer focus is central to Agile, with teams prioritizing the delivery of features that provide the most value to the customer.

Leadership plays a crucial role in Agile. Agile leaders are not traditional command-and-control managers; they are servant leaders who empower and support their teams. They create an environment where team members can collaborate effectively, make decisions autonomously, and continuously improve. Agile leaders focus on removing impediments, facilitating communication, and fostering a culture of trust and respect. They also champion the Agile mindset and principles throughout the organization, helping to create a culture of agility.

Test Your Understanding 7.8
Which Agile Manifesto value emphasizes adaptability in the face of unexpected changes?
A. Individuals and interactions over processes and tools
B. Working software over comprehensive documentation
C. Customer collaboration over contract negotiation
D. Responding to change over following a plan

Test Your Understanding 7.9
A project manager insists on following a strict process tool that limits team discussions and slows down decision-making. Which Agile principle is being overlooked in this situation?
A. Emphasizing customer collaboration
B. Prioritizing individuals and interactions
C. Delivering working software frequently
D. Supporting technical excellence

Test Your Understanding 7.10
During a sprint review, the customer requests a significant change in requirements. The team debates whether to accept it, as it was not in the original plan. According to Agile principles, what should the team do?
A. Reject the request since the plan has already been set.
B. Accept the request only if it does not affect the budget.
C. Welcome the change, adapting the backlog to reflect new priorities.
D. Escalate the decision to senior management for approval.

Test Your Understanding 7.11

In an Agile organization, the leader's role differs from traditional management. Which of the following best describes an Agile leader?
A. A servant leader who empowers teams and removes impediments.
B. A taskmaster who focuses primarily on schedules and budgets.
C. A command-and-control figure who enforces strict compliance.
D. A negotiator who prioritizes contracts over collaboration.

7.4 Scrum

Agile project management isn't a monolithic entity; it's implemented through various frameworks and methodologies, each with its own specific practices and terminology. Scrum is arguably the most popular and widely adopted Agile framework. It provides a structured yet flexible approach to managing complex projects, particularly software development (Grebić and Stojanović, 2021).

Scrum is characterized by its use of short, iterative cycles called sprints, typically lasting one to four weeks. It emphasizes empirical process control, meaning that decisions are based on observation and experimentation rather than detailed upfront planning. Scrum relies on transparency, inspection, and adaptation to manage complexity and risk. It's a lightweight framework that provides a structure for teams to self-organize and deliver value incrementally.

Within Scrum, there are three key roles: the Product Owner, the Scrum Master, and the Development Team. The *Product Owner* is the voice of the customer and is responsible for maximizing the value of the product. They manage the Product Backlog, a prioritized list of all the features, requirements, and user stories needed for the product. The Product Owner works closely with the stakeholders to understand their needs and translate them into actionable items in the Product Backlog. They are the champion for the customer and the business.

The *Scrum Master* is a servant leader who facilitates the Scrum process and helps the team remove impediments. They ensure that the team follows Scrum principles and practices and coaches the team to improve their performance. The Scrum Master is not a traditional project manager; they do not assign tasks or control the team. Instead, they focus on creating an environment where the team can self-organize and be most effective.

The *Development Team* is a cross-functional group of individuals responsible for building the product increment during each sprint. They are self-organizing, meaning they decide how to best accomplish the work within the sprint. The Development Team possesses all the skills necessary to deliver the product increment, including design, development, testing, and integration.

Scrum structures its iterative development process around a series of key events, each designed to serve a specific purpose in managing the sprint cycle. These events are time-boxed, meaning they have a fixed duration, and are essential for maintaining rhythm and focus within the Scrum process.

Sprint Planning kicks off each sprint, bringing the Product Owner and the Development Team together to collaboratively select a set of items from the Product Backlog to include in the current sprint. This selection forms the Sprint Backlog, which becomes the team's detailed plan for the upcoming sprint. It outlines the "what" -- the user stories or product backlog items they commit to deliver. Crucially, during Sprint Planning, the team also plans the "how" -- they determine how they will accomplish the work outlined in the Sprint Backlog. This involves breaking down larger stories into smaller tasks, estimating effort, and assigning responsibilities. The Sprint Planning meeting ensures that the team has a shared understanding of the sprint goals and a concrete plan for achieving them. It's a collaborative process that empowers the team to take ownership of their work.

The *Daily Stand-up* is a short, daily meeting (typically 15 minutes or less) for the Development Team members to synchronize their work and discuss any impediments they are facing. This is not a status report to the Scrum Master; it's a team-internal coordination session. Each team member typically shares what they accomplished since the last stand-up, what they plan to do today, and any roadblocks preventing them from making progress. The Daily Stand-up helps to identify potential issues early on, facilitates communication and collaboration within the team, and ensures that everyone is aligned on the sprint goals. It's a quick check-in that allows the team to adapt their plan as needed and stay on track. The Scrum Master facilitates the stand-up, ensuring it stays focused and productive.

The *Sprint Review* takes place at the end of each sprint. The Development Team demonstrates the working product increment they have developed during the sprint to the Product Owner and stakeholders. This provides an opportunity to gather feedback on the increment and ensure that it meets their needs. The Sprint Review is not just a demo; it's a collaborative discussion about the product and its progress. Stakeholders can provide valuable input, suggest changes, and help the team to refine the product backlog for future sprints. The Product Owner uses the feedback to assess if the delivered increment meets the sprint goal and if it is in line with the overall product vision.

Finally, the *Sprint Retrospective* follows the Sprint Review. This is a meeting dedicated to reflection and continuous improvement. The Development Team holds a retrospective to examine the sprint and identify areas for improvement in their processes, teamwork, and tools. The focus is on learning from the past and finding ways to make future sprints more effective. The retrospective is not about assigning blame; it's about creating a safe space for the team to discuss what went well, what could be improved, and what actions they can take to make those improvements. This continuous feedback loop helps Agile teams learn and adapt, becoming more efficient and effective over time. The Scrum Master facilitates the retrospective, encouraging open and honest communication and helping the team to develop concrete action items for improvement.

Scrum, beyond its defined events and roles, also utilizes three core artifacts that act as tangible representations of the work being done and the progress being made. These artifacts -- the Product Backlog, the Sprint Backlog, and the Increment -- are crucial for transparency, inspection, and adaptation within the Scrum framework.

As explained in Chapter 4, the *Product Backlog* is a single source of truth, a prioritized list of all the work that needs to be done to create the product. The *Sprint Backlog* is a subset of the Product Backlog. It contains the specific items that the Development Team has committed to complete during the current sprint. This commitment is made collaboratively during Sprint Planning, where the team and the Product Owner work together to select the most valuable and achievable items for the sprint. Additionally, the Sprint Backlog provides a more detailed plan than the Product Backlog, outlining the specific tasks required to complete the selected items.

The *Increment* is the potentially shippable product increment created during each sprint. It's the tangible outcome of the sprint, representing the sum of all the completed Sprint Backlog items. The Increment is "potentially shippable" because, ideally, it meets the team's definition of done and could be released to customers if desired. While not every increment is necessarily released, the goal is to create increments that are always in a releasable state. The Increment is more than just the code or software; it also includes any necessary documentation, testing, and integration work.

Test Your Understanding 7.12
Which principle of Scrum ensures that decisions are based on real-world results rather than upfront assumptions?
A. Predictive planning

B. Empirical process control
C. Critical path analysis
D. Earned value management

Test Your Understanding 7.13
During a Sprint Planning meeting, the team discusses how to break down large backlog items into smaller tasks and estimate effort. What is the result of this meeting?
A. The Product Backlog
B. The Sprint Retrospective
C. The Sprint Backlog
D. The Increment

Test Your Understanding 7.14
A Development Team member asks if the Daily Stand-up should be used to report progress to the Scrum Master. What is the correct guidance?
A. No, it is for the Development Team to synchronize work.
B. Yes, the Scrum Master uses it to track team performance.
C. Yes, but only if management requests status updates.
D. No, it is primarily for stakeholders to review progress.

Test Your Understanding 7.15
A software company finishes a sprint and demonstrates the working product increment to stakeholders. Stakeholders provide feedback and request new features. Which Scrum event is being described?
A. Sprint Planning
B. Sprint Review
C. Daily Stand-up
D. Sprint Retrospective

Test Your Understanding 7.16
At the end of a sprint, the Scrum Team meets to discuss what went well, what could be improved, and what actions they will take to improve future sprints. Which event is this?
A. Sprint Review
B. Sprint Retrospective
C. Backlog Refinement
D. Daily Stand-up

Test Your Understanding 7.17
A team delivers a working increment, but it is not released to customers immediately. Why is this still acceptable in Scrum?
A. Because every increment is potentially shippable.
B. Because only the Product Owner decides when to develop features.
C. Because Scrum avoids frequent integration to reduce costs.
D. Because testing is completed only at the end of the project.

Test Your Understanding 7.18
Which Scrum artifact represents the sum of completed work that meets the definition of done and is potentially releasable?
A. Product Backlog
B. Sprint Backlog
C. Increment

D. Burndown Chart

Test Your Understanding 7.19
A Development Team of five is self-organizing. Mid-sprint, a manager insists on assigning tasks to individual team members to improve efficiency. How should the Scrum Master handle this?
A. Allow the manager to assign tasks since they oversee resources.
B. Adjust the sprint scope so tasks are easier to allocate.
C. Ask the Product Owner to intervene and reassign tasks.
D. Remind the manager that task assignments are decided by the Development Team.

7.5 Kanban

Kanban is another popular Agile framework, offering a different approach to managing work compared to Scrum. While both are Agile, they differ significantly in their structure and emphasis. Kanban is a visual system for managing work as it moves through a process. It's particularly well-suited for projects or processes that involve a continuous flow of work, rather than distinct sprints.

At the heart of Kanban are several core principles and practices. It emphasizes visualizing the workflow, limiting work in progress (WIP), managing flow, making process policies explicit, and continuously improving. Unlike Scrum, Kanban doesn't prescribe specific roles or time-boxed iterations. Instead, it focuses on optimizing the flow of work through the system.

A central element of Kanban is the Kanban board. This visual tool typically takes the form of a board with columns representing different stages of the workflow. For example, a simple Kanban board might have columns like "To Do," "In Progress," "Testing," and "Done." Each task or work item is represented by a card (often a sticky note or a digital equivalent) that moves across the board as it progresses through the workflow. This visualization makes it easy to see the status of each task, identify bottlenecks, and track overall progress. The Kanban board provides transparency and shared understanding of the workflow (Alaidaros et al., 2021).

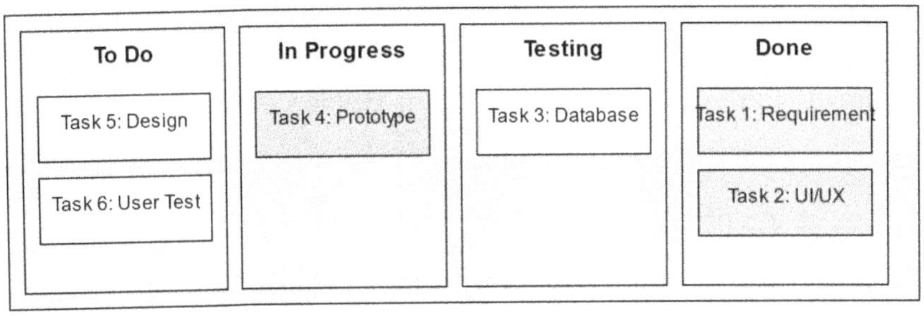

Figure 7.1 A sample Kanban board.

Managing workflow and limiting work in progress (WIP) are crucial aspects of Kanban. Limiting WIP means setting a maximum number of tasks that can be in progress at any given time in each stage of the workflow. This helps to prevent bottlenecks and improve flow by focusing the team's efforts on completing tasks rather than starting new ones. Limiting WIP also forces the team to address any impediments that are blocking progress, as they cannot start new work until the current work is completed. This focus on flow and completion helps to improve overall efficiency. To effectively manage and optimize this flow, Kanban teams often track two key metrics: cycle time and lead time.

The Cycle Time metric measures the time it takes for a task to move from the "In Progress" column to the "Done" column (or the equivalent final stage of the workflow). It focuses specifically on the time spent actively working on the task. Tracking cycle time helps the team identify bottlenecks within their active work stages. For example, if the cycle time for tasks in the "Testing" column suddenly increases, it indicates a potential problem in the testing process that needs to be addressed.

The Lead Time metric measures the total time it takes for a task to go from the moment it is requested or entered into the system (e.g., placed in the "To Do" column) all the way to the "Done" column. It encompasses the entire process, including any waiting time between stages. Lead time provides a broader view of the overall process efficiency and responsiveness to requests. A high lead time might be due to bottlenecks in any stage of the workflow, including the "To Do" stage, indicating that requests are waiting too long to be picked up.

Kanban also emphasizes making process policies explicit. This means clearly defining the rules and guidelines for how work moves through the system. For example, the criteria for moving a task from "In Progress" to "Testing" should be clearly defined. Making these policies explicit ensures that everyone on the team understands the process and helps to standardize the way work is handled. This clarity improves communication and reduces confusion.

Continuous improvement is another fundamental principle of Kanban. Teams regularly review their Kanban board and workflow to identify areas for improvement. This can involve adjusting WIP limits, refining process policies, or implementing other changes to optimize the flow of work. Kanban encourages a culture of continuous learning and adaptation, helping teams to become more efficient and effective over time.

Unlike Scrum's time-boxed sprints, Kanban's continuous flow allows for more flexibility and responsiveness to changing priorities. Work can be pulled into the system as needed, rather than being batched into sprints. This makes Kanban particularly well-suited for projects with a continuous flow of work, such as support and maintenance activities, or for teams that are constantly receiving new requests. While Scrum is often associated with software development, Kanban can be applied to a wide range of industries and processes, from manufacturing to marketing.

Test Your Understanding 7.20
Which of the following best describes the main purpose of a Kanban board?
A. To assign tasks to specific team members in advance
B. To visually represent the stages of work and track task progress
C. To enforce strict time-boxed iterations
D. To replace the Product Backlog used in Scrum

Test Your Understanding 7.21
A support team is constantly receiving new customer requests, making it difficult to plan fixed iterations. Which Agile framework would be more effective than Scrum in this case?
A. Kanban
B. PRINCE2
C. Lean Six Sigma
D. Extreme Programming (XP)

Test Your Understanding 7.22
What is the main reason for setting Work In Progress (WIP) limits in Kanban?
A. To maximize the number of tasks being worked on simultaneously
B. To reduce the need for testing and integration
C. To allow the Product Owner to control task assignments
D. To prevent bottlenecks and ensure focus on completing tasks

Test Your Understanding 7.23
Which metric measures the total time from when a task enters the "To Do" column until it reaches "Done"?
A. Cycle Time
B. Velocity
C. Lead Time
D. Burndown Rate

7.6 Extreme Programming (XP)

Extreme Programming (XP) is another influential Agile methodology, particularly known for its emphasis on technical excellence and a set of core practices designed to produce high-quality software efficiently. While it shares the Agile values of flexibility, collaboration, and responding to change, XP focuses heavily on the development practices within a team.

XP is characterized by its focus on short iterations, frequent releases, and close collaboration between developers and customers. It promotes a set of core practices that are designed to improve code quality, reduce defects, and increase developer productivity. Unlike Scrum, which focuses on project management and team organization, XP dives deep into the software development process itself (Akhtar et al., 2022).

Several core XP practices are central to its effectiveness. Test-Driven Development (TDD) is a practice where developers write automated tests before writing the code they are intended to test. This approach forces developers to think about the desired behavior of the code before implementing it, leading to clearer requirements and more robust code. TDD also serves as a form of continuous testing, ensuring that the code meets its specifications throughout the development process. If a test fails, the developer knows immediately that something is wrong and can fix it before moving on.

Pair Programming is another distinctive XP practice where two developers work together on the same code. One developer, the "driver," writes the code, while the other, the "navigator," reviews the code in real-time, offering suggestions and catching potential errors. This constant review helps to improve code quality, share knowledge within the team, and reduce the risk of introducing bugs. While it might seem like it would slow down development, studies have shown that pair programming can actually increase productivity due to the reduced number of defects and the improved knowledge sharing.

Continuous Integration (CI) is a practice where code changes are integrated into the shared codebase frequently, often multiple times a day. This integration is automated, with tests run automatically after each integration to ensure that the changes haven't introduced any regressions. CI helps to prevent integration problems and ensures that the codebase remains stable and working. It allows teams to identify and fix integration issues quickly, preventing them from becoming larger, more complex problems later on.

XP's strengths align well with projects exhibiting high technical complexity, evolving requirements, and a critical need for high code quality. Projects with high technical complexity often involve intricate systems, complex algorithms, or the integration of various technologies. These projects demand a high degree of technical expertise from the development team and require careful attention to design and code quality. XP's emphasis on practices like pair programming, test-driven development, and continuous integration helps to manage this complexity effectively. XP's focus on simple design and refactoring also helps to manage complexity by keeping the codebase clean and maintainable.

Evolving requirements are another key characteristic that makes XP a good fit. XP's iterative and adaptive nature allows teams to respond to these changes quickly and efficiently. Small releases and frequent feedback loops enable teams to incorporate new requirements and adjust the product direction as needed. The Planning Game, with its collaborative approach to prioritizing features, also helps to manage changing requirements by ensuring that the team is always working on the most valuable items.

Finally, XP is particularly well-suited for projects where high code quality is critical for success. This is often the case in projects where the software is safety-critical, mission-critical, or where long-term maintainability is essential. XP's emphasis on practices like test-driven development, pair programming, refactoring, and collective ownership helps to ensure high code quality.

Test Your Understanding 7.24
A development team is building a safety-critical medical device software system. The customer insists on very high code quality with minimal defects. Which XP practice would be most valuable in ensuring this requirement is consistently met?
A. Sprint Reviews
B. Pair Programming
C. Stand-up meetings
D. Kanban board visualization

Test Your Understanding 7.25
What is the main purpose of Test-Driven Development (TDD) in XP?
A. To reduce the time required for user acceptance testing
B. To encourage writing code without predefined requirements
C. To define desired code behavior before implementation
D. To eliminate the need for regression testing

Test Your Understanding 7.26
A team practicing XP notices frequent integration issues when merging code late in the sprint. What XP practice would best address this problem?
A. Continuous Integration
B. The Planning Game
C. Velocity tracking
D. Collective ownership

Test Your Understanding 7.27
Which of the following project environments is XP best suited for?
A. Projects requiring high technical excellence and adaptability
B. Projects with stable, unchanging requirements
C. Projects with minimal customer involvement
D. Projects where documentation is more important than working software

Test Your Understanding 7.28

A team is struggling with complex code that has become hard to maintain. According to XP principles, what should they prioritize?
A. Adding more developers to the project
B. Reducing customer involvement to focus on technical work
C. Extending iteration length to accommodate complexity
D. Implementing refactoring to simplify and clean the codebase

7.7 Other Agile Frameworks

While Scrum, Kanban, Lean Agile, and Extreme Programming (XP) are among the most widely used Agile methodologies, several other frameworks exist to address different scaling and organizational needs (Suvvari, 2019).

SAFe (Scaled Agile Framework) is a scaling framework designed specifically for large enterprises implementing Agile across multiple teams. It addresses the complexities of coordinating numerous Agile teams, aligning their efforts with strategic objectives, and managing dependencies across the organization. SAFe achieves this through a layered structure that aligns strategy with execution. This structure typically includes four levels: Team, Program, Large Solution, and Portfolio.

The Team level focuses on the core Agile principles and practices within individual development teams, often using Scrum or Kanban. The Program level coordinates multiple Agile teams working on a larger product or system. This level introduces the concept of the Agile Release Train (ART), a virtual team of teams that plans, develops, and delivers value incrementally. The Large Solution level is used for even larger initiatives involving multiple ARTs, often coordinating complex system development. Finally, the Portfolio level aligns all development efforts with the overall strategic themes and investment funding of the organization.

SAFe incorporates a blend of Lean principles, Agile development practices, and DevOps principles. Lean principles emphasize eliminating waste, maximizing value, and optimizing the flow of work. Agile development practices provide the foundation for iterative and incremental development, while DevOps principles focus on automating and streamlining the software delivery pipeline. SAFe also introduces structured roles and responsibilities to manage large-scale Agile projects. For example, the Release Train Engineer (RTE) is a key role at the Program level, responsible for facilitating the ART and ensuring that it delivers value predictably. The RTE acts as a servant leader for the ART, coordinating the work of multiple teams and removing impediments.

SAFe provides a comprehensive framework for scaling Agile, but its complexity can also be a challenge. Implementing SAFe requires significant organizational change and a commitment to adopting new ways of working. Organizations must carefully assess their needs and tailor the framework to their specific context. While SAFe offers a structured approach to scaling Agile, it's important to remember that it's not a rigid prescription. Successful SAFe implementations require flexibility and a willingness to adapt the framework to the organization's unique circumstances. Furthermore, effective leadership and a strong commitment to Agile principles are crucial for successful SAFe adoption.

Disciplined Agile Delivery (DAD), part of the Disciplined Agile (DA) toolkit, offers another approach to scaling Agile and integrates Agile, Lean, and DevOps principles into a flexible framework for scaling Agile. Unlike software-centric frameworks, DAD emphasizes end-to-end delivery, from project inception through production and operations, optimizing the delivery pipeline for speed, quality, and value. Its hybrid approach draws from Scrum, Kanban, XP, Lean, and DevOps, allowing teams to tailor practices to their context, project type, and organizational culture.DAD's focus on the full product lifecycle fosters collaboration among stakeholders, ensuring shared goals and effective delivery. It offers six lifecycles -- Agile (iterative, for evolving requirements), Lean (flow-based, for efficiency), Continuous Delivery: Agile (Agile with DevOps for frequent releases), Continuous Delivery: Lean (Lean with DevOps for value flow), Exploratory (for experimentation), and Program (for coordinating multiple teams). This flexibility makes DAD ideal for organizations seeking business agility across diverse contexts.

Test Your Understanding 7.29
Which SAFe level introduces the concept of the Agile Release Train (ART)?
A. Team level
B. Program level
C. Large Solution level
D. Portfolio level

Test Your Understanding 7.30
A large enterprise is struggling to coordinate multiple Agile teams working on the same product. They appoint someone to facilitate collaboration across teams, remove impediments, and ensure predictable value delivery. Which SAFe role best fits this description?
A. Product Owner
B. Scrum Master
C. Release Train Engineer
D. Portfolio Manager

Test Your Understanding 7.31

A company is experimenting with a new product idea and is uncertain about requirements. They want a lifecycle that encourages innovation and learning rather than strict predictability. Which DAD lifecycle should they use?
A. Exploratory Lifecycle
B. Continuous Delivery: Agile
C. Program Lifecycle
D. Lean Lifecycle

Test Your Understanding 7.32
An organization has multiple Agile teams working on complex systems. They need strong alignment with business strategy but also want to keep flexibility in tailoring practices to their context. Which framework might best suit their needs?
A. SAFe, because it provides a highly structured, layered approach to alignment
B. Kanban, because it emphasizes visual workflow without structured scaling
C. Scrum, because it is lightweight and works well with single teams
D. DAD, because it offers lifecycle flexibility and end-to-end focus

7.8 Agile Project Planning and Execution

Agile project planning and execution differ significantly from traditional, plan-driven approaches. Traditional planning, often associated with the Waterfall methodology, emphasizes detailed upfront planning and a fixed scope. Agile planning, on the other hand, is iterative and adaptive, focusing on delivering value incrementally and responding to change.

Agile planning revolves around the concept of user stories. Story mapping is a technique used to organize and prioritize user stories. It involves visually arranging user stories on a two-dimensional map, with the horizontal axis representing the flow of user activity and the vertical axis representing the priority of the stories. Story mapping helps to visualize the overall product backlog and identify dependencies between user stories. It also facilitates release planning by helping the team to identify which stories should be included in each release.

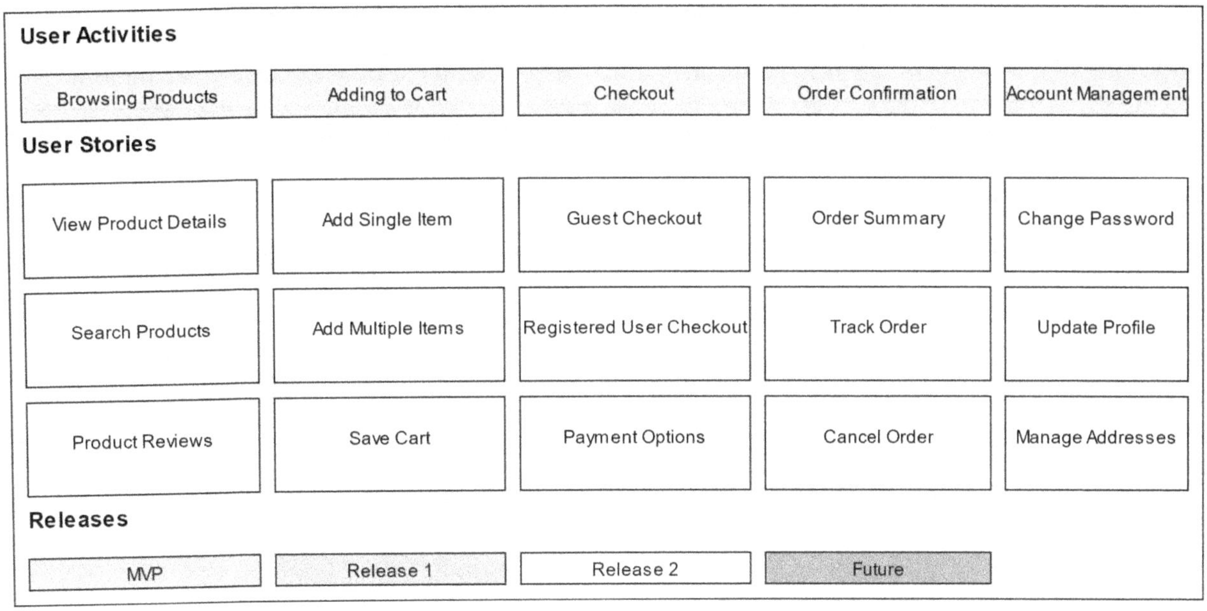

Figure 7.2 Sample story mapping.

Prioritization techniques in Agile planning ensure the most valuable features are delivered first. Since Agile projects are iterative and incremental, deciding which features to build first helps maximize return on investment and meeting customer needs. The MoSCoW method is a common prioritization technique that categorizes user stories based on their importance.

Weighted Shortest Job First (WSJF) is another, more sophisticated prioritization technique that considers both the value and the cost of delay of each user story. It's designed to maximize the economic value of the product by prioritizing the features that deliver the most value in the shortest amount of time. WSJF calculates a score for each user story using the following formula:

WSJF = (Value + Time Criticality + Risk Reduction/Opportunity Enablement) / Job Size

Let's break down each component:

Value: This represents the business value that the user story delivers. It can be measured in terms of revenue, cost savings, increased user engagement, or any other metric that is relevant to the business. It's important to have a consistent way of quantifying value across different user stories.
Time Criticality: This measures the urgency of the user story. How much will the business lose if this feature is not delivered soon? A feature that is time-critical might be tied to a market opportunity, a regulatory requirement, or a dependency on another project. A high time criticality score indicates that the feature should be prioritized.
Risk Reduction/Opportunity Enablement: This component accounts for the value of reducing risk or enabling future opportunities. Some user stories might not deliver immediate business value but are essential for mitigating risks or opening up new possibilities. For example, building a security feature might not generate direct revenue but can significantly reduce the risk of a data breach. Similarly, developing a core infrastructure component might not be

valuable in itself but can enable the development of many other valuable features in the future.
Job Size: This represents the relative size or effort required to complete the user story. It's typically estimated using story points or other relative sizing techniques. A smaller job size means that the feature can be delivered more quickly.

For example, imagine three user stories:

Story A: High value (10), high time criticality (10), low risk reduction (2), medium job size (5). WSJF = (10 + 10 + 2) / 5 = 4.4

Story B: Medium value (7), medium time criticality (7), medium risk reduction (5), small job size (2). WSJF = (7 + 7 + 5) / 2 = 9.5

Story C: Low value (3), low time criticality (3), high risk reduction (8), large job size (8). WSJF = (3 + 3 + 8) / 8 = 1.75

Based on WSJF, Story B would be prioritized first, followed by Story A, and then Story C. Even though Story A has higher value and time criticality than Story B, Story B's smaller job size makes it a more attractive option because it can be delivered more quickly, generating value sooner.

Estimating work in Agile often involves the use of story points, which are relative units of effort used to estimate the size and complexity of user stories. Unlike estimating in hours, which can be very precise but also time-consuming and inaccurate, story points provide a more flexible and relative measure of effort. A story point represents the relative effort required to complete a user story compared to other stories. For example, a story estimated at 2 story points is considered twice as much effort as a story estimated at 1 story point. This relative estimation helps to avoid getting bogged down in detailed estimations early in the project and allows the team to focus on delivering value quickly. While hours can be used in Agile estimation, they're often used at a lower level of planning within a sprint, not for initial story sizing.

Agile release planning is the process of planning the releases of working software increments to the customer. It involves identifying which user stories should be included in each release based on their priority and dependencies. Release planning is typically done at a higher level than sprint planning and focuses on delivering value to the customer over a longer timeframe.

The release plan is not fixed but rather evolves as the project progresses and more information becomes available. It provides a roadmap for delivering value incrementally and allows the team to adjust the release content based on feedback and changing priorities. Agile release planning is a collaborative effort involving the Product Owner, the Development Team, and stakeholders. It ensures that the releases are aligned with the overall product vision and deliver value to the customer. It's not a one-time event but rather an ongoing process that is revisited and adjusted regularly.

Test Your Understanding 7.33
Which of the following best describes the difference between Agile planning and traditional, plan-driven approaches?
A. Agile focuses on detailed upfront planning and fixed scope, while traditional planning adapts to change.
B. Traditional planning emphasizes iterative value delivery, while Agile planning emphasizes fixed deliverables.
C. Agile planning is adaptive and incremental, while traditional planning relies on fixed scope and upfront detail.
D. Both Agile and traditional planning rely primarily on user stories and story mapping.

Test Your Understanding 7.34
A product team is struggling to visualize how different user stories connect to the customer journey. They also need to prioritize which features to deliver in the next release. Which Agile technique would best help them?
A. Creating a work breakdown structure (WBS).
B. Building a story map.
C. Using burn-down charts.
D. Conducting a retrospective.

Test Your Understanding 7.35
In Weighted Shortest Job First (WSJF), which factor in the denominator reduces the priority of a user story if it is large?
A. Time Criticality
B. Risk Reduction
C. Business Value
D. Job Size

Test Your Understanding 7.36
Why are story points often preferred over hours in Agile estimation?
A. Story points provide a relative measure of effort and reduce time spent on detailed estimates.
B. Story points measure absolute effort which can be easily converted to the exact time.
C. Story points are more precise than hours and it is easy for stakeholders to understand.
D. Story points always ensure faster project completion when every team member agrees on it.

7.9 Agile Team Roles and Responsibilities

Agile teams operate differently than traditional project teams, emphasizing self-organization, collaboration, and shared responsibility. Agile teams are typically cross-functional, meaning they comprise individuals with diverse skills necessary to deliver a working product increment. This structure eliminates dependencies on external teams and fosters a sense of collective ownership.

Self-organizing teams are a hallmark of Agile. Unlike traditional teams where tasks are assigned by a project manager, Agile teams are empowered to decide how they will accomplish the work. They determine their own task assignments, schedules, and processes within the framework provided by the chosen Agile methodology (like Scrum or Kanban). This autonomy fosters greater ownership, motivation, and faster decision-making. Self-organization doesn't mean the team is without direction; it operates within the boundaries set by the Product Owner and guided by the Scrum Master (or Agile Coach).

The Product Owner is the voice of the customer and the business representative on the Agile team. They are responsible for defining and prioritizing the product backlog, ensuring it reflects the needs and desires of the users and stakeholders. The Product Owner works closely with the stakeholders to gather requirements, translate them into user stories, and prioritize them based on business value. They are the champion for the product and make decisions about what features will be included in each release. The Product Owner is not necessarily a technical expert but must have a deep understanding of the product and the market.

The Scrum Master (or Agile Coach) is a servant leader who facilitates the Agile process and helps the team remove impediments. They are responsible for ensuring that the team follows the chosen Agile framework and coaches the team to improve their performance. The Scrum Master is not a traditional project manager; they do not assign tasks or control the team. Instead, they focus on creating an environment where the team can self-organize and be most effective. They help remove any roadblocks that are preventing the team from making progress and facilitate communication between the team and the Product Owner. The Scrum Master also helps the team to continuously improve their processes and practices. In some organizations, this role might be called an Agile Coach, reflecting the focus on guidance and mentorship.

Developers, as members of the cross-functional team, are responsible for building the product increment. They are involved in all aspects of the development process, from design and coding to testing and integration. Agile teams often emphasize generalists over specialists, encouraging developers to have a broad range of skills and to be willing to contribute in different areas. This cross-functional nature of the team promotes shared understanding and reduces dependencies on individual specialists. Developers work closely together, often using practices like pair programming, to ensure code quality and share knowledge.

Test Your Understanding 7.37
Which of the following best describes a self-organizing team in Agile?

A. A team where the Scrum Master assigns tasks to ensure work is completed on time.
B. A team empowered to decide how tasks will be accomplished within Agile boundaries.
C. A team managed directly by stakeholders to align with business goals.
D. A team that works independently without any direction from Product Owner or Scrum Master.

Test Your Understanding 7.38
A company has an Agile team working on a new mobile app. Mid-sprint, the team encounters a recurring issue with their development environment, slowing progress. Who is primarily responsible for facilitating the removal of this impediment?
A. The Product Owner, since they define priorities.
B. The Scrum Master, as they remove roadblocks and facilitate the process.
C. The Developers, since they are responsible for coding and testing.
D. The Project Manager, since they oversee timelines and budgets.

Test Your Understanding 7.39
Which of the following is the *primary responsibility* of the Product Owner?
A. Assigning tasks to team members based on their expertise.
B. Ensuring code quality through pair programming practices.
C. Defining and prioritizing the product backlog to represent customer needs.
D. Managing the daily workflow and enforcing Agile rules.

7.10 Agile Tools and Techniques

Agile teams utilize a variety of tools and techniques, such as Kanban boards and daily standup, to effectively manage their work, track progress, and foster collaboration. Here are two such tools and techniques:

Backlog grooming and refinement is an ongoing process in Agile. It involves regularly reviewing and refining the product backlog, ensuring that it contains clear, concise, and actionable user stories. During backlog grooming sessions, the Product Owner, along with the development team, reviews the user stories, breaks down large stories into smaller ones, estimates their size, and prioritizes them. This process helps to keep the backlog organized and ensures that the team is working on the most valuable items. Backlog grooming is not a one-time event but rather a continuous activity that helps to keep the backlog up-to-date and relevant.

Velocity tracking and burndown charts are used to monitor the progress of the development team. Velocity measures the amount of work a team can complete in a sprint. It's calculated by summing the story points completed during a sprint. Tracking velocity helps the team to estimate how many sprints will be required to complete the project. Burndown charts provide a visual representation of the remaining work in the sprint or release. They show the ideal burndown (a straight line from the total story points at the start to zero at the end) compared to the actual burndown. Deviations from the ideal burndown can indicate potential issues or delays, allowing the team to take corrective actions.

Here is an example of a burndown chart. This chart represents a 5-day sprint with a total of 40 story points to complete. Each day, the team completes a certain number of story points, and the remaining work is plotted.

Data:

Total story points: 40

Daily completed story points: Day 1: 12, Day 2: 5, Day 3: 4, Day 4: 10, Day 5: 9

Remaining work: Day 0: 40, Day 1: 28 (40 - 12), Day 2: 23 (28 - 5), Day 3: 19 (23 - 4), Day 4: 9 (19 - 10), Day 5: 0 (9 - 9).

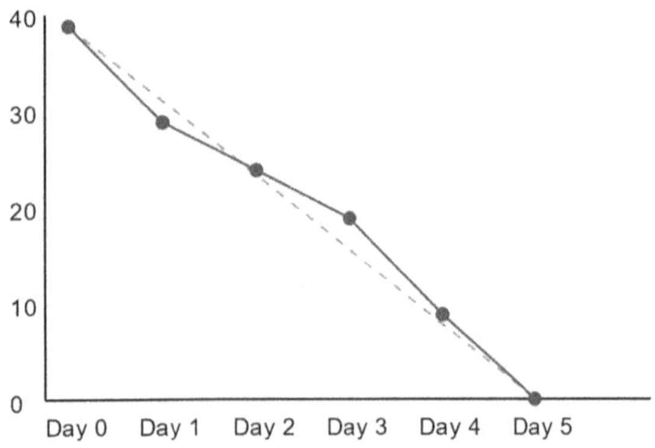

Figure 7.3 Sample burndown chart.

Explanation:

X-axis: Represents the days of the sprint (Day 0 to Day 5).

Y-axis: Represents the remaining story points (0 to 40).

Ideal burndown line (gray dashed): A straight line from the total story points (40) at Day 0 to 0 at Day 5.

Actual burndown line (blue): Plots the remaining story points each day based on the team's progress.

Test Your Understanding 7.40
Which of the following best describes the purpose of backlog grooming in Agile?
A. To finalize all user stories at the start of the project so no changes are needed later
B. To continuously review, refine, and prioritize user stories in the product backlog
C. To calculate velocity and track how many story points are completed each sprint
D. To ensure the Product Owner delegates coding tasks directly to developers

Test Your Understanding 7.41
Your Scrum team is in the middle of a sprint. The burndown chart shows that the actual burndown line is consistently above the ideal burndown line. What does this most likely indicate?
A. The team is completing work faster than planned and may finish early

B. The team is behind schedule and may not complete all sprint items on time
C. The Product Owner has been adding new user stories during the sprint
D. The team has overestimated story points and is progressing too slowly

Test Your Understanding 7.42
A Product Owner is trying to forecast how long it will take to deliver a feature set worth 120 story points. The team's past three sprint velocities have been: 38, 42, and 40. Based on this data, approximately how many sprints should the Product Owner plan for?
A. 1 sprints
B. 2 sprints
C. 3 sprints
D. 4 sprints

7.11 Self-Organizing Team

Self-organizing teams are a cornerstone of Agile methodologies, representing a significant departure from traditional hierarchical team structures. Self-organizing teams can be defined as groups of individuals who work together to achieve a common goal, and they have the autonomy to make decisions about how they will accomplish that goal, without constant managerial oversight. This doesn't mean they are leaderless or without direction; rather, they operate within clearly defined boundaries and are guided by the overall project vision and objectives, typically set by the Product Owner in Agile frameworks like Scrum (Perlak, 2019).

The importance of self-organizing teams in Agile stems from the need for speed, flexibility, and adaptability. In today's rapidly changing environments, projects often require quick responses to new information and evolving requirements. Self-organizing teams, with their distributed decision-making and ability to adapt quickly, are much better equipped to handle these challenges than traditional teams that rely on top-down direction.

Traditional hierarchical teams typically have a clear chain of command, with managers assigning tasks and controlling the team's work. While this structure can be effective in stable environments, it can be slow and cumbersome in dynamic situations. Information must flow up the hierarchy for decisions to be made, and then those decisions must be communicated back down, creating delays. Self-organizing teams eliminate these bottlenecks, allowing for faster responses and more efficient problem-solving.

Several key characteristics define self-organizing teams. *Autonomy* is perhaps the most prominent. Team members are given the freedom and responsibility to decide how they will approach their work. They determine their own task assignments, schedules, and processes within the constraints of the sprint or iteration goals. This autonomy empowers team members, increasing their motivation and ownership of the project.

Collaboration is another characteristic. Self-organizing teams thrive on high levels of teamwork and cross-functional cooperation. Team members work closely together, sharing knowledge, and supporting each other to achieve common goals. This collaborative environment fosters a sense of shared responsibility and encourages creative problem-solving.

Accountability is also crucial. While self-organizing teams have autonomy, they are also accountable for their work. Team members take ownership of their tasks and are responsible for delivering on their commitments. This sense of accountability is reinforced by the team's collective responsibility for the project's success.

Continuous improvement is a core value in Agile, and self-organizing teams embody this principle. They regularly reflect on their performance, identify areas for improvement, and adapt their processes accordingly. This continuous learning and adaptation help the team to become more efficient and effective over time.

Finally, *trust and respect* allow self-organizing teams to function effectively. Team members must trust and respect each other's skills and expertise. Open communication and shared responsibility are built on a foundation of trust, enabling the team to work together effectively and achieve its goals. Without trust, team members may be hesitant to share ideas or take risks, hindering the team's ability to self-organize and innovate.

In order to nurture these characteristics and drive agile success, leadership, facilitation, and balanced guidance must be in place. In contrast to traditional hierarchical structures, leadership in self-organizing teams isn't about command and control. Instead, Agile leaders adopt a servant leadership model, where their primary role shifts from directing tasks to empowering the team. They focus on creating an environment where team members can collaborate effectively, make their own decisions, and continuously improve, which is essential for fostering true self-organization.

Scrum Masters and Agile Coaches are key facilitators, not traditional managers. They guide the team through Agile processes, help remove impediments, and create a safe space for learning and experimentation. By asking insightful questions and encouraging collaboration, they empower the team to self-organize and find its own solutions, ensuring everyone understands the product vision and priorities.

Effective Agile leadership requires a delicate balance: providing clear direction without micromanaging. Leaders must communicate the project vision and strategic goals, setting clear boundaries and expectations. However, they must also trust the team's expertise to determine how to achieve those goals. The focus is on empowering the team to find their own path, experiment, and learn from their mistakes.

Self-organizing teams deliver significant benefits by empowering individuals and streamlining processes. Granting team members autonomy and ownership boosts their motivation and engagement, which directly translates into higher job satisfaction and better quality work. Decision-making and problem-solving become much faster because the people closest to the work are authorized to act, eliminating hierarchical delays.

This collaborative freedom also fosters greater innovation and adaptability, as teams can experiment with creative solutions and respond quickly to change. Ultimately, by cutting through bureaucratic bottlenecks and allowing teams to manage their own workflows, they achieve far greater productivity and efficiency.

Despite their benefits, self-organizing teams face several key challenges. A primary hurdle is maintaining alignment with organizational goals, as teams can falter without a clear vision from leadership and a well-defined backlog. The collective decision-making process can also spark internal conflicts, which requires effective resolution skills and an open communication culture to manage.

Furthermore, success hinges on a high level of individual discipline and responsibility, as each member must be self-motivated. Finally, a significant obstacle is often resistance from traditional managers reluctant to relinquish control. Overcoming this requires strong executive support and a dedicated commitment to shifting the organizational culture.

Test Your Understanding 7.43
Which of the following best describes a self-organizing team in Agile?
A. A team that works without any leadership or direction.
B. A group of individuals who decide how to achieve goals within set boundaries.
C. A team where a manager assigns tasks but members choose the schedule.
D. A group that experiments without any accountability.

Test Your Understanding 7.44
A project manager notices that decisions in her traditional team take several days because requests must move up and down the hierarchy. She considers shifting to an Agile approach. What is the primary advantage of using a self-organizing team in this situation?
A. Team members can make decisions directly, reducing delays.
B. Managers can still approve key decisions but at a faster pace.
C. Workflows will remain structured with minimal changes.
D. The team will no longer need guidance from leadership.

Test Your Understanding 7.45
A Scrum Master notices that the team is waiting for her approval before starting tasks, even though priorities are clear. What leadership adjustment would best encourage self-organization?
A. Provide direct task assignments to avoid confusion.
B. Ask the Product Owner to take over daily team decisions.
C. Reduce team autonomy to maintain stronger control.
D. Clarify the vision and step back to let the team decide how to proceed.

Test Your Understanding 7.46
During a sprint retrospective, a team identifies that their task handoff process causes delays. They decide to experiment with pair programming in the next sprint. What Agile principle are they demonstrating?
A. Top-down task management
B. Continuous improvement
C. Strict adherence to original processes
D. Eliminating accountability

7.12 Continuous Improvement

Continuous improvement is a core principle of Agile methodologies. Agile teams constantly strive to improve their processes, practices, and products. This commitment to continuous improvement helps adapt to change, maximize efficiency, and deliver high-quality value. Several techniques and philosophies contribute to this continuous improvement mindset within Agile.

Sprint retrospectives are a practice in Scrum for fostering continuous improvement. They are short meetings held at the end of each sprint where the team reflects on their performance, identifies areas for improvement, and plans actionable steps to implement those improvements in future sprints. The purpose of a retrospective is not to assign blame but rather to learn from the past and make positive changes (Sieckmann et al., 2021).

Retrospectives typically follow a structured format, often including the following elements: Setting the stage (establishing a safe and open environment), gathering data (reviewing what happened during the sprint), generating insights (identifying what went well, what could be improved, and what impediments were encountered), and deciding on actions (creating a plan for implementing specific improvements in the next sprint).

Several techniques can be used to make retrospectives more effective, such as "Start-Stop-Continue" (identifying what the team should start doing, stop doing, and continue doing), "Sailboat Retrospective" (visualizing the sprint as a sailboat, with anchors representing impediments and wind representing driving forces), and "Four Ls" (Liked, Learned, Lacked, Longed for). The key is to choose a technique that works well for the team and facilitates open and honest communication.

Kaizen, a Japanese term meaning "continuous improvement," is a philosophy that aligns perfectly with the Agile mindset. Kaizen emphasizes small, incremental changes implemented over time to achieve significant long-term improvements. It encourages teams to focus on making small, manageable changes rather than trying to implement large, disruptive overhauls. This incremental approach makes it easier to identify what works and what doesn't, allowing for adjustments along the way. Kaizen is about fostering a culture of continuous improvement where every team member is empowered to suggest and implement changes. It is a proactive approach to problem-solving and process optimization.

Metrics drive continuous improvement in Agile. As discussed earlier, metrics like velocity, cycle time, and lead time provide valuable insights into team performance and process efficiency. Tracking these metrics over time allows teams to identify trends, spot bottlenecks, and measure the impact of process improvements. For example, if the cycle time for a particular type of task is consistently high, the team can investigate the reasons for the delay and implement changes to streamline the process.

By regularly reviewing and analyzing these metrics, Agile teams can make data-driven decisions about how to improve their performance and deliver value more effectively. It's not enough to simply track the metrics; the team must also use them to identify areas for improvement and implement concrete actions to address any issues. This iterative cycle of measuring, analyzing, and improving is at the heart of continuous improvement in Agile. It's about constantly looking for ways to optimize the process and deliver greater value.

Test Your Understanding 7.47
What is the primary purpose of a sprint retrospective in Scrum?
A. To assign accountability for mistakes made during the sprint.
B. To reflect on performance, identify improvements, and plan actions.

C. To update the product backlog with new requirements.
D. To evaluate only the Product Owner's role during the sprint.

Test Your Understanding 7.48
A Scrum Master notices that her team struggles to engage during retrospectives because discussions often stay vague. Which technique would best help the team make their feedback more actionable and structured?
A. Start-Stop-Continue
B. Sailboat Retrospective
C. Four Ls
D. Daily Stand-up

Test Your Understanding 7.49
Which statement best describes the Kaizen philosophy in Agile?
A. It emphasizes large, disruptive changes to achieve quick results.
B. It requires management approval before any process changes are made.
C. It encourages teams to make small, incremental improvements over time.
D. It focuses on implementing changes at the end of a project to ensure stability during development.

7.13 Chapter Summary

This chapter introduces the Agile mindset, the foundation of Agile project management. It evaluates project management methodologies, explains Agile as a mindset, and explores key frameworks like Scrum, Kanban, and eXtreme Programming (XP). It also covers Agile team roles, responsibilities, tools, and techniques. The chapter concludes with two critical principles: self-organizing teams and continuous improvement.

7.14 Case Study

Revisit the case study in Chapter 1. Perform the following tasks:
Your team will conduct a sprint retrospective to evaluate the recently completed sprint. The retrospective will focus on analyzing team collaboration, processes, and outcomes, fostering self-organization, and proposing actionable improvements for the next sprint. Before the retrospective meeting, each team member should individually reflect on the sprint and prepare answers to the following questions: What went well in this sprint that helped us meet our goals or work effectively as a team? What challenges or obstacles did we face, and how did they impact our progress? What is one specific improvement we could make in the next sprint to enhance our collaboration, process, or deliverables? Write down 1-2 specific examples for each question, focusing on team dynamics, communication, or technical work (e.g., coding, testing, or client interactions).
Retrospective Meeting (Team, 60-90 minutes)
Schedule a team meeting facilitated by a designated Scrum Master (rotate this role if possible). Use one of the retrospective formats discussed in the chapter to structure the discussion.
Kaizen Focus (Team, 15-20 minutes of meeting)
Explicitly apply the Kaizen philosophy by selecting one small, incremental improvement to implement in the next sprint. Discuss: Why this improvement is feasible and impactful. How it supports the team's autonomy or collaboration. Who will be responsible for ensuring it's implemented.

Deliverable (Team, 1-2 pages, due 48 hours after the meeting)
Submit a written retrospective report summarizing: Key insights from the discussion (e.g., what went well, challenges faced). The chosen Kaizen improvement, including a clear action plan (what, how, who, and when). How this improvement aligns with self-organizing team characteristics (e.g., autonomy, collaboration) or Agile leadership principles (e.g., servant leadership, balanced guidance).
Any feedback on the retrospective process itself (e.g., was the format effective?). Use a shared document (e.g., Google Docs) to collaborate on the report, ensuring all team members review and contribute.

7.15 References

Akhtar, A., Bakhtawar, B., & Akhtar, S. (2022). Extreme programming vs scrum: A comparison of agile models. *International Journal of Technology Innovation and Management (IJTIM)*, *2*(2), 80-96.
Alaidaros, H., Omar, M., & Romli, R. (2021). The state of the art of agile kanban method: challenges and opportunities. *Independent Journal of Management & Production*, *12*(8), 2535-2550.
Alzahrani, A. A. (2024). Investigating Agile Values and Principles in Real Practices. *International Journal of Advanced Computer Science & Applications*, *15*(1).
Grebić, B., & Stojanović, A. (2021). Application of the Scrum framework on projects in IT sector. *Eur. Proj. Manag. J*, *11*(2), 37-46.
Perlak, J. (2019). Characteristics of self-organizing teams in agile project management: A case study. *Acta Universitatis Nicolai Copernici. Zarządzanie*, *46*(1), 19-27.
Sieckmann, F., Klatt, N., & Kohl, H. (2021, May). Managing Continuous Improvement with Agile Approaches: Case Study of an Industrial Learning Factory. In *Proceedings of the Conference on Learning Factories (CLF)*.
Suvvari, S. K. (2019). An exploration of agile scaling frameworks: Scaled agile framework (SAFe), large-scale scrum (LeSS), and disciplined agile delivery (DAD). *Int. J. Recent Innov. Trends Comput. Commun*, *7*(12), 9-17.

7.16 Solutions to Test Your Understanding

7.1 D; 7.2 C; 7.3 A; 7.4 D; 7.5 C; 7.6 A; 7.7 D; 7.8 D; 7.9 B; 7.10 C; 7.11 A; 7.12 B; 7.13 C; 7.14 A; 7.15 B; 7.16 B; 7.17 A; 7.18 C; 7.19 D; 7.20 B; 7.21 A; 7.22 D; 7.23 C; 7.24 B; 7.25 C; 7.26 A; 7.27 A; 7.28 D; 7.29 B; 7.30 C; 7.31 A; 7.32 D; 7.33 C; 7.34 B; 7.35 D; 7.36 A; 7.37 B; 7.38 B; 7.39 C; 7.40 B; 7.41 B; 7.42 C; 7.43 B; 7.44 A; 7.45 D; 7.46 B; 7.47 B; 7.48 A; 7.49 C;.

Chapter 8: Adaptive Approach

Chapter Learning Outcomes

8.1 Evaluate the advantages and disadvantages of adaptive and predictive, plan-based projects.
8.2 Assess the appropriateness of adaptive approaches in relation to the organizational structure.
8.3 Design a strategy for documenting project controls in an adaptive project.
8.4 Formulate a plan for preparing and implementing task management steps.

8.1 Adaptive vs. Predictive Methodologies

Project management approaches can be divided into two broad categories: predictive, plan-based projects and adaptive projects. Each approach has unique advantages and disadvantages that should be considered when selecting the best method for a project (Gareis, 2017; Kochenderfer and Chrisman, 2015). Predictive approaches, such as the traditional waterfall method, focus on detailed upfront planning and sequential execution. In contrast, adaptive approaches, like Agile, prioritize flexibility and iterative development, enabling adjustments as the project progresses.

Adaptive approaches, often associated with Agile methodologies, thrive in environments characterized by high uncertainty and evolving requirements. Think of software development projects where the initial vision might be somewhat vague and subject to change based on user feedback and technological advancements. These projects benefit from the iterative nature of adaptive approaches, allowing teams to deliver value in smaller, manageable increments. This incremental delivery enables continuous feedback from customers and stakeholders, ensuring the final product aligns with their evolving needs.

Furthermore, adaptive approaches are well-suited for complex projects operating in rapidly changing industries like technology and healthcare. The ability to adjust course quickly makes them invaluable in mitigating risks that emerge in these dynamic environments. For instance, a pharmaceutical company developing a new drug might use an adaptive approach to accommodate evolving research data and regulatory changes.

Conversely, predictive, plan-based approaches excel when requirements are stable and well-defined. Construction projects, for example, typically follow a detailed blueprint and adhere to strict schedules. The nature of these projects, with their well-established processes and minimal anticipated changes, makes a predictive approach ideal. Similarly, projects driven by regulatory requirements, such as government initiatives, often necessitate meticulous planning and documentation, making a predictive approach more suitable. These approaches also shine when dealing with fixed budgets and timelines, providing a structured framework for managing scope, cost, and deadlines. Manufacturing projects, with their focus on efficiency and standardization, often leverage predictive methodologies to ensure consistent product quality and timely delivery.

The table below compares key factors between adaptive approaches (e.g., Agile, Iterative) and predictive approaches (e.g., Waterfall, Plan-Based), highlighting differences in flexibility, planning, delivery models, stakeholder involvement, risk management, and typical project examples.

Factor	Adaptive Approach (Agile, Iterative)	Predictive Approach (Waterfall, Plan-Based)
Flexibility	High – accommodates changing requirements	Low – follows a fixed plan
Planning	Evolving – continuous refinement	Upfront – detailed project plan
Delivery Model	Incremental, frequent iterations	One-time final delivery
Stakeholder Involvement	High – continuous feedback loop	Low – mostly during planning phase
Risk Management	Adaptive – adjusts as risks emerge	Predictive – risks planned upfront
Project Examples	Software development, R&D, product design	Construction, engineering, government projects

Table 8.1 Comparing Adaptive vs. Predictive Approaches

Finally, it's important to recognize that a purely adaptive or predictive approach isn't always the best fit. Often, a hybrid approach, combining elements of both, can be the most effective strategy. For example, a large IT project might use an Agile approach for software development while adhering to a more traditional, plan-based approach for infrastructure deployment. Hybrid models allow organizations to tailor their project management methodology to the specific needs of the project and the organization. Industries like automotive and aerospace frequently use hybrid approaches, balancing the need for innovation with the rigor of established processes and regulatory compliance.

Test Your Understanding 8.1

A pharmaceutical company is developing a new drug. The research data and regulatory requirements are changing frequently. Which project management approach would be most suitable?

A. Predictive, because pharmaceutical projects always require strict planning
B. Adaptive, because it allows flexibility with evolving requirements
C. Hybrid, because it balances regulatory compliance and innovation equally
D. Predictive, because regulatory projects must follow fixed processes

Test Your Understanding 8.2
A construction company is building a new bridge. The requirements are clear, the design is finalized, and regulatory permits have been approved. Which project management approach would most likely ensure success?
A. Predictive, because the requirements are stable and well-defined
B. Adaptive, because changes may still arise during construction
C. Hybrid, because it always provides the best of both worlds
D. Adaptive, because incremental delivery reduces stakeholder risk

Test Your Understanding 8.3
An IT company is tasked with developing a new enterprise software platform. The project has two major parts:
Developing the software application, where user needs may evolve over time
Setting up the physical infrastructure, which requires strict deadlines and fixed budgets
Which project management approach would be most appropriate overall?
A. Fully adaptive approach for both software and infrastructure
B. Fully predictive approach for both components
C. Hybrid approach, adaptive for software and predictive for infrastructure
D. Predictive for software and adaptive for infrastructure

Test Your Understanding 8.4
Which of the following statements correctly contrasts adaptive vs. predictive approaches?
A. Adaptive approaches deliver value in a single final product release, while predictive approaches deliver incrementally
B. Predictive approaches involve stakeholders continuously, while adaptive approaches engage them only during planning
C. Adaptive approaches focus on iterative development and frequent feedback, while predictive approaches rely on detailed upfront planning and one-time delivery
D. Predictive approaches are best for uncertain environments, while adaptive approaches thrive with stable, fixed requirements

Test Your Understanding 8.5
A healthcare startup is launching a new digital health app. At the start, the requirements are unclear and depend heavily on user feedback. However, once regulatory approval is needed, strict compliance must be followed. Which approach would best align with these needs?
A. Adaptive for early app development, predictive once regulatory approval becomes critical
B. Predictive from the beginning to avoid rework later
C. Adaptive throughout the entire project to maximize flexibility
D. Predictive for app development and adaptive for regulatory compliance

8.2 Organizational Structure Suitability

The suitability of adaptive, Agile approaches varies significantly depending on an organization's structure (Agile Alliance, 2021). Different organizational structures present unique challenges and opportunities for Agile adoption.

Virtual organizations, characterized by geographically dispersed teams often working remotely, can benefit greatly from adaptive approaches. Agile frameworks like Scrum and SAFe are designed to facilitate remote collaboration through digital tools such as Jira, Trello, and Microsoft Teams. These tools support Agile workflows by enabling task management, communication, and progress tracking across distances. However, virtual teams face inherent challenges like communication barriers stemming from time zone differences and a lack of face-to-face interaction. Best practices for virtual Agile teams include daily stand-up meetings via video conferencing to maintain a sense of connection and shared purpose, along with a strong reliance on asynchronous collaboration tools for seamless information sharing.

Colocated teams, working together in the same physical location, also find adaptive approaches highly suitable. Face-to-face collaboration, a cornerstone of Agile methodologies, aligns perfectly with the dynamics of colocated teams. The proximity of team members facilitates quick decision-making, rapid feedback loops, and a strong sense of shared ownership. Colocated teams can further enhance their Agile practices by utilizing physical Kanban boards and task boards for real-time progress visualization. Regular Agile ceremonies, such as retrospectives and sprint reviews, are also more easily conducted and more impactful when teams are colocated, fostering a culture of continuous improvement.

Matrix organizations, which blend functional and project-based structures, present a more nuanced scenario for Agile adoption. In these organizations, employees report to multiple managers, creating a complex web of authority. Adaptive approaches can thrive in matrix structures when Agile teams are granted sufficient autonomy to make decisions and manage their work. However, conflicts can arise if Agile teams lack the necessary authority due to the influence of functional reporting lines. To mitigate these challenges, clear roles and responsibilities must be defined to avoid ambiguity and conflict. Utilizing Agile frameworks that integrate well with traditional management structures, such as Disciplined Agile Delivery (DAD), can also be beneficial. DAD helps bridge the gap between Agile principles and the existing organizational hierarchy.

Hierarchical or functional organizations, with their traditional top-down structure and rigid departmental divisions, often find Agile implementation more challenging. The command-and-control nature of these organizations can clash with the self-organizing principles of Agile. Direct implementation of Agile across the entire organization may encounter resistance and require significant cultural change. A more practical approach is to start with small Agile teams within departments, demonstrating the value of Agile on a smaller scale before attempting to scale it across the organization. Securing buy-in from leadership supports this gradual Agile transformation and fosters the necessary cultural shift.

Finally, *projectized organizations*, structured entirely around projects with project managers wielding significant authority, represent an ideal environment for adaptive approaches. The project-centric focus of these organizations aligns seamlessly with the principles of Agile. Teams can be fully Agile with minimal resistance, as the organization's structure inherently supports a project-based way of working. For large projects in projectized organizations, Agile scaling frameworks like SAFe and Large-Scale Scrum (LeSS) can be effectively employed to coordinate multiple Agile teams and ensure alignment with overall project goals. Strong cross-functional collaboration is essential in these environments, as teams from various departments come together to deliver project outcomes.

Test Your Understanding 8.6
A software development company operates as a virtual organization with teams spread across three continents. Despite adopting Scrum, the teams struggle with delayed communication due to time zone differences. Which BEST practice would most effectively address this issue?
A. Increase sprint length to allow more time for asynchronous work.
B. Conduct daily stand-up meetings via video conferencing to maintain team connection.
C. Rely exclusively on email communication to document all project decisions.
D. Assign one team leader in each region to manage communication across time zones.

Test Your Understanding 8.7
Which organizational structure provides the strongest natural alignment with Agile principles due to its project-centered focus?
A. Functional organizations
B. Virtual organizations
C. Matrix organizations
D. Projectized organizations

Test Your Understanding 8.8
A colocated team is adopting Agile practices. They want to reinforce collaboration and make progress visible at all times. Which approach would be MOST effective in this setting?
A. Using physical Kanban boards to track tasks in real-time.
B. Depending solely on digital task-tracking tools like Jira or Trello.
C. Replacing sprint reviews with weekly email status updates.
D. Avoiding retrospectives since face-to-face collaboration already ensures improvement.

Test Your Understanding 8.9
What is the primary challenge Agile teams face when working in a matrix organization?
A. Difficulty coordinating across different time zones.
B. Lack of authority due to competing functional and project managers.
C. Overreliance on physical Kanban boards for decision-making.
D. Resistance to Agile from project managers who favor traditional approaches.

8.3 Organizational Readiness for Adaptive Approaches

Adaptive approaches enable modern organizations to be flexible and solve problems dynamically, driving improved performance, efficiency, and outcomes. Their successful implementation relies on organizational process assets, such as established Agile frameworks, historical data, and knowledge repositories, as well as environmental factors like a collaborative culture, stakeholder support, and access to skilled teams. These elements create the foundation for organizations to effectively adopt and leverage adaptive methodologies.

Organizational Process Assets (OPAs) support project success, particularly when implementing adaptive, Agile approaches. OPAs encompass all internal assets within an organization that can influence how projects are executed. These can include formal documentation like policies and procedures, but also less tangible assets such as knowledge bases, historical data from past projects, and lessons learned. For organizations seeking to leverage the benefits of Agile, certain OPAs are particularly valuable in facilitating the adoption and effective use of adaptive methodologies (Azevedo et al., 2022).

One crucial OPA is an Agile-friendly project governance framework. This framework provides the high-level structure and guidelines for managing Agile projects within the organization. It defines how Agile projects align with overall organizational strategy, how funding is allocated, and how risks are managed within an Agile context. Having pre-defined guidelines for Agile implementation can significantly streamline the adoption process, ensuring consistency and reducing confusion. These guidelines might cover topics such as team formation, sprint planning, and stakeholder engagement.

Organizational knowledge repositories play a vital role in capturing and disseminating valuable information from past Agile projects. These repositories serve as a central hub for storing project data, lessons learned, best practices, and any other relevant information that can benefit future Agile teams. By leveraging this institutional knowledge, teams can avoid repeating past mistakes and build upon previous successes. For example, a knowledge repository might contain templates for user story mapping, sprint backlogs, or retrospective reports, saving teams time and effort.

Existing Agile process frameworks, such as documented workflows for Scrum, SAFe, or Kanban, provide a solid foundation for Agile project management. These frameworks offer a structured approach to implementing Agile principles and practices, ensuring that teams follow a consistent and effective process. Having pre-defined frameworks in place reduces the need for teams to reinvent the wheel and allows them to focus on delivering value.

Tools and templates designed specifically for Agile project management are invaluable OPAs. These tools can range from physical Agile task boards used for visualizing workflow to sophisticated software applications like Jira and Trello for managing backlogs, tracking progress, and facilitating collaboration.

Finally, the presence of training and Agile expertise within the organization is a critical OPA. This includes having access to experienced Agile coaches who can guide teams through the implementation process, providing workshops on Agile principles and practices, and supporting employees in obtaining Agile certifications. Investing in Agile training and expertise builds internal capability, ensuring that teams have the knowledge and skills necessary to succeed with adaptive approaches.

Enterprise Environmental Factors (EEFs) also shape project outcomes, and their influence is particularly pronounced when considering adaptive, Agile approaches. EEFs encompass both internal and external conditions that can impact project execution (Shtal et al., 2023).

Internally, an organization's structure can significantly influence the success of Agile adoption. Flat, cross-functional teams, where members from different departments collaborate closely, are ideal for Agile. These structures promote communication, collaboration, and shared ownership, all essential for Agile success. Conversely, rigid hierarchies with strong departmental silos can hinder Agile implementation, as information flow and decision-making can be slow and cumbersome.

The leadership mindset and organizational culture are equally critical. A leadership team that is open to change, experimentation, and continuous improvement creates a fertile ground for Agile to flourish. In contrast, a traditional command-and-control culture can stifle Agile initiatives. The organization's existing Agile maturity level also plays a crucial role. Organizations with prior experience using Agile methods have a distinct advantage. They have likely developed internal expertise, established best practices, and learned from past mistakes.

The availability of appropriate Agile tools and technology is another important internal EEF. Collaboration platforms like Slack or Microsoft Teams facilitate communication and information sharing among distributed teams. Continuous Integration/Continuous Delivery (CI/CD) pipelines automate the build, test, and deployment process, enabling faster and more frequent releases. Automated testing tools improve the quality and reliability of software products. Access to these tools and technologies empowers Agile teams to work more efficiently and effectively.

Externally, market conditions and competitive pressure can drive the adoption of adaptive approaches. In highly competitive markets, organizations need to be able to respond quickly to changing customer needs and competitive threats. Agile's iterative and incremental nature allows organizations to adapt rapidly, making it a valuable asset in dynamic environments.

The regulatory and compliance environment is another external EEF to consider. While Agile can be used in regulated industries, some sectors, like healthcare and finance, may require a hybrid approach. These industries often have strict documentation and compliance requirements, which may necessitate a combination of Agile practices and more traditional, plan-driven methods. For example, a pharmaceutical company developing a new drug might use Agile for the research phase but switch to a more predictive approach for the clinical trials and regulatory approval process.

Finally, customer expectations for flexibility and responsiveness can influence the suitability of Agile. In industries where customer requirements are constantly evolving, Agile offers a significant advantage. The ability to incorporate feedback and adapt to changing needs ensures that the final product or service meets customer expectations. Understanding and considering these internal and external EEFs improves the success of Agile implementation.

Test Your Understanding 8.10
Which of the following BEST describes Organizational Process Assets (OPAs) in the context of Agile adoption?
A. External pressures that shape project execution.
B. Internal assets such as frameworks, knowledge bases, and historical data.
C. Informal conversations and team dynamics.
D. Regulatory compliance requirements.

Test Your Understanding 8.11
A financial institution is adopting Agile but faces strict regulatory documentation requirements. Which approach is MOST appropriate?
A. Avoid Agile entirely and rely only on predictive methods.
B. Adopt Agile fully with no regard for compliance requirements.
C. Use a hybrid approach.
D. Delay Agile adoption until regulations change.

Test Your Understanding 8.12
Which of the following is an example of an Agile-friendly OPA that streamlines adoption?
A. A predefined governance framework outlining team formation, sprint planning, and risk management.
B. Competitive pressure from new market entrants.

C. Customer demand for rapid responsiveness.
D. A traditional command-and-control hierarchy.

Test Your Understanding 8.13
A colocated Agile team is starting a new project and wants to avoid repeating mistakes from previous efforts. Which OPA would be MOST useful?
A. Historical project data stored in the organization's knowledge repository.
B. Competitive analysis reports about industry trends.
C. Market research on customer expectations.
D. A directive from senior leadership to work faster.

Test Your Understanding 8.14
Which internal Enterprise Environmental Factor (EEF) MOST supports Agile adoption?
A. Hierarchical structure with centralized decision-making and formal communication channels.
B. A culture that prioritizes individual performance metrics over team collaboration.
C. Strict adherence to detailed, long-term project plans with minimal flexibility.
D. Flat, cross-functional teams with shared ownership.

Test Your Understanding 8.15
"Competitive market pressures demanding rapid adaptation" is an example of ____.
A. an internal organizational process asset supporting Agile adoption.
B. an internal technical factor enabling Agile adoption.
C. an external Enterprise Environmental Factor (EEF).
D. an internal governance structure facilitating Agile adoption.

8.4 Logical Units of Iterations

Logical units of iterations refer to the structured components or work items that break down a project into manageable, repeatable cycles (iterations). These units help teams organize, prioritize, and track progress within each iteration. They are "logical" because they represent meaningful groupings of work aligned with project goals, rather than arbitrary divisions.

In Agile development, particularly within iterative frameworks like Scrum, work is organized and managed using a hierarchy of logical units, each serving a distinct purpose in defining, planning, and executing the project. Understanding these units -- User Stories, Tasks, Features, Epics, and Themes -- is crucial for effective Agile project management. These units provide structure and clarity, ensuring that the development team focuses on delivering value incrementally and in alignment with overall project goals.

User stories represent discrete pieces of functionality that deliver value to stakeholders. They are small enough to be estimated and completed within a single iteration, making them ideal for iterative development.

Tasks are the actionable steps needed to complete a user story. They are the detailed "how" of implementing the "what" described in the user story. Tasks are typically identified and estimated by the development team during sprint planning. They break down user stories into smaller, manageable pieces of work that can be assigned to individual team members. For example, to implement the user story "As a customer, I want a login page to access my account securely," tasks might include "Design login page UI," "Create database schema for user authentication," "Implement login functionality in code," and "Test login functionality."

Features are larger functional components that span multiple user stories or even multiple iterations. They group related user stories together to deliver a cohesive capability or functionality. Features provide a higher level of organization than user stories, making it easier to manage and track the development of larger components. For example, "User authentication system" might be a feature that encompasses several user stories, including login, password reset, and security audit functionalities.

Epics are high-level requirements that are too large to be completed in a single iteration. They represent broad goals or initiatives that need to be broken down into smaller, more manageable pieces before they can be implemented. Epics provide a broad view of the project scope and help to organize the work at a higher level. For example, "Build an e-commerce platform" could be an epic that is later decomposed into smaller features, user stories, and tasks.

Themes are collections of related user stories, features, or epics that are aligned with a strategic goal or objective. They provide a way to organize work around shared objectives, such as "Improve user experience," "Enhance performance," or "Implement new regulatory requirements." Themes help to connect the work being done at the iteration level to the overall strategic direction of the project. They provide a context for prioritization decisions, ensuring that the team is always working on tasks that contribute to the most important strategic goals.

Distinguishing logical units of work aids effective project management, providing clarity, supporting prioritization, enabling progress tracking, and enhancing adaptability.Understanding the "why" behind these distinctions aids anyone working in an Agile environment. These logical units provide a structured yet flexible framework for managing the complexities of iterative development.

Clarity is a primary benefit. These units ensure that work is well-defined and aligned with stakeholder needs. By breaking down large initiatives (epics) into smaller, more manageable components (features and user stories), the work becomes more concrete and understandable. This breakdown also facilitates communication between the development team, the Product Owner, and stakeholders, ensuring everyone is on the same page regarding what needs to be done and why. The user story format, in particular, emphasizes the user perspective, focusing on the value delivered to the end-user.

Prioritization is greatly enhanced by distinguishing between these units. The hierarchical structure allows for prioritization at different levels. For example, the Product Owner can prioritize epics based on their strategic importance, then prioritize features within each epic based on business value, and finally prioritize user stories within each feature based on customer needs. This multi-level prioritization ensures that the team is always working on the highest-value items first.

Tracking progress becomes much more manageable when work is broken down into these logical units. Tasks, being the smallest unit of work, provide the most granular level of tracking. Teams can easily track the progress of individual tasks within a user story and use this information to monitor the overall progress of the sprint. Burndown charts and other visual tools can be used to track the completion of tasks and user stories, providing a clear picture of the team's performance. Tracking progress at the user story level helps to ensure that the team is delivering value incrementally.

Adaptability is facilitated by the modularity of these units. Because the work is broken down into smaller, independent units, it becomes easier to adjust the scope or reprioritize units as feedback emerges or requirements change. If a user story becomes less valuable or a new, higher-priority story appears, it can be easily swapped out without disrupting the entire project. This flexibility is a key advantage of Agile methodologies, enabling teams to respond quickly to changing circumstances.

Let's consider an example related to e-commerce functionality. The Iteration Goal might be: "Deliver a basic shopping cart." This goal provides a clear focus for the sprint.

The larger initiative, or Epic, could be: "E-commerce checkout system." This epic represents a broader set of functionalities related to the checkout process.

A specific component, or Feature, within that epic might be: "Shopping cart functionality." This feature encompasses all aspects of the shopping cart.

Individual User Stories related to this feature could include: "As a customer, I want to add items to my cart so that I can purchase multiple items in a single transaction." and "As a customer, I want to remove items from my cart so that I can correct mistakes or change my mind before finalizing my purchase." These user stories describe specific user needs and the desired functionality.

Finally, the Tasks required to implement these user stories could include: "Design cart UI," and "Implement backend cart logic." These tasks are the actionable steps the team will take to deliver the user stories and, ultimately, the shopping cart functionality. This example demonstrates how the logical units of work break down a large goal into manageable, value-driven increments.

Test Your Understanding 8.16
Which statement best describes “logical units of iterations” in Agile?
A. Arbitrary divisions of project work based on available resources
B. Structured components that break down projects into repeatable cycles
C. Random tasks chosen by the development team for flexibility
D. Fixed-length deliverables that cannot be reprioritized

Test Your Understanding 8.17
In Scrum, what is the primary role of user stories?
A. To define broad organizational goals and strategies
B. To describe detailed technical steps needed for implementation
C. To represent small, functional units that deliver stakeholder value
D. To group related features together into a higher-level capability

Test Your Understanding 8.18
During sprint planning, the team discusses how to implement a user story: “As a customer, I want a login page to access my account securely.” They identify items like designing the UI, creating a database schema, and coding authentication. What Agile unit are these items?
A. Tasks
B. Features
C. Themes
D. Epics

Test Your Understanding 8.19
Which Agile unit typically spans multiple user stories and may require several iterations to complete?
A. Task
B. Feature
C. User Story
D. Burndown Chart

Test Your Understanding 8.20
A product owner defines “Build an e-commerce platform” as a broad requirement. This item is too large for one iteration and must be decomposed. What type of Agile unit is this?
A. Epic
B. Feature

C. User Story
D. Theme

Test Your Understanding 8.21
A company sets a strategic goal of "Improve user experience." To align Agile work with this goal, related features and user stories are grouped under one unit. Which unit is being used?
A. Epic
B. Task
C. Theme
D. Story

Test Your Understanding 8.22
Which of the following units provides the most granular level of progress tracking in Agile?
A. Themes
B. Epics
C. Features
D. Tasks

Test Your Understanding 8.23
A team is delivering a "shopping cart" in an e-commerce platform. They identify the following:
Epic: E-commerce checkout system
Feature: Shopping cart functionality
User Stories: Adding and removing items from the cart
Tasks: Designing UI and implementing backend logic
What Agile concept does this breakdown illustrate?
A. The hierarchy of logical units of iterations
B. The principle of continuous delivery
C. The definition of a sprint backlog
D. The creation of a minimum viable product (MVP)

8.5 Pros and Cons of Iteration

Iterative planning offers several advantages that contribute to project success in dynamic and complex environments. These benefits help understand why Agile emphasizes iterative development.

One of the advantages of iterative planning is its inherent flexibility and adaptability. Because work is broken down into short cycles (iterations), adjustments can be made frequently based on feedback from stakeholders, testing, or changing market conditions. This allows the project to adapt to evolving requirements and incorporate new information as it becomes available. Instead of being locked into a rigid plan, teams can pivot and change direction as needed, ensuring that the final product aligns with the current needs of the customer and the market. This also reduces the risk of delivering outdated solutions, as the product is continuously being updated and refined based on the latest information.

Iterative planning also fosters continuous improvement and learning. The feedback loops built into each iteration, such as sprint reviews and retrospectives, provide opportunities for teams to reflect on their performance, identify areas for improvement, and adjust their processes accordingly. This iterative cycle of planning, doing, checking, and acting (PDCA) allows teams to learn from their experiences and continuously optimize their workflows. The ability to experiment with different approaches and make data-driven decisions based on feedback helps to improve team performance and product quality over time. Retrospectives, in particular, are valuable for process optimization, allowing teams to identify what went well, what could be improved, and what actions they can take to enhance their processes in future iterations.

Faster delivery of value is another significant benefit. By delivering incremental improvements rather than waiting for the final product, stakeholders can see progress early and provide valuable input throughout the development process. This early visibility helps to build trust and ensures that the product is meeting their needs. Iterative planning also facilitates the rapid development of a minimum viable product (MVP), a version of the product with just enough features to be usable by early customers who can then provide feedback for future product development. The MVP allows teams to validate their assumptions and get early feedback on the product's viability before investing heavily in developing all features. This approach reduces the risk of building a product that no one wants.

Risk mitigation is enhanced through iterative planning. By breaking the project into smaller iterations, issues are identified and addressed early in the project lifecycle, reducing the impact of failures. If a problem arises in one iteration, it can be contained and fixed before it affects the entire project. Iterative planning also provides frequent checkpoints for reassessing risks. At the end of each iteration, the team can review the project's risk profile and adjust their plans accordingly. This allows for proactive risk management and helps to prevent small problems from becoming big ones.

Finally, iterative planning leads to enhanced stakeholder engagement. Stakeholders are actively involved in reviewing progress at the end of each iteration, providing continuous feedback, and ensuring that the product aligns with business goals. This constant communication and collaboration reduces the risk of misalignment and increases stakeholder satisfaction. The greater transparency in the development process, facilitated by burn-down charts, Kanban boards, and regular demos, helps to build trust and ensures that everyone is on the same page. This close collaboration between the development team and stakeholders leads to a shared understanding of the product and its goals, resulting in a higher quality product that meets the needs of the business and its customers.

While iterative planning offers advantages, it also presents certain disadvantages and challenges that organizations must address to successfully implement Agile methodologies.

One significant challenge is the risk of scope creep. The frequent changes inherent in iterative planning can sometimes lead to uncontrolled expansion of the project scope. Because requirements are allowed to evolve, it can be difficult to define a fixed end date or a precise set of deliverables upfront. This can be particularly problematic for organizations accustomed to traditional project management approaches with fixed-price contracts.

Managing scope creep requires strong backlog management and prioritization. The Product Owner plays ensure that only the most valuable features are included in the product backlog and that lower-priority items are deferred to future iterations or releases. Regular backlog grooming sessions keep the backlog organized and prevent it from becoming a repository for every possible feature request. Clear communication with stakeholders about the potential for scope changes and the rationale behind prioritization decisions is also essential.

Iterative planning can also lead to higher resource and time demands. The active involvement of teams and stakeholders required by Agile methodologies can increase workload. Frequent meetings, sprint planning sessions, daily stand-ups, sprint reviews, and retrospectives, while valuable, can add to the team's workload. If not managed properly, this can lead to "iteration fatigue," where team members feel overwhelmed by the constant cycle of planning, execution, and review. To mitigate this risk, organizations should ensure that teams are adequately staffed and that meetings are focused and efficient. It's also important to create a sustainable pace for the team and avoid overloading them with too much work in each iteration.

Complexity in coordination can also be a challenge, especially in larger projects involving multiple teams. Effective collaboration across teams ensures that everyone is working towards the same goals and that dependencies between iterations are managed effectively. Dependencies between iterations can create bottlenecks if not properly identified and addressed. Hybrid models, which combine predictive (plan-driven) and iterative approaches, require particularly careful planning to ensure that the different parts of the project are integrated seamlessly.

Difficulty in cost estimation is another challenge. The evolving requirements inherent in iterative planning make it harder to estimate total project costs upfront. Traditional budgeting methods that rely on fixed scopes and detailed upfront planning may not be suitable for Agile projects. Organizations need to adopt a more flexible approach to budgeting, recognizing that costs may need to be adjusted as the project progresses and requirements change. This can be a significant challenge for organizations accustomed to fixed-price contracts, as they may need to adapt their contracting practices to accommodate the dynamic nature of Agile projects.

Finally, iterative planning requires strong Agile maturity within the organization. Teams need to be disciplined and committed to following iterative processes effectively. Implementing iterative planning often requires a mindset shift from traditional project management approaches, which can be a significant cultural change for some organizations. Overcoming this resistance to change requires strong leadership support, effective training, and a clear communication of the benefits of Agile. Organizations should invest in training their teams on Agile principles and practices and provide ongoing coaching and support to help them adopt iterative ways of working.

Test Your Understanding 8.24
During a project, a team receives new feedback from customers that significantly changes a product feature. How should an Agile team using iterative planning respond?
A. Reject the feedback until the end of the project to avoid disruptions.
B. Incorporate the feedback in the next iteration after reassessing priorities.
C. Apply the feedback immediately without consulting the Product Owner.
D. Pause all development work until a new master plan is approved.

Test Your Understanding 8.25
Which iterative process encourages continuous improvement and learning through regular reflection and adjustment?
A. PDCA (Plan-Do-Check-Act) cycle
B. Critical Path Method (CPM)
C. Earned Value Management (EVM)
D. Work Breakdown Structure (WBS)

Test Your Understanding 8.26
A Product Owner notices that the backlog has grown with many low-value feature requests. What should they do to prevent scope creep in an iterative project?
A. Include all features to satisfy stakeholders.
B. Freeze the backlog until the end of the project.
C. Transfer all non-critical tasks to another team.
D. Prioritize features by value and defer low-priority ones to later releases.

Test Your Understanding 8.27
In iterative planning, delivering a Minimum Viable Product (MVP) primarily helps a team to:
A. Complete the project faster without testing.
B. Reduce the need for future product updates.
C. Avoid changes by finalizing requirements upfront.

D. Validate assumptions and collect early feedback from users.

Test Your Understanding 8.28
Iterative planning reduces project risk primarily by:
A. Conducting all testing only at the end of the project.
B. Identifying and addressing issues early in smaller iterations.
C. Avoiding stakeholder reviews until the project is complete.
D. Assigning all risk management activities to the Product Owner.

Test Your Understanding 8.29
A large Agile program involves several teams working on interdependent components. What is the biggest coordination challenge likely to arise?
A. Excessive customer involvement
B. Reduced stakeholder communication
C. Managing dependencies between teams' iterations
D. Overuse of hybrid project management methods

Test Your Understanding 8.30
A company shifting from traditional project management to Agile experiences resistance from teams used to fixed plans. What is the best way to overcome this challenge?
A. Force immediate compliance with Agile practices.
B. Reduce retrospectives to minimize resistance.
C. Keep both Agile and traditional methods running separately.
D. Provide training, leadership support, and clear communication of Agile benefits.

8.6 From WBS to Iterations

Translating a traditional Work Breakdown Structure (WBS) into adaptive iterations facilitates transitioning to Agile methodologies. It bridges the gap between the familiar structure of a WBS and the iterative, incremental approach of Agile, providing a practical pathway for organizations moving from plan-driven to adaptive project management. It involves a series of well-defined steps to ensure a smooth transition and effective execution of Agile iterations.

The first step is to identify deliverables suitable for iterative development. Not all work packages in a WBS are equally suited for incremental development. The goal is to determine which packages can be broken down into smaller, independent pieces that can be developed and delivered iteratively. This often involves focusing on areas that require continuous feedback and improvement, such as user interface design or complex software components. High-priority deliverables should be identified for early iteration focus to deliver value quickly and gain early feedback.

Next, work packages are reorganized into iterations. This involves mapping the elements of the WBS to backlog items, typically user stories or features. Work packages are converted into these user-centric formats to ensure the team focuses on delivering value to the user. Tasks are then prioritized based on business value, ensuring that the most valuable features are developed first. Iteration goals are defined, clearly articulating what the team aims to achieve in each iteration. Ensure that each iteration delivers a usable increment. Iteration objectives should be aligned with the overall project roadmap, ensuring that each iteration contributes to the larger project goals.

Determining iteration length and scope is a next step. Iterations are typically time-boxed, meaning they have a fixed duration, commonly ranging from one to four weeks. The length of the iteration should be chosen based on the project's complexity, the team's experience, and the need for feedback. Tasks are then broken down to fit within the iteration constraints. This involves estimating the effort required for each task and ensuring that the team can realistically complete the selected tasks within the timebox. Dependencies across multiple iterations should be carefully considered. If one iteration's output is required for a subsequent iteration, this dependency must be factored into the planning process.

Assigning work and managing dependencies is the next step. WBS work packages are aligned with Agile roles, such as the Product Owner and the Scrum Team. The Product Owner is responsible for defining and prioritizing the product backlog, while the Scrum Team is responsible for executing the work within each iteration. Cross-functional dependencies between iterations should be managed proactively. This involves identifying both hard dependencies (tasks that must be done in sequence) and soft dependencies (tasks that can be parallelized). Hard dependencies require careful sequencing of iterations, while soft dependencies can be addressed through effective communication and collaboration between teams.

Finally, continuous monitoring and adaptation are essential throughout the process. Sprint reviews and retrospectives provide valuable opportunities for the team to reflect on their progress, identify areas for improvement, and refine the WBS breakdowns. Agile frameworks like Scrum and Kanban provide tools and techniques for refining iterations and managing the workflow. The product backlog should be continuously adjusted based on stakeholder feedback, ensuring that the project remains aligned with evolving needs and priorities. This iterative cycle of planning, execution, review, and adaptation is a hallmark of Agile and enables teams to deliver valuable products in dynamic environments.

Let's illustrate the translation of a traditional Work Breakdown Structure (WBS) into adaptive iterations with a practical example: a website development project. This example demonstrates how a structured WBS can be effectively transitioned into the iterative approach of Agile. This translation allows for incremental delivery, continuous feedback, and adaptation to changing requirements, core principles of Agile project management.

Step 1: Traditional WBS for Website Development

A traditional WBS for this project might look like this:

Level 1: Website Development Project
  Level 2: Frontend Development
    Level 3: UI/UX Design
    Level 3: HTML & CSS Development
    Level 3: JavaScript Functionality
  Level 2: Backend Development
    Level 3: Database Setup
    Level 3: API Development
    Level 3: Security Implementation

This WBS provides a hierarchical breakdown of the project scope, defining the different work packages required to complete the website. However, it doesn't inherently lend itself to the iterative nature of Agile.

Step 2: Translating into Adaptive Iterations

To translate this WBS into adaptive iterations, we need to reorganize the work packages into user stories or features and then prioritize them for development in specific iterations. The focus shifts from delivering all frontend work and then all backend work to delivering working slices of the website in each iteration.

Iteration 1: Build and Test Basic UI Components

Convert UI/UX Design into interactive wireframes for key pages (e.g., homepage, product page). This focuses on a tangible deliverable.
Develop homepage with basic layout and navigation using HTML and CSS. This creates a functional piece of the site.
Conduct initial usability testing on the homepage wireframes and basic layout. Early feedback is crucial.

This first iteration focuses on creating a functional, albeit basic, homepage. It allows stakeholders to see and interact with a working part of the website early on, providing valuable feedback and validating design decisions.

Iteration 2: Implement Core Backend Features

Set up the database schema for core data entities (e.g., users, products, orders). This lays the foundation for data-driven functionality.
Develop API endpoints for basic data retrieval (e.g., fetching product information). This enables the frontend to interact with the backend.
Ensure data storage and retrieval functionality is working correctly. This validates the backend infrastructure.

This iteration focuses on building the essential backend infrastructure required to support the website's core functionality. It sets the stage for integrating the frontend and adding dynamic features.

Iteration 3: Enhance Frontend and Add Dynamic Features

Implement JavaScript for user interactions (e.g., adding items to a shopping cart, filtering product listings). This enhances user experience.
Connect frontend with backend APIs to display dynamic data (e.g., product information, user accounts). This brings the site to life.
Develop and integrate a basic search functionality. This adds a key user feature.

This iteration builds upon the previous ones, enhancing the frontend with dynamic features and connecting it to the backend. It delivers a more complete and interactive user experience.

Iteration 4: Security Testing and Final Adjustments

Perform security audits and fix any vulnerabilities identified. This is crucial before launch.
Optimize website performance for speed and scalability. This ensures a smooth user experience.
Finalize deployment process and prepare for launch. This prepares the site for release.

This final iteration focuses on ensuring the website is secure, performs well, and is ready for launch. It represents the final polish before the product is delivered to the users.

By translating the WBS into these adaptive iterations, the project team can deliver working increments of the website frequently, gather feedback early, and adapt to any changes in requirements or priorities. This iterative approach reduces the risk of building a product that doesn't meet user needs and ensures that the website evolves to meet the changing demands of the market.

Test Your Understanding 8.31
When translating a traditional Work Breakdown Structure (WBS) into Agile iterations, what is the primary purpose of identifying deliverables suitable for iterative development?
A. To ensure that each iteration has the same number of tasks as determined by the time-box.
B. To divide work packages into smaller, independent, and valuable increments
C. To complete backend work before frontend tasks begin
D. To reduce the need for feedback from stakeholders

Test Your Understanding 8.32
Which of the following best describes how WBS work packages are transformed during Agile adoption?
A. Work packages are grouped into Gantt chart milestones
B. Work packages are converted into user stories or features within a backlog
C. Work packages are assigned directly to the Scrum Master
D. Work packages are replaced by Kanban swimlanes

Test Your Understanding 8.33
When determining iteration length, which factor should NOT primarily influence the decision?
A. The project's complexity

B. The team's experience
C. The need for feedback
D. The number of project stakeholders

Test Your Understanding 8.34
In a software project, the Product Owner notices that some tasks in Iteration 2 depend on outputs from Iteration 1. What should the team do to handle this effectively?
A. Combine both iterations into a single longer iteration
B. Delay Iteration 2 until Iteration 1 is fully completed
C. Factor dependencies into the iteration planning and adjust sequencing
D. Ignore dependencies since Agile teams are self-organizing

8.7 Input for Scope

Defining the scope of each iteration relies on several key inputs. These inputs provide the necessary context and information for making informed decisions about what work should be included in each iteration.

The *Project Scope Statement* provides a high-level overview of the project's objectives, deliverables, and boundaries. It serves as a guiding document for the entire project, including iterative planning. The product vision, articulated within the scope statement, influences the scope of individual iterations. However, in an Agile context, scope boundaries are not fixed; they are subject to adjustment during iterative execution. This adaptability allows the project to respond to changing requirements and market conditions.

The *Product Backlog* acts as an evolving repository of all the work that needs to be done to deliver the product. It's a dynamic document that is continuously updated and refined throughout the project lifecycle. Prioritizing backlog items is essential for ensuring that the most valuable features are developed first.

Requirements and stakeholder expectations are inputs for defining iteration scope. Gathering and refining requirements from business stakeholders, customers, and end-users is an ongoing process in Agile. User stories and their associated acceptance criteria serve as inputs for iteration planning. Managing evolving requirements through iterative feedback loops is an Agile principle. Feedback from stakeholders and users is incorporated into the product backlog and used to adjust the scope of future iterations.

The *WBS*, while traditionally used in plan-driven projects, can also be a valuable input for iterative planning. WBS components can be converted into smaller, iterative work units, such as user stories or tasks. Mapping WBS elements to sprints or time-boxed iterations helps to ensure that the work is organized and that each iteration delivers a meaningful increment.

The *Risk Register and Constraints* also define iteration scope. The iteration scope may need to be adjusted based on the risk assessment. For example, if a critical risk is identified, the team might choose to focus on mitigating that risk in the next iteration. Scope constraints, such as time, budget, and resources, must also be considered when defining the iteration scope. The team needs to ensure that the selected work can be realistically completed within the given constraints.

Finally, *lessons learned and retrospective data* from previous iterations provide insights for refining the scope of future iterations. Customer feedback helps identify necessary adjustments to project scope while enhancing the iterative planning process. Similarly, insights from retrospectives enable teams to make more informed decisions about scope in future cycles. This continuous improvement through iterative scope adaptation is a hallmark of Agile.

Defining the scope of an iteration requires careful consideration of various factors to ensure a successful and productive sprint. This process involves several key steps, each contributing to a well-defined and achievable iteration scope. A well-defined iteration scope sets the stage for the development team to deliver valuable increments and contributes to the overall project success.

The first step in defining iteration scope is reviewing business objectives and stakeholder priorities. The scope of each iteration should be directly aligned with the overarching business goals and stakeholder priorities. This ensures that the work performed during the iteration contributes to the overall strategic objectives of the project. Stakeholder input helps to ensure that the iteration scope reflects their needs and expectations. This collaborative approach fosters a shared understanding of the project goals and increases stakeholder buy-in.

Next, backlog items are selected and refined. The product backlog serves as the source for defining the iteration scope. Prioritization techniques are used to select the most valuable and appropriate items for the upcoming iteration. Ensure that the selected work items fit within the iteration constraints, primarily the timebox. The team must realistically assess the effort required for each item and ensure that they can be completed within the allocated time. This often involves breaking down larger user stories into smaller, more manageable tasks.

Identifying dependencies and constraints is another crucial step. Dependencies between backlog items must be mapped to ensure a smooth iteration workflow. Conflicts between dependencies or resource constraints may arise and need to be resolved. Constraints, such as budget, resource availability, or technical limitations, must also be considered when defining the iteration scope. The team needs to ensure that the selected work is feasible within the given constraints.

Finally, the scope is finalized for iteration planning. Once the backlog items have been selected, dependencies have been resolved, and constraints have been considered, the iteration scope is confirmed with the Product Owner or Project Sponsor. This confirmation ensures that everyone is aligned on the goals and deliverables of the iteration. Clear iteration goals are then set, providing the team with a focused objective for the sprint. The Definition of Done (DoD) is also established or reviewed at this stage. The DoD defines the criteria that must be met for a work item to be considered complete. A well-defined and agreed-upon DoD helps to prevent misunderstandings and ensures that the increment delivered is truly "done" and potentially shippable.

Let's illustrate the application of defining iteration scope with a mobile app development project.

Step 1: Key Inputs for Iteration Scope
In this scenario, the Project Scope Statement provides a high-level overview, stating the project's objective: "Develop a customer-facing mobile application with core functionalities including login, dashboard, and notifications." This statement sets the overall direction and provides a context for defining the scope of individual iterations.

The Product Backlog contains a list of features and functionalities to be developed, including "User authentication," "Dashboard UI," and "Push notifications." This backlog serves as the primary source for selecting items to be included in the iteration.

Stakeholder Input plays a crucial role. In this example, the CEO prioritizes a fully functional dashboard over push notifications. This input directly influences the prioritization of backlog items and the definition of the iteration scope. It emphasizes that the dashboard's functionality is more critical for initial releases.

Constraints also impact the scope. The limited team capacity of only two developers for this iteration imposes a practical constraint on how much work can be realistically accomplished within the iteration's timeframe.

Step 2: Defining Iteration Scope

Based on these key inputs, the iteration scope is defined. Given the CEO's prioritization and the limited team capacity, the following items are prioritized for Iteration 1:

Develop and test user authentication: This functionality is essential for any user-facing application and is a logical starting point. It provides a foundation for secure access to the app's features.
Create dashboard wireframe and UI components: Focusing on the dashboard's UI aligns with the CEO's priority and allows for early feedback on the user interface and user experience. Creating wireframes first allows for quick iteration and refinement of the design before moving to full development.

Although important, the "Push notifications" feature is deferred to later iterations due to CEO input and limited developer capacity. This decision prioritizes delivering the most valuable functionality first, while acknowledging resource constraints. By focusing on user authentication and dashboard UI, the team can release a functional core in the first iteration, demonstrating progress to stakeholders and gathering early feedback. This iterative approach enables adjustments in future iterations based on learnings and feedback received.

Test Your Understanding 8.35
In Agile projects, how are scope boundaries typically managed?
A. They remain fixed once approved by the sponsor.
B. They are flexible and adjusted through iterative feedback.
C. They are defined strictly through the initial WBS.
D. They are determined only after the final iteration.

Test Your Understanding 8.36
A project team discovers a high-risk technical dependency that could delay integration in the next sprint. According to Agile principles, what should they do when defining the next iteration's scope?
A. Proceed with the original plan to maintain schedule predictability.
B. Postpone addressing the risk until after the release.
C. Include work to mitigate the risk in the upcoming iteration.
D. Expand the iteration scope to add new tasks unrelated to the risk.

Test Your Understanding 8.37
During an iteration planning meeting, a team realizes that several backlog items exceed the iteration timebox. What is the most appropriate action?
A. Extend the iteration to fit all items.
B. Split large user stories into smaller, manageable tasks.
C. Remove the lowest-priority items without discussion.
D. Request additional resources to finish all items.

Test Your Understanding 8.38
A Product Owner wants to confirm that the team and stakeholders share the same understanding of what "done" means for each deliverable. Which tool or concept should be reviewed?
A. DoD
B. Product Vision Statement

C. Project Charter
D. Stakeholder Register

Test Your Understanding 8.39
After several sprints, the team reviews customer feedback and retrospective notes to refine the next iteration scope. Which Agile principle does this illustrate?
A. Continuous improvement through iterative adaptation
B. Strict adherence to the original plan
C. Reducing stakeholder involvement
D. Avoiding scope adjustments once iteration starts

Test Your Understanding 8.40
A new Agile team is defining the scope for Iteration 1 of a project. They have a Product Backlog, clear constraints, and stakeholder input. What should be their final step before beginning development?
A. Assign tasks without reviewing dependencies.
B. Begin coding immediately after backlog selection.
C. Add extra tasks to use all available capacity.
D. Confirm the iteration scope and goals with the Product Owner.

8.8 Project Tracking

Project tracking is defined as the process of monitoring and reporting on the progress of a project against its planned objectives. It involves systematically collecting data on project performance, analyzing that data to identify any deviations from the plan, and taking corrective actions to get the project back on track.

Effective project tracking allows project managers to monitor progress, ensuring that the project is proceeding according to schedule and within budget. It also enables early identification of potential problems in risk management and facilitates the development of mitigation strategies. Ultimately, project tracking ensures project success, as it provides the insights needed to make informed decisions and deliver the desired outcomes. The approach to project tracking differs significantly between predictive (plan-based) and adaptive (iterative/agile) methodologies, reflecting their contrasting philosophies.

In predictive (plan-based) project management, tracking is focused on measuring progress against a predefined project plan. This plan, often based on a structured WBS, outlines all the tasks, dependencies, and timelines for the project. Predictive tracking relies heavily on established project management tools and techniques, such as milestones, Gantt charts, and EVM. Milestones mark significant points in the project timeline, providing checkpoints for measuring progress. Gantt charts visually represent the project schedule, showing the start and end dates for each task and their dependencies. EVM is a more sophisticated technique that integrates cost, schedule, and scope performance to provide a comprehensive assessment of project health.

Predictive tracking offers several benefits. It provides a clear structure for the project, with defined tasks, schedules, and dependencies, making it easy to understand the project's plan and track its progress. The emphasis on upfront planning also makes it relatively easier to estimate budget and resources, as the scope is typically well-defined from the outset. Predictive tracking also facilitates early risk identification. By comparing actual progress against the plan, deviations can be identified quickly through variance analysis, allowing project managers to take corrective actions before problems escalate.

However, predictive tracking also has limitations. Its rigid process makes it difficult to accommodate changes in requirements or scope. Because the plan is considered the primary guide, any deviations from the plan often require formal change requests, which can be time-consuming and bureaucratic. Furthermore, predictive tracking has a high dependency on the accuracy of the initial plan. If the upfront planning is flawed or if unforeseen events occur, the plan can quickly become outdated, making tracking less effective. This can lead to a false sense of security, where the project appears to be on track based on the initial plan, but in reality, it is significantly behind or off-course. Finally, the adaptation to change in predictive tracking can be slow. The formal change request process, while providing control, can also be cumbersome and slow, hindering the project's ability to respond quickly to changing circumstances.

Adaptive (iterative/agile) project tracking takes a fundamentally different approach compared to predictive tracking. Instead of rigidly adhering to a pre-defined plan, adaptive tracking focuses on monitoring progress based on ongoing feedback and the iterative nature of the development cycles. It embraces change and uses it as an opportunity to refine the product and the process.

Adaptive tracking relies on several key tools and techniques, including burndown charts, velocity tracking, and Kanban boards, to provide visibility into project progress and team performance. Burndown charts visually represent the remaining work in an iteration or release. Velocity tracking measures the amount of work a team can complete in an iteration (typically a sprint in Scrum). It's calculated by summing the story points completed during a sprint. Kanban boards, as discussed previously, are visual tools used to manage the workflow, showing the status of each task and identifying any bottlenecks.

Adaptive tracking offers several key benefits. Its flexible scope allows the project to adjust based on stakeholder feedback and changing requirements. Because work is done in short iterations, changes can be incorporated quickly and efficiently, without requiring formal change requests or extensive replanning. This makes adaptive tracking particularly well-suited for projects where requirements are expected to evolve.

The frequent iterations also allow for a faster response to change. If a problem is identified or a new opportunity arises, the team can quickly adapt their plans and incorporate the necessary changes in the next iteration. Adaptive tracking also leads to increased stakeholder engagement. Regular reviews and demos ensure that stakeholders are actively involved in the development process and have frequent opportunities to provide feedback. This continuous feedback loop helps ensure that the project stays aligned with business needs and stakeholder expectations.

However, adaptive tracking also has limitations. The inherent flexibility can lead to less predictability in terms of scope and schedule. Because changes are embraced, the final scope and delivery date may shift frequently, making it challenging to provide precise estimates upfront. This can be a challenge for organizations that require fixed-price contracts or have strict deadlines.

Adaptive tracking also requires higher effort in continuous monitoring. Frequent team communication, tracking of progress, and regular reviews and retrospectives are essential for effective adaptive tracking. This can increase the workload for the team and requires a commitment to disciplined execution of Agile practices. Finally, there is a potential for scope creep if discipline is not maintained. While flexibility is a strength, without clear prioritization and a strong Product Owner to manage the backlog, adaptive tracking can lead to unstructured iterations and uncontrolled scope expansion. Teams must be diligent in managing the backlog and ensuring that only the most valuable features are included in each iteration.

Feature	Predictive Tracking	Adaptive Tracking
Planning Approach	Detailed upfront plan	Iterative and flexible
Scope Management	Fixed scope with change control	Scope evolves based on feedback
Tracking Metrics	Schedule variance, cost variance (EVM)	Velocity, cycle time, burndown charts
Risk Management	Identified early and controlled	Addressed dynamically as they arise
Stakeholder Involvement	Periodic reviews (milestones)	Continuous engagement (sprint reviews, demos)
Change Handling	Formal change requests	Changes integrated during iterations

Table 8.2 Key Differences Between Predictive and Adaptive Tracking

Test Your Understanding 8.41
A project manager notices that actual progress is lagging behind planned milestones in a predictive project. Which technique would most likely help her identify the variance source?
A. Velocity tracking

B. Earned Value Management (EVM)
C. Kanban board analysis
D. Sprint retrospective

Test Your Understanding 8.42
Which tool is primarily used in adaptive project tracking to visualize remaining work in a sprint?
A. Gantt chart
B. Burndown chart
C. Work Breakdown Structure
D. Milestone schedule

Test Your Understanding 8.43
Which combination correctly matches the metrics with their corresponding tracking approaches?
A. Velocity and EVM -- Predictive tracking
B. Schedule variance and burndown charts -- Predictive tracking
C. EVM and schedule variance -- Predictive tracking
D. Velocity and cost variance -- Adaptive tracking

Test Your Understanding 8.44
An Agile team frequently adds new features without reviewing priorities, causing delays. What is the most likely cause?
A. Lack of formal change requests from the team members
B. Insufficient milestone tracking by the Scrum Master
C. Excessive reliance on EVM metrics
D. Inadequate backlog management by the Product Owner

8.9 Project Control

Project controls, in general, can be defined as the processes and tools used to monitor and control project performance, ensuring that the project stays on track to meet its objectives. This involves tracking progress, managing risks, controlling costs, and ensuring quality. However, the way these controls are implemented differs significantly between predictive (plan-driven) and adaptive (iterative/agile) project management.

In predictive project management, project controls are heavily reliant on a detailed project plan created upfront. Progress is measured against this baseline plan, and any deviations are identified as variances. Formal change requests are typically required to adjust the plan. The focus is on minimizing deviations from the plan and maintaining strict control over scope, schedule, and cost. In contrast, adaptive project controls recognize that change is inevitable and embrace it as an opportunity to refine the product and the process. Instead of trying to control every detail upfront, adaptive controls focus on monitoring progress iteratively, gathering feedback frequently, and adjusting plans as needed. The emphasis is on responding quickly to change and delivering value incrementally.

The key difference between predictive and adaptive project controls lies in their approach to uncertainty. Predictive controls assume a relatively stable environment and focus on minimizing deviations from the plan. Adaptive controls, on the other hand, acknowledge that projects often operate in complex and dynamic environments where requirements and priorities can change rapidly. They are designed to handle this uncertainty by being flexible and adaptable. This difference in approach is reflected in the tools and techniques used for project control. While predictive controls rely on tools like Gantt charts, earned value management, and formal change control processes, adaptive controls utilize tools like burndown charts, velocity tracking, Kanban boards, and regular reviews and retrospectives.

Artifacts play a significant role in adaptive project management, serving as tangible representations of the project's progress, plans, and decisions. They provide transparency and facilitate communication among team members and stakeholders. In adaptive projects, artifacts are often lightweight and evolve over time, reflecting the iterative nature of the development process.

Category	Predictive Artifacts	Adaptive Artifacts
Scope Management	Scope Statement, WBS	Product Backlog, Sprint Backlog
Schedule Tracking	Gantt Charts, Milestones	Kanban Board, Burndown Charts
Progress Tracking	Earned Value Reports	Velocity Reports, Task Boards
Change Management	Change Requests	Backlog Refinement
Quality Control	Quality Audits	Definition of Done, Retrospectives

Table 8.3 Comparing Artifacts in Predictive vs. Adaptive Projects

Test Your Understanding 8.45
Which statement best describes the key difference between predictive and adaptive project controls?
A. Predictive controls assume that change is frequent, while adaptive controls try to prevent it through strict procedures.
B. Predictive controls focus on managing uncertainty, while adaptive controls assume a stable and predictable environment.
C. Predictive controls minimize deviations from a fixed plan, while adaptive controls embrace change and adjust iteratively.
D. Predictive controls use informal monitoring methods, while adaptive controls rely on detailed baseline tracking.

Test Your Understanding 8.46
A team in an adaptive project wants to improve transparency and communication about progress and priorities. Instead of producing detailed upfront documentation, they rely on evolving visual boards and regularly updated lists of work items. Which artifacts are they most likely using?
A. Scope Statement and Work Breakdown Structure
B. Product Backlog and Sprint Backlog

C. Quality Audit Reports and Variance Logs
D. Milestone Chart and Earned Value Report

8.10 Success Criteria

Defining success in adaptive projects requires a different lens than predictive project management. While time, cost, and scope remain important considerations, they are not the sole determinants of success in an Agile or iterative environment. In adaptive projects, success is more nuanced and multifaceted, focusing on delivering value incrementally, adapting to change, and maximizing stakeholder satisfaction.

Traditional project management often defines success primarily in terms of meeting the triple constraint: delivering the project on time, within budget, and according to the initial scope. While these metrics are still relevant in adaptive projects, they are viewed through a different perspective. For instance, "scope" in an Agile project is not a fixed entity but rather a continuously evolving set of features prioritized based on value. Therefore, delivering the initially defined scope might not be the ultimate goal if, during development, better or more valuable features emerge. Similarly, while adhering to a strict timeline is important, delivering value frequently and adapting to changes may take priority over rigidly sticking to the initial schedule, especially if market conditions or customer feedback necessitate a shift in direction.

In adaptive (Agile) projects, success is a multifaceted concept measured through value delivery, flexibility, and continuous improvement, rather than rigid adherence to an initial plan. This shift in perspective recognizes the dynamic nature of modern projects and the importance of responding to change effectively. Several key criteria contribute to success in adaptive projects, each reflecting the core values and principles of Agile methodologies.

Delivering Value to the Customer means ensuring that the project meets customer needs and delivers usable increments of the product at regular intervals. Success in this area is measured by several factors. Working product increments delivered at the end of each sprint provide tangible evidence of progress and value. Stakeholder satisfaction and feedback, gathered through sprint reviews, demos, and direct communication, are indicators of whether the project is meeting their expectations. Value-based prioritization in the backlog ensures that the team is always working on the most valuable features, maximizing the return on investment.

Meeting the Definition of Done (DoD) ensures quality and completeness of deliverables. The DoD is a predefined checklist that outlines the criteria a work item must meet to be considered "done." Components of a typical DoD might include code being peer-reviewed and tested, documentation being updated, and the feature being integrated and deployable. Adhering to the DoD ensures that all deliverables meet a consistent standard of quality and are ready for release. For example, a team might consider a new checkout feature complete only after unit tests, security reviews, and stakeholder sign-off have been obtained.

Adaptability and Response to Change are indicators of success in adaptive projects. This refers to the ability of the team to pivot based on feedback, evolving requirements, or external changes. Success in this area can be measured by the number of backlog refinements and sprint adjustments made in response to new information or changing priorities. The speed and effectiveness of implementing stakeholder feedback are also important indicators of adaptability. A low resistance to change within the team suggests a culture that embraces change and is able to adapt quickly.

Team Collaboration and Productivity drive project success. Ensuring effective teamwork, communication, and efficiency in delivering tasks contributes to a positive and productive team environment. Team velocity provides insights into the team's capacity and progress. The level of cross-functional collaboration between team members, such as developers, testers, and designers, is another important indicator. Team satisfaction and motivation, often assessed through surveys or retrospectives, contribute to overall team performance.

Stakeholder and End-User Satisfaction are ultimately the most important measures of project success. Ensure that project outputs align with customer and business expectations. Stakeholder feedback gathered during sprint reviews and other interactions provides valuable insights into their satisfaction levels. Metrics like the Net Promoter Score (NPS, a customer loyalty metric that measures how likely customers are to recommend a company's products or services to others) or customer satisfaction surveys can provide more formal measures of customer happiness. Usage metrics for delivered features can also indicate how well the product is meeting user needs.

Finally, Sustainable Work Practices (Avoiding Burnout) drive long-term project success. Ensuring that the team works at a sustainable pace, without overloading individuals, contributes to team morale and productivity. Metrics such as the frequency of overtime and work-life balance surveys can help to assess the team's workload and well-being. Team morale and engagement levels are also important indicators. Consistency in sprint velocity over time suggests a sustainable pace and a healthy team environment. A development team that completes each sprint without excessive overtime while maintaining consistent productivity is demonstrating sustainable work practices.

Success Factor	Predictive (Plan-Based)	Adaptive (Agile-Based)
Scope Management	Deliver full predefined scope	Deliver highest-value features first
Schedule Tracking	Follow a fixed project timeline	Adapt schedule based on priority
Budget Management	Stay within planned cost	Adjust scope to maximize ROI
Progress Tracking	Milestone completion	Working software at each sprint
Stakeholder Engagement	Periodic reviews (phase-gates)	Continuous collaboration
Change Management	Formal change control	Dynamic backlog refinement

Table 8.4 Comparing Success Criteria: Adaptive vs. Predictive

Test Your Understanding 8.47
In adaptive projects, success is primarily defined by which of the following?
A. Delivering the full predefined scope on time and within budget
B. Maintaining strict adherence to the initial plan and milestones
C. Delivering incremental value and adapting effectively to change
D. Preventing scope changes and minimizing backlog adjustments

Test Your Understanding 8.48
Which of the following best represents the Definition of Done (DoD) in Agile projects?
A. A document listing all project deliverables
B. A checklist specifying completion criteria for each work item
C. A timeline of completed sprints and milestones
D. A record of stakeholder approvals after release

Test Your Understanding 8.49
A team consistently delivers features that pass all tests but often works late nights to meet sprint goals. Over time, morale drops, and productivity declines. Which Agile success factor is most likely being neglected?
A. Adaptability and response to change
B. Team velocity tracking
C. Scope management
D. Sustainable work practices

Test Your Understanding 8.50
Which of the following metrics would be least useful in assessing success in an adaptive (Agile) project?
A. Frequency of backlog refinements
B. Working product increments delivered per sprint
C. Adherence to the original Gantt chart
D. Stakeholder feedback from sprint reviews

Test Your Understanding 8.51
A product owner notices that users are not engaging with a newly released feature despite positive stakeholder feedback. What should the team focus on next?
A. Reassess value delivery using usage metrics and customer feedback
B. Revert to the initial project scope to ensure alignment
C. Extend the next sprint to allow additional documentation
D. Increase the sprint velocity to release more features

8.11 Prioritize Tasks

Task prioritization in adaptive (Agile) project management is the process of determining the order in which tasks or user stories should be completed. Unlike traditional project management, where the plan is often fixed and prioritization is done mostly upfront, adaptive projects require continuous prioritization throughout the project lifecycle. This ongoing prioritization allows teams to respond effectively to new information, changing requirements, and shifting business priorities.

In Agile, task prioritization is not a one-time event; it's an iterative process that occurs at multiple levels. At the product level, the Product Owner is responsible for prioritizing the product backlog, ensuring that the most valuable features are developed first. This prioritization is based on a variety of factors, including business value, customer needs, technical feasibility, and risk. At the iteration level (e.g., sprint planning in Scrum), the development team works with the Product Owner to prioritize the tasks within the sprint backlog, determining the order in which they will be completed during the sprint.

The importance of prioritization in fast-changing environments cannot be overstated. Agile projects often operate in dynamic environments where requirements and priorities can shift rapidly. Effective prioritization allows teams to adapt to these changes quickly and efficiently, ensuring that they are always working on the most valuable tasks.

Prioritization also helps to manage risk. By focusing on the most critical tasks first, teams can mitigate the risk of delivering a product that doesn't meet core business needs. It also helps to maximize value delivery by ensuring that the most valuable features are delivered early in the project lifecycle.

The approach to prioritization differs significantly between predictive and adaptive project management. In predictive projects, prioritization is typically done upfront, during the planning phase. The project plan serves as the primary guide, and changes to the plan, including reprioritization, often require formal change requests.

In contrast, adaptive projects embrace change and use continuous prioritization as a mechanism for responding to it. This flexibility is a key advantage of Agile methodologies, enabling teams to deliver maximum value in the face of uncertainty. Adaptive prioritization relies on close collaboration between the Product Owner, the development team, and stakeholders, ensuring that everyone is aligned on the project goals and priorities.

There are several key steps to prioritize tasks in adaptive project management. The first step in prioritizing tasks in adaptive project management is to *define the project goals and objectives*. This involves understanding the project's purpose, scope, and the desired outcome. It is important to identify what needs to be achieved, why it needs to be achieved, and how success will be measured. This information provides a clear understanding of what tasks are required to achieve the project's goals and objectives.

The next step is to *identify all the tasks* that need to be completed to achieve the project's goals and objectives. This involves breaking down the project into smaller, more manageable tasks. Once the tasks have been identified, they should be *classified into different categories* based on their priority level.

Once the tasks have been classified, they should be *prioritized based on their importance and urgency*. The importance of a task refers to how critical it is to the project's success, while urgency refers to how quickly it needs to be completed. Urgent tasks are those that require immediate attention and should be given priority over non-urgent tasks. A simple way to determine urgency is to use a scale of 1 to 5, where 1 is not urgent and 5 is extremely urgent. Tasks that are both important and urgent should be given the highest priority, while tasks that are neither important nor urgent should be given the lowest priority.

A prioritization matrix is a useful tool that can be used to prioritize tasks in adaptive project management. It involves creating a grid with two axes: importance and urgency. Tasks are then plotted on the grid based on their importance and urgency, and given a priority ranking based on their position on the grid.

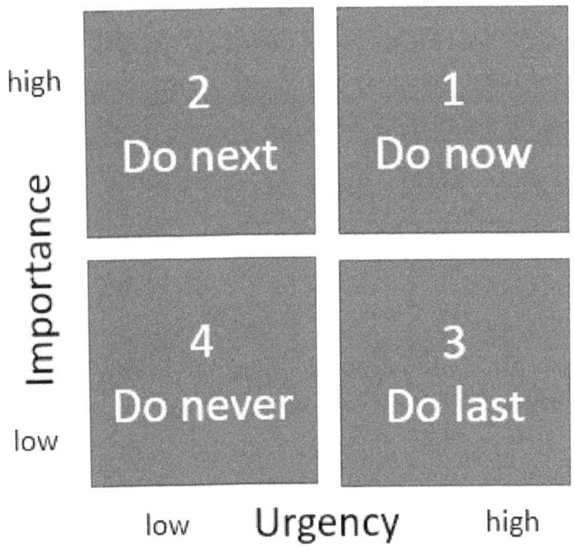

Figure 8.1 A prioritization matrix.

Stakeholders can help prioritize tasks. They can provide input on the importance of tasks, the urgency of tasks, and the impact of tasks. By involving stakeholders in the prioritization process, project managers can ensure that they are prioritizing tasks based on the needs and expectations of all stakeholders.

Finally, it is important to regularly review and adjust task priorities as the project progresses. This involves monitoring the project's progress and reassessing the importance and urgency of tasks as circumstances change. By regularly reviewing and adjusting priorities, the project manager can ensure that the project stays on track and that resources are allocated efficiently.

Test Your Understanding 8.52
A Product Owner notices that a key competitor has released a similar feature. The team decides to shift focus to a new, high-value capability during the next sprint. What Agile principle is being demonstrated through this decision?
A. Continuous prioritization to adapt to change
B. Fixed planning to maintain consistency
C. Avoiding stakeholder involvement in decision-making
D. Formal change control for all backlog modifications

Test Your Understanding 8.53
Who is primarily responsible for prioritizing the product backlog in Agile projects?
A. Scrum Master
B. Development Team
C. Product Owner
D. Project Sponsor

Test Your Understanding 8.54
During a sprint planning meeting, the team discusses the order of tasks for the next iteration. They decide to start with items that are both technically complex and high in business value. Which level of prioritization are they performing?
A. Portfolio-level prioritization
B. Product backlog prioritization
C. Sprint backlog prioritization
D. Strategic roadmap planning

Test Your Understanding 8.55
A project manager uses a grid to rank tasks based on their importance and urgency. Tasks rated “high importance” and “high urgency” are assigned top priority. What tool is the project manager using?
A. Work Breakdown Structure (WBS)
B. Prioritization Matrix
C. Gantt Chart
D. Burn-down Chart

8.12 Chapter Summary

This chapter further explores the agile approach to project management and compares it with the predictive approach. We explain the important role that organizational structure plays in determining the suitability of an adaptive project management approach. Additionally, we discuss how to determine the iterations and how to convert the work breakdown structure (WBS) of a predictive project to iterations of an agile project. Finally, we conclude the chapter by discussing how to prioritize tasks in the adaptive approach.

8.13 Case Study

Revisit the case study in Chapter 1. Perform the following tasks:
Produce a five-page document outlining how your team plans to control the project and carry out assigned tasks using an adaptive approach. In this document, describe the tools and techniques that will be used to ensure project success. Additionally, detail the processes that will be followed to execute tasks, including assigning roles and responsibilities, determining iteration goals, and adapting to changing requirements. It may also be helpful to include information on communication strategies, risk management plans, and quality control measures that are specific to the adaptive approach. Overall, the document should provide a comprehensive roadmap for executing the project in an adaptive manner.

8.14 MS Project Exercise 4

Progress Tracking and Report Creation

Ensure that "Exercise 3" is open before proceeding.

Part 1: Updating the Status Date
1. Once your project commences, navigate to the "Project" tab and select "Project Information".
2. In the "Project Information" dialog box, input the current date in the "Status Date" field. This step helps Microsoft Project track progress relative to the current date.

Part 2: Updating Task Progress
3. Return to the "Gantt Chart" view.
4. For each task that has commenced, open the "Task Information" dialog box by double-clicking on the task.
5. Navigate to the "General" tab within the dialog box.
6. Input the completion percentage in the "% Complete" field. This action informs Microsoft Project about the extent of task completion as of the "Status Date". Repeat this step for all tasks.

Part 3: Viewing Progress on the Gantt Chart
7. In the "Format" tab, check the "Project Summary Task" box in the "Show/Hide" section. This action displays a schedule bar on the Gantt chart for each task.
8. The schedule bar represents planned progress with a blue bar and actual progress with a darker bar. If a task is behind schedule, the end of the darker bar will be to the left of the current date line (usually red).

Part 4: Reviewing Project Progress
9. Navigate to the "Project" tab and select "Project Information".
10. In the "Project Information" dialog box, review key project progress statistics such as "Percent Complete", "Duration", "Start Date", "Finish Date", and "Cost".
10a. Check the project start date: The "Start date" field in the "Project Information" dialog box should match the start date set during project creation. If it doesn't, ensure that your tasks and dependencies are correctly set up.
10b. Check the project finish date: Similarly, verify the "Finish date" field. This date is calculated based on your tasks, their durations, dependencies, and the project calendar. If the finish date is later than expected, consider adjusting your plan.
10c. Go to Statistics: Click on the "Statistics" button in the "Project Information" dialog box to open the "Project Statistics" dialog box. Here, you can check the project duration and the percentage of completion. If the "% Complete" is less than 100% and all your tasks are complete, ensure that you've updated the "% Complete" for each task.

Part 5: Creating Reports
11. Navigate to "Project Overview": Click on "Report > Dashboards > Project Overview". This action opens the "Project Overview" report, providing a high-level view of your project, including the start date, finish date, percent complete, and cost.
12. Explore the different types of reports: Microsoft Project offers a variety of pre-built reports, categorized into "Dashboards", "Costs", "Work", "Resources", and "In Progress". Take some time to explore these categories and their respective reports. For instance, under "Costs", you'll find reports like "Cash Flow", "Budget", and "Overbudget Tasks".
13. Create a report of your choice: For this exercise, create a "Cash Flow" report. Navigate to "Report > Costs > Cash Flow". This report displays the cumulative cash flow for your project, broken down by costs and cumulative costs. It's a useful report for understanding when costs are incurred in your project.
14. Customize the report: You can tailor the report to your needs. Click anywhere in the report and then click Report Tools Design. From this tab, you can change the font, color, or theme of the whole report. You can also add new images (including photos), shapes, charts, or tables here. To change the data that Project shows in any part of a report, click the table or chart you want to change. Use the Field list pane on the right of the screen to pick fields to show and filter information. When you click a chart, three buttons also pop up directly to the right of the chart. Use the Chart Elements and Chart Filters buttons to quickly pick elements such as data labels and filter the information that goes into the chart.
15. Save the report: Don't forget to save the report once you're satisfied with it. Navigate to "Report > Export", click on "Visual Report" and follow the prompts to view or save the data.

8.15 References

Agile Alliance. (2021). Agile principles. Agile Alliance. Retrieved from https://www.agilealliance.org/agile101/agile-principles/
Azevedo, A., Jugdev, K., & Mathur, G. (2022). The impact of organizational support for the project management process on project and firm performance. *International Journal of Managing Projects in Business, 15*(7), 1013-1031.
Gareis, R. (2017). Project management: a systems approach to planning, scheduling, and controlling. John Wiley & Sons.
Kochenderfer, B. J., & Chrisman, J. J. (2015). Introduction to Decision Analysis. John Wiley & Sons.
Shtal, T., Pliekhanova, T., Kravets, K., & Ohiienko, N. (2023). Risk factors determination of enterprise external and internal environment during project implementation.

8.16 Solutions to Test Your Understanding

8.1 B; 8.2 A; 8.3 C; 8.4 C; 8.5 A; 8.6 B; 8.7 D; 8.8 A; 8.9 B; 8.10 B; 8.11 C; 8.12 A; 8.13 A; 8.14 D; 8.15 C; 8.16 B; 8.17 C; 8.18 A; 8.19 B; 8.20 A; 8.21 C; 8.22 D; 8.23 A; 8.24 B; 8.25 A; 8.26 D; 8.27 D; 8.28 B; 8.29 C; 8.30 D; 8.31 B; 8.32 B; 8.33 D; 8.34 C; 8.35 B; 8.36 C; 8.37 B; 8.38 A; 8.39 A; 8.40 D; 8.41 B; 8.42 B; 8.43 C; 8.44 D; 8.45 C; 8.46 B; 8.47 C; 8.48 B; 8.49 D; 8.50 C; 8.51 A; 8.52 A; 8.53 C; 8.54 C; 8.55 B;

Chapter 9: Business Analysis

Chapter Learning Outcomes

9.1 Identify the key concepts of business analysis.
9.2 Describe the roles and responsibilities of business analysts.
9.3 Explain how business analysis contributes to organizational strategy.
9.4 Recognize and list the core elements of Business Process Modeling Notation (BPMN).
9.5 Classify how business analysis activities align with different project management methodologies.

9.1 Introduction to Business Analysis

Business analysis is a disciplined approach to identifying business needs, understanding associated problems and opportunities, and devising effective, value-delivering solutions. It bridges the gap between business needs and technical solutions by understanding the "why" behind requests, ensuring alignment with strategic goals. This involves investigating the current state, defining the desired future state, and outlining the steps to achieve it.

The Business Analyst (BA) acts as a liaison among stakeholders, facilitates communication, and ensures projects align with overarching organizational strategy. BAs translate business needs into technical requirements and vice-versa, fostering shared understanding.

The scope of business analysis is broad, encompassing a wide range of activities from tactical process re-engineering and detailed requirements elicitation to strategic decision support involving enterprise-wide transformations. Several sub-disciplines exist, including enterprise analysis (focusing on organizational goals and strategies), requirements planning and management (defining, prioritizing, and managing requirements), and business process improvement (analyzing and redesigning processes).

Typical BA tasks include stakeholder interviews to gather information, workshops to collaboratively define solutions, and facilitating agile ceremonies like sprint planning and retrospectives. They must be adept at building consensus, managing expectations, and navigating conflicting priorities.

BAs are drivers of continuous improvement, analyzing current processes ("as-is" state) and designing improved future processes ("to-be" state). Tools like flowcharts and swimlane diagrams visualize these processes. Flowcharts illustrate the sequence of steps, while swimlane diagrams depict responsibilities. By identifying bottlenecks and inefficiencies, BAs help organizations streamline operations, reduce costs, and enhance customer satisfaction. They ensure technology investments deliver tangible business value, often developing business cases and measuring implemented changes' success.

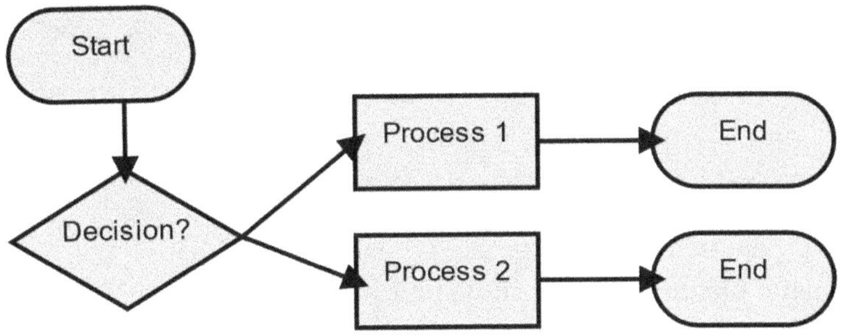

Figure 9.1 A sample flowchart

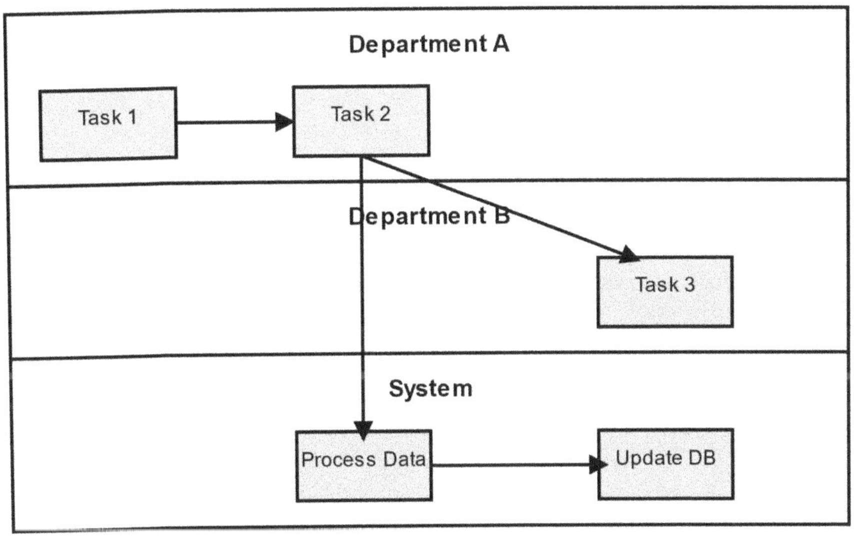

Figure 9.2 A sample swimlane diagram

By identifying bottlenecks, inefficiencies, and areas for improvement, BAs help organizations streamline operations, reduce costs, and enhance customer satisfaction. They ensure that technology investments deliver tangible business value and contribute to the achievement of strategic objectives. This often involves developing business cases to justify proposed solutions and measuring the success of implemented changes.

Test Your Understanding 9.1
A Business Analyst (BA) is primarily responsible for:
A. Managing project schedules and budgets to ensure timely delivery.
B. Writing detailed technical code to implement business solutions.

C. Bridging the gap between business needs and technical solutions.
D. Approving all strategic initiatives within the organization.

Test Your Understanding 9.2
You are a Business Analyst asked to improve the efficiency of the company's order fulfillment process. You map out the current process, identify redundant steps, and propose a streamlined version. Which approach are you using?
A. Enterprise analysis
B. Requirements planning and management
C. Business process improvement
D. Strategic portfolio alignment

Test Your Understanding 9.3
Which of the following best distinguishes a swimlane diagram from a flowchart in business analysis?
A. Swimlane diagrams focus on decision points, while flowcharts focus on parallel activities.
B. Swimlane diagrams assign responsibilities across participants, while flowcharts show process sequence.
C. Flowcharts display timelines, while swimlane diagrams depict data flows.
D. Flowcharts emphasize departments, while swimlane diagrams emphasize technology systems.

9.2 Gap Analysis

Gap analysis is a technique used in business analysis to evaluate the difference between the current state of a process, system, or strategy and the desired future state. It's a systematic approach to identifying deficiencies, opportunities, and areas for improvement. The "gap" represents the difference between where the organization is and where it wants to be (Kim and Ji, 2018). This analysis helps businesses understand what needs to be done to bridge that gap and achieve their goals.

Gap analysis helps understand the magnitude of the challenge, prioritize initiatives, and allocate resources effectively. It provides a clear picture of the current situation, highlights areas of weakness or underperformance, and identifies opportunities for growth and innovation.

In strategic planning, it could involve comparing the organization's current market share to its desired market share, identifying the necessary steps to achieve that growth. In technology upgrades, gap analysis might assess the capabilities of the current system against the requirements of a new system, highlighting the necessary customizations or integrations. It can also be used to evaluate employee skill levels against required competencies for a specific role or project.

Gap analysis is a valuable tool for BAs, supporting decision-making by providing concrete evidence of the need for change. By quantifying the gap, it helps prioritize initiatives based on their potential impact and feasibility. Gap analysis drives continuous improvement by highlighting areas where performance is lacking and prompting action to close the gap. It's not a one-time activity but rather an ongoing process that allows business to adapt to changing conditions and strive for excellence.

Gap analysis has a strong relationship with other business analysis techniques. It often works in conjunction with SWOT analysis, which helps identify strengths, weaknesses, opportunities, and threats. The "weaknesses" identified in a SWOT analysis often become the focus of a gap analysis. It also relates to requirements elicitation, as understanding the desired future state requires gathering requirements from stakeholders. The gap analysis helps to focus requirements elicitation efforts on the areas where the gaps are most significant.

The first step in gap analysis is thoroughly defining the "as-is" or current state. This involves documenting the existing processes, systems, or strategies in detail. Several techniques can be used for this purpose. Interviews with stakeholders, including employees, customers, and managers, provide valuable insights into how things currently work and what challenges are being faced. Process mapping, using tools like BPMN, visually represents the current workflow, highlighting bottlenecks, inefficiencies, and areas for improvement. Analyzing performance metrics, such as sales figures, customer satisfaction scores, or production output, provides objective data on the current performance level. For example, a BA might analyze customer service call logs to understand average handling time and identify areas where agents are struggling. Document review, including existing policies, procedures, and reports, can also provide valuable context and background information.

Next, the "to-be" or desired future state needs to be clearly envisioned. This involves defining what the organization wants to achieve and how it wants its processes, systems, or strategies to look in the future. Vision workshops, bringing together key stakeholders to collaboratively define the desired future state, can be highly effective. Stakeholder interviews can also be used to gather individual perspectives on the desired future state. Benchmarking, comparing the organization's performance or processes to industry best practices or competitors, can provide valuable insights into what is achievable and desirable. Market research and trend analysis can also help to understand future customer needs and technological advancements, informing the vision for the future state.

Once both the current and future states are clearly defined, the gaps between them can be identified. This involves systematically comparing the two states and quantifying and qualifying the differences. Quantitative gaps can be measured using metrics, such as the difference between current sales and target sales, or the reduction in processing time needed to achieve a specific goal. Qualitative gaps are more subjective and relate to aspects like employee morale, customer perception, or the quality of communication. Visual representations, such as charts and graphs, can be helpful for illustrating the gaps and communicating them to stakeholders.

After identifying the gaps, it's time to analyze the courses of gaps, or understand why they exist. Root cause analysis techniques, such as the "5 Whys" and Fishbone diagrams (Ishikawa diagrams), can be used to drill down to the underlying causes of the gaps. The "5 Whys" involves repeatedly asking "why" until the root cause is identified. A Fishbone diagram provides a visual framework for brainstorming and categorizing potential causes.

Not all gaps are created equal. Some gaps will have a greater impact on the organization's objectives than others. Therefore, it's crucial to prioritize the gaps based on several criteria, including their potential impact, feasibility of closing the gap, cost of closure, and the risk associated with not addressing the gap. A weighted scoring system can be used to objectively prioritize the gaps.

Once the gaps are prioritized, potential solutions and action plans need to be generated to bridge them. The step is usually called developing gap closure strategies. This involves brainstorming different approaches and evaluating their potential effectiveness. It's important to consider various options and involve stakeholders in the process to ensure buy-in.

The next step is to develop a detailed action plan for closing the prioritized gaps. This plan should outline the specific steps that need to be taken, assign responsibilities for each step, establish timelines for completion, and identify the resources required. The action plan should be realistic, achievable, and aligned with the organization's overall strategy.

The final step is to monitor the progress of the gap closure strategies and review their effectiveness. This involves setting Key Performance Indicators (KPIs) to track progress and establishing a feedback loop to monitor performance and adjust plans as needed. Regular reviews of the action plan should be conducted to ensure that it is still relevant and effective. If the desired results are not being achieved, the action plan may need to be revised.

Test Your Understanding 9.4

A Business Analyst at a logistics company identifies that delivery times average 5 days, while the company's goal is 2 days. Which of the following best describes what the analyst has discovered?
A. The organization's root cause.
B. The organization's performance benchmark.
C. A measurable gap between current and desired performance.
D. A qualitative improvement opportunity.

Test Your Understanding 9.5
Which of the following is typically the first step in conducting a gap analysis?
A. Prioritizing gaps based on impact and feasibility.
B. Defining the "as-is" or current state.
C. Developing a detailed action plan.
D. Monitoring KPIs to track results.

Test Your Understanding 9.6
During the gap analysis process, a Business Analyst uses the "5 Whys" technique. What is the purpose of this method?
A. To identify industry benchmarks for comparison.
B. To visualize stakeholder responsibilities.
C. To uncover the root causes of performance gaps.
D. To quantify the cost of closing identified gaps.

Test Your Understanding 9.7
How does gap analysis typically relate to SWOT analysis?
A. Gap analysis replaces SWOT analysis after implementation.
B. SWOT identifies threats that gap analysis eliminates.
C. SWOT provides KPIs used directly in gap analysis monitoring.
D. Weaknesses from SWOT often become areas of focus in gap analysis.

Test Your Understanding 9.8
Once gaps are identified, what should a Business Analyst do next to ensure effective action?
A. Prioritize the gaps based on impact, feasibility, cost, and risk.
B. Immediately assign tasks to responsible stakeholders.
C. Develop KPIs to track progress.
D. Conduct vision workshops to define future goals.

Test Your Understanding 9.9
A BA implements several initiatives to close identified gaps but finds that progress has stalled after six months. What should the BA do next?
A. Discontinue the action plan to avoid further resource loss.
B. Conduct a review of KPIs and revise the action plan if needed.
C. Wait another six months before taking further action.
D. Escalate the issue directly to senior management.

9.3 Business Case

A business case is a formal document that justifies a proposed project by outlining the problem or opportunity, proposed solution, costs, benefits, and alignment with organizational goals. It serves as a decision-making tool for stakeholders to evaluate the project's viability and strategic value.

A well-constructed business case secures funding, gains stakeholder buy-in, and ensures alignment with organizational success. It articulates the project's value proposition, addressing specific needs and expected benefits. For example, a CRM implementation case might detail inefficiencies in the current system, proposed functionalities, costs, projected gains in sales or customer satisfaction, and alignment with growth strategies.

By presenting evidence-based justifications and addressing concerns, a strong business case persuades stakeholders of the investment's merit, driving resource allocation and priority for high-return projects. It also identifies risks and mitigation strategies, improving project success likelihood.

Finally, it establishes benchmarks for benefits realization, enabling organizations to track outcomes and ensure intended value is delivered. A robust business case not only justifies investment but provides a roadmap for maximizing returns.

A robust business case comprises several key components that, together, provide a comprehensive justification for a proposed project. These components guide decision-making and ensure alignment with strategic objectives.

Executive Summary

The executive summary provides a concise overview of the entire business case. It highlights the proposal's key elements, including the problem or opportunity, the proposed solution, the most significant benefits, and how the project aligns with the organization's strategic direction. It's written for senior management and should be compelling enough to capture their attention and encourage them to delve into the details of the full document. This section is usually written last, after all other sections are complete.

Problem Statement/Opportunity

This section clearly articulates the business need or problem that the project aims to address. It explains the current situation, its negative impacts, and the potential consequences of inaction. Conversely, if the business case focuses on an opportunity, this section describes the opportunity, its potential benefits, and why it should be pursued. Data and evidence should support the claims made in this section, demonstrating the significance of the problem or opportunity. For example, a business case for a new marketing automation system might highlight the current inefficiencies in lead generation and the lost revenue due to manual processes.

Analysis of Alternatives

This section presents a range of potential solutions to the problem or opportunity, including the "do nothing" scenario (i.e., continuing with the status quo). Each alternative is evaluated and compared based on its benefits, costs, and risks. This analysis should be objective and data-driven, providing a clear comparison of the different options. For instance, the marketing automation system business case might compare the proposed system to alternative solutions, such as upgrading the existing system, outsourcing marketing activities, or maintaining the status quo. The analysis would consider factors like cost, functionality, integration capabilities, and potential ROI for each option.

Financial Analysis

A thorough financial analysis demonstrates the economic viability of the project. This section includes a cost-benefit analysis, comparing the project's costs (development, implementation, maintenance) to its anticipated benefits (increased revenue, cost savings, improved efficiency). Key financial metrics, such as Return on Investment (ROI), Net Present Value (NPV), and break-even analysis, are calculated and presented to demonstrate the project's financial attractiveness. This analysis provides a clear picture of the project's potential financial impact and helps stakeholders assess its value.

Risk Assessment

This section identifies potential risks and challenges associated with the project, such as technical risks, market risks, or operational risks. For each identified risk, the potential impact and likelihood are assessed, and mitigation strategies are outlined. A risk assessment helps stakeholders understand the potential downsides of the project and how those risks will be managed. This section might include a risk register, which lists the identified risks, their descriptions, impact, probability, and mitigation plans.

Implementation Plan and Timeline

This section outlines the key milestones, phases, and resource requirements for implementing the project. It provides a high-level roadmap for how the project will be executed, including timelines for each phase and the resources (personnel, budget, equipment) required. This section demonstrates that the project is well-planned and that the organization has a clear understanding of the steps involved in its implementation.

Benefits Realization

This section defines the expected outcomes of the project and how they will be measured over time. It establishes clear metrics for tracking the realization of benefits, such as increased sales, reduced costs, or improved customer satisfaction. This section also outlines the plan for monitoring and reporting on the benefits, ensuring that the project delivers the intended value. It connects back to the initial problem or opportunity, demonstrating how the project will achieve the desired outcomes and close the identified gap.

Test Your Understanding 9.10
The primary purpose of a business case is to:
A. Provide detailed technical specifications for a new system.
B. Justify a proposed project by outlining its value, costs, and alignment with goals.
C. Serve as a contractual agreement between the project sponsor and team.
D. Present marketing materials to promote the organization's image.

Test Your Understanding 9.11
After a project's completion, a company tracks customer satisfaction, operational efficiency, and sales growth to confirm that the expected benefits are achieved. Which section of the original business case guides this process?
A. Implementation Plan and Timeline
B. Problem Statement
C. Executive Summary
D. Benefits Realization

9.4 Strategic Alignment

Organizational strategy defines a company's long-term vision, goals, and market positioning to achieve sustainable competitive advantage. Business analysis aligns IT initiatives, process improvements, and projects with these strategic objectives, ensuring effective resource allocation, prioritized projects, and focused efforts to maximize value and drive business success.

Digital transformation has significantly redefined traditional strategies, placing a greater emphasis on agility, innovation, and data-driven decision-making. In today's rapidly changing digital landscape, organizations must be able to adapt quickly to new technologies, evolving customer expectations, and emerging competitive threats (Elmuti and Kathawala, 2001).

Innovation helps stay ahead of competition and create new customer value. Digital transformation generates vast amounts of data, which, when analyzed effectively, can provide valuable insights for strategic decision-making. Business analysis ensures that organizations leverage these insights to inform their strategies and drive innovation.

Several key responsibilities enable BAs to effectively contribute to strategic alignment. BAs act as strategic partners, ensuring that proposed solutions, directly support the company's long-term goals. They bridge the gap between high-level strategic objectives defined by the C-suite and the operational execution of those strategies. BAs translate the vision and goals set by senior management into actionable initiatives that can be implemented by project teams.

BAs drive strategic alignment by eliciting requirements from senior management, analyzing how processes support or hinder strategic goals, and creating roadmaps that link initiatives to objectives for better prioritization and resource allocation.

BAs integrate business analysis into strategic planning by participating in strategy sessions, contributing to reviews, and ensuring project portfolios align with goals. They evaluate projects for strategic impact and optimize resource allocation. Continuous feedback loops, such as agile retrospectives and performance reviews, help BAs adapt processes and solutions to evolving strategies, ensuring organizational agility.

To measure strategic alignment, BAs use KPIs like ROI on IT projects, process improvement metrics (e.g., cycle time reduction, cost savings), and customer satisfaction scores. Feedback from these metrics and stakeholders refines BA practices and strategic initiatives, ensuring continuous improvement and sustainable success in a dynamic environment.

Test Your Understanding 9.12
A retail company wants to align its new e-commerce platform with its strategic goal of expanding into international markets. As the business analyst on the project, what should your primary focus be to ensure strategic alignment?
A. Designing the platform's user interface to match the company's brand identity
B. Translating the company's expansion strategy into actionable system requirements and project initiatives
C. Managing vendor contracts for web development services
D. Conducting training sessions for customer support staff

Test Your Understanding 9.13
You are a BA working in a company that recently implemented an AI-powered customer support system. Senior management wants to know whether this initiative supports strategic goals. Which approach should you take?
A. Review KPIs such as ROI, process efficiency, and customer satisfaction to assess strategic impact
B. Ask the IT department for system uptime data to evaluate reliability
C. Gather employee opinions about the new system's usability

D. Conduct a competitor analysis to benchmark technology adoption rates

9.5 Process Modeling with BPMN

Process modeling is a skill for BAs, enabling them to visually represent and analyze business processes. Business Process Modeling Notation (BPMN) has become the de facto standard for graphically representing business processes. It's more than just a drawing tool; it's a powerful language for describing, analyzing, and improving how work gets done. BPMN offers a standardized set of symbols and rules, ensuring that process models are easily understood by everyone involved, from BAs and developers to managers and even end-users (Zarour et al., 2020).

Its history dates back to the Business Process Modeling Initiative (BPMI) in the early 2000s, evolving through several versions to become the widely adopted standard it is today, now maintained by the Object Management Group (OMG). BPMN's importance stems from its ability to bridge the gap between business and IT. By providing a common language, it enables business stakeholders to clearly articulate their process requirements, and IT professionals to effectively translate those requirements into system implementations. BPMN isn't just about documenting existing processes; it's about creating a foundation for change.

The benefits of using BPMN in business process modeling are numerous. First and foremost, it brings standardization and clarity. Before BPMN, organizations often used a variety of ad-hoc methods for documenting processes, leading to confusion and miscommunication. BPMN provides a consistent and well-defined notation, ensuring that everyone interprets process diagrams in the same way.

BPMN also significantly enhances communication among stakeholders. Because the diagrams are visually intuitive and use a standardized language, they are accessible to both technical and non-technical audiences.

BPMN enhances process analysis and optimization by visually mapping processes to pinpoint inefficiencies and redundancies. Its simulation tools enable "what-if" scenario testing, supporting data-driven decisions for process improvements. For instance, a company can model its order fulfillment process, identify shipping bottlenecks, and simulate solutions like adding staff or automation to reduce fulfillment time.

BPMN diagrams are built using a core set of elements that work together to represent a business process. These elements can be broadly categorized into several groups. Flow Objects are the core building blocks that define the flow of a process. These include Events, which represent triggers or outcomes in the process (like a customer order being received or a product being shipped); Activities, which represent the work being performed (such as "Process Payment" or "Ship Order"); and Gateways, which control the flow of the process based on conditions or events (like a decision to approve or reject a loan application).

Connecting Objects link the Flow Objects together, defining the sequence of activities. Sequence Flow shows the normal order of activities, Message Flow represents the exchange of messages between different participants (like a customer sending an email to customer service), and Associations connect Artifacts to Flow Objects, showing how data or information is related to the process. Swimlanes provide a way to visually organize the process by participant. Pools represent major participants in the process, often external to the organization (like a customer or supplier), while Lanes represent internal actors or departments within the organization (like the sales department or the shipping department).

Finally, Artifacts provide additional information about the process. Data Objects represent data that is used or produced by the process (like a customer order or an invoice), Groups visually group related elements of the process, and Annotations provide textual descriptions or comments about specific parts of the diagram.

Understanding BPMN's specific symbols enables accurate creation and interpretation of process diagrams. Start Events, depicted as a thin circle, mark the beginning of a process. End Events, represented by a thick circle, indicate the completion of a process. Tasks, shown as a rounded rectangle, represent individual activities performed within the process. Sub-processes, also rounded rectangles but with a plus sign inside, are used to decompose complex tasks into smaller, more manageable sub-processes.

Figure 9.3 Symbols of start and end events, task and sub-process.

Intermediate Events, represented by double-lined circles, capture occurrences such as delays (timer events), messages, errors, or escalation points during the process, making them critical for modeling exceptions and signaling transitions. Additionally, Pools and Lanes structure BPMN diagrams by grouping participants: Pools represent entire organizations or participants, while Lanes subdivide these Pools to denote specific roles or departments, thereby clarifying responsibility and facilitating the visualization of cross-functional workflows and accountability.

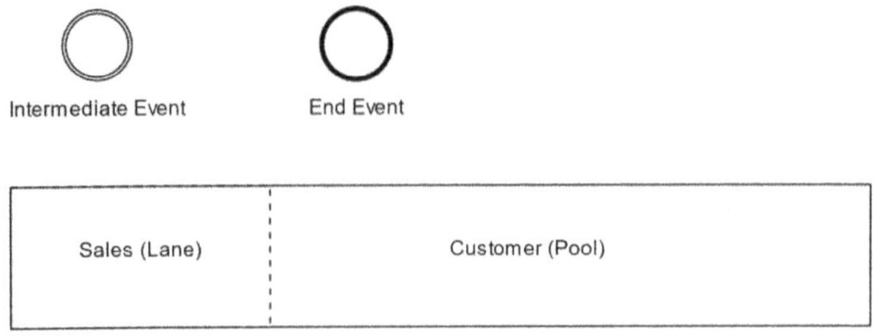

Figure 9.4 Symbols of intermediate and end events, lans and pool.

Decision points, represented by diamond-shaped Gateways, control the flow of the process based on conditions. Exclusive Gateways (diamond with an "X") represent a decision where only one path can be taken (like approving or rejecting a loan). Inclusive Gateways (diamond with a circle containing a plus sign) allow for multiple paths to be taken. Parallel Gateways (diamond with a plus sign) split the flow into multiple parallel paths, all of which must be completed.

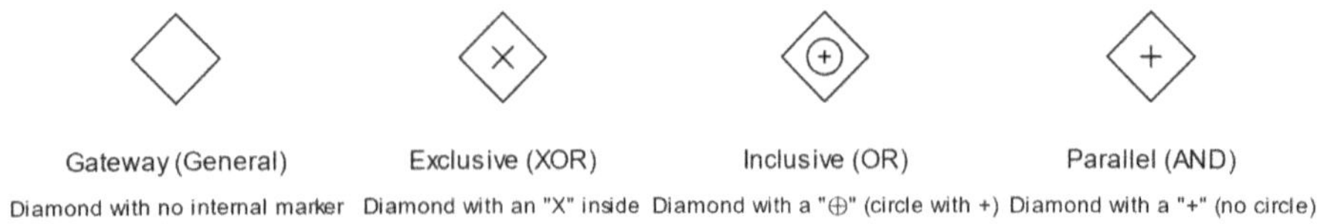

Figure 9.5 Symbols of decision points

Data Objects, shown as a rectangle with a folded corner, represent data that is used or produced by activities. Data Stores, depicted as a cylinder, represent locations where data is persistently stored, like a database or file system.

Figure 9.6 Symbols of data object and data store.

By understanding these core BPMN elements and symbols, BAs can effectively model a wide range of business processes. This visual representation allows for clear communication, facilitates process analysis and improvement, and supports the automation of business processes.

Creating effective BPMN diagrams involves a systematic approach. The process typically begins with defining the scope of the process being modeled. This involves identifying the start and end points of the process, as well as the key activities and participants involved. Next, the flow of the process is mapped out, starting with the initial event and progressing through the various activities and gateways, connecting them with sequence flows. As the diagram is developed, it's important to identify any data objects that are used or produced by the activities, and connect them using data associations. Swimlanes are then added to the diagram to represent the different participants involved in the process, clarifying roles and responsibilities. Finally, annotations can be added to the diagram to provide additional context or explanations.

Consider modeling a retail order fulfillment process in BPMN, where a customer orders a product online. The process includes receiving the order, processing payment, picking and packing the product, shipping, and confirming delivery. BPMN modeling visualizes the activity flow, identifies bottlenecks or inefficiencies, and highlights automation opportunities. The result is a clear, standardized diagram for communication, analysis, and optimization, fostering shared understanding among sales, warehouse, and shipping stakeholders.

Creating the BPMN diagram begins by defining the process boundaries. The start event is the "Order Placed" by the customer, and the end event is "Delivery Confirmed." Next, the key tasks are mapped out in sequence. These might include "Receive Order," "Process Payment," "Check Stock Availability," "Pick and Pack Product," "Ship Order," and "Send Shipping Confirmation." Decision points, represented by gateways, are incorporated to handle conditional logic. For example, a gateway after "Process Payment" would check for "Payment Approval." If approved, the process continues; if rejected, the process might branch to a "Payment Declined" path.

Another decision point after "Check Stock Availability" would determine if the item is in stock. If in stock, the process proceeds to "Pick and Pack Product"; if not, it might branch to a "Backorder" or "Out of Stock" path. Data objects, such as "Order Details," "Payment Information," and "Shipping Address," are added to the diagram and connected to the relevant tasks using data associations. Swimlanes are used to represent the different departments or systems involved, such as the "Online Store," "Payment Gateway," "Warehouse," and "Shipping Carrier." Message flows can be used to show communication between these participants, like the "Shipping Confirmation" sent from the "Shipping Carrier" to the "Online Store."

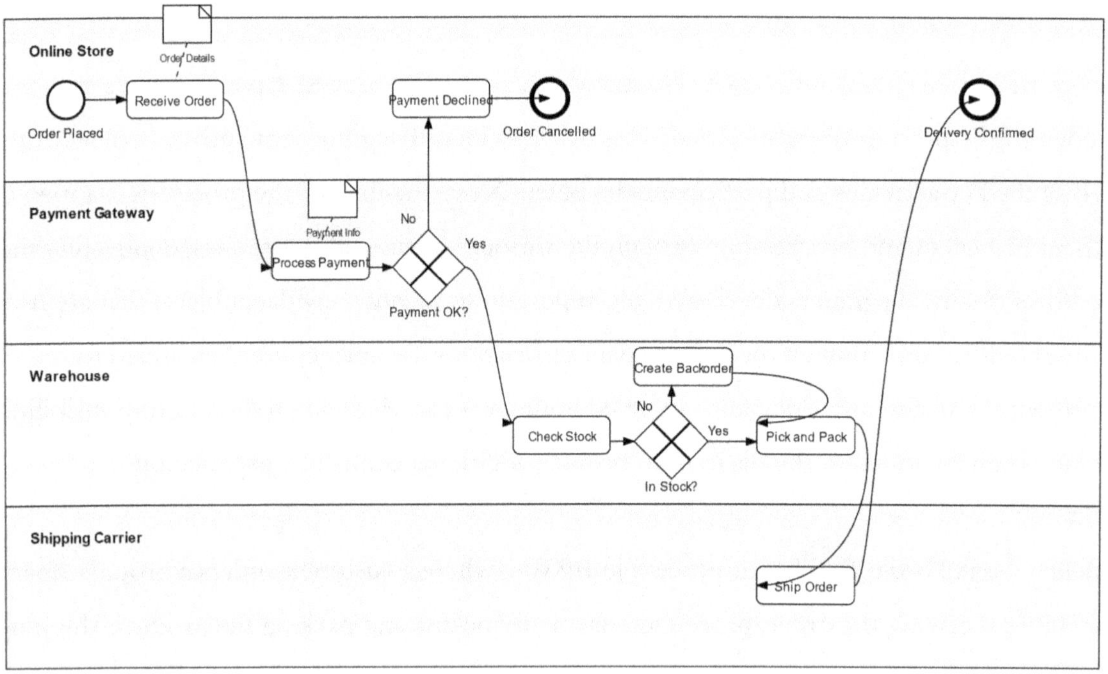

Figure 9.7 Sample BPMN.

Once the BPMN diagram is created, it's important to review and validate it with stakeholders. This involves sharing the diagram with representatives from all departments involved in the order fulfillment process, such as sales, warehouse, shipping, and customer service. During the review, stakeholders should be asked to verify the accuracy of the process flow, ensuring that all steps are correctly represented and that no important activities are missing. They should also check for completeness, ensuring that all relevant details, such as decision points, data objects, and participants, are included.

It's helpful to walk through the diagram step-by-step with the stakeholders, discussing each activity and decision point to ensure everyone understands the process and agrees with its representation. Encourage stakeholders to provide feedback and suggestions for improvement. This collaborative review process not only validates the diagram but also fosters a shared understanding of the process. After incorporating stakeholder feedback, the BPMN diagram can be considered validated and ready for use in further analysis, optimization, or automation efforts.

Test Your Understanding 9.14
Which of the following best describes the primary purpose of Business Process Modeling Notation (BPMN)?

A. To create artistic diagrams of organizational processes
B. To provide a standardized visual language for describing, analyzing, and improving processes
C. To automate software code generation from business requirements
D. To replace project documentation with visual models

Test Your Understanding 9.15
In BPMN, which type of Flow Object represents a trigger or outcome within a process?
A. Activity
B. Gateway
C. Event
D. Pool

Test Your Understanding 9.16
Which BPMN symbol represents a decision point where only one path can be taken, such as approving or rejecting a loan?

A. Inclusive Gateway (◉)
B. Parallel Gateway (+)
C. Exclusive Gateway (X)
D. Complex Gateway (*)

Test Your Understanding 9.17
You are modeling a process that includes receiving an order, checking stock, and branching to either fulfillment or backorder depending on availability. Which BPMN element should you use to represent this branching?
A. Activity
B. Gateway
C. Event
D. Pool

Test Your Understanding 9.18
In BPMN, what is the difference between a Pool and a Lane?
A. Pools represent entire organizations or participants, while Lanes represent departments or roles within them
B. Lanes represent external entities, while Pools represent internal systems
C. Pools are for data storage; Lanes are for data flow
D. There is no functional difference between them

Test Your Understanding 9.19
During a process review, a stakeholder asks what the "cylinder" symbol represents in a BPMN diagram. What should the BA explain?
A. It represents an Activity
B. It represents a Pool
C. It represents a Gateway
D. It represents a Data Store

Test Your Understanding 9.20
You are modeling a "Loan Approval" process. After "Review Application," a decision must be made -- if approved, continue to "Disburse Funds"; if rejected, proceed to "Notify Applicant." Which BPMN element should represent this step?

A. Event
B. Sub-process
C. Task
D. Exclusive Gateway

Test Your Understanding 9.21
A BA is developing a BPMN diagram for a supply chain process involving multiple external suppliers and internal departments. To clearly show communication between them, the BA should use:
A. Message Flows
B. Sequence Flows
C. Gateways
D. Data Objects

9.6 Wireframing and Prototyping Tools

Wireframing and prototyping are essential steps in translating business requirements into tangible user interface designs. Wireframes are low-fidelity representations of user interfaces, focusing on layout and functionality rather than visual aesthetics. They serve as a blueprint for the user interface, outlining the placement of elements like buttons, forms, and navigation menus.

Wireframes bridge the gap between business requirements and technical specifications. They provide a visual representation of how the system will function from the user's perspective, allowing stakeholders to validate the design and ensure it meets their needs. For example, a wireframe for a mobile banking app might show the layout of the account summary screen, including where the balance, transaction history, and bill pay options will be located. This allows business stakeholders to review the design and provide feedback before any actual coding begins, preventing costly rework later in the development process. Wireframes are typically created using simple tools or even just pen and paper, emphasizing speed and ease of iteration.

Prototyping takes wireframes a step further, transforming them into interactive, clickable mockups. Prototypes simulate the user experience, allowing stakeholders to interact with the interface and get a feel for how the system will work. This interactivity enables more thorough testing and validation of the design, uncovering usability issues and refining the user flow. Various tools are available for wireframing and prototyping, each with its strengths and weaknesses. Balsamiq is a popular choice for creating rapid, low-fidelity mockups. Its focus is on speed and simplicity, allowing BAs to quickly sketch out user interface ideas and iterate on designs based on stakeholder feedback.

Figma, on the other hand, is a more powerful and versatile tool, suitable for creating both low-fidelity wireframes and high-fidelity, interactive prototypes. Figma's collaborative features make it ideal for team-based design, allowing multiple stakeholders to contribute to the design process in real time. Its advanced features also enable the creation of more detailed and realistic prototypes, including animations and transitions, providing a more accurate representation of the final product. The choice between Balsamiq and Figma, or other similar tools, often depends on the project's specific needs, the level of fidelity required, and the team's familiarity with the software. For quick, early-stage prototyping, Balsamiq might be sufficient. For more complex projects requiring detailed, collaborative design, Figma might be a better fit.

Test Your Understanding 9.22
Which of the following best describes the primary purpose of a wireframe?
A. To create a fully functional version of the final user interface for user acceptance testing.
B. To provide a visual layout focusing on structure and functionality, not aesthetics.
C. To demonstrate the performance of the system under load.
D. To finalize the color scheme and branding elements of the interface.

Test Your Understanding 9.23
A business analyst is working with stakeholders to design a new online shopping cart system. The stakeholders want to quickly see where items, prices, and the "checkout" button will appear, but they are not concerned about colors or graphics yet. What should the analyst create first?
A. A high-fidelity prototype using Figma
B. A coded user interface in HTML and CSS
C. A low-fidelity wireframe sketch
D. A detailed usability test plan

Test Your Understanding 9.24
During a design review, stakeholders request the ability to click through screens and experience how users would navigate the app. The business analyst decides to move beyond static layouts. Which approach should the analyst take next?
A. Convert the wireframes into an interactive prototype.
B. Redesign the layout using a new wireframing tool.
C. Begin developing the app using front-end code.
D. Add color and branding to the existing wireframes.

9.7 Scenario Analysis and Decision Tables

Scenario analysis and decision tables are techniques used by BAs to understand and model complex decision-making processes. *Scenario analysis* is a structured approach to predicting and evaluating the potential outcomes of different business decisions under various conditions. It involves developing plausible "what-if" situations or scenarios that represent different possible future states. These scenarios consider various factors, such as market trends, competitive pressures, technological advancements, and regulatory changes, to assess their potential impact on the business.

By mapping out these different scenarios, BAs can help organizations understand the risks, opportunities, and dependencies associated with different strategic choices. For example, a company considering launching a new product might develop scenarios that consider different levels of market demand, competitor response, and supply chain disruptions.

Scenario Analysis: TechNova's Smart Home Hub Launch
Product: Smart Home Hub priced at $200 per unit.

Key Variables & Assumptions:
1. Market Demand (Units Sold):
   - High Demand: 100,000 units (10% of Total Addressable Market).
   - Moderate Demand: 50,000 units (5% of TAM).
   - Low Demand: 20,000 units (2% of TAM).
2. Competitor Response (Market Share Capture):
   - No Response: TechNova captures 30% of demand.
   - Moderate Response: TechNova captures 20%.
   - Aggressive Response: TechNova captures 10%.
3. Supply Chain Costs (Per Unit):
   - No Disruption: $120.
   - Minor Disruption: +10% ($132).
   - Severe Disruption: +25% ($150).
4. Fixed Costs: $1 million (marketing, R&D, etc.).

Scenario 1: Best Case
- Market Demand: High (100,000 units).
- Competitor Response: None (30% share → 30,000 units sold).
- Supply Chain: No disruptions ($120/unit).
Calculations:
- Revenue: 30,000 × $200 = $6 million.
- Variable Costs: 30,000 × $120 = $3.6 million.
- Profit: $6M – $3.6M – $1M (fixed) = $1.4 million profit.

Scenario 2: Base Case
- Market Demand: Moderate (50,000 units).
- Competitor Response: Moderate (20% share → 10,000 units sold).
- Supply Chain: Minor disruption ($132/unit).
Calculations:
- Revenue: 10,000 × $200 = $2 million.
- Variable Costs: 10,000 × $132 = $1.32 million.
- Profit: $2M – $1.32M – $1M = -$0.32 million loss.

Scenario 3: Worst Case
- Market Demand: Low (20,000 units).
- Competitor Response: Aggressive (10% share → 2,000 units sold).
- Supply Chain: Severe disruption ($150/unit).

Calculations:
- Revenue: 2,000 × $200 = $0.4 million.
- Variable Costs: 2,000 × $150 = $0.3 million.
- Profit: $0.4M – $0.3M – $1M = -$0.9 million loss.

Key Takeaways for Decision-Makers:
1. Profitability Range: Outcomes vary from +$1.4M to -$0.9M, highlighting significant risk.
2. Critical Levers:
   - Competitor response has the largest impact on market share (e.g., 30% vs. 10% capture).
   - Supply chain resilience is crucial to avoid cost spikes (e.g., $120 vs. $150/unit).
3. Mitigation Strategies:
   - Secure pre-orders to validate demand.
   - Diversify suppliers to reduce disruption risk.
   - Develop a competitive pricing strategy to counter rivals.

This analysis can help them assess the potential profitability of the product launch under various conditions and identify potential mitigation strategies for identified risks. Scenario analysis is not about predicting the future with certainty, but rather about preparing for different possibilities and making informed decisions based on a range of potential outcomes.

Decision tables provide a structured way to represent complex decision rules and ensure consistency in decision-making. They are particularly useful when dealing with situations involving multiple conditions and corresponding actions. A decision table lists the different conditions that might arise, along with the actions that should be taken in each case. Each row in the table represents a specific combination of conditions, and the corresponding entry in the table specifies the appropriate action. For example, a decision table for approving loan applications might consider conditions like credit score, income, and loan amount. Based on different combinations of these conditions, the table would specify whether the loan should be approved, rejected, or referred for further review.

Decision Table: Loan Approval Process
Context: A bank uses a decision table to automate loan application decisions.
Conditions: Credit score, annual income, and loan amount.
Decision Table with Rules and Outcomes (Thresholds and actions are simplified for illustration)

Rule	Credit Score	Annual Income	Loan Amount	Action
1	≥ 750	≥ $80,000	≤ $50,000	Approve
2	≥ 750	≥ $80,000	>$50,000	Approve with higher rate
3	700–749	≥ $60,000	≤ $75,000	Refer for manual review
4	700–749	≥ $60,000	> $75,000	Reject
5	650–699	≥ $50,000	≤ $25,000	Refer for manual review
6	650–699	≥ $50,000	> $25,000	Reject
7	< 650	Any	Any	Reject

Table 9.1 Example Applications with Numbers

1. Applicant A:
   - Credit Score: 780, Income: $95,000, Loan Request: $40,000; Decision: Rule 1 → Approve
2. Applicant B:
   - Credit Score: 720, Income: $65,000, Loan Request: $80,000; Decision: Rule 4 → Reject
3. Applicant C:
   - Credit Score: 680, Income: $55,000, Loan Request: $20,000; Decision: Rule 5 → Manual review
4. Applicant D:
   - Credit Score: 600, Income: $120,000, Loan Request: $30,000; Decision: Rule 7 → Reject

Decision tables clarify complex decision logic, making it easier for stakeholders to understand how decisions are made. They also promote consistency by ensuring that the same decision rules are applied consistently across different situations. Furthermore, decision tables can be easily translated into computer code, facilitating the automation of decision-making processes. By using both scenario analysis and decision tables, BAs can provide valuable support for strategic planning and operational decision-making, helping organizations make informed choices and improve their overall performance.

Test Your Understanding 9.25
A BA is using scenario analysis to evaluate the impact of market trends and competitor actions on a new product launch. What is the *primary goal* of using scenario analysis in this context?
A. To accurately predict the most likely future outcome
B. To prepare for a range of possible future situations and make informed decisions
C. To eliminate uncertainty by modeling all possible market variables
D. To determine the single best financial forecast for the company by comparing all possible outcomes

Test Your Understanding 9.26
What is one key advantage of decision tables for business analysis?
A. They eliminate the need for data validation.
B. They visually represent future market conditions.
C. They promote consistent decision-making.
D. They predict financial outcomes under different demand levels.

Test Your Understanding 9.27
Which statement best distinguishes scenario analysis from decision tables?
A. Scenario analysis focuses on operational automation, while decision tables focus on strategic planning.
B. Scenario analysis models potential future conditions, while decision tables outline rules for consistent decisions.
C. Both techniques are used exclusively for financial forecasting.
D. Decision tables are more suitable for long-term strategy than scenario analysis.

9.8 Align with Predictive Methodology

The BA's role is significantly influenced by the project management methodology used. Each methodology has distinct approaches to planning, execution, and change management, directly impacting the BA's activities. Understanding these nuances drives BA success.

Predictive project management, often associated with the Waterfall model, emphasizes detailed upfront planning and documentation. The BA defines and documents requirements thoroughly before development begins. This approach aims to minimize changes and establish a clear understanding of the project scope from the outset. The BA's responsibilities in this environment center around thoroughness, precision, and comprehensive documentation.

In a predictive approach, the BA conducts extensive requirements gathering and stakeholder interviews. This involves engaging with a broad range of stakeholders, from business users and subject matter experts to management and IT professionals, to elicit their needs and expectations. The BA employs various techniques, including structured interviews, questionnaires, workshops, and document analysis, to gain a comprehensive understanding of the requirements. The goal is to capture all relevant information, including functional requirements (what the system should do), non-functional requirements (performance, security, usability), and business rules.

Developing detailed process models is another key activity. The BA uses tools like Business Process Modeling Notation (BPMN) and flowcharts to visually represent business processes, both current ("as-is") and future ("to-be"). These models serve as a communication tool, helping stakeholders understand how the system will interact with existing processes and support their work. For instance, a BPMN diagram of the customer onboarding process could show the steps involved in registering a new customer, verifying their information, and setting up their account. This diagram can then be used to identify bottlenecks, inefficiencies, and areas for improvement. Process models also serve as a basis for defining system requirements, ensuring the system supports the desired business processes.

Creating a comprehensive Business Requirements Document (BRD) is a central deliverable. The BRD serves as the project's baseline, documenting all agreed-upon requirements clearly, concisely, and structurally. It acts as a contract between business stakeholders and the development team, ensuring shared understanding of the project scope and objectives.

The BRD typically includes sections on business objectives, scope, functional and non-functional requirements, business rules, use cases, and data requirements. While it's a living document subject to change control procedures, the emphasis is on minimizing changes after finalization. The BRD is used throughout the project lifecycle, from design and development to testing and implementation, ensuring the final product meets documented requirements. It's a reference point for the development team and serves as a basis for acceptance testing.

In a predictive project environment, the BA and project manager (PM) collaborate closely, leveraging their expertise for project success. Their collaboration aligns the project plan with business goals and technical capabilities. The BA focuses on understanding and documenting the "what" and "why" (business needs and requirements), while the PM focuses on the "how" and "when" (project plan, schedule, and resources).

The BA collaborates with the PM throughout the project lifecycle, starting with initial planning. They jointly define the project scope, ensuring alignment with business objectives and technical feasibility. The BA provides the PM with detailed business requirements. This information informs the PM's development of the project plan, including the work breakdown structure, schedule, and resource allocation. The BA also works with the PM to identify potential risks and develop mitigation strategies.

Emphasis on sign-off milestones and review checkpoints is a hallmark of predictive project management. Sign-off milestones are key points where deliverables, like the BRD, are formally reviewed and approved by stakeholders. The BA ensures deliverables are complete, accurate, and meet agreed-upon requirements. They facilitate the review process, gathering feedback and incorporating revisions. The sign-off milestone signifies formal agreement, providing a clear baseline for subsequent activities.

Review checkpoints are smaller, more frequent reviews throughout the project, offering opportunities to track progress, identify issues, and make adjustments. The BA participates, providing requirements updates and ensuring development aligns with specifications. By emphasizing sign-off milestones and review checkpoints, the BA and PM ensure the project stays on track, meets business needs, and delivers expected value. This structured approach minimizes change risk and ensures stakeholder alignment.

A predictive approach ensures stability and minimizes change. The goal isn't to eliminate change but to manage it effectively and minimize its disruptive impact. This requires proactive scope management and a well-defined change control process.

Strategies for maintaining scope and controlling change include a clear and comprehensive BRD as the project baseline. A well-defined scope makes it easier to identify and resist "scope creep." Another strategy is a formal change control process, outlining how requirement changes will be requested, evaluated, and approved. This typically involves a Change Control Board (CCB) that reviews and approves change requests, assessing their impact on project scope, schedule, budget, and resources.

The BA facilitates formal change requests and impact analyses. When a stakeholder requests a change, the BA documents it, clearly describing the proposed change and rationale. The BA then conducts an impact analysis, assessing the potential consequences on project scope, schedule, budget, and other requirements. The BA presents the impact analysis to the CCB. If the change request is approved, the BA updates the BRD and other relevant documentation. They also work with the PM to update the project plan and schedule. By following a formal change control process and conducting impact analyses, the BA helps ensure changes are managed effectively and the project remains on track. This structured approach minimizes disruptions and maintains stability.

Test Your Understanding 9.28
In a predictive (Waterfall) project management environment, what is the *primary focus* of the Business Analyst's (BA's) role during the planning phase?
A. Iteratively developing prototypes for stakeholder feedback
B. Thoroughly defining and documenting detailed business requirements upfront
C. Adjusting project scope continuously based on emerging business needs and customer requests
D. Managing daily project schedules and resource allocations

Test Your Understanding 9.29
A BA is creating a Business Requirements Document (BRD) for a new accounting system. The PM emphasizes that the BRD will serve as the "project baseline." What does this mean for the BA?
A. The BRD will guide all change requests and serve as the reference point for scope management.
B. The BRD will only be used for testing and implementation phases.
C. The BRD will replace all other project documentation.
D. The BRD can be freely updated by any stakeholder without formal approval.

Test Your Understanding 9.30
Which statement best describes how the BA and Project Manager (PM) collaborate in a predictive project?
A. The BA focuses on the "what" and "why," while the PM focuses on the "how" and "when."
B. The BA manages scope and scheduling, while the PM handles requirements elicitation.
C. Both focus primarily on testing deliverables against requirements.
D. The BA defines tasks, and the PM validates business needs.

Test Your Understanding 9.31
During a project review, a stakeholder requests a new report feature not included in the approved BRD. What should the BA do first according to predictive practices?
A. Add the new requirement directly to the project scope to maintain stakeholder satisfaction.
B. Document the change request and perform an impact analysis on project scope, schedule, and budget.
C. Escalate the issue to the development team for immediate implementation.
D. More than likely, reject the change outright to prevent scope creep.

Test Your Understanding 9.32
Why are sign-off milestones and review checkpoints critical in predictive project management?
A. They provide opportunities for stakeholders to make unapproved changes.
B. They enable iterative development cycles and flexible adaptation.
C. They ensure deliverables are reviewed, approved, and aligned with requirements at key stages.
D. They reduce documentation requirements by eliminating the need for formal reviews.

Test Your Understanding 9.33
A stakeholder requests a change after the BRD is finalized. The BA follows the change control process, conducts an impact analysis, and the Change Control Board (CCB) approves the modification. What is the BA's next step?
A. Update the BRD and related documentation, and coordinate with the PM to adjust the project plan.
B. Implement the change directly in the system to save time.
C. Reopen the requirements-gathering phase for all stakeholders.
D. Record the change and proceed without updating other documents.

9.9 Align with Agile Methodology

Agile methodologies, like Scrum, emphasize iterative development and continuous feedback. In an Agile environment, the BA's work is iterative and incremental, focusing on ongoing refinement of user stories and acceptance criteria. Requirements are captured in smaller chunks, often as user stories, prioritized and refined throughout the project. The BA collaborates closely with the product owner and development team, participating in sprint planning, daily stand-ups, and sprint reviews. The focus is on delivering working software in short cycles (sprints), adapting to change as needed. The BA's role shifts from extensive upfront documentation to facilitating communication and collaboration, ensuring development aligns with evolving business needs. This is akin to building a house one room at a time, incorporating homeowner feedback after each room's completion, and adapting the design for subsequent rooms (Gobov and Titlova, 2023).

In today's dynamic business landscape, Agile approaches have transformed the BA role, emphasizing flexibility, collaboration, and proactivity. The traditional BA as a solely upfront requirements gatherer is outdated. Instead, the Agile BA is integral to the development team, working closely with stakeholders, developers, and the Product Owner throughout the project lifecycle to deliver value iteratively.

The Agile BA facilitates communication between stakeholders and development teams, ensuring business needs are translated into actionable requirements. They support Agile ceremonies like sprint planning, backlog refinement, and sprint reviews by providing detailed requirements and clarifications, while the Scrum Master facilitates these events and the Product Owner prioritizes the work. The BA collaborates with the Product Owner to refine requirements into user stories and acceptance criteria, aligning the product backlog with business priorities.

Unlike the Product Owner, who owns the product vision and backlog prioritization, the BA focuses on analyzing and detailing requirements for effective delivery. Eliciting, refining, and prioritizing user stories is an ongoing process. The BA gathers stakeholder needs, translates them into user stories, and adds them to the product backlog, which the Product Owner manages and prioritizes based on business value. During sprint planning, the BA works with the Product Owner and development team to refine user stories for the upcoming sprint, adding acceptance criteria to define completion. This ensures the team focuses on high-value features, with the product evolving iteratively based on feedback.

As a change agent, the Agile BA supports continuous improvement by encouraging feedback, identifying optimization opportunities, and facilitating change implementation. They manage scope changes, assess their impact, and work with the Product Owner to update the backlog and communicate changes to the team. By championing adaptability, the BA ensures the project aligns with evolving business needs and delivers maximum value.

Agile BAs require a unique blend of skills. Flexibility is paramount. Adaptive BAs must be comfortable with ambiguity and adjust their approach as needed. Requirements are likely to evolve, requiring the BA to adapt quickly and efficiently, remaining open to new ideas, experimenting, and embracing iterative development. They must shift gears as priorities change and re-prioritize tasks. This adaptability keeps the project aligned with evolving business needs.

Critical thinking is also essential. Agile BAs must analyze information quickly and make sound judgments. They need to evaluate user stories, identify risks, and propose solutions, asking probing questions, challenging assumptions, and thinking creatively. They must see the big picture while attending to details. Critical thinking enables informed decisions that contribute to project success.

Effective collaboration is crucial. Agile BAs work closely with various stakeholders, including product owners, developers, testers, and business users. This requires strong communication skills, relationship building, and teamwork. BAs must facilitate discussions, resolve conflicts, and build consensus, acting as a bridge between business and technical teams, ensuring everyone works towards a common goal. Collaboration is key to creating shared product understanding and ensuring project value delivery.

Proficiency in agile tools and techniques is also important. Tools like Jira and Confluence are widely used for managing user stories, tracking progress, and facilitating communication. BAs should be familiar with these tools. Techniques like user story mapping are valuable for visualizing the product backlog and planning releases, helping break down large epics into smaller user stories and prioritizing them. BAs should be proficient in these techniques and stay up-to-date with the latest Agile practices and tools.

Test Your Understanding 9.34
Which statement best describes the relationship between the Agile BA and the Product Owner?
A. The Product Owner defines business value and backlog priorities, while the BA details and analyzes requirements.
B. The BA owns the product vision and backlog prioritization, while the Product Owner supports documentation.
C. The BA manages the development team, while the Product Owner manages stakeholders.
D. The BA and Product Owner have identical responsibilities in the Agile framework.

Test Your Understanding 9.35
Which skill is most critical for Agile BAs when priorities and requirements frequently shift?
A. Flexibility and adaptability
B. Strong documentation skills
C. Deep technical expertise in coding
D. Strict adherence to the initial plan

Test Your Understanding 9.36
Which of the following tools or techniques is most relevant for Agile BAs managing user stories and backlog visualization?
A. Microsoft Project for Gantt chart scheduling
B. Earned Value Management (EVM) analysis
C. Jira and user story mapping
D. Critical Path Method (CPM) modeling

9.10 Maximizing Project Impact

Successful change implementation hinges on effective training and documentation. Even the best-designed system or process will fail if end-users don't understand how to use it. Training ensures users understand new systems, processes, and tools, and appreciate their benefits. BAs design training programs and create clear, concise, and accessible documentation, bridging the gap between technical jargon and non-technical language. Effective training and documentation minimize resistance to change, accelerate user adoption, and maximize ROI.

Documentation best practices emphasize a variety of formats to cater to different learning styles. User manuals offer comprehensive system information, features, and usage instructions. Quick reference guides provide concise summaries of key tasks, ideal for quick reminders. Video tutorials demonstrate specific tasks, offering a visual and engaging learning experience. Frequently Asked Questions (FAQs) address common user queries and provide quick solutions. Crucially, documentation must be "living," regularly updated as the system evolves. Outdated documentation leads to confusion and hinders user adoption. A well-maintained knowledge base can serve as a central repository for all documentation, facilitating easy access.

Training modalities should be carefully considered. Traditional classroom training, while effective, can be expensive and time-consuming. Online and blended learning offer greater flexibility and accessibility. Interactive e-learning modules, incorporating multimedia and quizzes, enhance engagement and retention. Hands-on workshops allow users to practice in a safe environment, reinforcing learning and building confidence. Simulation exercises mimic real-world scenarios, allowing users to apply knowledge and develop problem-solving skills.

The best approach often combines modalities, tailored to user needs and system complexity. For example, a new CRM system implementation might involve online tutorials for basic navigation, hands-on workshops for sales processes, and a comprehensive user manual for advanced features. Investing in effective training and documentation empowers end-users, ensuring a smooth transition and maximizing technology investment benefits.

A post-implementation review (PIR) provides a structured evaluation of project success. Its purpose is threefold: determining if the project met objectives, assessing the delivered solution's quality, and evaluating the extent of realized benefits. A PIR is not simply a post-mortem; it's a valuable learning opportunity. Collecting quantitative and qualitative feedback is essential. Quantitative data, like KPIs (ROI, cost savings, processing time improvements), provides objective performance measures. For example, if a project aimed to reduce customer onboarding time by 20%, the PIR analyzes actual onboarding times. Qualitative feedback, gathered through surveys, interviews, and focus groups, offers insights into user satisfaction, usability, and overall impact, revealing unforeseen issues or opportunities.

Benefits realization actively ensures expected project benefits are delivered. It's not enough to implement a solution; organizations must manage benefit realization, whether cost savings, increased efficiency, improved user satisfaction, or other goals. This involves defining clear benefit metrics upfront, tracking them throughout the project lifecycle and beyond, and taking corrective actions.

Benefits realization is ongoing, requiring continuous monitoring and improvement. Regular benefit metric reviews, coupled with stakeholder feedback, help maintain value and ensure projects deliver intended results. By focusing on benefits realization, organizations maximize ROI and ensure projects contribute to strategic objectives (Zwikael et al., 2019).

Test Your Understanding 9.37
During the rollout of a new payroll system, several employees struggle to use the interface and revert to old manual processes. As the Business Analyst, what should you focus on to address this issue?
A. Implementing stricter enforcement policies to ensure system compliance
B. Enhancing training programs and updating documentation for clarity
C. Redesigning the entire payroll system to make it more intuitive
D. Conducting additional testing sessions with the development team

Test Your Understanding 9.38
Which of the following documentation formats is best suited for users seeking quick answers to common system issues?
A. Comprehensive user manuals
B. Quick reference guides
C. Video tutorials
D. Frequently Asked Questions (FAQs)

Test Your Understanding 9.39
A company is implementing a new CRM system. The BA proposes using online tutorials for basic functions, workshops for sales processes, and manuals for advanced features. What principle does this approach best represent?
A. Cost reduction through uniform training
B. Standardization of all training across departments
C. Combining modalities to tailor training to user needs
D. Relying on documentation to replace live instruction

Test Your Understanding 9.40
Which statement best describes the purpose of a Post-Implementation Review (PIR)?
A. To assess project objectives, quality, and realized benefits
B. To determine team performance for future promotions
C. To finalize remaining deliverables before closing the project
D. To identify new requirements for the next project phase

Test Your Understanding 9.41
Which of the following best illustrates effective benefits realization?
A. Measuring ROI at the project's completion
B. Tracking benefit metrics and adjusting actions post-implementation
C. Documenting expected benefits during initiation, especially mentioned in the project charter
D. Focusing solely on user satisfaction as a success measure

9.11 Chapter Summary

This chapter expands on business analysis concepts, building upon the foundations of requirement management and stakeholder communication established earlier in the book. It integrates key business analysis principles, beginning with gap analysis, which evaluates the difference between a process, system, or strategy's current and desired future states. The chapter then explores the importance of developing a compelling business case and aligning business analysis activities with various project management methodologies. Finally, it concludes by examining strategies for maximizing project impact.

9.12 Case Study

Revisit the case study in Chapter 1. Perform the following task:
Write a business case that includes the sections outlined in the chapter. Tailor the content to reflect the specific scope, features, and context of your project. Use your understanding of the project's requirements and stakeholders to make the case relevant and persuasive.

9.13 References

Gobov, D., & Titlova, O. (2023). Towards identifying challenges in business analysis on IT projects–a practical study. *Radioelectronic and Computer Systems*, (2), 193-206.
Elmuti, D., & Kathawala, Y. (2001). An overview of strategic alliances. *Management decision*, *39*(3), 205-218.
Kim, S., & Ji, Y. (2018). Gap analysis. *The international encyclopedia of strategic communication*, *8*, 1-6.
Zarour, K., Benmerzoug, D., Guermouche, N., & Drira, K. (2020). A systematic literature review on BPMN extensions. *Business Process Management Journal*, *26*(6), 1473-1503.
Zwikael, O., Meredith, J. R., & Smyrk, J. (2019). The responsibilities of the project owner in benefits realization. *International Journal of Operations & Production Management*, *39*(4), 503-524.

9.14 Solutions to Test Your Understanding

9.1 C; 9.2 C; 9.3 B; 9.4 C; 9.5 B; 9.6 C; 9.7 D; 9.8 A; 9.9 B; 9.10 B; 9.11 D; 9.12 B; 9.13 A; 9.14 B; 9.15 C; 9.16 C; 9.17 B; 9.18 A; 9.19 D; 9.20 D; 9.21 A; 9.22 B; 9.23 C; 9.24 A; 9.25 B; 9.26 C; 9.27 B; 9.28 B; 9.29 A; 9.30 A; 9.31 B; 9.32 C; 9.33 A; 9.34 A; 9.35 A; 9.36 C; 9.37 B; 9.38 D; 9.39 C; 9.40 A; 9.41 B;

Chapter 10: Executing and Closing Projects

Chapter Learning Outcomes

10.1 Design a plan for following and executing planned strategies.
10.2 Explain common problem-solving tools and techniques.
10.3 Understand project initiation framework
10.4 Elaborate on the concept of project closure and transitions.

10.1 Follow and Execute Planned Strategies

Strategy execution is the bridge between strategic planning and tangible results. A brilliant strategic plan is worthless without the ability to effectively put it into action. It's the "how" that transforms the "what" of strategic planning into reality. Think of it like a blueprint for a house; the blueprint itself is just a plan, but strategy execution is the construction process that brings the house to life. This process involves a complex interplay of people, processes, and resources, all working in concert towards a shared vision (De Oliveira et al., 2019).

Successful strategy implementation hinges on several key components. First and foremost, clear communication is paramount. Everyone involved, from senior management to frontline teams, must understand the strategic goals, their individual roles, and how their work contributes to the overall objective. This includes not only disseminating information but also fostering open dialogue and feedback channels.

Secondly, resource alignment is essential. This means allocating the necessary financial, human, and technological resources to support the strategic initiatives. Without the right resources, even the best-laid plans will falter. Thirdly, establishing clear accountability mechanisms is crucial. This involves defining roles and responsibilities, setting measurable targets, and tracking progress regularly. This ensures that everyone is answerable for their contributions and that corrective actions can be taken when necessary.

Fourthly, change management plays a significant role. Strategic implementation often requires significant changes to existing processes, systems, and even organizational culture. Effectively managing this change, addressing resistance, and building buy-in are essential for successful execution. Finally, continuous monitoring and evaluation are vital. This allows organizations to track progress against their strategic goals, identify any roadblocks, and make necessary adjustments along the way. This iterative process of planning, executing, and evaluating is what drives successful strategy implementation.

Moving from plan to action is rarely a smooth process. Organizations often encounter numerous challenges during strategy execution. One common hurdle is a lack of clarity or alignment. If the strategic goals are not clearly defined or if different parts of the organization are working at cross-purposes, execution will suffer. Another challenge is resistance to change. People are often comfortable with the status quo, and implementing new strategies can disrupt established routines and power structures. Overcoming this resistance requires effective communication, empathy, and demonstrating the benefits of the change.

Resource constraints can also hinder strategy execution. If the necessary resources are not available, or if they are not allocated effectively, initiatives may stall or fail altogether. Furthermore, poor communication can create confusion, misunderstandings, and a lack of coordination, all of which can derail even the most promising strategies. Finally, a lack of accountability can lead to a lack of ownership and a failure to achieve desired outcomes. When no one is clearly responsible for specific tasks or outcomes, it becomes easy for things to fall through the cracks.

The project manager plays a crucial role in strategy execution. They are the orchestrators, ensuring that the various elements of the strategic plan are translated into concrete actions. Project managers are responsible for defining project scope, developing project plans, managing project budgets, and tracking project progress. They also play a critical role in communicating with stakeholders, managing risks, and resolving issues. In essence, they are the glue that holds the execution process together. They act as a liaison between the strategic level and the operational level, ensuring that projects align with the overall strategic goals. Furthermore, project managers often have to manage cross-functional teams, requiring them to have strong leadership, communication, and interpersonal skills. They must be adept at motivating team members, resolving conflicts, and fostering a collaborative environment. By effectively managing projects, project managers contribute significantly to the successful execution of the organization's strategy.

Test Your Understanding 10.1

Which of the following best describes the relationship between strategic planning and strategy execution?

A. Strategic planning focuses on defining objectives, while strategy execution turns those objectives into results.

B. Strategic planning ensures proper resource allocation, while execution determines market positioning.

C. Strategic planning handles operations, while strategy execution develops the long-term vision.

D. Strategic planning evaluates success, while strategy execution creates performance metrics.

Test Your Understanding 10.2
During the implementation of a new strategic initiative, a manager notices that some employees are resisting new workflows because they prefer existing processes. Which aspect of strategy execution should the organization strengthen?
A. Accountability mechanisms
B. Change management
C. Continuous evaluation
D. Resource allocation

Test Your Understanding 10.3
A manufacturing company launches a cost-reduction strategy but soon realizes that several departments are duplicating efforts and working at cross-purposes. What is the *most likely* cause of this problem?
A. Overemphasis on performance metrics
B. Inadequate leadership support
C. Insufficient resource allocation
D. Poor communication and lack of alignment

Test Your Understanding 10.4
Which statement best reflects the project manager's role in strategy execution?
A. They create the organization's strategic vision.
B. They translate strategic plans into actionable projects and ensure alignment with organizational goals.
C. They focus solely on financial reporting and resource budgeting.
D. They primarily manage technical teams without engaging stakeholders.

10.2 Project Initiation Framework

Project initiation lays the foundation for a successful project. It's the first step that sets the stage for everything that follows. This framework essentially answers the question: "Should we do this project, and if so, how do we get started?" A key element of initiation, already covered in detail in a previous chapter, is project charter development. A well-crafted charter serves as a guiding document throughout the project lifecycle. It's the bridge between the strategic vision and the project execution (Zaveri et al., 2022).

Building upon the charter, effective project initiation involves several components. One is stakeholder identification and analysis. This involves identifying all individuals or groups impacted by the project, understanding their interests and influence, and developing strategies to effectively engage them. A stakeholder register is a useful tool for documenting this information.

Another element is initial scope definition. While the scope will be further refined during planning, It helps to set boundaries and prevent scope creep later on. This initial definition is often documented in a scope statement. Furthermore, the initiation phase involves identifying high-level resource requirements. This includes estimating the human resources, budget, and other resources needed to execute the project. These are preliminary estimates, and they will be refined during the planning phase.

A preliminary risk assessment is conducted during initiation. This involves identifying potential risks that could impact the project and developing initial strategies for mitigating those risks. This is a proactive approach that helps to anticipate potential problems and avoid them or minimize their impact.

A vital part of project initiation, often overlooked, is benefit planning. Projects are undertaken to achieve specific benefits, and it's essential to define these benefits clearly from the outset. Project benefits can be tangible, such as increased revenue or cost savings, or intangible, such as improved customer satisfaction or brand reputation (Ahmed et al., 2025).

A key step is creating a benefits realization plan. This plan outlines how the project's benefits will be achieved, measured, and sustained over time. It should identify specific activities, timelines, and responsibilities for realizing the benefits. It's also essential to define Key Performance Indicators (KPIs) to measure and track the benefits. Benefits mapping techniques can be used to visually represent the relationship between project activities, outputs, and outcomes, ultimately linking them to the desired benefits. This helps to ensure that the project is aligned with the organization's strategic goals and that the benefits are clearly understood by all stakeholders.

Let's illustrate the concept of a benefits realization plan with an example: a company implementing a new Customer Relationship Management (CRM) system.

Scenario: "Abcd Retail," a mid-sized retailer, decides to implement a new CRM system to improve customer engagement and drive sales. Their strategic goals include increasing customer lifetime value and improving customer retention.

Benefit: Increased customer lifetime value.

Benefits Realization Plan:

Benefit Statement: Increase customer lifetime value by 15% within 12 months of CRM implementation.

Activities:
Phase 1 (0-3 months): Data migration and CRM system setup. Responsibility: IT Department. Timeline: Completed within 3 months.

Phase 2 (3-6 months): Sales and marketing team onboarding and training on the new CRM system. This includes initial training sessions, development of training materials, follow-up support, and a period for teams to become proficient with the system. While the formal training component is estimated to be completed within one month (e.g., during months 3 or 4), the overall onboarding and support period will continue through month 6 to ensure effective adoption. Responsibility: Training Department, with support from Sales and Marketing Management. Timeline: Onboarding and support activities occur throughout the 3-6 month period, with formal training completed within the first month of this phase.

Phase 3 (6-12 months): Targeted marketing campaigns using the CRM system to personalize offers and improve customer engagement. Responsibility: Marketing Department. Timeline: Ongoing from month 6 to 12.
Phase 4 (Ongoing): Regular monitoring of customer behavior and feedback to optimize CRM usage and campaign effectiveness. Responsibility: Sales and Marketing Departments Timeline: Ongoing.

Key Performance Indicators (KPIs):
Customer Lifetime Value (CLTV): Measured by calculating the total revenue generated by a customer over their relationship with the company. Target: 15% increase. Measurement Frequency: Quarterly.
Customer Retention Rate: Percentage of customers who continue to purchase from Abcd Retail over a specific period. Target: 5% increase. Measurement Frequency: Monthly.
Average Order Value: The average amount spent per order. Target: 8% increase. Measurement Frequency: Monthly.

Responsibilities: Clearly defined for each activity, ensuring accountability. The plan would specify who is responsible for data migration, training, campaign management, and ongoing monitoring.

Timeline: Specific timelines are attached to each activity, creating a roadmap for benefits realization. The phased approach allows for a controlled rollout and ensures that each stage is completed before moving on to the next.

Benefits Mapping: Abcd Retail could create a visual map showing how the CRM system (output) leads to improved customer engagement (intermediate outcome), which in turn leads to increased customer lifetime value and improved customer retention (final outcomes), directly supporting the strategic goals. This map would also illustrate the link between targeted marketing campaigns (activity) and increased average order value (intermediate outcome).

Measurement and Tracking: Regular monitoring of KPIs (CLTV, retention rate, average order value) provides data to track progress toward the desired benefits. This data is used to make adjustments to the CRM usage and marketing campaigns as needed.

Sustaining Benefits: The ongoing monitoring and optimization (Phase 4) ensure that the benefits are sustained over time. Regular training refreshers and updates to the CRM system are also essential for long-term benefits realization.

By developing and following this benefits realization plan, Abcd Retail can ensure that their CRM implementation delivers the intended value and contributes to their strategic goals. They have a clear roadmap, defined responsibilities, measurable KPIs, and a mechanism for tracking progress and making adjustments. This structured approach maximizes the chances of achieving the desired benefits and demonstrates the value of the project to stakeholders.

Test Your Understanding 10.5
During the project initiation phase, which of the following best describes the purpose of the project charter?
A. It lists detailed technical specifications for all deliverables.
B. It serves as a contract between the customer and supplier.
C. It bridges the organization's strategic vision and project execution.
D. It provides a step-by-step plan for project implementation.

Test Your Understanding 10.6
You're managing a project to launch an online service platform. During initiation, you identify that server capacity issues could delay deployment. You document this and propose early load testing as a response. Which best describes your action?

A. Conducting a preliminary risk assessment
B. Developing the project schedule
C. Defining deliverables in the scope statement
D. Performing stakeholder analysis

Test Your Understanding 10.7
During Phase 2 of Abcd Retail's CRM project, the training department leads employee onboarding while the marketing team provides support. This is an example of:
A. Benefit mapping
B. Resource allocation and responsibility definition
C. Benefit mapping and KPI measurement
D. Preliminary scope definition

Test Your Understanding 10.8
How does benefits mapping contribute to project initiation?
A. It shows how project activities, outputs, and outcomes connect to desired benefits.
B. It calculates the financial feasibility of a project and map them to the desired benefits.
C. It identifies all external vendors and suppliers.
D. It documents the initial project scope boundaries.

Test Your Understanding 10.9
After Abcd Retail completes its CRM rollout, the project manager sets up regular customer feedback reviews and quarterly KPI monitoring to sustain improvements. Which phase of the benefits realization plan does this represent?
A. Initial setup and data migration
B. Stakeholder engagement and communication
C. Risk assessment and mitigation
D. Sustaining benefits through ongoing monitoring

10.3 Introduction to Project Problem-Solving

Project problem-solving is an integral part of project management. It's not merely about reacting to issues as they arise; it's about proactively anticipating potential problems and developing effective solutions. From technical glitches and resource constraints to stakeholder conflicts and changing requirements, project managers are constantly faced with problems that need to be addressed. The success of a project often hinges on how well these problems are identified, analyzed, and resolved.

Critical thinking is the bedrock of effective project problem-solving. It's more than just common sense; it's a structured approach to analyzing information, evaluating options, and making sound judgments, especially when the pressure is on. In a project context, this means several key things. First, it involves actively questioning assumptions. Don't just accept information at face value. For example, if a team member reports a delay, don't just accept "technical difficulties" as the explanation. Instead, probe deeper: What specific technical difficulties? Why are they occurring? What steps are being taken to resolve them? This questioning helps to uncover the real root cause, which might be something entirely different, like inadequate training or faulty equipment.

Second, critical thinking means separating facts from opinions. Project discussions can be filled with interpretations and assumptions. A skilled project manager uses critical thinking to sift through this noise and identify the objective facts. For instance, instead of "the testing is taking too long," a fact-based statement would be "testing has taken 15 days so far, exceeding the planned 10 days by 50%." This allows for more accurate problem definition and avoids emotional reactions.

Third, it requires considering multiple perspectives. A problem might look different depending on who you ask. A developer might see a bug as a coding issue, while a user might see it as a usability problem. Critical thinking encourages project managers to seek out these different viewpoints and understand the problem from all angles. This might involve talking to different stakeholders, conducting surveys, or even role-playing different scenarios (Carmeli et al., 2021).

Fourth, critical thinking helps in evaluating the broader implications of a problem. A seemingly small issue in one area of the project can have ripple effects in other areas. For example, a delay in design might not only impact the development phase but also the testing and deployment phases. Critical thinking allows project managers to anticipate these downstream effects and develop solutions that minimize disruption across the entire project. This might mean adjusting the schedule, reallocating resources, or even renegotiating deadlines with stakeholders.

Finally, critical thinking assists informed decision-making, especially in complex or ambiguous situations. Projects are rarely black and white, and project managers often have to make decisions with incomplete information. Critical thinking provides a framework for evaluating the available information, identifying potential risks and rewards, and choosing the best course of action. This might involve using decision-making tools like cost-benefit analysis, SWOT analysis, or decision trees. By applying these critical thinking skills, project managers can move beyond simply reacting to problems as they arise and instead adopt a proactive and strategic approach, anticipating potential issues and developing effective solutions before they escalate.

A systematic approach to problem identification is crucial for effective project management. It's not enough to just know that there's a problem; you need to understand what the problem truly is, why it's occurring, and how it's impacting the project. This requires a structured approach, which typically involves several key steps.

First, clearly defining the problem is paramount. This goes beyond stating the obvious. Instead of saying "the website is slow," a better definition would be "the website's average page load time has increased by 40% over the last two weeks, impacting user experience and potentially leading to a decrease in conversion rates." This specific definition provides measurable parameters and highlights the impact of the problem. It's also essential to define the boundaries of the problem. What is included in the scope of the problem, and what is not? This helps to focus the investigation and avoid scope creep.

Second, gathering relevant data helps understand the problem's scope and nature. This might involve collecting quantitative data, such as website analytics, system logs, or user feedback surveys. It can also involve gathering qualitative data through interviews with stakeholders, focus groups, or observations. For example, in the website speed example, data could be gathered on server performance, network latency, browser usage, and user location. This data helps to paint a comprehensive picture of the problem and identify potential contributing factors.

Third, analyzing the root cause is critical. This is where you dig beneath the surface symptoms to identify the underlying reasons for the problem. Several techniques for this (e.g. root cause analysis, fishbone diagrams, and brainstorming) will be discussed in a later section.

Fourth, developing potential solutions should be based on the identified root cause, not just the symptoms. Once the root cause is understood, the project team can brainstorm and evaluate potential solutions. For the website speed example, solutions might include upgrading the server RAM, optimizing the website code, or switching to a different vendor. Each solution should be evaluated based on its feasibility, cost, impact, and risks.

Finally, documenting the entire problem-solving process is vital. This includes documenting the problem definition, the data gathered, the root cause analysis, the potential solutions, and the chosen solution. This documentation serves as a valuable record for future reference and can help to prevent similar problems from occurring in the future. By following this systematic approach, project managers can effectively identify and solve problems, minimizing their impact on the project and increasing the likelihood of success.

Collaborative problem-solving is often essential in project contexts. Projects typically involve diverse teams with different skills and perspectives. Bringing these perspectives together can lead to more creative and effective solutions. Collaborative problem-solving encourages open communication, knowledge sharing, and a sense of shared ownership. It can also help to build team morale and improve stakeholder engagement.

However, collaborative problem-solving also requires effective facilitation and communication skills to ensure that all voices are heard and that decisions are made efficiently. Project managers should foster a culture of open communication and encourage team members to contribute their ideas and expertise to the problem-solving process. By embracing a systematic and collaborative approach to problem-solving, project managers can navigate the inevitable challenges that arise during a project and increase the likelihood of achieving project success.

Test Your Understanding 10.10
Which of the following best demonstrates critical thinking in a project management context?
A. Accepting reports from team members as accurate to save time.
B. Relying on prior experience to make quick judgments.
C. Questioning assumptions and verifying facts before making decisions.
D. Delegating decision-making to subject matter experts.

Test Your Understanding 10.11
During a project meeting, a developer states, "The testing phase is taking too long." Which response demonstrates critical thinking by the project manager?
A. Asking for exact data on how long testing has taken compared to the plan.
B. Asking the developer to speed up testing immediately.
C. Reporting the delay to the sponsor without further inquiry.
D. Reassigning the testing team to a different task.

Test Your Understanding 10.12
A project manager learns that the design phase is delayed. Instead of only focusing on the design team, she considers how this might affect testing, deployment, and stakeholder expectations. Which critical thinking skill is she demonstrating?
A. Evaluating broader implications
B. Root cause analysis
C. Separating facts from opinions
D. Brainstorming solutions

Test Your Understanding 10.13
A project manager is facilitating a problem-solving session with her team. She encourages participants to share different viewpoints -- from developers to end users -- before identifying a solution. What critical thinking principle is she applying?
A. Root cause analysis
B. Decision tree evaluation
C. Quantitative data collection
D. Considering multiple perspectives

Test Your Understanding 10.14
Which of the following best illustrates a systematic approach to problem-solving in a project?
A. Fixing each problem as soon as it appears to maintain momentum.
B. Using intuition and prior experience to quickly decide on actions.
C. Defining the problem, collecting data, analyzing causes, and evaluating solutions.
D. Delegating issue resolution to subject matter experts.

Test Your Understanding 10.15
A project manager wants to encourage open communication during a complex issue-resolution meeting. She ensures all team members -- including junior developers -- feel comfortable contributing ideas and perspectives. What key concept is she demonstrating?
A. Collaborative problem-solving
B. Delegated authority
C. Rapid decision-making
D. Change control management

10.4 Collaborative Meeting

Collaborative meetings are vital for project success, but their effectiveness relies on careful planning and execution. Knowing the types of meetings and their purposes is key. For instance, status meetings regularly update team members on progress, address roadblocks, and coordinate tasks.

Problem-solving sessions bring together relevant stakeholders to identify, analyze, and resolve specific project issues. These sessions often require brainstorming and critical thinking to generate effective solutions. *Decision-making meetings*, as the name suggests, are designed to make key project decisions. These meetings should involve the appropriate decision-makers and focus on evaluating options and reaching a consensus.

Information sharing gatherings aim to disseminate information to a group of stakeholders, such as project updates, training materials, or new policies. These meetings can be more informational and less interactive than other types. Finally, *strategic planning meetings* are focused on defining project goals, setting priorities, and developing high-level strategies. They often involve brainstorming and visioning exercises.

Evaluating the effectiveness of collaborative meetings ensures they are a productive use of time and resources. Several key metrics should be considered when assessing meeting success. First and foremost, did the meeting achieve its intended objectives and outcomes? This requires clearly defined objectives before the meeting starts. For example, if the objective was to make a decision on a vendor, was that decision made? If the objective was to brainstorm solutions to a problem, were several viable solutions generated?

Measuring the achievement of objectives is the most direct way to evaluate meeting success.

Participant engagement metrics are also important. A meeting where only a few people speak while others remain silent is not a truly collaborative meeting. Metrics like the number of participants who actively contributed to the discussion, the frequency of contributions, and the diversity of viewpoints expressed can be helpful. Observing body language and facial expressions can also provide insights into engagement levels. Are people attentive and interested, or are they distracted and disengaged? Encouraging participation from everyone, perhaps through techniques like round-robin discussions or asking specific individuals for their input, can improve engagement.

Time management efficiency is another crucial factor. Was the meeting time used wisely? Did the meeting start and end on time? Was the discussion focused and on track, or were there unnecessary tangents and distractions? Tracking the time spent on each agenda item can help identify areas where time management can be improved. Using a timer or assigning a timekeeper can also help to keep the meeting on schedule. If meetings consistently run over time, it might be necessary to re-evaluate the agenda, the meeting format, or the facilitation techniques used.

Action item completion rates provide a tangible measure of meeting effectiveness. Meetings often generate action items that need to be completed after the meeting. Tracking the completion rate of these action items provides insight into whether the meeting had a real impact. Clearly assigning responsibility for each action item and setting deadlines can improve completion rates.

Cost-effectiveness analysis is also a relevant consideration. Meetings consume resources, including the time of the participants, the cost of the meeting room, and any materials or equipment used. It's important to weigh these costs against the benefits of the meeting. Was the meeting worth the investment? Could the same outcomes have been achieved through a less costly means, such as email or a quick phone call? If meetings are consistently not cost-effective, it might be necessary to re-evaluate the need for meetings or explore alternative communication methods.

Finally, gathering feedback through meeting satisfaction surveys can provide valuable insights into participant perspectives. Surveys can ask about various aspects of the meeting, such as the clarity of the objectives, the effectiveness of the facilitation, the level of participant engagement, and the overall value of the meeting. This feedback can be used to identify areas for improvement and to make future meetings more effective. Anonymous surveys can encourage honest feedback. By regularly evaluating meeting effectiveness using these metrics, project managers can ensure that meetings are a valuable tool for collaboration and project success.

To maximize meeting effectiveness, several best practices should be followed. Pre-meeting preparation is critical. This includes clearly defining the meeting objectives, identifying the necessary participants, and distributing any relevant materials in advance. Developing a detailed agenda keeps the meeting focused and on track. The agenda should outline the topics to be discussed, the time allocated for each topic, and the desired outcomes.

Effective meeting facilitation techniques ensure that all participants have an opportunity to contribute and that discussions are productive. This might involve using techniques like round-robin discussions, brainstorming, or voting. Proper documentation methods are essential for capturing meeting minutes, action items, and decisions. This ensures that everyone is on the same page and that there is a record of what was discussed and agreed upon (Abd Al-Salam et al., 2024).

Finally, following up after the meeting ensures that action items are completed and that decisions are implemented. This might involve sending out meeting minutes, tracking progress on action items, and communicating any updates to stakeholders. By adhering to these best practices, project managers can ensure that meetings are valuable and contribute to project success.

Test Your Understanding 10.16
A project manager conducts a session where multiple stakeholders collaborate to identify the reasons behind a recurring issue and generate potential solutions. What type of meeting is being described?
A. Problem-solving session
B. Status meeting
C. Decision-making meeting
D. Strategic planning meeting

Test Your Understanding 10.17
During a team meeting, the project manager notices that only two senior members are actively speaking while others remain silent. What action would best improve engagement?
A. Shorten the meeting to maintain focus.
B. Ask specific individuals for their input using a round-robin approach.
C. Move future meetings to a virtual format.
D. Increase the meeting frequency to encourage participation.

Test Your Understanding 10.18
After a meeting, the project manager tracks whether all assigned action items were completed by the agreed deadlines. What aspect of meeting effectiveness is being measured?

A. Participant engagement
B. Time management efficiency
C. Action item completion rate
D. Cost-effectiveness

Test Your Understanding 10.19
A company notices that their weekly meetings consume significant staff time but rarely produce actionable results. The project manager decides to analyze whether similar outcomes could be achieved via email. Which evaluation metric is being applied?
A. Cost-effectiveness analysis
B. Engagement assessment
C. Objective achievement review
D. Facilitation effectiveness

10.5 Types of Meetings

In project management, various meetings facilitate communication and collaboration among team members and stakeholders. Understanding the purpose of these meetings helps teams work more effectively to achieve project goals. Effective communication and collaboration are crucial for project success, and different meeting types support these efforts.

A *focus group* is a research technique used to gather in-depth qualitative data from a small group of people about a specific topic. Think of it as a guided conversation where a moderator facilitates a discussion among participants to explore their perspectives, opinions, attitudes, and experiences. It's not about getting statistical data like a survey; it's about understanding the "why" behind people's thoughts and behaviors. Focus groups are particularly valuable for understanding customer needs, exploring reactions to new products or services, or gathering feedback on project proposals.

Imagine a company wants to understand how users feel about a new mobile app they've developed. They could use a focus group. They would recruit a small group of people (typically 6-10) who represent their target users and bring them together for a moderated discussion. The moderator would guide the conversation, asking open-ended questions about the app's features, usability, and overall experience. The participants would share their thoughts and interact with each other, providing rich qualitative data about their interactions and perceptions of the app.

The process of conducting a focus group involves several key steps. First, you need to clearly define the purpose and objectives. What exactly do you want to learn from the focus group? For our app example, the objective might be to understand user satisfaction with the app's navigation and identify any usability issues. These objectives will guide the entire process.

Next comes the planning and preparation phase. This involves developing a discussion guide, which is a list of questions and topics that the moderator will use to guide the discussion. The questions should be open-ended, encouraging participants to share their thoughts and experiences in detail. For the app example, questions might include, "What do you like most about the app's navigation?" or "What, if anything, did you find confusing about using the app?" You also need to select a comfortable and quiet location for the focus group and recruit participants who represent your target audience. In our example, participants would likely be smartphone users who are familiar with similar apps. Incentives, like gift cards, are often offered to encourage participation.

The actual focus group session is where the magic happens. A trained moderator facilitates the discussion, ensuring that everyone has a chance to speak and that the conversation stays on track. The moderator's role is to encourage interaction, ask clarifying questions, and probe deeper into interesting responses. They are not there to lead the discussion in a particular direction but rather to facilitate a natural and productive conversation. The session is typically recorded (with participant consent) so that the data can be analyzed later.

After the session, the data needs to be analyzed. This involves reviewing the transcripts and recordings, identifying key themes, patterns, and insights. For our app example, the analysis might reveal that many users found the app's menu structure confusing or that certain features were difficult to find. This analysis often involves coding the transcripts, which is a process of tagging and categorizing responses to identify recurring themes and patterns.

Finally, the findings are summarized in a comprehensive report. This report should present the key insights gleaned from the focus group, supported by quotes from participants and illustrative examples. It should also highlight any limitations of the study and offer recommendations for action. In our app example, the report might recommend redesigning the app's navigation or adding clearer instructions for certain features. The insights from the focus group can then be used to inform product development, marketing strategies, or other business decisions.

Stand-up meetings, a staple of Agile methodologies, are brief, focused gatherings designed to keep team members aligned and projects moving forward. They embody several core Agile principles, such as frequent communication, self-organization, and adaptation. These meetings are meant to be short and to the point, typically lasting no more than 15 minutes, encouraging concise updates and quick problem-solving. Their frequency, often daily, allows teams to address impediments rapidly and maintain a consistent rhythm of work.

A common and effective format for stand-up meetings revolves around three key questions: What did I do yesterday? What will I do today? What impediments are blocking me? This structure ensures that each team member provides a concise update on their progress, outlines their plans for the current day, and highlights any roadblocks they are encountering.

Effective time management keeps stand-up meetings concise and productive. Sticking to a strict time limit, often enforced by physically standing, helps to prevent the meeting from straying into lengthy discussions. It's helpful to have a designated timekeeper to ensure the meeting stays on track. Encouraging team members to keep their updates brief and focused is essential. If a particular topic requires more in-depth discussion, it should be taken offline after the stand-up meeting, involving only the relevant team members.

Remote stand-up meetings present unique challenges. Maintaining engagement and ensuring everyone has an opportunity to contribute can be more difficult when team members are geographically dispersed. Video conferencing is highly recommended for remote stand-ups, as it allows for face-to-face interaction and helps to build rapport. It's also important to establish clear ground rules for remote meetings, such as muting microphones when not speaking and using visual cues to indicate a desire to speak. Tools like shared online whiteboards or project management software can be used to visualize progress and track action items.

Several common pitfalls can hinder the effectiveness of stand-up meetings. One common issue is allowing the meeting to become a status reporting session to management, rather than a collaborative update among team members. Another pitfall is letting the meeting stray into lengthy discussions of specific issues. As mentioned earlier, these discussions should be taken offline. Other pitfalls include lack of preparation by team members, inconsistent attendance, and a lack of follow-up on identified impediments. To avoid these pitfalls, it's essential to clearly communicate the purpose and format of stand-up meetings to the team, enforce time limits, and ensure that action items are assigned and tracked. Regularly reviewing the effectiveness of stand-up meetings and soliciting feedback from the team can help to identify and address any issues.

Brainstorming sessions are a powerful tool for generating creative ideas and solutions in a collaborative setting.

Several different brainstorming techniques can be employed, each with its own strengths and weaknesses. Traditional brainstorming, the most common approach, involves a group of individuals generating ideas freely and spontaneously. The focus is on quantity over quality, encouraging participants to share whatever comes to mind, no matter how outlandish it may seem. This open and non-judgmental environment fosters creativity and can lead to innovative solutions. A facilitator typically guides the session, encouraging participation and capturing the ideas generated.

Electronic brainstorming utilizes computer-based tools and networks to facilitate idea generation. Participants can submit their ideas anonymously and simultaneously, which can reduce inhibitions and encourage more diverse contributions. Electronic brainstorming can also be useful for geographically dispersed teams. Various software platforms are available that support electronic brainstorming, often including features like idea rating and categorization. This method can be particularly effective for large groups or when dealing with sensitive topics.

The nominal group technique (NGT) is a structured approach that combines individual idea generation with group discussion and voting. Participants first generate ideas individually and silently. Then, each participant shares their ideas with the group, and the ideas are recorded. After all ideas have been presented, the group discusses and clarifies them. Finally, participants vote anonymously to rank the ideas in order of priority. NGT is useful for reducing the influence of dominant personalities and ensuring that all ideas are considered fairly. This method is particularly effective when dealing with complex problems or when consensus is important.

The Crawford slip method is another structured technique that involves having participants write down their ideas on individual slips of paper. These slips are then collected and sorted into categories. The categories are then discussed by the group, and the ideas within each category are further developed. This method is useful for generating a large number of ideas quickly and can be particularly effective for large groups. It also helps to organize and categorize ideas, making them easier to analyze and evaluate.

By understanding and applying these various brainstorming techniques, project managers can effectively leverage the collective intelligence of their teams to generate innovative solutions and improve project outcomes.

Test Your Understanding 10.20

Which of the following best describes the main purpose of a focus group in a project context?
A. To collect quantitative data from a large sample
B. To brainstorm creative solutions to project problems and solutions
C. To gather qualitative insights into people's opinions and experiences
D. To present final project deliverables to stakeholders

Test Your Understanding 10.21
A project team is developing a new e-commerce platform. To understand user frustrations with the current website, they organize a small, moderated discussion with frequent customers. What technique are they using?
A. Focus group
B. Nominal group technique
C. Mind mapping
D. Crawford slip method

Test Your Understanding 10.22
In a focus group, the moderator's primary role is to:
A. Control the discussion and ensure their opinion is heard
B. Facilitate balanced discussion and probe deeper into responses
C. Collect quantitative metrics from participants
D. Ensure participants agree with the project's proposed ideas

Test Your Understanding 10.23
Which characteristic best defines a stand-up meeting in Agile project management?
A. In-depth discussions lasting about an hour
B. A brief, daily meeting focused on progress and impediments
C. A long-term planning session held monthly to solve monthly remaining problems
D. A brainstorming session for new product ideas

Test Your Understanding 10.24
What are the three standard questions asked during a stand-up meeting?
A. Who completed what? What's next? Who's responsible?
B. What went well? What didn't? What can we improve?
C. What's the project budget? Who is attending? What's our deadline?
D. What did I do yesterday? What will I do today? What's blocking me?

Test Your Understanding 10.25
During a daily stand-up, one developer begins discussing a complex bug in detail, causing the meeting to go over time. What should the project manager do?
A. Allow the discussion to continue for team learning
B. End the meeting immediately without resolving the issue
C. Ask the developer to discuss the issue offline with relevant members
D. Schedule another stand-up immediately

Test Your Understanding 10.26
A project manager wants to avoid dominant personalities influencing idea generation. Team members first write ideas individually, then share and vote on them anonymously. Which brainstorming technique is being used?
A. Traditional brainstorming
B. Nominal group technique

C. Mind mapping
D. Electronic brainstorming

10.6 Problem-solving Tools and Techniques

Project management involves a great deal of problem-solving, as project managers must identify and resolve issues that arise during the course of a project. To be effective, project managers must have a range of tools and techniques at their disposal to help them diagnose problems and find solutions.

Here are some common problem-solving tools and techniques used in project management. When choosing the right tool or technique for a given problem, project managers must consider the specific circumstances and goals of their projects.

Root cause analysis (RCA) is a structured, problem-solving approach designed to pinpoint the fundamental reasons why a problem occurs, rather than just treating its symptoms. It's about digging deeper than the surface level to uncover the underlying triggers. Instead of simply noticing a project is behind schedule, RCA helps you understand why it's behind schedule.

Let's take the example of a software development project falling behind schedule. Instead of panicking and throwing more resources at the problem, let's use RCA. First, define the problem clearly. "The project is behind schedule" is too vague. Be specific. "The Alpha module of the project is two weeks behind schedule, specifically in the user interface development phase." This clarifies the scope of the problem.

Next, gather data. This is where you collect evidence. Don't rely on assumptions. Examples include reviewing the original schedule, current progress, and any deviations (schedule data); analyzing developer workload, availability, and skill sets (resource data); examining communication logs, meeting minutes, and email threads (communication data); looking at code quality metrics, bug reports, and testing results (performance data); and talking to developers, testers, project managers, and even stakeholders (interviews). Ask open-ended questions like, "What are the biggest challenges you're facing?" or "What could be improved to make the process smoother?"

Based on the data, brainstorm potential contributing factors. Examples include a lack of qualified developers, unclear requirements or frequent changes to requirements, inadequate testing resources or delayed testing cycles, communication breakdowns between teams, technical challenges or unforeseen dependencies, inefficient development processes or tools, and a lack of management support or unclear priorities.

Now, drill down to the root cause. This is where the "5 Whys" technique can be useful. For each possible cause, ask "Why?" repeatedly until you reach the underlying issue. For example: The Alpha module is behind schedule. Why? The UI development is behind. Why? Developers are spending too much time fixing bugs. Why? The code quality is low. Why? Developers are under pressure to deliver features quickly and don't have time for thorough testing. Why? Management is prioritizing feature delivery over code quality (Root Cause).

Once you've identified the root cause, develop solutions to address it. Examples include implementing code reviews and automated testing to improve code quality; providing developers with training on best practices and coding standards; adjusting project timelines to allow for proper testing; improving communication processes between development and testing teams; and re-evaluating management priorities and emphasizing code quality.

Finally, implement and monitor. Put the solutions into action and monitor their effectiveness. Track key metrics to ensure the problem is being addressed and doesn't recur. By following this structured approach to RCA, you can move beyond simply reacting to problems and proactively address their root causes, leading to more efficient and successful projects.

Fishbone Diagram, also known as an Ishikawa diagram or cause-and-effect diagram, is a visual tool for organizing the factors that may contribute to a problem. By using a fishbone diagram, project managers can identify the factors that are contributing to a problem and prioritize them for further analysis. For example, a construction project is over budget and behind schedule, and the project manager wants to determine the cause. By using a fishbone diagram, the project manager identifies the factors that are contributing to the problem, including poor weather conditions, a shortage of skilled labor, and a lack of clear communication between the construction and engineering teams.

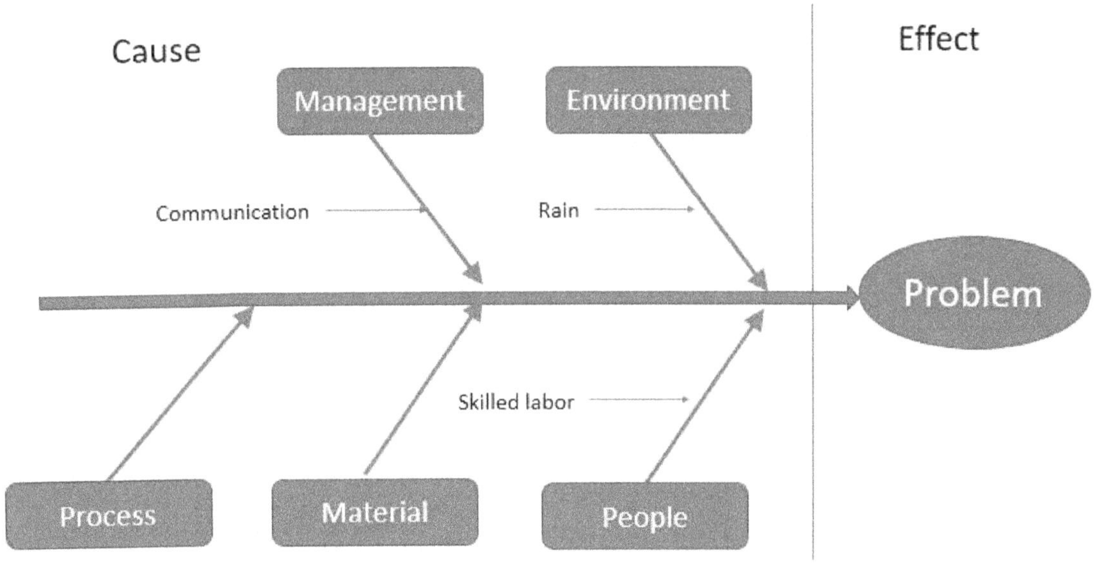

Figure 10.1 Fishbone diagram.

SWOT analysis is a tool that is used to identify an organization's strengths, weaknesses, opportunities, and threats. Project managers can use SWOT analysis to identify potential problems that may arise during a project and develop strategies to mitigate those risks. For example, a marketing project is about to launch, and the project manager wants to identify potential risks and opportunities. By using SWOT analysis, the project manager determines that the project's strengths include a well-defined target market and a strong brand reputation, while the weaknesses include a limited budget and a lack of experience in launching similar projects.

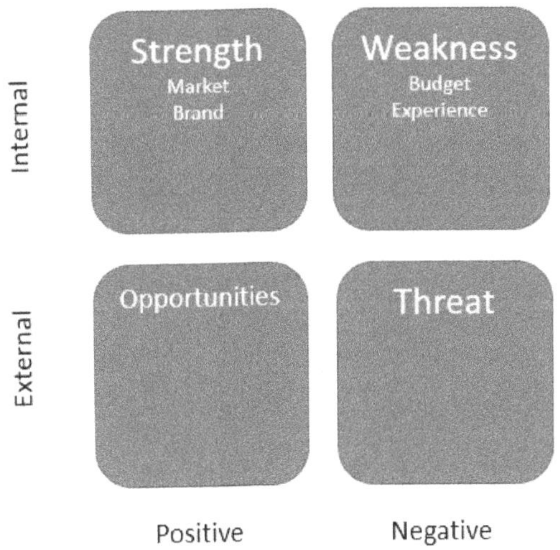

Figure 10.2 SWOT analysis.

Mind mapping is a visual tool that is used to organize and present information. Project managers can use mind mapping to identify problems, brainstorm solutions, and develop action plans. For example, a product development project is facing a problem with product design, and the project manager wants to identify potential solutions. By using mind mapping, the project manager organizes the information related to the problem and identifies several potential solutions, including outsourcing product design, hiring a new product designer, and incorporating user feedback into the design process.

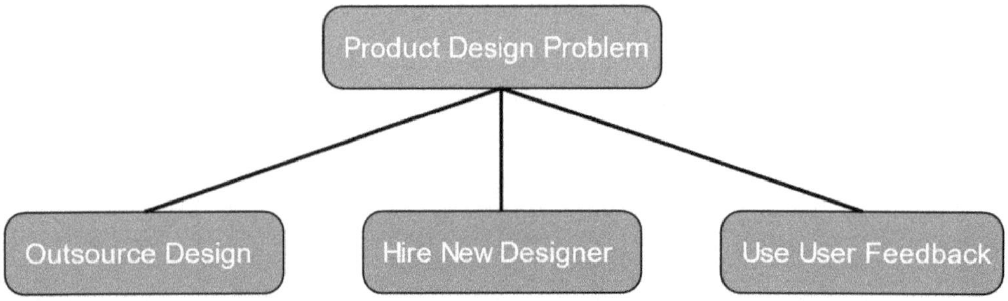

Figure 10.3 Mind mapping.

Pareto analysis is a statistical technique that is used to prioritize problems based on their relative importance. Project managers can use Pareto analysis to identify the most critical problems and allocate resources accordingly. For example, a software development project has several bugs that need to be fixed, and the project manager wants to prioritize them. By using Pareto analysis, the project manager determines that 20% of the bugs are responsible for 80% of the issues, and prioritizes those bugs for immediate attention.

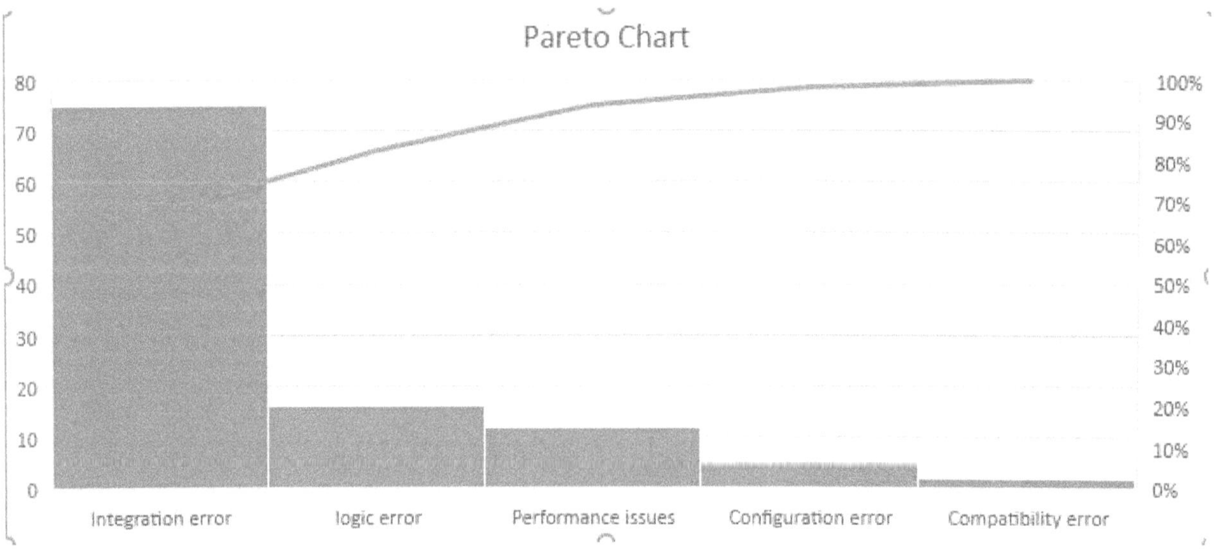

Figure 10.4 Pareto chart.

Test Your Understanding 10.27

A project manager notices that their project is behind schedule. They decide to investigate the underlying reasons instead of just adding more resources. Which problem-solving tool or technique are they applying?
A. SWOT Analysis
B. Root Cause Analysis
C. Fishbone Diagram
D. Mind Mapping

Test Your Understanding 10.28
During a construction project, the team identifies several contributing factors to cost overruns: poor weather, labor shortages, and miscommunication between teams. Which visual tool would best help organize and display these causes?
A. Pareto Chart
B. Mind Map
C. Fishbone Diagram
D. SWOT Matrix

Test Your Understanding 10.29
A marketing project manager wants to identify the internal and external factors that could affect an upcoming campaign. Which tool should they use?
A. SWOT Analysis
B. Pareto Analysis
C. Root Cause Analysis
D. Ishikawa Diagram

Test Your Understanding 10.30
A project manager discovers that 20% of reported bugs are responsible for 80% of system failures. Which technique is being used to identify and prioritize issues?
A. Pareto Analysis
B. Root Cause Analysis
C. Mind Mapping
D. SWOT Analysis

Test Your Understanding 10.31
A project manager wants to quickly generate and categorize ideas for solving a product design problem with input from the whole team. Which tool would best support this?
A. Mind Mapping
B. Pareto Analysis
C. Root Cause Analysis
D. SWOT Analysis

Test Your Understanding 10.32
In Root Cause Analysis, which step should come immediately after identifying the problem clearly?
A. Brainstorming potential solutions
B. Gathering data and evidence
C. Implementing corrective actions
D. Creating a Pareto chart

10.7 RTM & Product Backlog for Requirement Validation

Integrating the Requirements Traceability Matrix (RTM) and the Product Backlog drives effective requirements management, validation, and ultimately, project success. These tools complement each other: the RTM ensures traceability from requirements to testing, showing how each requirement is addressed and validated, while the Product Backlog prioritizes and organizes work items for development, providing a roadmap for the project team. This alignment allows project managers to effectively manage requirements throughout the project lifecycle.

Mapping requirements from the RTM to the backlog involves several steps. First, each RTM requirement should be clearly defined, documented (description, priority, acceptance criteria), and then translated into user stories or other work items added to the product backlog. Each user story should be linked back to its corresponding RTM requirement, ensuring traceability. The product owner prioritizes these user stories based on business value and dependencies. As the development team works, they refer to the RTM to ensure they meet the defined requirements and acceptance criteria. This focuses development on the most valuable features and ensures all requirements are addressed.

This integration determines project and product readiness. Several criteria must be met before release or launch: complete requirement coverage (verified by the RTM), all high-priority items resolved (tracked in the backlog), and successful validation of test cases (linked to requirements in the RTM). Gaps in the RTM indicate missing functionality or unvalidated requirements. High-priority items must be completed and tested. Each requirement should have associated test cases, and passing these, especially for high-priority items, builds confidence that the product meets acceptance criteria.

These readiness criteria relate directly to acceptance criteria (specific conditions for deliverable acceptance), sign-off milestones (stakeholder approvals tied to key deliverables or phases, often coinciding with completed high-priority items and validated test cases), and quality thresholds (acceptable levels of quality like defect rates, performance, and usability). Meeting these thresholds, alongside the other criteria, ensures the project is on track and the product is ready.

The validation process itself uses the RTM and backlog during sprint reviews and project sign-offs. The RTM allows stakeholders to verify that all requirements have been addressed and tested. Tracing requirements through the RTM to user stories and test results demonstrates that the product meets acceptance criteria. The prioritized backlog provides context for completed work and progress. Reviewing both documents provides a comprehensive readiness assessment.

Discrepancies between the RTM and backlog can occur (e.g., a requirement in the RTM not in the backlog, or a completed user story not linked to a requirement). Reconciling these involves reviewing both documents, identifying the root cause (often through discussions with business analysts, developers, and stakeholders), creating missing user stories or updating the RTM, and linking them appropriately. Regular synchronization meetings can prevent these issues.

The combined RTM and backlog approach offers numerous benefits: enhanced visibility into project progress and requirement coverage (tracking requirement status and identifying gaps), and improved communication between stakeholders, business analysts, and development teams (using the RTM and backlog as common reference points). This shared understanding fosters collaboration and reduces misunderstandings, ultimately contributing to delivering a product that meets stakeholder needs and project objectives.

Test Your Understanding 10.33
A project team finds that one of the requirements in the RTM does not appear in the Product Backlog. What should the project manager do first?
A. Remove the requirement from the RTM since it is not in the backlog.
B. Re-prioritize the backlog to focus on other user stories.
C. Investigate the discrepancy and create a user story linked to the RTM requirement.
D. Delay the project release until all missing requirements are deleted.

Test Your Understanding 10.34
Which criterion is most important to confirm product readiness before release?
A. Completion of all documentation regardless of testing results
B. Verification that all requirements are covered and validated in the RTM
C. Closure of all low-priority tasks in the backlog to ensure the highest value delivered
D. Elimination of all defects, even minor ones

Test Your Understanding 10.35
During a sprint review, stakeholders notice that several completed user stories are not linked to RTM requirements. What risk does this situation present?
A. It may cause duplication of test cases.
B. It could indicate missing or unvalidated requirements.
C. It shows that the team overestimated sprint capacity.
D. It suggests that traceability between user stories and requirements may be incomplete.

10.8 Project Closure and Transitions

Project closure and transitions refer to the final stage of a project in project management. It involves formally closing the project and transitioning the project deliverables to the stakeholders who will use them.

The purpose of project closure and transitions is to ensure that the project has achieved its objectives and that all stakeholders are satisfied with the outcome.

Project closure and transitions formally finalize a project and ensure a smooth handover of deliverables. Here's a streamlined and practical breakdown of the key steps:

Verification of Completion & Deliverables: The project manager and team conduct a comprehensive review to confirm that all objectives, deliverables, and planned tasks are completed to standard. This final phase extends beyond basic verification, requiring evidence of functional performance, alignment with acceptance criteria, and stakeholder satisfaction. Deliverables undergo rigorous evaluation through walkthroughs, live demonstrations, and user acceptance testing (UAT), ensuring they meet predefined expectations. Simultaneously, all project documentation -- including requirements, design specifications, test outcomes, and user guides -- is meticulously audited for accuracy, clarity, and completeness. By integrating hands-on validation with systematic record checks, the team ensures a seamless project closure and fulfills stakeholder requirements.

Formal Stakeholder Acceptance: Securing formal stakeholder sign-off is essential to validate acceptance of deliverables and confirm the project's successful completion. This process begins with a final presentation, where the team summarizes outcomes, demonstrates deliverables, and explicitly ties results to the project's original objectives. This session also provides an opportunity to address final questions or concerns, ensuring stakeholders fully understand and agree with the work delivered. Following this, a sign-off meeting is held to formalize approval, often involving stakeholders signing acceptance documents or completion certificates. This step legally or contractually acknowledges that requirements have been met and marks the project's official closure. By emphasizing transparency and documented agreement, the process reduces post-project disputes, reinforces accountability, and fosters trust for future collaborations.

Contract Closure & Financial Reconciliation: Formally closing all project-related contracts is a mandatory step to ensure financial and legal accountability. This involves two critical actions: finalizing payments (settling all outstanding invoices and releasing funds to vendors/contractors) and completing contract documentation. The latter requires verifying that all obligations are fulfilled, resolving disputes (if any), and reconciling project financials to confirm budget alignment. By prioritizing these steps, organizations minimize post-project risks, maintain compliance, and preserve positive relationships with external partners.

Deliverable Transfer & Training: Transferring ownership and accountability for deliverables to stakeholders ensures their successful adoption and long-term use. This transition hinges on a structured handover process, where the team systematically shares documentation, transfers knowledge, and provides training to stakeholders responsible for operating and maintaining the deliverables. Equally important is the delivery of comprehensive user manuals, training guides, and support resources tailored to the stakeholders' needs. These materials bridge gaps in expertise, minimize disruption during the transition, and empower users to troubleshoot issues independently. By prioritizing clarity, accessibility, and hands-on guidance, this approach fosters stakeholder confidence and ensures deliverables achieve their intended impact.

Project Archiving & Knowledge Capture: Systematically archiving all project records -- such as plans, reports, financial data, and lessons learned -- preserves organizational knowledge and drives continuous improvement. This involves securely storing data in accessible, protected locations (e.g., cloud platforms or internal databases) to ensure long-term availability while maintaining confidentiality. Equally important is the structured documentation of lessons learned, which goes beyond informal discussions to formally capture successes, challenges, and actionable insights. This deliberate reflection helps teams refine strategies, avoid past pitfalls, and enhance future project outcomes. By prioritizing thorough archiving practices, organizations not only ensure transparency and simplify audits but also build a foundation for more informed, efficient, and resilient project execution. The knowledge base established through these efforts can serve as a valuable resource for AI systems, as explored in the next two chapters. This captured knowledge enables organizations to leverage data-driven insights for future innovation and strategic decision-making.

Project Celebration & Team Recognition: Acknowledging the team's efforts and celebrating project success is important for morale and team building. This can be as simple as a team lunch or a more formal recognition event. This fosters a positive team environment and reinforces the value of their contributions.

Test Your Understanding 10.36
Which of the following best describes the primary purpose of project closure and transitions?
A. To finalize financial reports and terminate all vendor contracts
B. To ensure the project objectives are met and deliverables are accepted by stakeholders
C. To archive all documents for audit compliance
D. To plan the next phase of the project lifecycle and move on

Test Your Understanding 10.37
During a project's final review, the team performs live demonstrations and user acceptance testing (UAT) to confirm functionality. Which closure activity does this describe?
A. Contract Closure & Financial Reconciliation

B. Formal Stakeholder Acceptance
C. Verification of Completion & Deliverables
D. Deliverable Transfer & Training

Test Your Understanding 10.38
A project manager schedules a final meeting with the client to summarize results, link them to original objectives, and obtain a signed completion certificate. Which step in the closure process is being carried out?
A. Contract Closure & Financial Reconciliation
B. Project Archiving & Knowledge Capture
C. Formal Stakeholder Acceptance
D. Deliverable Transfer & Training

Test Your Understanding 10.39
A project team has completed all work, but several vendor invoices remain unpaid and one minor dispute is unresolved. What should the project manager do next?
A. Proceed to deliverable transfer since work is finished
B. Document the issue as a lesson learned and move on
C. Skip contract closure until the next project review cycle
D. Close contracts and reconcile finances before final closure

Test Your Understanding 10.40
During handover, the project team provides stakeholders with user manuals, training sessions, and troubleshooting resources. What is the main goal of this activity?
A. Ensuring stakeholders can independently operate and maintain deliverables
B. Collecting performance feedback for the next project
C. Reinforcing contractual obligations and payment terms
D. Preparing for post-project audits

Test Your Understanding 10.41
A company stores all project documents, financial records, and lessons learned in a secure internal database after closure. Which benefit is most directly achieved by this action?
A. Improved project budgeting for future initiatives
B. Enhanced transparency and organizational learning
C. Reduced need for stakeholder sign-off
D. Faster project delivery timelines

10.9 Chapter Summary

This chapter explores the execution and closure phases of projects. It offers an overview of common problem-solving tools and techniques, such as focus groups, stand-up meetings, and brainstorming. Topics related to integrating the Requirements Traceability Matrix (RTM) and the Product Backlog for requirement validation are discussed. Finally, the chapter concludes with insights into project closure and transitions.

10.10 Case Study

Revisit the case study in Chapter 1. Perform the following tasks:
Write a three-page project closure report that clearly summarizes the project's accomplishments, challenges, and outcomes. This report provides a comprehensive final overview of the project's success and offers recommendations for future improvements. Include the following sections:
Project Overview: Briefly introduce the project, outlining its objectives, scope, and key stakeholders.
Project Results: Summarize the project's outcomes, highlighting achievements, challenges faced, and key lessons learned.
Deliverables: List all completed project deliverables, including relevant metrics or performance indicators.
Budget and Resource Utilization: Provide an overview of the project's budget and resource usage, noting any variances and explaining their causes.
Risks and Issues: Summarize identified risks and issues, along with the mitigation strategies implemented to address them.
Stakeholder Satisfaction: Evaluate stakeholder satisfaction with the project and its outcomes, incorporating feedback received and any actions taken in response.
Lessons Learned and Recommendations: Offer recommendations for future projects or improvements to the project management process based on lessons learned. Additionally, assess the accuracy of your story points and their impact on project planning.

10.11 References

Abd Al-Salam, M., Killen, C., & Forsythe, P. (2024). A Novel Method for Exploring Collaboration in Project Meetings. In *Design Methods and Practices for Research of Project Management* (pp. 143-156). Routledge.
Ahmed, S., Musawir, A. U., & Nauman, S. (2025). Beyond benefits realization: towards a framework for sustaining and enhancing project benefits. *International Journal of Managing Projects in Business*, 1-23.
Carmeli, A., Levi, A., & Peccei, R. (2021). Resilience and creative problem-solving capacities in project teams: A relational view. *International Journal of Project Management*, *39*(5), 546-556.
De Oliveira, C. A., Carneiro, J., & Esteves, F. (2019). Conceptualizing and measuring the "strategy execution" construct. *Journal of Business Research*, *105*, 333-344.
Zaveri, T., Patel, M., Shah, V., Patel, N., Shastri, S., & Kiran, M. B. (2022). Challenges in Project Initiation. In *Sydney: Proceedings of the First Australian International Conference on Industrial Engineering and Operations Management, Sydney* (pp. 2561-2569).

10.12 Solutions to Test Your Understanding

10.1 A; 10.2 B; 10.3 D; 10.4 B; 10.5 C; 10.6 A; 10.7 B; 10.8 A; 10.9 D; 10.10 C; 10.11 A; 10.12 A; 10.13 D; 10.14 C; 10.15 A; 10.16 A; 10.17 B; 10.18 C; 10.19 A; 10.20 C; 10.21 A; 10.22 B; 10.23 B; 10.24 D; 10.25 C; 10.26 B; 10.27 B; 10.28 C; 10.29 A; 10.30 A; 10.31 A; 10.32 B; 10.33 C; 10.34 B; 10.35 B; 10.36 B; 10.37 C; 10.38 C; 10.39 D; 10.40 A; 10.41 B;

Chapter 11: AI in Project Management

Chapter Learning Outcomes

11.1 Define artificial intelligence.
11.2 Identify fundamental concepts of artificial intelligence.
11.3 Describe ethical considerations of AI.
11.4 Recognize AI-driven project management principles.

11.1 Introduction to Artificial Intelligence

Artificial intelligence (AI) is rapidly transforming industries, and project management is no exception. At its core, AI refers to the ability of a computer or machine to mimic human cognitive functions such as learning, problem-solving, and decision-making. It's about creating systems that can perceive their environment, process information, and act rationally to achieve a specific goal, much like a human would.

This ability to mimic cognitive functions is realized through a diverse set of techniques and subfields. While popular culture often portrays AI as sentient robots, the practical application of AI focuses on developing tools that augment human capabilities and automate tasks. This augmentation is achieved through specialized areas like machine learning, which enables computers to learn from data without explicit programming, and deep learning, which uses neural networks to analyze complex data. These subfields directly translate the core definition of AI -- mimicking cognitive functions -- into tangible tools that can perceive, process, and act upon information.

The field of AI is broad and encompasses various subfields, each contributing in unique ways to the overall goal of creating intelligent machines. Natural language processing (NLP) allows computers to understand, interpret, and generate human language, enabling tasks like sentiment analysis and text summarization. Computer vision empowers machines to "see" and interpret images and videos, crucial for applications like object recognition and quality control. These are just a few examples, and the landscape of AI subfields is constantly evolving.

While the concept of artificial beings has existed in mythology and fiction for centuries, the formal study of AI as a scientific discipline began in the mid-1950s. The Dartmouth Workshop in 1956 is widely considered the birth of AI as a field, where leading researchers like John McCarthy, Marvin Minsky, Claude Shannon, and Nathaniel Rochester gathered to explore the possibility of creating machines that could "think."

Early AI research centered on symbolic reasoning, using rules and symbols to represent knowledge and solve problems, such as playing chess or proving mathematical theorems. Progress was uneven, with periods of optimism followed by "AI winters" in the late 1960s to 1980s, when unmet expectations led to reduced funding and interest. These downturns were later countered by renewed enthusiasm as new techniques and improved hardware emerged.

Recent AI advancements, driven by powerful computing, vast datasets, and breakthroughs in machine learning -- particularly deep learning -- have transformed the field. Moving away from rule-based systems, data-driven approaches now excel in complex tasks like image recognition, natural language processing, and predictive analytics, marking a new era of AI innovation.

Several AI concepts are particularly relevant to project management, offering powerful tools to enhance efficiency and decision-making. *Predictive analytics* uses AI to analyze historical project data, forecasting potential risks, delays, and cost overruns. *Machine learning* algorithms can be trained to identify patterns in this data, enabling project managers to make more informed decisions about resource allocation, task prioritization, and risk mitigation. *Natural language processing* (NLP) automates tasks like analyzing project documents, summarizing meeting notes, and even generating reports, freeing up project managers for more strategic work. *Optimization* algorithms further contribute by optimizing resource allocation, scheduling, and task dependencies for maximum efficiency.

Beyond these, *generative AI* is emerging as a significant force. It can assist in brainstorming project ideas, generating creative solutions to challenges, and even drafting project documentation. Imagine AI tools that can generate different project plans based on varying constraints, allowing project managers to explore a wider range of options.

Furthermore, consider the role of *computer vision* -- a field of AI that enables computers to interpret and process visual data, like images or videos. In projects involving physical infrastructure or construction, computer vision can analyze images and videos from job sites to monitor progress, identify safety hazards, and ensure quality control. This can lead to more accurate tracking and proactive problem-solving.

Understanding these core AI concepts -- predictive analytics, machine learning, NLP, optimization, generative AI, and computer vision -- enables project managers to effectively leverage AI tools and techniques. Today, AI is no longer a futuristic fantasy but a tangible force reshaping how we live and work, and its potential impact on project management is only beginning to be realized.

Test Your Understanding 11.1
Artificial Intelligence (AI) can best be defined as:
A. Machines that perform repetitive tasks more efficiently than humans like robots on assembly line.
B. Systems designed to mimic human cognitive functions like learning and decision-making.
C. Computers programmed with pre-determined rules to follow human instructions.
D. Robots capable of replacing humans in all industries.

Test Your Understanding 11.2
A project manager is using an AI-powered tool that reviews historical project data to predict future cost overruns and schedule delays. Which AI concept is being applied here?
A. Natural Language Processing (NLP)
B. Predictive Analytics
C. Computer Vision
D. Generative AI

Test Your Understanding 11.3
Deep learning primarily differs from traditional machine learning because it:
A. Uses rule-based reasoning instead of data-driven learning.
B. Relies on symbolic logic to solve mathematical problems.
C. Employs neural networks to process and interpret complex data patterns.
D. Focuses on visual data like images and videos and treat everything as numbers.

Test Your Understanding 11.4
A construction project team uses drones to capture real-time images of the job site. An AI system then analyzes the images to detect safety hazards and monitor progress. Which AI subfield enables this functionality?
A. Computer Vision
B. Natural Language Processing
C. Predictive Analytics
D. Optimization Algorithms

Test Your Understanding 11.5
A project manager wants an AI system that can create multiple project plan versions based on changing deadlines, budgets, and resources. Which AI subfield would best support this need?
A. Generative AI
B. Predictive Analytics
C. Machine Learning
D. Symbolic Reasoning

11.2 What Project Managers Need to Know About AI

Today's project managers navigate a complex, data-driven landscape. You don't need to be an AI expert, but understanding key principles will help you use these tools effectively. This section builds on the concepts from the previous section, focusing on those most relevant to project managers.

11.2.1 Machine Learning

Machine learning (ML) is a subset of AI where computers learn from data without explicit programming. Instead of relying on pre-defined rules, ML algorithms identify patterns, make predictions, and improve their performance over time by being exposed to more data. Think of it like training a dog -- you don't program every single command, but through repetition and feedback, it learns to respond appropriately. This learning process can be broadly categorized into different types, with two of the most common being supervised and unsupervised learning.

Supervised learning is like having a teacher guide the learning process. The algorithm is trained on a labeled dataset, meaning the data includes both the input features and the correct output (or "label"). The goal is for the algorithm to learn the mapping between inputs and outputs so that it can accurately predict the output for new, unseen inputs. A common example is predicting project timelines. The algorithm might be trained on historical project data, where the inputs are factors like team size, budget, and task dependencies, and the label is the actual project duration. Once trained, the algorithm can predict the duration of new projects based on their characteristics.

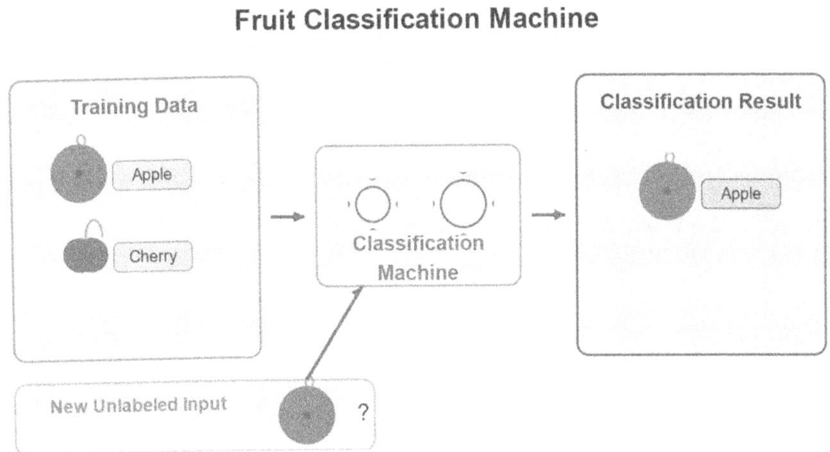

Figure 11.1 Superised Learning

Unsupervised learning, on the other hand, is like learning without a teacher. The algorithm is given an unlabeled dataset and must find patterns and structure on its own. There are no correct answers provided. Clustering is a typical example of unsupervised learning. Imagine having project data without knowing which projects are similar. An unsupervised learning algorithm could group projects based on their characteristics, revealing clusters of similar projects that might share common risk factors or resource requirements. This can be invaluable for project managers in identifying trends and making informed decisions.

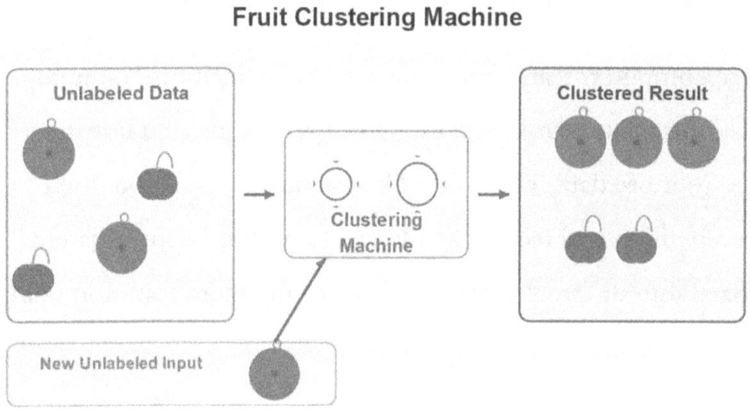

Figure 11.2 Unsupervised Learning.

Beyond these, there are other types of machine learning, such as reinforcement learning, which involves an agent learning to interact with an environment through trial and error. While supervised and unsupervised learning are more commonly used in project management today, the field is constantly evolving, and new applications of different ML techniques are always emerging.

Predictive analytics is a key application of machine learning combined with traditional statistical methods in project management. By analyzing historical project data and identifying patterns, AI can forecast potential risks, delays, and cost overruns. This enables project managers to address issues proactively rather than reacting after they occur. For example, AI can predict the likelihood of a task delay based on past data and current project conditions, allowing managers to intervene and prevent setbacks.

Test Your Understanding 11.6
Which of the following best describes the main goal of supervised learning in machine learning?
A. To group data into clusters without prior knowledge of their labels.
B. To learn from labeled data and predict outcomes for new, unseen inputs.
C. To interact with an environment and learn through rewards and penalties.
D. To identify relationships between unlabeled variables using trial and error.

Test Your Understanding 11.7
A project management team wants to categorize hundreds of past projects based on characteristics like budget, duration, and complexity, but they don't have predefined labels for these projects. Which machine

learning approach should they use?
A. Supervised learning
B. Reinforcement learning
C. Unsupervised learning
D. Deep learning

Test Your Understanding 11.8
The book compares training a machine learning model to training a dog. What is the key idea behind this analogy?
A. Both require a set of explicit rules to operate correctly.
B. Both are fully autonomous from the beginning.
C. Both can function without any external supervision.
D. Both rely on repetition and feedback to improve performance.

11.2.2 Deep Learning

Deep learning (DL) is a specialized area within machine learning that utilizes artificial neural networks with multiple layers (hence "deep") to analyze complex data. These networks, inspired by the structure of the human brain, can learn intricate patterns and representations, making them particularly effective for tasks that are challenging for traditional machine learning algorithms. Think of it like this: a single-layer neural network might be able to identify simple shapes in an image, but a deep learning network with multiple layers can learn to recognize entire objects, like a cat or a dog, by breaking down the image into hierarchical features -- edges, textures, shapes, and finally, the complete object.

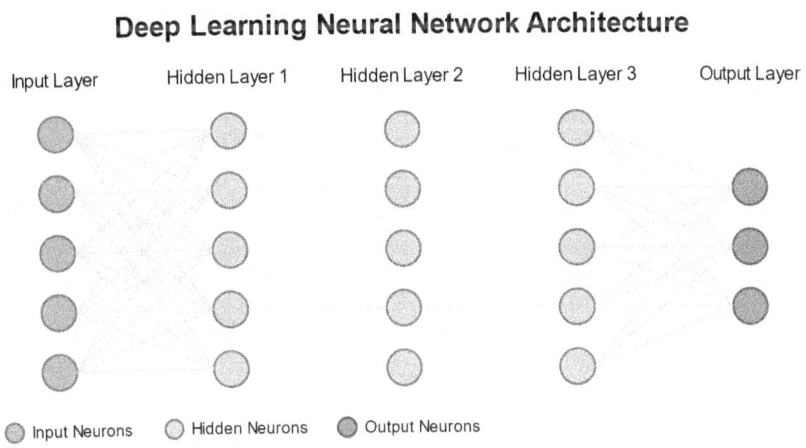

Figure 11.3 Sample deep learning model.

The "deep" in deep learning refers to the multiple layers of interconnected nodes in the neural network. Each layer learns a different level of abstraction from the data. For example, in image recognition, the first layer might detect edges, the second layer might combine those edges into shapes, the third layer might combine shapes into parts of an object, and the final layer might combine those parts into a complete object. This hierarchical learning allows deep learning models to capture very complex relationships in data. In a project context, this could be used to automatically analyze images from construction sites to monitor progress, identify safety violations, or assess the quality of work.

Test Your Understanding 11.9
What does the term "deep" in deep learning primarily refer to?
A. The large size of the dataset used for training.
B. The complex mathematical equations used in the algorithm.
C. The multiple layers of interconnected nodes in the neural network.
D. The high computational cost of running the model.

Test Your Understanding 11.10
According to the book, how does a deep learning model improve upon a single-layer neural network?
A. It replaces human supervision entirely.
B. It uses fewer computational resources to achieve similar accuracy.
C. It eliminates the need for large amounts of data.
D. It can identify higher-level features by combining simpler patterns learned at earlier layers.

11.2.3 Natural Language Processing

Natural Language Processing (NLP) focuses on enabling computers to understand, interpret, and generate human language. This automates tasks that involve text and speech, making it a powerful tool for project management. Instead of just seeing words as strings of characters, NLP allows computers to understand the meaning and context behind the words, much like humans do. NLP techniques often rely on machine learning algorithms, including deep learning models, to achieve these capabilities. For example, deep learning can be used to train NLP models to recognize complex grammatical structures or understand the nuances of sentiment in text. Let's break down some specific examples of how NLP can be used in project management:

Analyzing Project Documentation: Imagine having to sift through hundreds of pages of project proposals, contracts, and technical documents. NLP can automate this process by extracting key information, identifying important dates, summarizing key points, and even flagging potential risks or inconsistencies. For example, NLP could identify all mentions of specific deliverables, deadlines, or budget constraints within a set of documents, creating a concise summary for the project manager.

Summarizing Meeting Notes: Long, rambling meeting notes can be a chore to review. NLP can automatically summarize these notes, highlighting key decisions, action items, and discussion points. This saves project managers valuable time and ensures that everyone is on the same page. Imagine an NLP tool that can take a recording of a meeting, transcribe it, and then generate a bullet-point summary of the key takeaways.

Generating Reports: NLP can even help generate reports. By analyzing project data and combining it with natural language generation techniques, NLP can create reports that are easy to read and understand. For example, NLP could automatically generate a weekly progress report that summarizes key milestones achieved, challenges encountered, and planned activities for the following week.

Sentiment Analysis: Understanding team morale is critical for project success. NLP can analyze emails, chat logs, and other forms of communication to gauge the overall sentiment of the team. Are people feeling positive and motivated, or are there signs of frustration or concern? NLP can identify patterns in language that suggest positive or negative sentiment, allowing project managers to proactively address potential issues. For example, if NLP detects a rise in negative sentiment related to a specific task, the project manager can intervene and address the underlying concerns.

Chatbots for Project Support: NLP powers chatbots that can answer common project-related questions, provide updates on project status, or even help team members find relevant documentation. This can free up project managers from repetitive tasks and provide team members with instant access to information.

Test Your Understanding 11.11
How can sentiment analysis support project management?
A. By tracking project budgets in real-time.
B. By identifying emotional tone in team communications.
C. By calculating project completion probabilities.
D. By generating task lists for project milestones.

Test Your Understanding 11.12
A project support chatbot can instantly answer questions like "When is the next deadline?" or "Where can I find the project charter?" Which AI technology enables this?
A. Natural Language Processing.
B. Predictive analytics.
C. Symbolic reasoning.
D. Reinforcement learning.

11.2.4 Generative AI

Generative AI takes NLP a step further by enabling AI models to create new content, whether it's text, images, code, or even music. Instead of just analyzing existing data, generative AI models learn the underlying patterns and structures of that data and then use that knowledge to create entirely new, original content. Here are some tangible examples of how generative AI could be used in a project context:

Generating Project Proposals: Imagine needing to create multiple project proposals tailored to different clients or stakeholders. Generative AI could take a few key inputs, such as the project scope, budget, and target audience, and then generate a first draft of a compelling project proposal. This frees up the project manager to focus on refining the content and adding their personal touch, rather than starting from scratch. For example, the AI could generate different versions of the proposal, highlighting different aspects of the project based on the target audience.

Creating Marketing Materials: Need to create eye-catching marketing materials for a new project? Generative AI can create marketing copy, social media posts, or even design mockups for brochures or websites. Imagine an AI that can generate different taglines, descriptions, and even visual layouts for a marketing campaign, allowing the project team to quickly explore multiple options.

Developing Training Content: Creating engaging training materials can be time-consuming. Generative AI can assist by generating scripts for training videos (even the videos itself can be created), creating quizzes, or even designing interactive training modules. For example, the AI could generate different training scenarios or case studies based on the project's specific context.

Generating Code: While still an evolving area, generative AI is showing promise in generating code snippets or even entire programs. This could be used to automate the creation of software tools or scripts needed for a project. Imagine an AI that can generate the initial code for a data analysis tool based on a description of the desired functionality.

Brainstorming and Ideation: Generative AI can even be used for brainstorming and ideation. By providing the AI with a problem or challenge, it can generate a range of potential solutions or ideas that the project team can then evaluate and refine. For example, the AI could generate different approaches to solving a specific technical challenge within the project.

It's important to remember that generative AI is still a developing field. The content it generates may require human review and editing. However, the potential of generative AI to automate content creation and boost project efficiency is immense, and it's likely to play an increasingly important role in project management in the future.

Test Your Understanding 11.13
A marketing team needs several tailored promotional materials for a new project campaign. They provide the AI with key inputs like project goals and target audience. Which capability is being applied here?
A. NLP-based sentiment detection.
B. Predictive analytics using regression models.
C. Generative AI for content creation.
D. Supervised learning for classification.

Test Your Understanding 11.14
A project manager uses generative AI to draft a project proposal, but before submitting it, they carefully review and revise the AI's draft. Why is this step important?
A. Because generative AI models always produce incorrect data.
B. Because AI-generated proposals are not legally acceptable.
C. Because AI cannot generate content longer than a certain number of pages.
D. Because AI-generated content may need human validation for accuracy and tone.

11.2.5 Automation and AI Agents

Automation and AI Agents are key benefits of AI in project management, allowing project managers to streamline repetitive tasks and free up time for strategic work. Automation uses predefined rules to execute tasks automatically, while AI agents take it further by leveraging AI to analyze data, adapt workflows, or generate insights autonomously.

Together, they enhance efficiency across various project management functions, from scheduling and resource allocation to risk tracking and reporting. For example, automation can update project schedules based on real-time progress data, while an AI agent might predict potential delays and suggest adjustments before they become major issues. The best part? You don't need to be a developer to make this happen. Using intuitive no-code and low-code platforms, you can build powerful automation "recipes" or "workflows" -- and even tap into AI agent capabilities -- to manage your projects with greater efficiency and precision.

Think of no-code automation platforms like Zapier, or the built-in automation features in tools like Asana, monday.com, and Trello, as your personal digital assistants. Some platforms also integrate AI agents for smarter task management, such as generating summaries or optimizing schedules. These tools operate on a simple but powerful principle: "When this happens (trigger), do that (action)." By connecting the different apps you already use (like email, calendars, project management software, and team chat), you can create seamless workflows that handle administrative busywork for you.

Let's say your team receives project requests through a Google Form. Manually transferring that information into your project management tool is time-consuming and prone to error. Here's how you can automate it in just a few steps using a tool like Zapier:

Set the Trigger: The trigger is a "New Form Response" in Google Forms. This tells the automation to start whenever someone submits a request.

Define the Action: The first action is to "Create a Task" in your project management tool (e.g., Asana). You can map the fields from the form directly to the task details:

The form's "Project Name" field becomes the Asana Task Title.

The "Description" field becomes the Asana Task Description.

You can even set rules. For instance, if the form's "Department" field is "Marketing," automatically assign the task to the Marketing Lead.

Add Another Action: To ensure everyone is informed, add a second action to "Send a Channel Message" in Slack or Microsoft Teams. The message could be, "New project request just came in: '[Project Name]'. It has been assigned to [Assignee Name]."

With this simple workflow, a new request is captured, assigned, and communicated to the team instantly, without you lifting a finger.

By leveraging these no-code and low-code automation tools and AI agents, you can streamline the administrative backbone of your projects. This shift frees you from being a task-tracker and allows you to become a true strategic leader, focusing on problem-solving, team motivation, and stakeholder management -- the high-value work that truly drives project success.

Test Your Understanding 11.15

In automation tools like Zapier, what does the concept "When this happens (trigger), do that (action)" represent?

A. A command-line script for workflow control.

B. The basic logic behind how automation workflows function.

C. The decision-making algorithm in deep learning.

D. The manual input process for scheduling.

Test Your Understanding 11.16
A project manager wants to provide stakeholders with real-time updates on project progress, team workload, and overdue tasks without creating manual reports. Which automation feature would best achieve this?
A. AI-generated summaries in Slack.
B. Email-based progress notifications.
C. Predictive scheduling alerts.
D. Automated dashboards connected to project management software.

11.3 Ethical Considerations in AI

The increasing prevalence of AI across various aspects of our lives necessitates a careful examination of the ethical considerations it raises. As AI systems become more sophisticated and influential, ensuring their responsible development and deployment is paramount.

One area of concern is *bias and fairness* in AI algorithms (Modi, 2023). AI systems learn from data, and if that data reflects existing societal biases, the algorithms will perpetuate and even amplify those biases. For example, facial recognition systems have been shown to be less accurate for people with darker skin tones, potentially leading to discriminatory outcomes in areas like law enforcement and security. Addressing this requires careful data curation, algorithm design, and ongoing monitoring to ensure fairness and avoid discriminatory outcomes. It's not just about the data itself; the way the algorithm is designed and trained can also introduce bias. Therefore, developers must be vigilant in identifying and mitigating potential biases throughout the AI development lifecycle.

Data *privacy and security* are critical ethical considerations (Paul, 2024). AI systems often rely on vast amounts of personal and business proprietary data to function effectively. Protecting this data from unauthorized access and misuse is essential. Robust security measures, including encryption and access controls, are necessary to safeguard sensitive personal and proprietary information.

Furthermore, data sovereignty, or data autonomy is another ethical consideration. Individuals should have control over their data and be informed about how it is being used by AI systems. Regulations like the General Data Protection Regulation (GDPR) in Europe aim to give individuals greater control over their personal data and hold organizations accountable for its protection. Beyond technical safeguards, ethical guidelines and best practices are needed to ensure responsible data handling and respect for individual privacy. This includes anonymizing data whenever possible, minimizing data collection, and being transparent about data usage (Patil et al., 2025).

Anonymizing data is a technique for protecting individual privacy when using data for AI development and deployment. It involves transforming data in such a way that it can no longer be directly linked to a specific individual. This can be achieved through various methods, such as removing or masking identifying information like names, addresses, and social security numbers. Other techniques include generalizing data (e.g., instead of specific ages, using age ranges), aggregating data (e.g., combining individual data points into group statistics), and shuffling data (e.g., rearranging data points to break the link between individual records and their original order). Effective anonymization allows data to be used for analysis and model training without compromising individual privacy. However, it's important to note that anonymization is not always perfect, and there's always a risk of re-identification, especially with large and complex datasets.

Re-identification, the process of linking anonymized data back to individuals, threatens data privacy despite anonymization efforts. Sophisticated techniques and auxiliary data sources can exploit residual attributes, such as age, gender, location, and purchase history, to create unique "fingerprints" that identify individuals. Risks escalate with dataset size, complexity, and the availability of external data for cross-referencing. Data breaches and publicly accessible data further amplify these risks (Ye et al., 2024).

To safeguard privacy, robust anonymization must pair with ongoing monitoring and a holistic strategy that considers data context and potential integration with other datasets. Practical measures include adopting differential privacy, secure data enclaves (specialized areas within a processor or system that provide a secure, isolated space for sensitive data and applications to run), and regular updates to anonymization protocols. Researchers and data handlers must proactively address re-identification risks through technical safeguards and ethical data practices.

Furthermore, even anonymized data should be handled responsibly and ethically. Best practices include implementing strict access controls to limit who can access the data, regularly auditing anonymization procedures to ensure their effectiveness, and establishing clear guidelines for data usage. A comprehensive approach to data privacy is necessary, which includes not only anonymization but also other measures like data minimization, purpose limitation, and transparency.

Transparency and accountability in AI decision-making are also critical (Cheong, 2024). As AI systems are increasingly used to make important decisions in areas like healthcare, finance, and criminal justice, it's essential to understand how these decisions are being made. "Black box" AI systems, where the decision-making process is opaque, raise concerns about accountability and trust. If an AI system makes a mistake, it's crucial to understand why it happened so that corrective measures can be taken.

Explainable AI (XAI) is a growing field that focuses on developing AI systems that are more transparent and understandable. XAI techniques aim to provide insights into the factors that contribute to AI decisions, making them more accountable and trustworthy. This transparency is not only important for ensuring fairness and accountability but also for building trust in AI systems. If people understand how AI systems work, they are more likely to accept and use them. Ultimately, navigating these ethical considerations helps realize the full potential of AI while mitigating its risks and ensuring its responsible use for the benefit of society (Dwivedi et al., 2023).

Test Your Understanding 11.17
Which of the following best describes the main ethical challenge of bias in AI systems?
A. AI systems make random errors that can amplify existing societal biases and difficult to remove
B. AI systems may inherit and amplify existing societal biases found in training data
C. Bias in AI is primarily caused by software bugs rather than data issues
D. Bias in AI systems can be fully eliminated once they are deployed

Test Your Understanding 11.18
A facial recognition system used in airport security consistently misidentifies passengers with darker skin tones. What is the most appropriate step developers should take?
A. Replace the system with manual human checks for passengers of darker skin tones
B. Collect more diverse and representative training data and review algorithm design
C. Limit the system's use to passengers of lighter skin tones
D. Encrypt the data to prevent bias in recognition

Test Your Understanding 11.19
Which of the following best describes data sovereignty?
A. The right of organizations to own and sell user data
B. The ability of AI systems to make decisions without human involvement
C. The control individuals have over their personal data and how it is used
D. The technical process of encrypting and storing data securely

Test Your Understanding 11.20
Anonymization in AI development is primarily used to:
A. Enhance algorithm speed and accuracy
B. Prevent hackers from accessing proprietary company data
C. Store more data in a smaller space
D. Remove or obscure personal identifiers to protect privacy

Test Your Understanding 11.21
Which of the following strategies provides additional protection against re-identification risks in AI systems?
A. Using differential privacy and secure data enclaves

B. Publishing anonymized datasets for public use
C. Reducing data size by deleting random records
D. Allowing unrestricted researcher access for transparency

Test Your Understanding 11.22
A hospital uses an AI system to recommend patient treatments but cannot explain how the recommendations are generated. Which ethical issue is most relevant here?
A. Data minimization
B. Algorithmic fairness
C. Transparency and accountability
D. Encryption and data security

Test Your Understanding 11.23
Explainable AI (XAI) contributes to ethical AI practices primarily by:
A. Improving the speed of AI model training
B. Allowing humans to understand and trust AI decisions
C. Reducing the need for data collection
D. Preventing bias during data input

11.4 AI-Driven Project Planning

AI is transforming project planning by enhancing traditional methodologies with machine learning, predictive analytics, and natural language processing. These capabilities drive data-driven decision-making, where insights guide planning strategies. AI also automates tasks like data collection, analysis, and report generation, allowing planners to focus on strategic thinking and problem-solving. Predictive analytics and forecasting, powered by machine learning, improve accuracy in estimating timelines, costs, and risks, optimizing project outcomes.

The integration of AI with traditional planning methods is not about replacement, but rather augmentation. AI complements established methodologies like Waterfall, Agile, and Hybrid approaches by addressing their limitations. For instance, while Waterfall provides a structured framework, it can be inflexible to changes. AI can introduce adaptability by continuously analyzing data and adjusting plans as needed.

Similarly, Agile's iterative approach can benefit from AI's predictive capabilities, allowing for more accurate sprint planning and resource allocation. AI also addresses the challenge of manual estimation in traditional planning. The shift from manual estimation to automated forecasting is a significant leap forward. AI algorithms can analyze vast amounts of historical data, market trends, and external factors to generate more accurate and dynamic forecasts, leading to better resource allocation and risk management.

Techniques like regression models, which establish relationships between variables, and time series forecasting, which analyze data points collected over time, are commonly employed. For example, a regression model could predict project cost based on factors like team size and material expenses, while time series forecasting can predict a project's completion date by analyzing the temporal sequence of past progress data, such as task completion rates over time. These models empower project managers to anticipate potential roadblocks and proactively adjust plans.

Furthermore, AI-driven optimization algorithms are transforming project scheduling and resource allocation. Techniques like genetic algorithms (GA), which mimic natural selection to find optimal solutions, and simulation, which creates virtual project environments to test different scenarios, can significantly improve efficiency. Imagine a construction project where AI optimizes the scheduling of various tasks, considering resource availability, dependencies, and potential delays. This can lead to reduced project duration and enhanced resource utilization, minimizing idle time and maximizing productivity. For instance, AI could determine the most efficient sequence for concrete pouring, considering weather conditions and crew availability, leading to significant time and cost savings.

Risk identification and management also benefit significantly from AI. AI algorithms can analyze vast amounts of data, including historical project data, news feeds, and even social media sentiment, to predict and quantify potential project risks. This allows project managers to identify and mitigate risks proactively, minimizing their impact on project success. Moreover, AI-powered tools can monitor real-time data from various sources, such as Internet of Things (IoT) sensors on construction sites or project management software, to dynamically adjust project plans in response to unforeseen events. If a delay occurs in one task, the AI system can automatically reschedule subsequent tasks to minimize the overall impact on the project timeline.

The practical application of AI in project planning is further facilitated by the emergence of specialized AI tools and platforms. Popular project management software like Microsoft Project is increasingly incorporating AI integrations, offering features like predictive analytics and automated scheduling. Cloud-based platforms like Smartsheet are also leveraging AI to enhance collaboration and provide intelligent insights. AI-powered dashboards, reporting, and visualization tools provide project managers with a comprehensive overview of project status, risks, and potential issues.

These tools can generate interactive reports that highlight key performance indicators, visualize project dependencies, and even predict potential delays, enabling data-driven decision-making and proactive project management. By embracing these AI-driven techniques and tools, project managers can significantly improve project outcomes, delivering projects on time, within budget, and to the required quality standards.

Test Your Understanding 11.24
Which of the following best describes how AI enhances traditional project planning methods?
A. By completely replacing manual planning methodologies like Waterfall and Agile
B. By automating all project decisions without human input
C. By augmenting traditional methods with predictive analytics and automation
D. By removing the need for iterative processes in Agile

Test Your Understanding 11.25
A project manager notices that her Agile team frequently underestimates sprint durations. She decides to implement an AI-driven tool to improve estimation. What capability of AI would be most useful in this situation?
A. Regression analysis to identify patterns between team velocity and sprint length
B. Automated duration report generation for completed sprints
C. Sentiment analysis to evaluate team morale how it affects a sprint duration
D. Simulation to visualize post-project results

Test Your Understanding 11.26
A construction project uses AI to determine the most efficient sequence for concrete pouring, considering weather and crew availability. Which AI technique is this scenario demonstrating?
A. Neural network analysis
B. Genetic algorithms for optimization
C. Regression forecasting
D. Sentiment-based decision modeling

Test Your Understanding 11.27
A project team is using time series forecasting to estimate project completion dates. Which type of data would this model most likely analyze?
A. Historical resource availability across projects
B. Sequence of task completion rates over time
C. Relationship between cost and team experience
D. Feedback from project stakeholders

11.5 AI Techniques for Project Estimation

Accurate project estimation drives successful project management, and AI offers a powerful toolkit to enhance this process. Machine learning models are at the forefront of this transformation. Supervised learning offers two primary approaches: regression and classification. Regression models predict continuous values, like project cost or duration, based on historical data. For example, a regression model could analyze past projects to identify correlations between project size, team experience, and budget, and then use these correlations to estimate the cost of a new project. Classification models, on the other hand, predict categorical values, such as whether a project will be completed on time or not. This can be useful for risk assessment and resource allocation.

Unsupervised learning, particularly clustering techniques, can significantly enhance project estimation by grouping similar projects based on shared characteristics, without requiring predefined labels. For instance, algorithms like k-means or hierarchical clustering can analyze historical project data -- such as scope, team size, duration, resource allocation, and complexity metrics -- to identify patterns and group projects with comparable attributes. This clustering is valuable for effort prediction, as projects within the same cluster are likely to share similar effort requirements, risks, and resource needs. Additionally, unsupervised learning can uncover hidden patterns, such as common causes of delays or budget overruns, enabling project managers to refine estimates and proactively address risks.

Reinforcement learning (RL) is particularly suited for dynamic project estimation scenarios, where conditions evolve rapidly, such as in software development projects with frequently changing requirements. An RL agent can be trained to optimize project estimates by learning from historical and real-time data, adapting to variables like scope creep, resource availability, task dependencies, and team performance. For instance, the agent operates within an environment defined by project metrics (e.g., task completion rates, budget consumption) and receives rewards based on outcomes like meeting deadlines or staying within budget. Over time, through trial-and-error interactions, the RL agent learns to adjust estimates dynamically -- reallocating resources, revising timelines, or prioritizing tasks -- to maximize project success. Practically, this could involve an RL model integrated into project management tools like Microsoft Project, where it continuously refines estimates as new requirements emerge or unexpected delays occur. For example, if a client adds new features mid-project, the RL agent can assess the impact on effort and schedule, suggesting optimal adjustments to minimize disruptions. By leveraging RL, project managers can achieve more resilient and adaptive planning, improving delivery accuracy in complex, unpredictable environments.

Natural Language Processing (NLP) can be used to analyze project requirements. NLP algorithms can process textual requirements documents, extracting key information like project scope, deliverables, and dependencies. This information can then be used to automatically generate initial project estimates or to identify potential risks and ambiguities in the requirements. For example, NLP could analyze user stories in an Agile development project to estimate the effort required for each story or to identify dependencies between stories. NLP can also be used to analyze communication within the project team, such as emails and meeting transcripts, to gain insights into project progress and potential issues.

AI-driven project estimation relies heavily on the availability of high-quality data. Historical project data forms the foundation, providing a record of past projects that the AI can learn from. This data should include details about project scope, duration, budget, team composition, and outcomes. Cost and effort metrics help train models to predict these key project parameters. These metrics can include actual costs incurred, hours worked by team members, and resource utilization.

Risk and uncertainty factors, such as potential delays, resource constraints, and market fluctuations, should also be captured, as these can significantly impact project outcomes. External data, like economic indicators or industry trends, can also be valuable for incorporating broader contextual factors into the estimation process. For example, if estimating the cost of a construction project, data on material prices and labor costs would be essential.

However, raw data is rarely perfect and often requires cleaning and preprocessing before it can be used for AI model training. Data cleaning involves identifying and correcting errors, inconsistencies, and duplicates in the data. This might include standardizing data formats, correcting typos, and removing outliers. Data preprocessing involves transforming the data into a format that is suitable for the AI algorithm. This might involve scaling or normalizing the data to ensure that all features have a similar range of values, or encoding categorical variables into numerical representations. For example, a project's location might be encoded as a numerical value for the AI model to process.

Handling missing and incomplete data is another critical step. Missing data can arise due to various reasons, such as incomplete records or data entry errors. Several techniques can be used to address missing data, including imputation (filling in missing values with estimated values), deletion (removing records with missing values), or using algorithms that can handle missing data directly. The choice of method depends on the amount and pattern of missing data, as well as the specific AI algorithm being used. For instance, if a small percentage of data is missing, imputation using the mean or median value might be sufficient. However, if a significant portion of data is missing, more sophisticated techniques like K-Nearest Neighbors imputation or even creating a separate category for "missing data" might be necessary.

Feature engineering, the process of selecting, transforming, and creating relevant features from the raw data, improves the accuracy of AI predictions. This involves identifying the most important variables that influence project outcomes and creating new features that might be more informative for the AI model. For example, instead of just using the start and end dates of a task, a feature representing the task duration might be more relevant.

Feature engineering often requires domain expertise and a deep understanding of the project management domain. It can involve creating interaction terms between existing features, transforming features using mathematical functions, or even creating entirely new features based on expert knowledge. Effective feature engineering can significantly improve the performance of AI models for project estimation, leading to more accurate and reliable predictions.

Test Your Understanding 11.28
Which statement best distinguishes regression from classification in supervised learning for project estimation?
A. Regression predicts continuous values, while classification predicts categorical outcomes.
B. Regression predicts project risks, while classification predicts cost overruns.
C. Regression is used only when data is unlabeled, while classification requires labeled data.
D. Regression models are more accurate than classification models for time predictions.

Test Your Understanding 11.29
A project manager wants to group similar past projects to improve cost estimation for new ones. Which AI approach should they use?
A. Supervised learning using regression
B. Supervised learning using classification
C. Unsupervised learning using clustering
D. Reinforcement learning

Test Your Understanding 11.30
In which scenario would reinforcement learning (RL) be most useful for project estimation?
A. When estimating static projects with fixed requirements
B. When dealing with rapidly changing project conditions and requirements
C. When grouping projects based on historical similarities
D. When analyzing completed project data for risk categorization from the historical data

Test Your Understanding 11.31
A project management software integrates an AI agent that updates project schedules in response to scope changes. What kind of AI technique is this most likely using?
A. Supervised regression
B. Unsupervised clustering
C. Reinforcement learning
D. Natural language processing

Test Your Understanding 11.32
A project analyst uses NLP to review user stories in an Agile project to estimate effort and identify dependencies. What key NLP function is being applied?
A. Clustering text data
B. Parsing and extracting structured information from text
C. Reinforcement-based task allocation

D. Regression-based cost analysis, forecasting, and validating

Test Your Understanding 11.33
A project manager notices several missing entries in the project cost column of a dataset. Which strategy is most appropriate if only 2% of the data is missing?
A. Delete all records with missing values
B. Rebuild the dataset from scratch
C. Ignore missing values entirely
D. Replace missing values with the mean or median cost

Test Your Understanding 11.34
During model development, the team standardizes all numeric features to have similar ranges before training. What process are they performing?
A. Feature scaling
B. Feature selection
C. Data augmentation
D. Feature encoding

Test Your Understanding 11.35
A project AI model uses "team size," "project duration," and a new derived variable called "duration per team member." This process illustrates which concept?
A. Data cleaning
B. Data normalization
C. Feature engineering
D. Clustering

11.6 AI Techniques for Resource Optimization

Resource optimization, the process of efficiently allocating and managing resources to maximize project success, is significantly enhanced by AI techniques. By analyzing historical project data, including past resource usage, project characteristics, and external factors, machine learning models can predict future resource needs. Time series forecasting techniques, like ARIMA models or Prophet, can be particularly useful for predicting resource demand over time, considering seasonal trends or cyclical patterns.

Unlike traditional methods that rely on pre-defined rules, reinforcement learning agents can learn to dynamically allocate resources based on the current state of the project and the project's overall goals. Imagine a complex project with multiple interconnected tasks and limited resources. A reinforcement learning agent can learn to allocate resources in real-time, adapting to changing project conditions and prioritizing tasks to maximize project completion rate or minimize project duration. This dynamic and adaptive approach to resource allocation can significantly improve project efficiency and resilience.

Optimization algorithms inspired by nature are powerful tools for managing resources in project management. For example, genetic algorithm (GA), which mimic natural selection, work by testing and improving different resource allocation plans over time, like evolving the best schedule for assigning team members to tasks. Similarly, simulated annealing, inspired by the cooling process of metals, starts with a flexible approach to explore various solutions and gradually narrows down to a near-optimal plan, avoiding getting stuck on less ideal options. These algorithms are great for solving tricky resource allocation problems, such as scheduling workers across multiple projects while balancing limited budgets, tight deadlines, and available equipment. For instance, a project manager could use a GA in software like Microsoft Project to determine the best way to assign developers to tasks across several software development projects, ensuring deadlines are met without overloading the team. These tools make complex planning easier by finding efficient solutions tailored to your project's needs.

Selecting the most suitable optimization algorithm depends on the unique challenges of the project management problem. GAs are ideal for discrete resource allocation tasks, such as assigning team members with specific skills to tasks across multiple projects while minimizing idle time. For example, GAs can evolve schedules that balance developer workloads in an IT portfolio, ensuring no single team is overburdened.

Particle swarm optimization (PSO), by contrast, thrives in continuous optimization scenarios, such as dynamically reallocating budget or shared equipment (e.g., cloud servers) across concurrent projects as priorities shift. This mimics how a project manager might redistribute funds from a delayed project to one nearing its deadline.

Simulated annealing (SA) is particularly effective for highly constrained, multi-objective problems, such as optimizing construction project timelines while accounting for fluctuating material costs, labor availability, and permit deadlines -- scenarios where rigid schedules risk costly bottlenecks. Hybrid approaches, like combining GA and PSO, can address mixed problems, such as simultaneously optimizing task sequencing (discrete) and budget allocation (continuous) in a product launch. The choice ultimately hinges on whether the problem prioritizes flexibility (e.g., agile rescheduling) or rigor (e.g., minimizing financial risk).

Natural Language Processing (NLP) can provide valuable insights for resource scheduling. By analyzing textual data, such as project plans, meeting transcripts, and communication logs, NLP algorithms can extract information about resource requirements, dependencies, and potential conflicts. For example, NLP could analyze meeting transcripts to identify potential resource bottlenecks or conflicts between team members. It could also be used to automatically extract resource requirements from project documentation, reducing the manual effort involved in resource planning. Furthermore, NLP can be used to analyze feedback from team members about resource allocation, providing valuable insights for improving resource management practices.

AI-driven resource optimization relies heavily on the availability of comprehensive and high-quality data. Several types of data help build effective AI models. Workforce skills and availability data are crucial for matching the right resources to the right tasks. This data should include information about each team member's skills, experience, certifications, and availability. For example, knowing which team members are proficient in specific programming languages or have experience with certain types of projects drives effective resource allocation.

Project complexity and workload distribution data are also vital. This data should capture the complexity of different project tasks, their dependencies, and the estimated workload associated with each task. Understanding the distribution of workload across the project timeline avoids resource bottlenecks and ensures smooth project execution. For instance, projects with a sudden surge in workload at a specific phase require careful resource planning to prevent delays.

Historical resource utilization data provides valuable insights into how resources have been used in past projects. This data can be used to identify patterns in resource usage, predict future resource needs, and optimize resource allocation strategies. For example, analyzing historical data on software development projects can reveal the typical resource utilization patterns for different project phases, allowing project managers to better plan for future projects. Beyond these core data types, contextual information like project deadlines, budget constraints, and even external factors like market conditions can also be valuable for building more robust AI models.

Like other AI-driven project management techniques, data collection, cleaning, and preprocessing form the foundation of preparing data for AI-driven resource optimization. For example, consistent naming conventions for skills and certifications ensure accurate matching of resources to tasks. Similarly, encoding a team member's experience level as a numerical value (e.g., years of experience) allows AI models to process this information effectively.

Handling uncertainty and dynamic changes in data is a challenge in resource optimization. Project environments are often dynamic, with changes in requirements, priorities, and resource availability occurring frequently. AI models need to be able to adapt to these changes and make informed decisions in the face of uncertainty. Several techniques can be used to address this challenge, including using robust AI algorithms that are less sensitive to noise and outliers, incorporating uncertainty estimates into the model, and using real-time data feeds to update the model dynamically.

For example, if a key team member becomes unavailable due to unforeseen circumstances, the AI system should be able to quickly adjust resource allocation to minimize the impact on the project. Reinforcement learning algorithms, which can learn to adapt to changing environments, are particularly well-suited for handling dynamic resource allocation scenarios. By addressing these data requirements and challenges, project managers can leverage the power of AI to optimize resource allocation, leading to more efficient project execution, reduced costs, and improved project outcomes.

Test Your Understanding 11.36
Which AI technique is best suited for predicting resource demand over time considering trends and seasonality?
A. Genetic Algorithm
B. Reinforcement Learning
C. Time Series Forecasting
D. Particle Swarm Optimization

Test Your Understanding 11.37
A project manager wants an AI system that can continuously reallocate team members as project priorities shift in real time. Which approach is most appropriate?
A. Supervised regression models
B. Reinforcement learning
C. K-means clustering
D. Simulated annealing

Test Your Understanding 11.38
In a large construction project, the manager wants to optimize schedules considering changing material prices and limited labor availability. Which algorithm is most effective?
A. Genetic Algorithm
B. Simulated Annealing
C. Time Series Forecasting
D. Natural Language Processing

Test Your Understanding 11.39
Which of the following best describes the strength of Genetic Algorithms (GA) in project resource optimization?
A. GAs are best for analyzing unstructured textual data.
B. GAs perform better with continuous resource reallocation.
C. GAs are used mainly for predicting time series data.
D. GAs can evolve near-optimal schedules for discrete allocation problems.

Test Your Understanding 11.40
A company needs to manage shared cloud resources across several simultaneous projects, reallocating them as needs change. Which optimization technique is most suitable?
A. Genetic Algorithm
B. Particle Swarm Optimization
C. Simulated Annealing
D. Time Series Forecasting

Test Your Understanding 11.41
A company encodes team experience levels numerically and standardizes skill naming conventions before model training. What process are they performing?
A. Feature engineering and data cleaning
B. Model validation and tuning
C. Data visualization and storytelling
D. Clustering and regression

11.7 AI for Cost Estimation and Budget Forecasting

Accurate cost estimation and budget forecasting drive successful project management, and AI offers a range of powerful techniques to enhance these processes. Machine learning models offer sophisticated methods for cost prediction. Regression models, including linear, polynomial, and decision trees, are commonly used to establish relationships between project characteristics and costs. For instance, a linear regression model might predict project cost based on factors like project size and team experience, while a polynomial regression could capture more complex, non-linear relationships. Decision trees can identify key cost drivers by partitioning the data based on different project attributes, making the model more interpretable.

Neural networks can provide even more accurate cost estimations, especially in projects with many interacting variables. For example, a neural network could be trained on historical project data to predict the cost of a new software development project, taking into account factors like team size, technology stack, and complexity of features.

Clustering techniques can be used to group similar projects together based on their cost patterns. This can be valuable for identifying cost benchmarks and estimating the cost of new projects based on their similarity to past projects. For example, if a new project is clustered with past projects that had high development costs, the project manager can anticipate potential cost overruns and take proactive measures.

Natural Language Processing (NLP) can analyze cost drivers and process textual data, such as project requirements documents, contracts, and meeting transcripts, to extract information about factors that influence project costs. For example, NLP could analyze a contract to identify specific clauses that might lead to increased costs or analyze meeting minutes to identify potential scope creep, which often leads to budget overruns. This information can then be used to refine cost estimations and proactively manage cost risks. NLP can also be used to analyze market trends and news articles to identify external factors that could impact project costs, such as changes in material prices or labor costs.

Reinforcement learning enables dynamic budget optimization. In dynamic project environments where requirements and priorities change frequently, reinforcement learning agents can learn to adjust project budgets in real-time. This dynamic budget optimization can help project managers to adapt to changing circumstances and maximize project value.

Probabilistic models and Bayesian networks provide a framework for cost forecasting that incorporates uncertainty. Instead of providing a single point estimate, these models provide a range of possible cost outcomes along with their associated probabilities. This allows project managers to make more informed decisions about risk management and contingency planning.

Bayesian networks can be used to model the dependencies between different cost factors and to update cost forecasts as new information becomes available. For example, a Bayesian network could be used to model the impact of potential delays on project costs, allowing project managers to estimate the probability of exceeding the project budget. By combining these AI techniques, project managers can develop more accurate, dynamic, and robust cost estimations and budget forecasts, leading to better project planning and execution.

Like other AI-driven project management techniques, AI-driven cost estimation relies heavily on the availability of comprehensive and high-quality data. Historical project cost data forms the foundation, providing a record of past project costs that the AI can learn from. This data should include detailed breakdowns of costs for various project activities, phases, and deliverables. The more granular and detailed the historical data, the better the AI can learn to identify patterns and relationships between project characteristics and costs.

Labor, material, and overhead costs are components of project costs and should be tracked meticulously. Labor costs include salaries, wages, and benefits for project team members. Material costs encompass the cost of raw materials, equipment, and supplies used in the project. Overhead costs include indirect costs associated with the project, such as rent, utilities, and administrative expenses.

Accurate tracking of these cost components helps build reliable cost estimation models. Market trends and inflation data are also important, as they can significantly impact project costs. Inflation data is essential for adjusting historical cost data to current market conditions and for forecasting future cost escalations. External data sources, like industry benchmarks or economic indicators, can also provide valuable context for cost estimation. For instance, comparing project costs to industry averages can help identify potential cost overruns or areas for improvement.

As with other AI-driven project management techniques mentioned earlier, data collection, cleaning, and preprocessing form the backbone of preparing data for AI-driven cost estimation. For example, consistent units of measurement for material costs (e.g., dollars per unit) ensure accurate analysis. During preprocessing, project complexity might involve numerical representation based on factors such as task count, dependencies, and team size. Additionally, identifying the root causes of missing or inconsistent data is key, not only to address gaps effectively (e.g., through imputation or deletion,) but also to refine future data collection workflows. Imputation fills in missing data using statistical or machine learning methods, preserving data integrity without introducing bias from deletions or zeros.

Test Your Understanding 11.42
Which type of machine learning model would be most appropriate for predicting continuous project costs based on team size and project complexity?
A. Clustering model
B. Regression model
C. Reinforcement learning agent
D. Bayesian network

Test Your Understanding 11.43
A project manager wants to understand which factors most influence project costs to explain results to stakeholders. Which model offers the best interpretability?
A. Decision trees
B. Neural networks
C. Bayesian networks
D. Polynomial regression

Test Your Understanding 11.44
A software company is estimating costs for a new project. They have data on similar past projects that share the same technology stack and complexity level. Which AI technique would be most useful here?
A. Clustering
B. Reinforcement learning
C. Time series forecasting

D. Linear regression

Test Your Understanding 11.45
Which of the following best illustrates how Natural Language Processing (NLP) supports AI-driven cost estimation?
A. NLP models historical cost data to calculate average labor costs.
B. NLP automatically adjusts inflation rates based on external indices.
C. NLP extracts cost-related risks and factors from contracts and meeting transcripts.
D. NLP clusters projects into cost groups for benchmarking.

Test Your Understanding 11.46
A project's budget must adapt to frequent changes in requirements and priorities. Which AI approach is best suited for dynamically adjusting the budget in real time?
A. Reinforcement learning
B. Neural networks
C. Clustering
D. Polynomial regression

Test Your Understanding 11.47
A project manager wants to estimate the probability of exceeding the budget if a delay occurs. Which AI approach would be most appropriate?
A. Linear regression
B. Reinforcement learning
C. Bayesian networks
D. Clustering

Test Your Understanding 11.48
A company is developing an AI-driven cost forecasting model using 10 years of project data. What is the most important preprocessing step to ensure consistency in material cost data?
A. Encode team experience as categorical data
B. Randomly delete incomplete data entries
C. Apply clustering to remove duplicate entries
D. Use consistent measurement units such as dollars per unit

11.8 AI-Based Risk Management

AI offers a powerful toolkit to enhance risk assessment process. Machine learning models are at the forefront of this advancement, offering techniques for risk prediction. Supervised learning can be used for risk classification. For example, a supervised learning model could be trained on historical project data, labeled with whether each project experienced specific risks (e.g., schedule delays, cost overruns), to predict the likelihood of similar risks occurring in new projects. Algorithms like logistic regression, support vector machines, or random forests can be employed for this purpose.

Unsupervised learning can be used for anomaly detection, identifying unusual patterns in project data that might indicate potential risks. For instance, an unsupervised learning algorithm could analyze project metrics like resource utilization and task dependencies to identify projects that deviate significantly from the norm, flagging them for further investigation. Clustering algorithms can group projects with similar risk profiles, allowing project managers to learn from past experiences with similar projects.

Natural Language Processing (NLP) algorithms can analyze textual data as explained earlier. For example, NLP could analyze project requirements to identify ambiguities or inconsistencies that could lead to misunderstandings and project delays. It could also analyze communication logs to identify negative sentiment or emerging conflicts within the project team, which could escalate into risks. Furthermore, NLP can be used to analyze news articles and industry reports to identify external risks, such as changes in regulations or market conditions, that could impact the project.

Deep learning excels at uncovering hidden risk patterns in large-scale projects by analyzing unstructured or interconnected data that traditional methods often miss. For instance, in a multi-phase construction project, a deep learning model could process historical data on delays (e.g., weather patterns, supplier reliability, permit approvals) alongside real-time sensor data from equipment to predict bottlenecks before they occur. Unlike basic machine learning, these models can detect nonlinear relationships, like how a minor design change in one task might cascade into cost overruns in another due to overlapping dependencies. In software development, a model trained on past sprint outcomes, code commit patterns, and stakeholder feedback could flag high-risk features prone to scope creep. By integrating such insights, teams can prioritize audits or reallocate resources proactively, turning reactive risk management into a strategic advantage.

Effective AI-based risk management hinges on the availability of comprehensive and high-quality data. *Historical project data*, including past project plans, execution records, and post-project reviews, provides valuable insights into previously encountered risks and their impact. This data allows AI models to learn from past experiences and identify patterns that might indicate potential risks in new projects.

Project characteristics data, such as project size, complexity, team composition, and technology used, are also essential. These characteristics can significantly influence the types and likelihood of risks that a project might face. For example, larger and more complex projects typically have a higher risk of schedule delays and cost overruns.

External data sources, such as market trends, economic indicators, regulatory changes, and even social media sentiment, can provide valuable context for risk assessment. These external factors can introduce new risks or exacerbate existing ones.

Risk registers, which document identified risks, their potential impact, and mitigation strategies, are a valuable source of information for training AI models. These registers capture expert knowledge and provide a structured representation of potential risks.

Real-time data streams provide valuable information for dynamic risk assessment. Data from various sources, such as IoT sensors, social media feeds, and project management systems, can provide real-time updates on project status, potential issues, and emerging risks. For example, real-time data from construction site sensors could provide early warnings of potential safety hazards. Social media monitoring could reveal negative sentiment about the project, which could indicate reputational risks. Integrating these real-time data streams into AI-based risk management systems allows for dynamic risk assessment and proactive risk mitigation.

Data collection, cleaning, and preprocessing prepare data for AI-driven risk management. For example, ensuring consistent terminology for risk categories and impact levels drives accurate analysis. Handling incomplete and uncertain data is a challenge in risk management. Risk data is often incomplete, as it's impossible to anticipate all potential risks, and it's inherently uncertain, as the likelihood and impact of risks are often difficult to predict precisely.

Several techniques can be used to address these issues, including imputation (filling in missing values with estimated values), using fuzzy logic to represent uncertain information, and employing probabilistic models that can handle uncertainty. For example, if the probability of a specific risk is uncertain, a range of probabilities could be used instead of a single point estimate.

Test Your Understanding 11.49
A project manager wants to predict the likelihood of schedule delays in upcoming projects using historical data. Each past project is labeled as having experienced a delay or not. Which AI approach would be most suitable?
A. Unsupervised learning
B. Supervised learning
C. Reinforcement learning
D. Deep learning without labels

Test Your Understanding 11.50

An organization uses an AI system to scan project communication logs for negative sentiment and early signs of team conflict. Which AI technique is primarily being used in this scenario?
A. Natural Language Processing (NLP)
B. Deep learning on structured data
C. Clustering algorithms
D. Reinforcement learning

Test Your Understanding 11.51
A multinational construction firm uses sensors on equipment to monitor real-time operations. Their AI system predicts bottlenecks by analyzing sensor data along with historical supplier performance and weather patterns. Which AI technique best describes this approach?
A. Deep learning
B. Logistic regression
C. Unsupervised clustering
D. Fuzzy logic modeling

Test Your Understanding 11.52
A project team uses clustering algorithms to group projects with similar characteristics and risk profiles. How does this help in risk management?
A. It ensures every project has unique risks.
B. It replaces the need for expert judgment.
C. It eliminates uncertainty in risk predictions.
D. It allows managers to apply past mitigation strategies to similar projects.

Test Your Understanding 11.53
A project's risk assessment AI model produces inconsistent results because some project reports use different terms for the same risk category (e.g., "cost risk" vs. "budget issue"). What data preparation step could best improve model accuracy?
A. Increasing the sample size
B. Normalizing risk terminology
C. Reducing the number of features
D. Ignoring inconsistent records and focus on the keyword

Test Your Understanding 11.54
Your company develops an AI-driven system that continuously monitors real-time data from social media and IoT devices to identify potential project risks as they emerge. What is the main advantage of integrating such real-time data streams?
A. It replaces the need for human supervision
B. It guarantees 100% accuracy in risk predictions
C. It allows for dynamic and proactive risk assessment
D. It reduces the need for historical data

11.9 AI-Driven Risk Identification, Categorization, and Mitigation

AI is transforming risk management by providing tools for risk identification and categorization. One of the key advantages of AI is its ability to distinguish between known and emerging risks. Known risks are those that have been identified and documented through traditional risk assessment methods. AI can analyze historical project data and risk registers to identify recurring patterns and predict the likelihood of these known risks occurring in new projects.

Emerging risks are new or unforeseen challenges that can impact a project. AI can leverage techniques like anomaly detection and NLP to identify these risks. For instance, AI can use anomaly detection to monitor project performance metrics, such as task completion rates or budget expenditures, and flag unusual patterns -- like a sudden spike in costs or delays in a specific phase --that may indicate emerging risks. Simultaneously, NLP can analyze unstructured data, such as team communications on platforms like Slack or emails, to detect sentiment shifts or recurring concerns, like mentions of resource shortages or vendor issues, that could signal potential risks.

AI also enables automated risk classification. By training machine learning models on labeled data, where risks are categorized based on their type, impact, and likelihood, AI can automatically classify new risks as they are identified. This automated classification can significantly speed up the risk assessment process and ensure consistency in risk categorization. For instance, AI can automatically categorize a risk as "schedule risk," "cost risk," or "technical risk" based on its characteristics. This categorization can then be used to prioritize risks and assign appropriate mitigation strategies.

AI-powered risk heat maps and visualizations provide project managers with a clear and concise overview of the project's risk landscape. Risk heat maps visually represent the likelihood and impact of different risks, allowing project managers to quickly identify the most critical risks that require immediate attention.

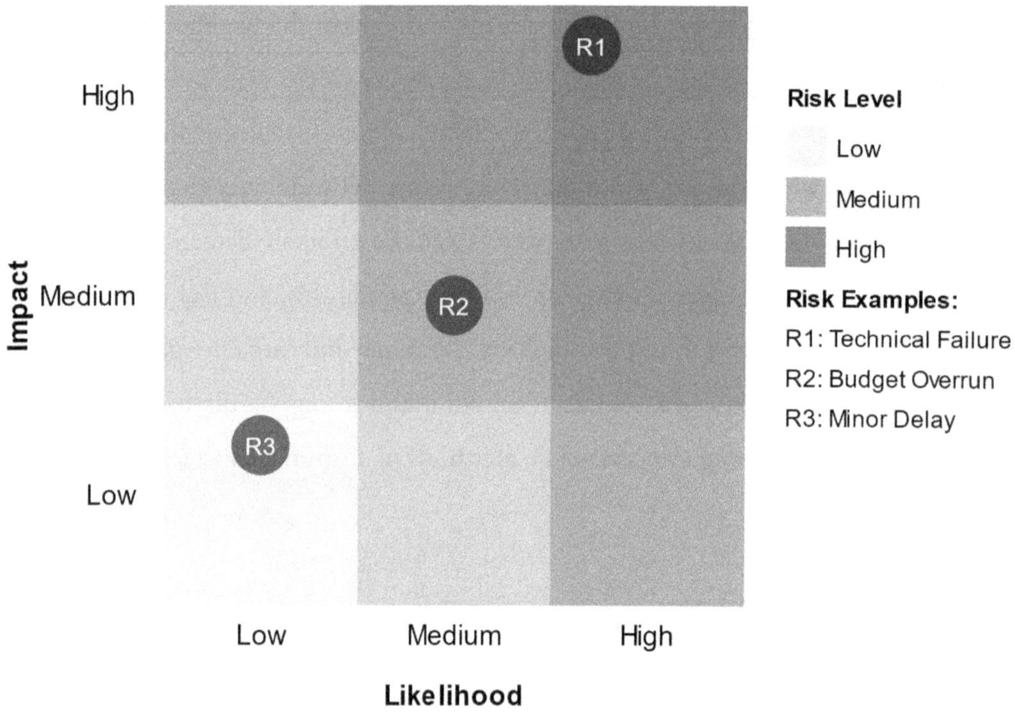

Figure 11.4 A Sample Project Risk Heat Map

AI can automatically generate these heat maps based on the risk assessments performed by the AI models. Furthermore, AI can create interactive visualizations that allow project managers to drill down into the details of each risk, explore the relationships between different risks, and track the effectiveness of risk mitigation strategies. These visualizations can improve communication about project risks among stakeholders and facilitate data-driven decision-making.

AI is not only transforming risk identification and assessment, but also revolutionizing how organizations develop and implement risk mitigation strategies. AI empowers proactive risk mitigation by analyzing historical project data and identifying patterns that indicate potential risks before they materialize. For example, AI can analyze project schedules and resource allocation to identify potential bottlenecks that could lead to delays and suggest proactive measures to mitigate these risks, such as re-allocating resources or adjusting task dependencies.

Reinforcement learning offers a powerful approach for adaptive risk response. In dynamic project environments where risks can emerge unexpectedly, reinforcement learning agents can learn to dynamically adjust risk mitigation strategies in real-time. Imagine a complex project with multiple interconnected tasks and various potential risks. A reinforcement learning agent can learn to select the most appropriate risk response based on the current state of the project and the project's overall goals.

AI-powered contingency planning enables the development of robust contingency plans that can be activated when specific risks occur. By analyzing historical project data and simulating various risk scenarios, AI can help project managers identify the most effective contingency plans for different types of risks. These contingency plans can be automatically triggered when the corresponding risks materialize, ensuring a swift and coordinated response.

Predictive analytics can be used to develop early risk warning systems. By continuously monitoring project data and external factors, AI can identify early warning signs of potential risks. For example, AI can analyze real-time data from IoT sensors on a construction site to detect early signs of structural problems. It can also monitor social media feeds and news articles to identify emerging reputational risks. These early warning systems allow project teams to take proactive measures to mitigate risks before they escalate and cause significant damage.

AI also enhances scenario planning and decision support. By simulating various risk scenarios and their potential impact on the project, AI can help project managers make more informed decisions about risk mitigation strategies. For example, AI can simulate the impact of different weather conditions on a construction project and help project managers decide whether to postpone certain activities.

AI can also be used to evaluate the cost-effectiveness of different risk mitigation strategies and to select the optimal combination of strategies to minimize project risk. By providing decision support based on data analysis and scenario simulations, AI empowers project managers to make more informed and strategic decisions about risk management. By combining these AI-driven approaches, organizations can develop more proactive, adaptive, and effective risk mitigation strategies, leading to improved project outcomes and reduced losses from unforeseen events.

Test Your Understanding 11.55
A project manager notices a sudden spike in material costs during the procurement phase. Which AI technique would most likely identify this as an emerging risk?
A. Reinforcement learning
B. Natural Language Processing (NLP)
C. Anomaly detection
D. Predictive analytics

Test Your Understanding 11.56
A project manager uses an AI system that continuously monitors IoT sensor data to detect early signs of structural weakness in a bridge construction project. What AI concept is being applied?
A. Reinforcement learning for early warning
B. Predictive analytics for early warning
C. Automated risk classification
D. Scenario simulation

Test Your Understanding 11.57
Which of the following best illustrates reinforcement learning in risk management?
A. An AI model that adapts risk mitigation strategies dynamically as project conditions change.
B. An AI system that classifies risks into cost, schedule, and technical categories.
C. A neural network that identifies sentiment trends in stakeholder communications.
D. A static model that ranks risks based on their initial probability and impact.

Test Your Understanding 11.58
During a project review, the team uses an AI-generated heat map that visually displays the impact and likelihood of all identified risks, helping prioritize responses. What is the main benefit of this visualization?
A. It automates project scheduling.
B. It eliminates the need for human analysis.
C. It predicts emerging risks automatically.
D. It improves stakeholder communication and decision-making.

11.10 Chapter Summary

This chapter begins by defining artificial intelligence and its key subfields, including machine learning, deep learning, natural language processing, generative AI, and predictive AI. It then explores the ethical considerations of AI. The second half of the chapter examines various AI-driven technologies for project planning, estimation, cost and budget forecasting, risk assessment, and strategies for risk identification, categorization, and mitigation.

11.11 Case Study

Revisit the case study in Chapter 1. Perform the following tasks:
Task 1: Enhancing the Risk Register with AI
1. Retrieve the risk register you created in Chapter 5.
2. For at least three risks in your register, write a short paragraph for each explaining how a specific AI technique discussed in the chapter could have helped you identify, categorize, or mitigate that risk more effectively. Be specific.

Task 2: Using Generative AI for Project Documentation
1. Choose one of the following tasks for your project:
   Write a brief project status update for a stakeholder.

Draft a short user guide for the "course registration" feature.
Brainstorm a list of potential new features for the system.

2. Use a generative AI tool (like Google's Gemini or others) to complete the task you chose. Provide a clear prompt to the AI.
3. Submit three things:
   The prompt you used
   AI's full, unedited response.
   The edited document by you.

11.12 References

Cheong, B. C. (2024). Transparency and accountability in AI systems: safeguarding wellbeing in the age of algorithmic decision-making. *Frontiers in Human Dynamics*, *6*, 1421273.

Dwivedi, R., Dave, D., Naik, H., Singhal, S., Omer, R., Patel, P., ... & Ranjan, R. (2023). Explainable AI (XAI): Core ideas, techniques, and solutions. *ACM computing surveys*, *55*(9), 1-33.

Modi, T. B. (2023). Artificial Intelligence Ethics and Fairness: A study to address bias and fairness issues in AI systems, and the ethical implications of AI applications. *Revista Review Index Journal of Multidisciplinary*, *3*(2), 24-35.

Patil, A., Mishra, B., Chockalingam, S., Misra, S., & Kvalvik, P. (2025). Securing financial systems through data sovereignty: a systematic review of approaches and regulations: A. Patil et al. *International Journal of Information Security*, *24*(4), 159.

Paul, J. (2024). Privacy and data security concerns in AI. *ResearchGate, November.*

Ye, M., Shen, W., Zhang, J., Yang, Y., & Du, B. (2024). Securereid: Privacy-preserving anonymization for person re-identification. *IEEE Transactions on Information Forensics and Security*, *19*, 2840-2853.

11.13 Solutions to Test Your Understanding

11.1 B; 11.2 B; 11.3 C; 11.4 A; 11.5 A; 11.6 B; 11.7 C; 11.8 D; 11.9 C; 11.10 D; 11.11 B; 11.12 A; 11.13 C; 11.14 D; 11.15 B; 11.16 D; 11.17 B; 11.18 B; 11.19 C; 11.20 D; 11.21 A; 11.22 C; 11.23 B; 11.24 C; 11.25 A; 11.26 B; 11.27 B; 11.28 A; 11.29 C; 11.30 B; 11.31 C; 11.32 B; 11.33 D; 11.34 A; 11.35 C; 11.36 C; 11.37 B; 11.38 B; 11.39 D; 11.40 B; 11.41 A; 11.42 B; 11.43 A; 11.44 A; 11.45 C; 11.46 A; 11.47 C; 11.48 D; 11.49 B; 11.50 A; 11.51 A; 11.52 D; 11.53 B; 11.54 C; 11.55 C; 11.56 B; 11.57 A; 11.58 D;

Chapter 12: Data Integration and Automation

Chapter Learning Outcomes

12.1 Identify the role of data integration in AI-driven project management
12.2 Describe how AI can be added to existing workflows
12.3 Recognize the basics of human-AI collaboration

12.1 Data Integration

Data integration is the backbone of AI-driven project management. AI systems, at their core, thrive on data. They require vast quantities of information, both structured and unstructured, to learn, adapt, and ultimately provide valuable insights. Structured data, like project schedules with start and end dates, resource allocations, and budget figures, provides a clear framework for AI to analyze.

Unstructured data, such as meeting notes, emails, and even social media chatter related to the project, offers a richer, more nuanced understanding of the project's dynamics, including team sentiment and potential roadblocks. The AI sifts through this data, identifying patterns, correlations, and anomalies that would be nearly impossible for a human project manager to detect manually. This analysis enables the AI to generate predictions about project timelines, potential risks, and resource needs. It can also provide personalized recommendations for optimizing workflows, improving communication, and ultimately increasing the likelihood of project success.

One aspect of leveraging AI in project management is ensuring a seamless flow of data between existing project management tools and the AI systems (Adamantiadou and Tsironis, 2025). Many organizations already use project management software to track progress, manage tasks, and allocate resources. Rather than replacing these systems, the ideal scenario involves integrating them with AI platforms. This integration allows the AI to access the historical project data stored within these tools, providing it with a valuable training ground. Furthermore, it allows for real-time data exchange, ensuring that the AI is working with the most up-to-date information.

This real-time connection enables AI to provide timely alerts, make dynamic adjustments to project plans, and offer proactive solutions to emerging challenges. This integration not only enhances the capabilities of existing project management tools but also empowers project managers with AI-driven insights, leading to more informed decision-making and more effective project execution. Think of it as adding a powerful analytical engine to your existing project management infrastructure, turning it from a simple tracking tool into a proactive, intelligent project partner.

However, integrating data for AI-driven project management presents a multitude of challenges. One of the most significant hurdles stems from the fact that project-related data is often scattered across a variety of disparate sources. Think about it: project schedules might live in one system, budget information in another, customer relationship management (CRM) data in a third, and team communications in yet another collaboration tool. This fragmentation makes it difficult for AI systems to get a holistic view of the project.

Spreadsheets, while ubiquitous, often become isolated islands of data, difficult to integrate with more formal systems. Enterprise Resource Planning (ERP) systems, while comprehensive, may not always capture the nuances of project-specific information. This data fragmentation creates what are often referred to as "data silos," where information is trapped within individual systems, inaccessible to others, including the AI.

These data silos are often exacerbated by compatibility issues. Different systems may use different data formats, making it technically challenging to combine the information. Legacy systems, while still functional, may lack the modern APIs or data export capabilities necessary for seamless integration. These older systems might also be built on outdated technologies that are difficult to connect with newer AI platforms.

Even when data can be technically integrated, ensuring its quality and consistency is another major concern. Data from different sources may contain inconsistencies, errors, or duplicates, which can significantly impact the accuracy and reliability of AI-driven insights. For example, a project task might be named differently in two systems, leading the AI to misinterpret its status or dependencies. Data cleaning and transformation are therefore crucial steps in the data integration process.

Beyond the technical hurdles, data integration for AI in project management must also address considerations related to data privacy, security, and regulatory compliance. Regulations like the General Data Protection Regulation (GDPR) in Europe and the California Consumer Privacy Act (CCPA) impose strict requirements on how organizations collect, store, and process personal data.

Project data often includes sensitive information, such as employee details, client data, and financial records. Integrating this data with AI systems requires robust security measures to prevent unauthorized access, data breaches, and misuse. Organizations must ensure that their data integration processes comply with all applicable regulations, including data anonymization, encryption, and access control. Failing to address these privacy and security concerns can lead to significant legal and reputational risks. Therefore, building a secure and compliant data integration pipeline is not just a technical challenge, but a critical business imperative.

Test Your Understanding 12.1
AI-driven project management primarily depends on data integration because:
A. It allows AI systems to automatically generate project budgets.
B. AI systems rely on large amounts of data to learn and make predictions.
C. It ensures that all team members use the same project management tool.
D. It prevents project managers from having to use spreadsheets.

Test Your Understanding 12.2
A project manager uses an AI-powered project dashboard that tracks milestones, analyzes meeting notes, and predicts schedule risks. Which combination of data types is the AI most likely analyzing?
A. Both structured data and unstructured data.
B. Only unstructured data.
C. Only structured data.
D. Numerical data.

Test Your Understanding 12.3
Integrating AI with existing project management tools provides which of the following primary benefits?
A. It replaces human project managers entirely if successful.
B. It enables the AI to provide real-time, data-driven insights and proactive recommendations.
C. It removes the need for project managers to update project schedules.
D. It no longer needs the large amount of historical data available for training AI systems.

Test Your Understanding 12.4
A company's project data is spread across spreadsheets, CRM tools, and email systems. When attempting to deploy an AI analytics system, the AI cannot generate complete insights. What is the most likely issue?
A. The AI lacks sufficient computing power.
B. The company used too much structured data and not enough unstructured data.
C. The project team failed to define project goals clearly.
D. The company's data is trapped in isolated systems, creating data silos.

Test Your Understanding 12.5
Legacy systems can hinder data integration with AI platforms mainly because they:
A. Contain excessive structured data that AI cannot process.
B. Use modern APIs that are incompatible with older databases.
C. Lack APIs or data export capabilities needed for seamless integration.
D. Automatically enforce GDPR and CCPA compliance, limiting integration.

12.2 Components of Data Integration

Successful data integration for AI-driven project management begins with a thorough identification of all relevant data sources. This involves mapping out where project-related information resides, both within and outside the organization. Internal data sources are the foundation, providing a rich repository of information about project activities, resources, and performance. Project management software, such as Jira, Asana, or Trello, often serves as the central hub, containing details about tasks, timelines, dependencies, and assigned individuals.

Resource planning tools like Microsoft Project or Smartsheet capture information about resource allocation, availability, and cost. Communication platforms like Slack or Microsoft Teams provide valuable insights into team interactions, discussions, and decisions. Financial systems, such as SAP or QuickBooks, track project budgets, expenses, and revenue. Integrating data from these diverse internal systems creates a comprehensive picture of the project's internal dynamics.

Beyond these core internal systems, external data sources can provide valuable contextual information. Vendor and customer feedback systems, for example, offer insights into stakeholder satisfaction, potential issues, and areas for improvement. This feedback can identify potential risks and adjust project plans accordingly. The rise of the Internet of Things (IoT) presents new opportunities for data integration in certain project contexts. For example, in construction projects, sensors embedded in equipment can provide real-time data on usage, performance, and maintenance needs, allowing for proactive maintenance scheduling and optimized resource allocation.

In other industries, data from third-party APIs, such as weather forecasts or market trends, can provide valuable external context for project planning and execution. For example, weather data could affect scheduling outdoor activities in a construction project, while market trends could influence the development roadmap for a new product launch. Identifying and integrating these external data sources can provide a more holistic view of the project environment and enable more informed decision-making. The key is to consider all potentially relevant sources, both internal and external, to ensure that the AI system has access to the broadest range of information possible for generating meaningful insights. This comprehensive approach to data source identification allows for building a truly intelligent project management system.

Once the relevant data sources have been identified, the next step in data integration is ensuring data compatibility and standardization. Different systems often store data in different formats, creating a significant challenge for AI systems that require consistent and structured input. For example, one system might use CSV (Comma Separated Values) files, another JSON (JavaScript Object Notation), and yet another a SQL database. AI models, regardless of their sophistication, need data in a format they can understand. Therefore, a part of data integration involves mapping these diverse data formats to the specific requirements of the chosen AI model. This might involve converting data from one format to another, parsing complex data structures, and extracting relevant information.

Beyond format compatibility, data standardization is equally important. Even if data is in a compatible format, inconsistencies in how data is represented can create problems. For instance, date formats might vary across systems (e.g., MM/DD/YYYY vs. DD/MM/YYYY), or units of measurement might differ (e.g., meters vs. feet). These seemingly minor inconsistencies can lead to significant errors in AI analysis. Therefore, data integration must include a process for resolving these inconsistencies. This might involve converting all dates to a standard format, standardizing units of measurement, and ensuring that all data adheres to a consistent set of rules.

Data normalization and schema alignment help transform inconsistent data into a valuable asset. Data normalization, a foundational step in this pipeline, rescales numerical features such as project timelines (e.g., 30–180 days) and budget variances (e.g., -50kto+50kto+200k) to a standardized range (e.g., [0, 1] or z-scores). For instance, in a construction project, normalizing daily equipment costs (ranging from 5,000 to 50,000) and worker productivity scores (1–10 ratings) prevents machine learning models from overemphasizing cost data when predicting delays. This ensures balanced inputs for AI tools forecasting critical path risks.

Meanwhile, schema alignment addresses structural inconsistencies between datasets. Schemas define the structure of data, such as column headers or field names. For instance, a logistics company merging shipment data with differing field names (e.g., "Item_Code" vs. "ProductID") requires schema alignment to create a unified inventory report. Tools like Microsoft SQL Server, map mismatched fields to a common structure, ensuring data from disparate sources can be merged for reliable forecasting and compliance reporting. AI can also aid in this process by identifying relationships and resolving discrepancies.

Test Your Understanding 12.6

You are managing a construction project using an AI-powered project management system. IoT sensors on equipment start sending performance data showing increasing maintenance needs. What should the AI system ideally do with this data?

A. Automatically reschedule the project by delaying the task until equipment is replaced.

B. Proactively schedule maintenance and reallocate resources to avoid downtime.

C. Ignore the data since it doesn’t affect the financial system.

D. Convert the data into visual charts for presentation purposes.

Test Your Understanding 12.7
Which of the following best describes the purpose of schema alignment during data integration?
A. Mapping fields with different names or structures to a unified format.
B. Converting text data into numeric form for machine learning models.
C. Normalizing numerical values into a standardized range.
D. Eliminating redundant records from the dataset.

Test Your Understanding 12.8
A global logistics company wants to merge shipment data from two regions: one system uses "Item_Code" while another uses "ProductID." Which step should the data integration team take before feeding the data into the AI model?
A. Perform data normalization to rescale numeric values.
B. Remove one of the datasets to avoid conflicts.
C. Convert the data into z-scores for comparison.
D. Conduct schema alignment to unify data field structures.

Test Your Understanding 12.9
When integrating data for an AI project management system, which issue can occur if data formats are inconsistent across platforms (e.g., CSV, JSON, SQL)?
A. The AI system may overemphasize numerical data.
B. The AI model may fail to process data properly.
C. The system may generate redundant reports.
D. The project data will automatically standardize itself.

Test Your Understanding 12.10
An AI project forecasting model shows inconsistent results after integrating data from multiple countries' project databases. Investigation reveals one database uses DD/MM/YYYY while another uses MM/DD/YYYY for date fields. What caused this issue?
A. Incorrect normalization of numerical data
B. Inconsistent schema alignment
C. Lack of data standardization
D. Overfitting during model training

Test Your Understanding 12.11
Why is data normalization essential before feeding data into AI models for project management?
A. It ensures all data is stored in text format for compatibility.
B. It balances the influence of different numerical variables in model training.
C. It increases the storage capacity of the database.
D. It eliminates qualitative data from the dataset.

12.3 Data Governance and Security

Effective data integration for AI-driven project management hinges not only on technical implementation but also, crucially, on robust data governance and security practices. Data governance provides the framework for managing data as a valuable organizational asset. It involves defining clear roles and responsibilities for data ownership, establishing access controls to ensure that data is only accessible to authorized individuals, and implementing audit trails to track data usage and changes.

Defining data ownership enhances accountability. Data owners are responsible for the quality, accuracy, and security of the data they own. They also define data access policies and ensure compliance with regulatory requirements. Access controls, such as role-based access or attribute-based access, restrict data access based on user roles or specific data attributes. This helps prevent unauthorized access to sensitive project information. Audit trails provide a record of data access and modifications, which helps security monitoring, compliance audits, and identifying potential data breaches.

Aligning data governance with organizational policies and regulatory requirements is paramount. Organizations must ensure that their data integration practices comply with relevant regulations, such as GDPR, CCPA, HIPAA (for healthcare projects), or industry-specific regulations. This includes implementing data anonymization or pseudonymization techniques when dealing with personal data, ensuring data encryption both in transit and at rest, and providing mechanisms for data subjects to exercise their rights, such as access, rectification, or erasure.

Beyond regulatory compliance, data governance should also align with internal organizational policies related to data quality, data retention, and data security. For example, organizations might have policies regarding data backup and recovery, data retention periods, or acceptable use of data. A well-defined data governance framework provides a clear roadmap for managing data throughout its lifecycle, from creation to disposal, ensuring that data is used responsibly, ethically, and in compliance with all applicable rules and regulations. This not only mitigates legal and reputational risks but also fosters trust among stakeholders, including project teams, clients, and partners.

Securing project data requires robust security to prevent unauthorized access and breaches. Encryption ensures that data is protected both in transit and at rest. Data in transit, such as when it's being transferred between systems or over a network, should be encrypted using protocols like TLS/SSL. This prevents eavesdropping and tampering during data transmission. Data at rest, meaning data stored on servers, databases, or other storage devices, should also be encrypted. This protects the data even if the storage system is compromised. Encryption algorithms convert data into an unreadable format, making it unintelligible to anyone without the decryption key. This ensures that even if a data breach occurs, the stolen data remains unusable.

Role-based access control (RBAC) is another security measure. RBAC restricts access to project data based on the roles and responsibilities of individual users. Different users have different levels of access, depending on their job function and project involvement. For example, a project manager might have full access to all project data, while a team member might only have access to the data relevant to their specific tasks. This principle of least privilege ensures that users only have access to the information they absolutely need to perform their duties, minimizing the potential impact of a security breach.

When dealing with personally identifiable information (PII), anonymization techniques protect individual privacy. PII includes any data that can be used to identify an individual, such as names, addresses, social security numbers, or email addresses. Anonymization techniques remove or replace PII with pseudonyms or other identifiers, making it difficult or impossible to link the data back to a specific individual. This is particularly important when using project data for AI training or analysis, as it allows researchers and analysts to work with the data without compromising individual privacy.

Techniques like data masking, tokenization, and differential privacy can be used to anonymize PII while preserving the utility of the data for analytical purposes. By implementing these security measures, organizations can create a secure environment for data integration in AI-driven project management, protecting sensitive information and maintaining the trust of stakeholders.

Test Your Understanding 12.12
A project manager is preparing to integrate financial and HR data into an AI-driven project management platform. To prevent unauthorized access, the team decides to assign data permissions based on users' job functions. Which approach are they implementing?
A. Attribute-Based Encryption (ABE)
B. Role-Based Access Control (RBAC)
C. Differential Privacy
D. Data Masking

Test Your Understanding 12.13
Your organization's AI model uses historical project data that includes employee names and contact details. To comply with GDPR before sharing this dataset with external analysts, what should you do?
A. Apply anonymization or pseudonymization techniques
B. Encrypt only the financial fields and ignore employee information
C. Allow analysts to access all original data under a confidentiality agreement
D. Back up the dataset and store it unmodified for transparency

Test Your Understanding 12.14
An AI-driven project management tool experiences a potential breach, but the stolen files are unreadable. Investigators discover that the compromised data had been encrypted. What most likely prevented the

attackers from accessing usable information?
A. Data encryption was used.
B. Data masking was used to scramble the dataset.
C. Access controls prevented the breach from occurring.
D. Audit trails automatically erased the compromised files.

12.4 Building Automated Data Pipelines

Automating data pipelines could realize the full potential of AI in project management. Building automated workflows allows for seamless integration between AI tools and project management platforms, ensuring that AI models are continuously updated with the latest project data and that AI-driven insights are readily available to project managers.

Triggers and webhooks are key components of workflow automation. Triggers are events that initiate a specific action. For example, a change in a task's deadline in a project management system could trigger a specific workflow. Webhooks are a mechanism for applications to notify other applications of events in real-time. When a trigger event occurs, the project management platform can send a webhook notification to the AI system, informing it of the change. This real-time communication enables the AI system to react dynamically to changes in the project environment.

A practical example of workflow automation is auto-updating risk prediction models when task deadlines change. Imagine a project management system where task deadlines are regularly updated as the project progresses. Whenever a task deadline is modified, the system can trigger a webhook that sends a notification to the AI system responsible for risk prediction. Upon receiving the notification, the AI system can automatically retrieve the updated task data, along with other relevant project information, and rerun its risk prediction model. This ensures that the risk predictions are always based on the most current project schedule. The updated risk assessment can then be presented to the project manager, allowing them to proactively identify and mitigate potential risks.

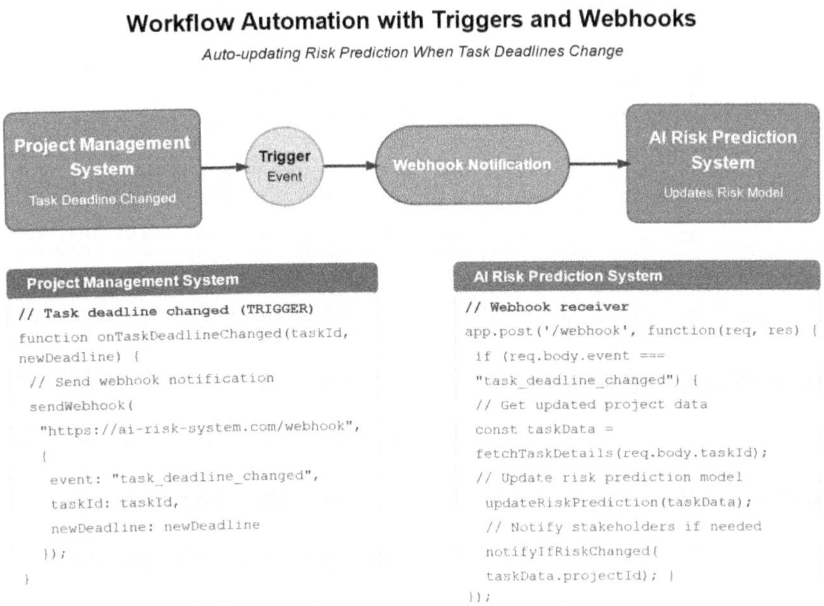

Figure 12.1 Trigger and webhook.

This automation eliminates the need for manual intervention to update the risk model, saving time and ensuring that risk assessments are always timely and accurate. Furthermore, automated data pipelines can be used to integrate AI tools with other project management functions, such as resource allocation, budget forecasting, and communication management, creating a truly intelligent and adaptive project management environment. By automating these data flows, organizations can empower project managers with real-time insights, enabling them to make more informed decisions and improve project outcomes.

Building automated data pipelines is only the first step. Maintaining their health and ensuring they continue to function effectively over time is equally crucial. Monitoring and maintenance help identify and resolve issues that can arise in data pipelines, ensuring a continuous flow of high-quality data to AI systems. Real-time data pipeline health checks can detect anomalies, bottlenecks, or failures. Tools like Datadog and Prometheus provide comprehensive monitoring capabilities, allowing organizations to track key metrics such as data latency, throughput, and error rates.

These tools can generate alerts when issues are detected, enabling prompt intervention to prevent disruptions to data flow. For example, if the data pipeline experiences a sudden spike in latency, indicating a potential bottleneck, the monitoring system can alert the operations team, who can then investigate and address the issue. Proactive monitoring helps prevent minor issues from escalating into major problems that could impact the accuracy and reliability of AI-driven insights.

Beyond monitoring the technical health of the data pipeline, maintaining the effectiveness of AI models over time is also important. AI models are trained on historical data, and as project dynamics and external factors change, the model's performance can degrade. Therefore, AI models require periodic retraining with updated datasets. The frequency of retraining depends on the specific application and the rate at which the underlying data changes. For example, a model predicting project risks might need to be retrained more frequently in a rapidly changing environment than in a stable one.

Automated retraining pipelines can be implemented to automatically trigger model retraining when new data becomes available or when the model's performance falls below a certain threshold. This ensures that the AI models are always up-to-date and reflect the latest project realities. Furthermore, monitoring the performance of AI models after retraining is also important. Metrics such as accuracy, precision, and recall should be tracked to ensure that the retrained model is performing as expected.

Test Your Understanding 12.15
A project management system automatically updates its AI risk model every time a task deadline changes. The system sends an event notification that prompts the AI model to rerun its predictions. Which technology enables this real-time update?
A. Data warehouse
B. API endpoint
C. Webhook
D. Data masking

Test Your Understanding 12.16
Which of the following best describes a trigger in workflow automation?
A. A manual approval step before data processing begins
B. A time delay between data updates
C. An event that initiates a specific automated action or workflow
D. A monitoring tool that tracks system performance metrics

Test Your Understanding 12.17
An organization's AI model for resource forecasting begins to show declining accuracy over time due to new project conditions. What should the organization implement to address this issue?
A. Reduce data collection frequency to avoid overload.
B. Automate model retraining.
C. Disable real-time triggers to stabilize results.
D. Switch to a manual reporting process.

12.5 AI-Driven Workflow Automation

AI-driven workflow automation marks a significant departure from traditional rule-based systems, employing machine learning for dynamic adaptation. Rather than relying on scripted approaches limited to predefined scenarios, AI systems analyze historical data to optimize processes and make context-aware decisions (Karamthulla et al., 2024).

The core difference lies in adaptability. While traditional automation handles repetitive tasks, such as sending deadline reminders, AI-driven systems predict outcomes and proactively prevent issues. For example, an AI system might forecast delays by recognizing patterns in project data and automatically suggest rescheduling options, transitioning from reactive notifications to proactive risk mitigation (Ronak, 2024).

The increasing complexity of modern projects, combined with the growing pressure to deliver on time and within budget, underscores the criticality of AI-driven workflow automation. Today's projects often involve numerous teams, diverse data sources, and intricate dependencies, making it difficult for project managers to maintain oversight and control. The sheer volume of information can be overwhelming, leading to errors, delays, and cost overruns. AI addresses these challenges by automating routine tasks. Additionally, AI analyzes vast amounts of project data to identify patterns and trends that would be challenging for humans to detect, providing valuable insights for optimizing resource allocation, managing risks, and enhancing overall project performance.

By automating workflows with AI, organizations can achieve significant improvements in efficiency, scalability, and error reduction. For instance, AI can automate the process of generating project reports, tracking progress against milestones, or even predicting potential roadblocks. This not only saves time and resources but also reduces the risk of human error, leading to more accurate and reliable project outcomes.

AI enhances operational efficiency by automating intelligent task execution, systematically reducing manual effort spent on repetitive workflows. This efficiency gain allows teams to reallocate human resources to high-value strategic initiatives like creative problem-solving and stakeholder engagement.

Real-time adaptability is another benefit. Unlike traditional automation systems that rely on pre-defined rules, AI can dynamically adjust workflows based on changing project conditions. AI algorithms can analyze real-time data from various sources, such as project schedules, resource availability, and risk assessments, to identify potential issues and adjust workflows proactively. This real-time adaptability allows project teams to respond quickly to unexpected events and minimize their impact on project timelines and budgets.

Error reduction is an advantage, especially in tasks that are prone to human error, such as data entry, scheduling, and report generation. AI systems can perform these tasks with a high degree of accuracy and consistency, minimizing the risk of errors that can lead to project delays, cost overruns, or even project failure.

The benefits of AI-driven workflow automation extend to cost savings as well. By optimizing resource allocation and improving time management, AI helps organizations lower operational costs. For example, AI can analyze project data to identify optimal resource assignments, ensuring that the right people are working on the right tasks at the right time. This prevents resource bottlenecks and maximizes resource utilization. AI can also optimize project schedules, identifying critical paths and potential delays, allowing project managers to take proactive steps to prevent delays (Kokala, 2024).

Finally, scalability is a significant advantage, particularly for large-scale projects that involve high-volume processes. AI can automate these processes, ensuring that they are executed efficiently and consistently, regardless of the project size or complexity. This scalability enables organizations to take on larger and more complex projects without significantly increasing their overhead costs.

Test Your Understanding 12.18
Compared to traditional rule-based automation, AI-driven workflow automation offers which of the following key advantages?
A. It operates strictly according to human-defined scripts.
B. It focuses only on repetitive, low-level data entry tasks.
C. It dynamically adapts to real-time project changes using data-driven insights.
D. It replaces all human decision-making in project management.

Test Your Understanding 12.19
A project involves multiple teams across time zones. Frequent manual report generation causes delays and inconsistencies. The project manager deploys an AI system that automatically compiles and distributes real-time progress reports. What two main benefits are achieved?
A. Improved efficiency and reduced human error
B. Enhanced creativity and increased workload
C. Static workflows and higher adaptability
D. Increased data quality and lower software costs

12.6 Strategies for Integrating AI into Workflows

Successful AI integration into project management requires a strategic, phased approach, starting with comprehensive process mapping. Organizations must audit existing workflows to differentiate between rule-based tasks -- like routing approvals or scheduling meetings, which are best suited for traditional automation tools (e.g., Robotic Process Automation) -- and complex activities demanding pattern recognition or adaptive decision-making.

Prioritizing implementation in repetitive, time-intensive areas, such as cross-functional report compilation or stakeholder feedback analysis, enables teams to reduce manual effort and improve decision quality through AI-driven insights. This ensures automation investments address both efficiency gaps and strategic intelligence needs.

For instance, instead of manually collecting status updates, AI can automatically gather information from various systems, consolidate it, and generate progress reports. Similarly, AI can streamline the approval process by routing requests to appropriate individuals based on predefined criteria.

However, not all workflows are created equal when it comes to AI integration. It's essential to prioritize workflows that offer the highest return on investment (ROI) for AI integration. This means focusing on workflows that are not only suitable for automation but also have a significant impact on project outcomes. For example, automating the process of identifying and mitigating project risks might offer a higher ROI than automating a less critical task like scheduling team meetings. AI enhances project risk management by analyzing data to identify potential risks and recommend mitigation strategies.

By prioritizing workflows with the highest ROI, organizations can maximize the benefits of AI integration and ensure that their efforts are focused on areas that will have the greatest impact on project success. This might involve conducting a cost-benefit analysis for different workflows, considering factors such as the time saved, the reduction in errors, and the potential impact on project timelines and budgets. A well-defined prioritization strategy ensures that AI is integrated strategically, delivering tangible results and contributing to overall project performance.

Furthermore, starting with smaller, well-defined projects or workflows can provide valuable experience and insights before scaling AI integration to larger and more complex projects. This iterative approach allows organizations to learn from their experiences and refine their strategies as they progress.

The choice of the right AI tools will impact the success of AI integration efforts. Several criteria should be considered when evaluating AI tools. Compatibility with existing project management systems is paramount. The chosen AI tools must be able to seamlessly integrate with the project management platforms already in use within the organization. This ensures smooth data flow and prevents data silos from forming.

Ease of customization is another important factor. Project management processes vary across organizations, and even within the same organization, different projects may have unique requirements. Therefore, the AI tools should be flexible enough to be customized to fit the specific needs of the project and the organization. This might involve configuring the AI algorithms, defining custom rules, or integrating with other specialized tools.

Scalability is also a key consideration. As the organization grows and project complexity increases, the AI tools should be able to scale accordingly. This means that the tools should be able to handle increasing volumes of data and more complex workflows without compromising performance.

Cost is another obvious but important factor. Organizations need to carefully evaluate the cost of acquiring, implementing, and maintaining the AI tools. This includes not only the upfront licensing fees but also ongoing costs for support, training, and infrastructure.

Finally, ease of use ensures adoption. The AI tools should be user-friendly and intuitive, making it easy for project managers and team members to understand and use them effectively. A steep learning curve can hinder adoption and limit the benefits of AI integration.

Several types of AI-powered platforms can be used for workflow automation. Platforms like Zapier and UiPath offer pre-built connectors for a wide range of applications, making it easier to integrate AI with existing systems without requiring extensive coding. Zapier is particularly well-suited for connecting different web applications and automating simple workflows. UiPath is a more robust platform for building and deploying robotic process automation (RPA) solutions, which can automate complex, rule-based tasks.

For more specialized needs, organizations might opt for custom-built AI solutions. These solutions can be tailored to the specific requirements of the organization and can leverage cutting-edge AI techniques. However, custom-built solutions typically require more development effort and expertise. The choice between pre-built platforms and custom solutions depends on factors such as the complexity of the workflows, the available budget, and the in-house AI expertise.

As explained earlier, preparing data for AI training is a crucial step in integrating AI into existing project management workflows. AI models are only as good as the data they are trained on, so ensuring clean, structured, and relevant data is paramount. Beyond cleaning and structuring, data relevance is also critical. The data used for AI training should be relevant to the specific task the AI model is intended to perform.

Feature engineering, discussed earlier, also plays a significant role in data preparation. Creating new features from existing data can significantly improve the performance of AI models. For example, calculating task duration from start and end dates can provide the AI model with more direct information about the time involved in completing the task.

Integrating AI into existing project management workflows is not just a technical challenge; it's also a cultural one. Effective change management ensures smooth adoption and maximizing the benefits of AI. A key aspect of change management is training teams to collaborate effectively with AI systems. Project managers and team members need to understand how the AI tools work, how to interact with them, and how to interpret the insights they provide.

Training programs should focus on practical applications of AI in project management, providing hands-on experience with the AI tools and demonstrating how they can improve project outcomes. The training should be tailored to the specific needs of different user groups, ensuring that everyone has the skills and knowledge necessary to work effectively with AI.

Perhaps the most significant hurdle in AI integration is overcoming resistance to change. Some project teams might be hesitant to embrace AI, fearing that it will replace their jobs or make their roles obsolete. Transparent communication about AI's role addresses these concerns. It's important to emphasize that AI is intended to be an enhancer, not a replacement for human project managers and team members. AI can automate routine tasks, provide valuable insights, and assist with decision-making, but it cannot replace the human element of project management, such as leadership, communication, and problem-solving.

Communicating success stories and demonstrating the tangible benefits of AI can help build trust and acceptance. Open communication channels should be established to address any concerns or questions that team members might have about AI. This might involve regular meetings, Q&A sessions, or online forums where team members can share their thoughts and receive feedback. By proactively addressing concerns and providing adequate training and support, organizations can facilitate a smooth transition to AI-driven project management and ensure that project teams embrace AI as a valuable tool for enhancing their work.

Test Your Understanding 12.20
Before integrating AI into project management, organizations should first:
A. Purchase AI tools with the most advanced features
B. Map and audit existing workflows
C. Automate all repetitive tasks immediately
D. Assign all AI integration responsibilities to IT departments

Test Your Understanding 12.21
Which type of workflow task is best suited for traditional automation tools like Robotic Process Automation (RPA)?
A. Predicting project risks
B. Forecasting project completion delays
C. Analyzing stakeholder sentiment
D. Scheduling meetings and routing approvals

Test Your Understanding 12.22
Which of the following is the most critical factor when selecting AI tools for project management?
A. Compatibility with existing systems
B. Visual design and interface color scheme
C. Social media integration features
D. Vendor marketing reputation

Test Your Understanding 12.23
A project management office (PMO) is evaluating two AI tools. One is powerful but hard to customize; the other is flexible and adaptable. Which criterion is being prioritized?
A. Scalability
B. Ease of customization
C. Cost efficiency
D. Compatibility

Test Your Understanding 12.24
A large multinational company expects its data and projects to grow rapidly over the next two years. Which AI tool characteristic should it prioritize most?
A. Scalability
B. Low licensing cost
C. Minimal training requirements
D. Offline functionality

12.7 Introduction to Human-AI Collaboration

Integrating AI into project management isn't just about replacing project managers with robots; it's about augmenting human capabilities with the power of AI. To understand where we're going, it's helpful to look at the evolution of AI's role in project management. While the concept of using computers to assist with project tasks has been around for decades, truly intelligent systems that can learn and adapt are a more recent development. Early applications focused on basic scheduling and resource allocation, but now, AI is being used for everything from risk assessment and predictive analytics to team collaboration and communication (Diameh et al., 2025).

The integration of AI is no longer a futuristic concept; it's a necessity for project success in today's rapidly changing world. Projects are becoming increasingly complex, generating vast amounts of data that are difficult for humans to process and analyze effectively. AI excels at this, identifying patterns, trends, and potential issues that might be missed by the human eye.

Moreover, AI can help optimize resource allocation, ensuring that the right people are working on the right tasks at the right time, leading to increased efficiency and productivity. In practical terms, this could mean an AI system suggesting the best team members for a particular task based on their skills and experience, or even predicting the optimal time to schedule a critical activity based on dependencies and resource availability.

By embracing AI, project managers can free themselves from tedious, repetitive tasks and focus on more strategic activities, such as stakeholder management, creative problem-solving, and fostering team morale. Ultimately, the successful projects of tomorrow will be those that leverage the combined strengths of human intelligence and artificial intelligence.

Human-AI collaboration within project management frameworks creates a powerful synergy. This partnership isn't about replacing project managers, but rather equipping them with intelligent tools to elevate their performance. The benefits of this collaboration are numerous and far-reaching, impacting virtually every aspect of project management. One of the most significant advantages is enhanced decision-making. AI algorithms can analyze vast datasets, including historical project data, market trends, and resource availability, to provide project managers with data-driven insights. This allows for more informed and strategic decisions, moving beyond gut feelings and relying on concrete evidence.

Furthermore, human-AI collaboration significantly boosts efficiency. AI can automate repetitive tasks, such as scheduling updates, progress tracking, and report generation, freeing up project managers to focus on higher-level activities. Imagine an AI system that automatically updates task dependencies based on real-time progress reports, or one that generates weekly status reports with minimal human input. This not only saves time but also reduces the risk of human error.

Another key benefit lies in risk mitigation. AI algorithms can identify potential risks and issues early on, allowing project managers to take proactive measures to prevent or mitigate them. For instance, an AI system might analyze project data to identify potential bottlenecks in the critical path or predict the likelihood of resource conflicts. By identifying these risks early, project managers can adjust their plans and avoid costly delays or disruptions.

Beyond these tangible benefits, human-AI collaboration also reduces the cognitive load for project managers. Managing complex projects can be incredibly demanding, requiring project managers to juggle multiple tasks, track numerous dependencies, and communicate with various stakeholders. AI can alleviate some of this burden by automating routine tasks, providing real-time insights, and streamlining communication. This allows project managers to focus on strategic thinking, problem-solving, and relationship management, which increase project success. Essentially, AI acts as a powerful assistant, augmenting human capabilities and enabling project managers to work more effectively and strategically. This synergy between human intuition and AI's analytical power is the key to unlocking the next level of project management excellence.

While the potential benefits of human-AI collaboration are significant, successful integration requires careful consideration of several hurdles. One of the most common challenges is resistance to change. Introducing AI into project management workflows can be met with skepticism or even outright opposition from team members who are accustomed to traditional methods. This resistance often stems from a fear of job displacement, a lack of understanding about AI's capabilities, or simply a general discomfort with new technologies.

Overcoming this resistance requires proactive communication, education, and training. Project managers need to clearly articulate the benefits of AI, address concerns about job security, and provide ample opportunities for team members to learn how to work effectively with AI tools. Demonstrating the practical applications of AI and showcasing its positive impact on project outcomes can go a long way in building buy-in and fostering a culture of acceptance.

Another significant challenge is the trust gap. For human-AI collaboration to be truly effective, project managers and team members need to trust the insights and recommendations provided by AI systems. This trust isn't built overnight. It requires transparency about how AI algorithms work, clear explanations of the data used to train these systems, and consistent demonstration of their accuracy and reliability.

Addressing concerns about bias in AI algorithms is also crucial. Project managers should be aware of the potential for bias in the data used to train AI systems and take steps to mitigate it. This might involve using diverse datasets, carefully evaluating the outputs of AI systems, and incorporating human oversight to ensure that decisions are fair and unbiased (Jagannathan et al., 2025).

Finally, skill mismatches can pose a significant challenge to AI integration. Effectively leveraging AI in project management requires a new set of skills, including data literacy, AI fluency, and the ability to interpret and apply AI-generated insights. Project managers and team members need to be trained on how to use AI tools, understand the limitations of AI, and develop the critical thinking skills needed to evaluate AI-driven recommendations. This may involve investing in training programs, hiring new talent with AI expertise, or partnering with external consultants.

Bridging the skill gap ensures that project teams can effectively collaborate with AI systems and maximize their potential. Successfully navigating these challenges -- resistance to change, trust gaps, and skill mismatches -- is critical for realizing the full potential of human-AI collaboration in project management. Addressing these issues proactively and thoughtfully will pave the way for a smoother and more successful integration of AI into existing workflows.

Test Your Understanding 12.25
The main purpose of integrating AI into project management is to:
A. Replace project managers with automated systems
B. Eliminate human decision-making from projects
C. Augment human capabilities and enhance decision-making
D. Remove the need for traditional project planning methods

Test Your Understanding 12.26
Which of the following best describes the evolution of AI's role in project management?
A. From automating basic scheduling to enabling adaptive, intelligent decision-making
B. From managing human resources to replacing entire project teams
C. From data storage to virtual communication platforms
D. From manual project documentation to automated budgeting

Test Your Understanding 12.27
How does AI contribute to risk mitigation in project management?
A. By creating backup project teams for emergencies
B. By identifying potential risks early through data analysis
C. By eliminating all project uncertainties
D. By relying on human intuition and past experiences

Test Your Understanding 12.28
During a large infrastructure project, the AI system predicts potential bottlenecks in the supply chain. What should the project manager do first?
A. Ignore the alert until an actual delay occurs
B. Ask the AI to handle supplier negotiations directly
C. Disable the AI tool to reduce project noise
D. Take proactive measures to adjust plans and prevent disruption

Test Your Understanding 12.29
One of the indirect benefits of AI integration is reducing cognitive load. This means that:
A. AI decreases the number of team members needed
B. AI removes the need for stakeholder communication
C. AI replaces critical thinking with automation
D. AI helps project managers focus on strategic, high-value tasks

Test Your Understanding 12.30
A project team resists the introduction of AI tools, fearing job loss and unfamiliar workflows. What is the best course of action for the project manager?
A. Enforce mandatory AI usage without explanation
B. Delay AI adoption indefinitely
C. Communicate AI's role as a supportive tool and offer training opportunities
D. Replace resistant team members with AI specialists

Test Your Understanding 12.31
The trust gap in human-AI collaboration can be best addressed by:
A. Concealing AI's decision-making logic to simplify adoption
B. Ensuring transparency about AI processes and consistent accuracy in outputs
C. Delegating all decisions to AI without human oversight
D. Using AI tools that require minimal user interaction

Test Your Understanding 12.32
Bias in AI algorithms can be mitigated by:
A. Using diverse datasets and applying human oversight
B. Training AI only on internal company data
C. Allowing AI to self-correct without supervision
D. Ignoring outliers during model development

Test Your Understanding 12.33
Bridging the skill gap in AI-enabled project management primarily involves:
A. Outsourcing all AI-related tasks
B. Training teams in data literacy and AI fluency
C. Hiring only data scientists as project managers
D. Relying solely on AI vendors for technical expertise

12.8 Chapter Summary

This chapter begins by exploring the role of data integration in AI-driven project management. It outlines the key components of data integration, explains the tools and techniques used in the process, and discusses the importance of strong data governance and security practices to support effective data integration. Next, the chapter shifts to AI-driven project management, focusing on process automation. It covers the tools, techniques, and strategies for integrating AI into existing project management workflows. The chapter wraps up by presenting a framework for human-AI collaboration, highlighting how people and AI can work together effectively.

12.9 Case Study

Revisit the case study in Chapter 1. Perform the following task:
Designing an AI Agent Workflow for Project Management Using MS Project. Specifically, building an AI Agent with MCP to Automate Project Monitoring in Microsoft Project. First, choose a Project Workflow for AI Automation (This task may require you to pay for the API):
Using the MS Project file as the source, design one of the following AI automation workflows.

Workflow Type	AI Agent Purpose	Example MCP Connector Use
Status Report Generator	Automatically read task progress from MS Project and create a concise weekly status summary.	MCP connector pulls "% complete," "late tasks," and "milestone" data. Agent summarizes and formats report for email or Teams.
Risk and Delay Detector	Scan MS Project tasks for overdue or dependent items at risk of delay.	MCP connector reads task baselines, compares with current progress, and triggers alert messages.
Stakeholder Notifier	Automatically notify stakeholders when a critical path task changes.	MCP watches for updates in MS Project via API and sends notifications through Outlook or Teams using another connector.
Resource Load Analyzer	Detect resource over-allocation and recommend schedule adjustments.	MCP connector fetches resource usage table and highlights conflicts.

Next, define the Agent Workflow in AgentKit by using OpenAI's Agent Builder (AgentKit):

1. Create a new agent workflow.
2. Add the following nodes (components):
   Reasoning Node: Handles logic and decision-making prompts.
   MCP Connector Node (to Microsoft Project): Fetches data using sample CSV export.
   Action Node: Sends the output summary to email, Slack, or Teams (using another connector).
   Guardrail Node: Ensures sensitive data (budgets, employee info) isn't shared externally.
   Output Node: Generates formatted output (status report, alert, or dashboard entry).
3. Define Prompts & Logic Example (for a Status Report Agent):
   Prompt 1:
   "Analyze the following MS Project data and summarize project progress. Identify tasks that are delayed, list milestones achieved, and generate a 5-bullet executive summary."
   Prompt 2 (Conditional Logic Node):
   "If more than 3 tasks are delayed, generate a risk warning and notify the project manager."
4. Map the MCP Connector
   Input: MS Project file data or API endpoint.
   Output: Parsed task list for reasoning node.

5. Simulate and Evaluate
   Run the agent in Preview Mode using a sample MS Project file (exported to CSV or JSON).
   Observe how the agent processes task data and produces a status summary.
6. Test edge cases (e.g., project ahead of schedule, missing data).
7. Adjust prompts, thresholds, and logic nodes for better results.

Last, provide the following deliverables:

1. Visual Workflow Diagram (screenshot from Agent Builder).
2. Documentation of Workflow Components
   Description of each node (reasoning, MCP, output, guardrail).
   Prompts and decision logic used.
3. Sample Input and Output (MS Project data snippet and generated report).
4. Reflection Report (500–700 words).

12.10 References

Adamantiadou, D. S., & Tsironis, L. (2025). Leveraging artificial intelligence in project management: A systematic review of applications, challenges, and future directions. *Computers*, *14*(2), 66.

Diameh, J. T., Oluwatobi, B. T., Daniels, C., Ekaette, O., Sunday, N., Azumah, C., & Mariama, Q. (2025). Integrating AI-driven predictive analytics in project risk management to optimize decision-making and performance efficiency. *Int. J. Eng. Technol. Res. Manag*, *9*, 373-389.

Jagannathan, J., Kanishka, S., Thanushree, S., & Bhuvaneswari, M. S. (2025, April). Collaboration of AI with Project Management. In *2024 International Conference on IT Innovation and Knowledge Discovery (ITIKD)* (pp. 1-4). IEEE.

Kokala, A. (2024). Business process management: The synergy of intelligent automation and AI-driven workflows. *International Research Journal of Modernization in Engineering Technology and Science*, *6*, 12.

Karamthulla, M. J., Muthusubramanian, M., Tadimarri, A., & Tillu, R. (2024). Navigating the future: AI-driven project management in the digital era. *International Journal for Multidisciplinary Research*, *6*(2), 1-11.

Ronak, B. (2024). Ai-driven project management revolutionizing workflow optimization and decision-making. *International Journal of Trend in Scientific Research and Development*, *8*(6), 325-338.

12.11 Solutions to Test Your Understanding

12.1 B; 12.2 A; 12.3 B; 12.4 D; 12.5 C; 12.6 B; 12.7 A; 12.8 D; 12.9 B; 12.10 C; 12.11 B; 12.12 B; 12.13 A; 12.14 A; 12.15 C; 12.16 C; 12.17 B; 12.18 C; 12.19 A; 12.20 B; 12.21 D; 12.22 A; 12.23 B; 12.24 A; 12.25 C; 12.26 A; 12.27 B; 12.28 D; 12.29 D; 12.30 C; 12.31 B; 12.32 A; 12.33 B;

www.ingramcontent.com/pod-product-compliance
Lightning Source LLC
LaVergne TN
LVHW060022210926
848481LV00013B/3771
* 9 7 9 8 3 4 9 5 5 8 5 9 7 *